KURT COBAIN

Christopher Sandford

An Orion paperback

First published in Great Britain in 1995
by Victor Gollancz
This paperback edition published in 1996
by Vista

Reissued in 2001
by Orion Books Ltd,
Orion House, 5 Upper St Martin's Lane,
London WC2H 9EA

11

ISBN-13 978-0-7528-4456-5
ISBN-10 0-7528-4456-3

Printed and bound in Great Britain by
Clays Ltd, St Ives plc

The Orion Publishing Group's policy is to use papers that
are natural, renewable and recyclable products and
made from wood grown in sustainable forests. The logging
and manufacturing processes are expected to conform to
the environmental regulations of the country of origin.

www.orionbooks.co.uk

To Adam and Julie

Contents

Acknowledgements

I first came to Seattle in 1961. In visiting and writing about Cobain's adopted town, I have piled up debts of such size that I despair of ever meeting them. Still, the attempt must be made.

The list begins with those I relied on heavily during the last year: Monty Dennison, Jane Farrar, Gillian Gaar, Al Meyersahm, Jim Meyersahm, John Prins and Nancy Roller. I am also grateful to Judy Hentz and all at Tower 801.

For insights into Cobain and his music, I am indebted to: Miti Adhikari, Grant Alden, Michael Andeel, Les Blue, William S. Burroughs, Jackie Busse, Patrick Campbell-Lyons, Noel Chelberg, Art Cobain, Beverley Cobain, Don Cobain, Ernest Cobain, Iris Cobain, Leland Cobain, Toni Cobain, Mike Collier, Marco Collins, Francis Coughlin, Jack Daugherty, Jan Even, Larry Fancher, Robert Gess, James Grauerholz, Jeff Griffin, Amy Griggs, Judy Groez-inger, Tony Groves, David Haig, Cheryl Han, Geraldine Hope, Randi Hubbard, Robert Hunter, Claude Iosso, Betty Kalles, Megan Kern, Donna Kessler, Chuck Leavell, Al Levine, Julia Levy, Myer Loftin, Patrick MacDonald, Warren Mason, Sam Mayne, Slim Moon, Maria Novoselic, Wendy O'Connor, Lisa Orth, John Peel, Charles Peterson, Jeff Pike, Leo Poort, 'Johnny Renton', Tim Rice, Celia Ross, Kate Rous, Jeff Sanford, Michael Schepp, Lamont Shillinger, Stephen Towles, Alice Wheeler and Graham Wright.

On an institutional note, source material on Cobain and

Nirvana was provided by: Aberdeen *Daily World*, Aberdeen High School, Daniel Freeman Marina Hospital, Grays Harbor County Court, Harborview Medical Center, Dr Nikolas Hartshorne, Montesano High School, the Performing Rights Society, *The Rocket*, Seattle, New York and British Libraries, Seattle Department of Construction and Land Use, Seattle Police Department, Seattle *Post-Intelligencer*, Seattle *Times*, Sub Pop and the Washington State Department of Health. I would like to thank David Geffen Company and Gold Mountain Entertainment for proving that even the most anarchic punk icon has his corporate guardians. Suffice it to say, in this context, that in the last three years I have dealt professionally with Mick Jagger's office and I have dealt with Cobain's. Jagger's was easier.

Finally, personally, I should again thank: Kathleen Anderson, Peter Barnes, Judy Baskey, Jeanne and Ray Bates, Asunción Batlle Brossa, Robert Bruce, Ken and Cindy Crabtrey, the Crocodile Café, Janice Crotch, Celia Culpan, Miles Dennison, Focus Fine Arts, Malcolm Galfe, Erin Hennessey, Johnny Johnson, Betty and Carl Knecht, Terry Lambert, Belinda Lawson, Barbara Levy, Julie and George Madsen, Amina McKay, Kurt Meyersahm, Lucille Noel, Robin Parish, Noelle Prins, Jonathan Raban, Keith Richards, Amanda Ripley, my father Sefton Sandford, Sue Sims-Hilditch, Hilary Stevens, Ti-Fa, Jacob van de Rhoer, Von's, Tom Wallace, Katrina Whone, Richard Wigmore and, not least, Victoria Willis Fleming.

C.S.
1995

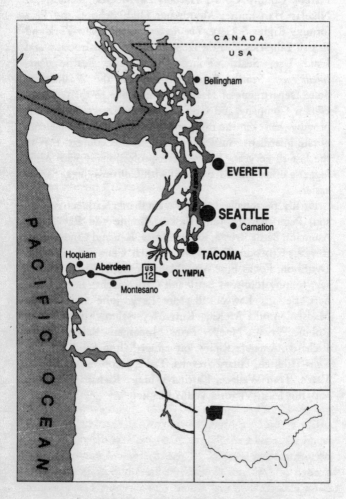

WESTERN WASHINGTON STATE, USA

1

Kurt Cobain

The Peaceable Kingdom isn't the first place one would have looked for Kurt Cobain. Of all the ironies and confusions of his life, none was as pointed as his choosing to kill himself in a room overlooking that sign. Coming down East Denny Way in Seattle, with its view of the lake and the mountains beyond, the trees sending chopped-up sun on to the Weyerhaeuser and Boeing executives' mansions of Cobain's neighbours, you see his house from an angle altogether different from that of the grainy photographs: a pale, shake-sided villa low at the foot of a hill, the eye drawn to the detached garage with its upstairs room where, one spring evening, Cobain took a shotgun and blew his brains out.

The body lay there for two and a half days. It was only the last in a long series of ironies that Cobain, who in the words of his father 'desperately needed saving from himself', was found by a man sent to install an alarm system. When Gary Smith arrived at the house that morning he approached the back of the garage, looked to see if he had a way to route in a wire and noticed the body through a glass opening in the door. Dressed in a light-coloured shirt and jeans, Cobain was on his back in the northwest corner of the room. A shotgun lay across him, his left hand still wrapped around the barrel. According to the doctor who performed the autopsy, 'it was the act of someone who wanted to obliterate himself, to literally become nothing'. Later Cobain's widow would tell a reporter that police could identify her husband only through fingerprints.

Dental records were no use, because nothing was left of his mouth.

No one can say for certain what went through Cobain's mind in the hours before his death. There was, of course, the fact that he had lost interest in almost every aspect of his life. Cobain's musical tastes were changing, and he had little sympathy for the nostalgic feelings that lingered among the more sentimental of his fans. As he said to a cousin just a month before the end, 'I feel like I'm performing in a circus.' It is known that, after struggling to overcome his addiction, Cobain had again fallen prey to heroin. The toxicology report confirmed that, along with traces of Valium, there were 1.52 milligrams of the drug in his blood, three times the normal fatal dose. He suffered well-documented, though misdiagnosed, stomach cramps, and the same family member believes 'he may have done it, plain and simple, to put a stop to the pain'. A relative named Beverley Cobain, a practising psychiatric nurse, adds: 'Kurt was, without doubt, bipolar – he had a psychological disorder which caused him to swing from wild ecstasy to manic despair. In trying to self-medicate with heroin, he almost certainly made the problem worse. That was the background to his shooting himself.'

That leaves the question of a motive. Since the decision to commit or not to commit suicide can be taken in an instant, it is tempting to look for a specific reason for Cobain to have killed himself. There may not be one. The combination of professional frustration, depression and drug addiction would have been enough to make a healthier man than Cobain consider his options. All the same, it is possible to imagine the reaction of someone who made a personal campaign of his loathing of rape and of the exploitation of children – and whose horror of organized religion was proverbial – when he opened the morning paper delivered to his home on the last day of his life:

MINISTER ENTERS GUILTY PLEA TO RAPING GRANDDAUGHTER

In a barely audible voice, a burly Port Orchard minister pleaded guilty yesterday to charges of molesting, raping and kidnapping his 9-year-old granddaughter.

Faced with a choice of eighteen years in prison or a court trial in which he could have faced another alleged victim, Frederick Aylward, 51, signed a plea agreement in Kitsap County Superior Court.

Aylward's attorney said the term constituted 'a life sentence' for his client, who weighs 375 pounds, has heart trouble, high blood pressure and diabetes ... His wife Mary has filed for divorce.

When, later that afternoon, Cobain sat in his study watching television, he would have seen the all-day 'Praise-A-Thon' airing on cable, an extended '700 Club' and yet a third programme inviting viewers to send $200 to hear their prayer read on air. He would have noted the opening of the baseball season, a ritual he always dreaded, with its threat of conformity and male competitiveness. It is known, through police reports, that the set had been tuned to a channel showcasing Disney (who emerges as a semi-tutor to Cobain), and when, at four o'clock, shortly before he wrote his rambling suicide note, pumped his veins full of heroin and went upstairs to shoot himself – the station would have been playing the 'Andy Griffith Show', a sixties sitcom so inane he could not keep from parodying it in a song*, and which he told his cousin was 'exactly the world I'm running away from' – even he must have been struck by the pathos of the scene: a millionaire drug addict sitting alone in his room confronted by the demons and vestiges of his youth, and no way to exorcise them but with the gun.

* * *

* 'Floyd The Barber'.

For the 6,000 fans who gathered in a candlelit vigil for Cobain, venting their sense of betrayal by chanting a chorus of 'You fucker' led by his widow, it was a loss comparable to that of Hendrix or Lennon. 'He died for your sins,' bellowed one overwrought girl to her fellow mourners. A local man shot himself in an apparent copycat suicide. And a twelve-year-old named Helki Wald wrote in the Seattle *Post-Intelligencer*: 'You may not have cared for Kurt Cobain but we, his friends, fans and family, will have to put up with the fact that a great, great man and genius is gone forever ... Life is a sick game and he helped us express that. Many say he was weak to kill himself, no, Kurt was our voice, he helped us in more ways than he will ever know.'

Cobain's fans were a various body and not all were strangers themselves to depression, but, in view of the fact that her letter also contained references to 'helplessness' and 'utter despair', not many of them would have endorsed the theory of a pre-teenage girl that 'life is a sick game'. Apart from those who considered it an act of wanton stupidity, there were two distinct views of Cobain's death. For many who had actually known him, it was a shocking but not illogical development. Overwhelmed by his success, Cobain had long declared that stigma of the creative conscience, an 'artistic crisis'. There is evidence that he was bored by the formulaic structure that made his songs so familiar and that Cobain himself satirized as 'Verse Chorus Verse'. He said as much to *Rolling Stone*. His widow would tell a television reporter that Cobain was desperately unhappy with his group, adding to her, 'I hate it. I can't play with them any more,' and that the only thing he wanted was to collaborate with Michael Stipe. According to this reading of Cobain's life, an heroic but fragile talent, hemmed in by the demands of the market and already walking the self-caricature tight-rope on record and in concert, took the only way out to maintain his dignity and preserve the legend.

The other reaction to Cobain's death was more personal. Among his mourners were a large number of those, like Helki Wald some of them younger than twelve years old, only now experiencing loss for the first time. To them the news they heard on that April day destroyed the idea of having a friend for life, swindling them out of an emotional involvement and thus of their hopes for a reasonably tolerable adolescence. Theirs were among the voices raised loudest in protest at Cobain's vigil. Added to a sense of personal betrayal was a broad streak of anger and disbelief as the details emerged of their hero's last days. For nearly two years both his record company and his management, not to mention his immediate family and friends, had aggressively maintained that 'Kurt doesn't do drugs'. No such constraint, it now seemed, had been embraced by Cobain himself. There was surprise, too, that a man apparently dedicated to the slacker lifestyle had met his end while living the yuppie dream in a $1.5 million mansion in the most exclusive part of Seattle. Among the many reactions voiced that long weekend there was genuine shock that, as a fourteen-year-old named Alison Coe put it, 'Kurt was faking it all along.'

It is not impossible to feel sympathy for his younger fans, the ones who were told by tricksters in the form of respectable journalists that, with Cobain's marriage and the birth of his daughter, everything had finally changed for the better. When words like 'spokesman' or 'agent' are mentioned, one thinks of an organization, offices, a reporting structure and the like. Those things were all part of the conspiracy to protect Cobain's name, but in that world it is easy to forget the most important element – people. It wasn't an entity called Gold Mountain that insisted just weeks before Cobain's death that his unwrapping and swallowing fifty high-dosage Rohypnol tablets and a bottle of champagne 'was definitely not a suicide attempt, [but] a celebration of seeing his wife after so long', it was human beings, and in the outpouring of grief and shock that followed a month later, the harshest words were kept for those who had known of Cobain's condition and had not, perhaps, done enough to treat it.

The other disclosure – that Cobain enjoyed a traditional rock star lifestyle – should have come as no surprise. For several years, efforts had been made to stress (in his wife's words) 'Kurt's sweet, Jimmy Stewart side', that he was by no means out of touch with ordinary people, and, to prove it, that he could be seen out walking his dog, paying with his own money in the local restaurant and, to crown it all, getting it right three times out of four. The hoped-for image was of a man at ease with himself and comfortable with his local community. In fact the general feeling in Seattle was that Cobain had long since become unknowable. As success came, he expressed loathing of his fame by commenting angrily on the conceits of rock stars while indulging those conceits all the more. He bought a large house and, for the first time in his life, hired a bodyguard. Begging letters and requests for autographs went unanswered. On tour Cobain frequently stayed in a separate hotel from the rest of the group, travelling in a limousine that made Mick Jagger's seem apologetic by comparison. There was never anything as innocent or self-denying about Cobain as some supposed. He may have offended elements of the rock establishment, brilliantly realizing his talent for satire and parody and setting up a rallying-point for disaffected youth, but in the process he risked the threat that all this would help his career.

That Kurt Cobain was gifted needs no restating. As well as his voice – an extraordinary, full-bodied instrument that was both savage and tuneful – his songs were invariably based on old-fashioned musical virtues. Along with the raucous guitar and cryptic lyrics went faithful reworkings of early pop melodies. An album like *Nevermind* owes as much to the Beatles as to any number of the post-punk groups of the 1980s. Where Cobain succeeded and they failed was in his mingling of sing-along hard rock with manic punk energy and a singular talent for 'putting himself across' to an audience. If the results became increasingly stale and formulaic – and by the end of his life Cobain would admit, 'I've been working [on it] for so long that it's literally boring for me' – for at least a year or two his was one of the few distinctive voices in an industry anaesthetized by Bros and Kylie Minogue.

Cobain's musicianship and ear for a pop hook were, however, only half the story. Anyone in the performing arts is prone to the accusation of egotism and vanity, but when it comes to Cobain the stench overpowers anything that has gone before. It took nerve to complain, at the height of his fame, that 'I can't believe that people wouldn't listen to this music and think more highly of me than they do', or to insist that the names of former colleagues be removed from his, album covers. This was the man who shouted at chauffeurs and assistants, who insulted friends who tried to help him, and who reneged on a binding contract by demanding that his share of Nirvana's publishing royalties be more than doubled, and that the deal be retrospective.

Only in America would a twenty-five-year-old millionaire complain of being under-valued. Apologists and free-marketeers can muster numerous arguments to justify such vast rewards. Cobain undoubtedly generated far more than his salary for the managers, accountants and record executives who came to rely on him. Other rock stars have earned as much or more. Cobain was accountable to the press, his audience and to a large body of loyal, impressionable fans for whom his songs represented an act of faith. Even so, to describe him as one author did as 'saintly in his avoidance of all rock star bullshit' defies belief. To the much-publicized egalitarianism Cobain welded an unshakeable faith in his own worth. One of his most striking qualities was his ability to simulate near-anarchy while ensuring that the management of his image and his money proceed along orthodox lines. 'He *could* be modest,' says Charles Peterson, a man involved with Cobain throughout his career, 'but he knew exactly where he was going and what he wanted. You don't get to be that famous by accident.'

There are several mysteries about Kurt Cobain, prince of grunge and unwitting mouthpiece for a generation: the chief one being that he seemed to be several different people. Conjuring a picture of him from the cuttings file and obituaries, one might imagine a figure with the vision of a Lennon and the joyous derangement of a Dylan, snarling punning lyrics while strumming an agitated yet tuneful guitar. The type who might also play the harmonica.

Yet another image was that of the young, tormented demi-Christ – a perception Cobain angrily denied yet hastened to play up to – whose early death was somehow of a piece with a violent, beleaguered life. This, too, was something of a simplification, and a reaction set in among older commentators for whom, in Bernard Levin's words, 'it would be pointless to tell [Cobain's] fans that they will have forgotten him in a year or two, and that he will be replaced in their affections by a similar figure, who in turn will succumb to booze, coke and adulation' – or, in Andy Rooney's, that 'Kurt Cobain was a loser'. Yet another view was that Cobain, an admittedly rare and fragile talent, had betrayed his radical ideals, as if by becoming so successful, and thus by inference 'selling out', he had in some way impoverished his gifts. This was a theory heard frequently in Seattle.

Cobain in person was nothing like Cobain the legend. He was an intensely shy man, poorly educated, and prone to the same vanities and excesses he despised in others. Like all his family he was over-sensitive and never forgot a word of criticism. Like anyone who grows up feeling more intelligent and more put-on than everyone else, he was afflicted with a strange mix of ego and insecurity. As *Nevermind* sat at Number One on both sides of the Atlantic Cobain worried constantly about being exposed as a fake. He knew he could list fifty groups who were, in his opinion, more talented than Nirvana and yet could not have landed a hit record had they taped a free backstage pass to the cover; on other occasions he talked about himself as 'the greatest poet-musician in the world'. He had the little boy's longing to shock and contributed something to the history of sculpture by his clay-baked dolls with diseased body parts. That Cobain was no artist hardly matters, for incongruity and 'activating the space' were his stocks in trade. His whole approach to performance was a scream for attention. It must have been galling to have achieved his ambition and realize it still wasn't enough. He could be ecstatic, and experienced the brief illusion of happiness. What Cobain never knew was contentment.

There is a Kurt Cobain today on every street corner in Seattle: a morose pale-skinned man dressed in a winter coat whatever the weather, hunched, mumbling, and raging against *something*. Cobain succeeded because, unlike theirs, his voice tapped the eternal themes of frustration, bewilderment and anger. Suddenly a sizeable part of the world's youth had a hero figure they could relate to. The adulation had just the opposite of the desired effect on Cobain. When he realized that, for the first time in his life, perfect strangers not only admired but worshipped him, he was confronted with all his old feelings of inadequacy and doubt, and it was this weakness that killed him.

2

'Twin Peaks Without the Excitement'

Aberdeen, Washington, is an unlovely place without external graces.

As the traffic flows west into the city towards the Pacific Ocean, the road crosses a zone of flea markets and trailer parks before entering a valley flanked by smelters, chimneys, pipes and the rusted-up Weyerhaeuser lumberyard. The shops are pre-fabricated shacks selling auto parts and furniture; acres of dead railroad track and bridges mark the centre of town, where the sole new buildings are fast-food restaurants and funeral parlours. According to Kurt Cobain's father, 'it may be the bleakest single spot on the west coast'.

When Donald Leland Cobain married Wendy Fradenburg in Coeur d'Alene, Idaho, on 31 July 1965, neither party had reached their twenty-first birthday. A year later the couple moved west in search of work and settled briefly in Hoquiam, a logging town adjacent to Aberdeen (population 17,000), where their first child was born in the Grays Harbor Community Hospital on 20 February 1967. Although the Cobains were of humble means – the house in Hoquiam could not have been a worse one – the family were loving and protective of their son. 'I was totalled out on him,' says Wendy. A friend named Francis Coughlin remembers her 'fussing about the boy almost unnaturally', holding him in a quilted pink blanket and raising eyebrows among the more roughly hewn neighbours.

On the morning Kurt Donald Cobain was born the rain in Aberdeen cleared and the temperature reached 50 degrees. It was a fine winter's day, crisp with bright sunshine. The news that Monday in the *Daily World* was of Vietnam, where 25,000 US troops launched Operation Junction City against the enemy stronghold north of Saigon; of New Orleans, where a district attorney named Garrison reaffirmed his belief that arrests would be made in the Kennedy assassination probe; of Washington, where the Civil Rights Commission urged Congress to take immediate steps to end school segregation; of Kentucky, where Cassius Clay's effort to be re-classified as a Black Muslim minister to avoid military conscription was rejected by a Selective Service Board; and of Aberdeen itself, where the talk was of blueberry festivals, pet shows and chain-saw competitions.

This was an America still celebrating the fifties more than it anticipated the seventies. Words like militancy and counterculture, with their threat of drugs and draft-dodging, hardly existed in Hoquiam. Within limits men were allowed to let their hair grow longer than the old marine cuts. An occasional marijuana plume drifted up from Lions City Park, next to the high school. Don Cobain himself enjoyed a party, sometimes stopping on Lincoln Street to purchase what a neighbour says were 'probably cigarettes'. But in its clinging to old-fashioned values and conservative notions of God and country Hoquiam might still have belonged to the Eisenhower era, somewhere, as Francis Coughlin puts it, 'you watched Pat Boone with the family after supper' and the 7th Street Theater showed *The Sound of Music* for the ninety-ninth consecutive week.

The area *was* bleak. Built in the 1860s by French and Germans to cut timber from the region's vast forests and now little inhabited by their descendants, the sawmills were all closed and so gloomy that the electric lights along 8th Street would be turned on even in summer. To the residents of Hoquiam, even neighbouring Aberdeen, with its museums and occasional bowling alley, had a sort of glamour, while Seattle, 110 miles to the northeast, enjoyed almost imperial status. As a relative says, 'the place was a virtual time-warp, still suffering from the Depression', only grudgingly aware of events in the outside world.

Among them was the growth and rapid accessibility of pop music. On 20 February 1967, the day Kurt Cobain was born, the Beatles were at work in Abbey Road recording the title track of *Sergeant Pepper*; their single 'Strawberry Fields' had been released three days earlier. Two seminal British groups, Cream and The Who, were about to make their US debuts in New York, where in April the first Human Be-In symbolically launched the Summer of Love. Jimi Hendrix was playing his first club dates in London. In a sign of which way the pop *zeitgeist* was moving, Mick Jagger and Keith Richards had been arrested that week on drugs charges, a case prompting a sympathetic leader in *The Times* and polarizing at a stroke attitudes towards the new hedonism. It would be tempting to think that Aberdeen and Hoquiam, because of their positions as harbours, tradition-ally the marginal places where lifestyles meet, would be receptive to the stirrings from abroad, making the west coast of Washington analogous to, say, Liverpool ten years before. The truth is that the influence was an oblique one. No one in Aberdeen, a Cobain relative says, had given up on traditional values, 'although people everywhere were suscep-tible to new ideas'. When, after two years, *The Sound of Music* closed at the 7th Street Theater, it was replaced in short order by *Blow-up* and *The Knack*. The Doors' 'Break on Through', a definite stepping-up of rock's subversive power, was voted best single by the students at Hoquiam High, while the owner of Rosevear's Music Shop in Aber-deen confirms that 'suddenly, kids were demanding electric guitars instead of flutes and violins'. All this, without being recognized as a revolution at the time, took place in the late winter and spring of 1967. If ever there was a child of his

times, someone who lived by the code of personal noncon-
formity and avoidance of dull, boring, conventional reality
made possible by the likes of Hendrix, the Doors and Cream,
it was Kurt Cobain. As his cousin puts it, 'He was fortunate
to have been born at a time things were loosening up, and
to have parents who allowed and even enjoyed rock music.
Not that he would have ever admitted it. Being lucky was
the last thing Kurt ever thought he was.'

Cobain was full-blooded Irish on his father's side (the name
is a form of Coburn, of Gaelic and Northumbrian origins)
and some of that race's assertiveness spoke as he grew up. In
August 1967 the family made the upward move to Aberdeen,
where Don found work at the Chevron station, eventually
settling in a green, four-room dwelling at 1210 East 1st
Street, an area of old-fashioned wooden box homes and
daubed graffiti. The first indication that the boy might be
no shrinking violet came in 1969, when a seventy-eight-
year-old neighbour complained that Cobain had tried to
bite his ear off. In a second incident that winter a policeman
called at East 1st Street in response to a complaint that a
woman's cat had been tortured. Even as young as three,
Cobain showed a marked aversion to authority in general
and the law in particular. 'Corn on the cops!', a term of
abuse he illustrated by a well-aimed bottle or rock, was his
standard response to the sight of a patrol car. His few dealings with children of his own age were equally violent. 'I
picked on them,' he later remembered, an admission that,
if anything, downplays an outlook bordering on the psychotic. As Beverley Cobain says, 'You have to remember he
was Irish on his father's side and German on his mother's,
from whom he also got his emotional, hyper-sensitive streak.
It's a volatile combination.' Some of the wilder stories of
Cobain's upbringing are in the realm of myth, since detailed
accounts of incidents – in one case his sexual tormenting of

a little girl – are given without attribution, but the general Aberdeen view is that he was both a loner and a bully, someone even at the age of three whose type was cast.

The other side of Cobain was the weak, clinging child – what he later called his Pisces genes – doting on his family, inquisitive, brooding, with sad-looking, pale blue eyes. This was the boy who drew and painted animals and wrote love odes addressed to his mother. On the quality of Cobain's output, it is kindest to be silent. Even compared to the efforts of other young children, it was neither startling nor original. But it does convey an almost abnormal fixation on one parent – all the poems were dedicated to Wendy and none to Don – and a sense of betrayal (Cobain later used the word) dating from 24 April 1970, when he was presented with a sister, Kimberly.

That night Cobain went missing from home and was found by a neighbour, cowering under a bridge, howling and sobbing.

In the new decade Cobain entered a transitional phase when his aggressive side had run out of steam, but there was no clear-cut replacement. According to his grandmother Iris, 'between the ages of four and five, he seemed to withdraw. He shrank into himself.' Cobain invented an invisible companion, an uncontrollable ball of manic energy he named Boddah, at which he stared fixedly at meals (Boddah was given his own place-setting) or walked with along the banks of the Wishkah River. Don's brother James remembered that 'this was the time we began to seriously worry about the boy'. Cobain's other fantasy was that he was an alien, sent to earth to study the natives and not subject to the same morals or values as humans. 'That one took him twenty years to shake off,' says Beverley.

The same tendency to withdraw, to set up an image of himself as irreparably odd, was obvious at school. Barbara Mallow, a relief teacher at Robert Gray kindergarten in

Aberdeen, remembers him as quiet, with an aptitude for drawing and poetry. A student at the school who prefers anonymity says there was 'a kind of menace about him. When he gave you that blinkered look it was straight out of *The Exorcist* or one of those Satanic-worship films.' This particular feature is remarked on repeatedly by Cobain's peers. His narrow white face gave him the look of being angry, even when he wasn't; his eyes, according to his cousin, were 'cold and pale' and gave those on whom Cobain turned the uncomfortable feeling of being x-rayed. His blonde hair accentuated the sallowness of his skin. The milky flecked shoulders and delicate bony hands might have belonged to a girl.

By the time Cobain transferred to junior high school his reputation had grown. He was firmly from the 'problem child' tradition, wary of friends and hostile to teachers, although with a sentimental streak that expressed itself towards animals. He acquired several pets. On his best form he had an almost messianic quality of his own, coaxing home rabbits and squirrels, befriending strays in the street and feeding birds from his palm. Many of these were committed to the ever-present sketch pad. 'The artistic bent came from Don,' says his cousin Ernest Cobain. 'All the family dabbled with painting or photography, probably because it's a solitary kind of hobby.' His ex-wife Toni agrees that 'art appealed to Kurt's furtive side. He used to disappear for hours and come back with a drawing of a man alone in a boat or a lighthouse in a wild storm.' The bleak renditions 'weren't the stuff of other kids'.

Don's other influence on his son was musical. Beverley Cobain has a memory of her cousin vigorously playing an Hawaiian-style guitar, and Don himself admits to a fondness for old Beatles and Monkees hits. Here was a subject on which the Cobains and Fradenburgs could agree: pop music was something Wendy understood, and for a time her brother Chuck drummed in a semi-professional group performing fifties hits around the ocean resorts and Aberdeen pool halls. Another sister, Mary Fradenburg, played guitar and was once placed second in a local talent contest. According to Don's mother Iris: 'It's fair to say Kurt got his visual art from us, and his love of music from the Fradenburgs. But his mother encouraged drawing and his father enjoyed music. There weren't closed doors.'

The other thing Cobain inherited from his mother was the highly strung, brittle personality remarked on to his death. According to an Aberdeen reporter named Claude Iosso, 'Interviewing Wendy is like being in a car with two gears – overdrive and reverse. She tends to either talk non-stop or say nothing. Incredibly sensitive to criticism. You don't have to be a geneticist to work out where Kurt got his personality.' One of the chief characteristics of both mother and son was an unquenchable belief in their own ability, welded to a feeling that this was either unappreciated or exaggerated by others. A teacher in Aberdeen remembers 'Kurt *ranting* at another child because she couldn't understand one of his paintings'. Yet when Cobain appeared in October 1973 with a copy of the school paper featuring his artwork on the cover, he was incensed because it was 'no good'. 'His attitude toward adults changed because of that,' says Wendy. 'Everybody was telling him how much they loved his art and he was never satisfied with it' – an observation that was to prove particularly acute two decades later.

Cobain's belief that he was different was encouraged by his parents. Don upgraded the family home (giving it a 'Godawful, fake European look', according to one visitor, sharply at odds with the stark, run-down tone of the neighbourhood), while Wendy, her son later said, 'told me to stay away from poor kids'. A resident of Young Street, adjoining the Cobains, believes them to have had 'delusions of grandeur. You should have seen the way (Wendy) dressed up

Kurt for school. He looked like Little Lord Fauntleroy.'

There has long been a tradition of temperamental, artistically minded boys, pampered by their mothers and instinctively feared by other children – most American mass-killers fit the description – and Cobain belonged in the category. Wendy, one of eight children herself, was a strikingly attractive blonde who in later years might have passed for her son's protective elder sister. 'She just melted around Kurt,' says his father. With nine aunts and uncles and two sets of doting grandparents competing to babysit him, it was hardly surprising Cobain grew up spoilt. His father, a self-confessed blue-collar, all-American type with a penchant for basketball and baseball, was conscious as early as 1974 that he was never his favourite parent. A letter from one Cobain cousin to another that winter opens with the line, 'Kurt seems to be more of a Mommy's Dear than ever,' and continues in the same vein from there. In a town where some shopkeepers still took their payment in gold, women in tight skirts loitered in doorways on State Street and loggers drank and gambled away their wages, it was inevitable that gossip would accumulate around the bouffant-haired seven-year-old with the fluffy pink sweater.

It did accumulate. Aberdeen in the mid-1970s was a virtual ghost town, where every bar was infested with louche and mutant characters of the roughest sort: desperadoes and thugs, the riff-raff of a community beached in a primitive place and drinking away the afternoon. The city's chief characteristics were its near-constant rain and a suicide rate among the highest in the country. For a boy uninterested in sport and with the conviction he was an alien, the prospects were the opposite of rosy. When father and son drove together on errands it was to suburbs with names like Satsop and Humptulips and Elma, tree-lined and dripping outposts on which, the lumberyards now closed, a doom seemed to have fallen, or, as Cobain later put it, 'like *Twin Peaks* without the excitement'. Cobain's grandmother is only the most compelling witness to the view that 'Aberdeen affected Kurt for the rest of his days' and that the 'Fascinating Activities' listed in the *Daily World* or the Montesano *Vidette*, with their accent on pet shows, bake-ins, parking restrictions and amateur beauty contests, were 'what he was running from all his life'. According to Claude Iosso, 'Something happens in Aberdeen all the time. This week it's rain; next week, rain also . . . It's a decent enough place to settle and raise a family, but it must be hell to anyone with the slightest sense of claustrophobia.' It may be stretching belief to suggest that something gloomy about the place communicated itself to its earliest settlers, but every schoolchild is taught that when George Vancouver led an expedition along the Washington coast in 1792 he bypassed Grays Harbor and Aberdeen, a fact celebrated annually on Undiscovery Day, and that when Robert Gray later chanced upon the spot, although their ship remained for several weeks, neither captain nor crew chose to disembark.

Cobain began his lifelong dependency on drugs in 1974, when he was prescribed first Ritalin, a form of amphetamine, then with sedatives to help him sleep. Finally Don and Wendy made the decision to remove all sugar from his diet. Cobain's parents, speaking with a rare unanimous voice, played a key mediation role in making suggestions to his school. For a time Cobain was excused the compulsory exercise he loathed. Special meals were prepared for him. The entire family engulfed him in art supplies – his room took on the look of a studio – until, as Wendy admits, 'It got crammed down his throat. We almost killed it for him.'

Prescribing drugs established a precedent for Cobain to which he conformed for the rest of his life. The boy's teacher in Aberdeen claims that 'Kurt's health was and remained a concern'. The main issue was his reliance on prescription medicine, a rigorous avoidance of all sport, as well as his belief that 'every difficulty in life could be solved with a pill'. Compounding the problem was the very real possibility that Cobain had been mis-diagnosed. His cousin remembers the phrase 'attention deficit' being chanted like a mantra to describe his condition. 'It was an article of faith that Kurt could be cured by drugs,' she says. 'Like most kids of his generation he was given the wrong medication. Kurt's problem, pure and simple, was a condition that caused him to swing from mania to despair. The Ritalin and sedatives didn't help. In fact they made things worse by setting up a pattern he clung to in later life.' A second family member, close to Cobain in the 1970s, agrees that 'the heroin addict really grew out of the seven-year-old pill-head'.

For years Cobain had been banging on pots and pans, using spoons as percussive instruments and making sounds his grandmother says would have done credit to Ringo Starr. Now, bowing to the inevitable, his parents bought him a bass drum. Cobain was transfixed. For a year, according to Iris, 'you never saw Kurt without it strapped around his chest'. A neighbour, Megan Kern, also remembers him 'marching up and down 1st Street, banging and hollering, and accompanying himself on Beatles songs'. Given the fact that his other proclivities were for flailing a cheap plastic guitar and imitating the stuntman Evel Kneivel, it is possible to agree with Kern that Cobain's behaviour was of a kind with 'a manic personality, misunderstood by his parents and indulged by well-meaning relatives'. Because such behaviour took place in Aberdeen – culturally dominated by elderly couples and hard-bitten loggers with little time for hyper-active children – attitudes began to harden against Cobain. 'He was regarded as a pest,' says Kern. Cobain's grand-mother also believes he played the drums not only because he liked them, but to annoy other people, something he effortlessly achieved in the streets of north Aberdeen.

Cobain's fate always to be the outsider was thus prefigured at an early age. His father inhabited a male, sports-oriented world he despised, and his mother developed an instinct so fiercely protective of her son that for years he was not allowed to mix with other children. Under the circumstances, it was hardly surprising he developed a preference for his own company, for invisible companions or for abstracts like music and art. Opinions vary as to whether, within the limitations of his upbringing, Cobain was happy or unhappy as a boy. Wendy insisted to the author Michael Azerrad that 'he got up every day with such joy that there was another day to be had'. Cobain himself told the same source, 'I was an extremely happy child . . . I was constantly screaming and singing.' His cousin, on the other hand, is among those who believe 'Kurt mistook being manic for being content'. Iris agrees that 'he was basically cheerful, but there was a rage to him'. Perhaps displaying just such a mood, Cobain would later tell the *Los Angeles Times*, 'I was a seriously depressed kid.'

All this changed greatly for the worse in 1976.

For at least a year things had gone downhill between Cobain's parents. Although the court documents refer merely to 'certain differences [having] arisen' and Don Cobain prefers not to discuss the matter, Wendy gave Azerrad the impression she divorced her husband because he 'simply wasn't around very much'. Another family member believes it was a mistake from the start, a marriage that might have survived in an earlier era but that stands as a good example of 'what happened in the sixties when women like Wendy began asserting themselves'. Whatever the cause, the effect was a catastrophic shock for Cobain, who remembered 'all of a sudden not being the same person, feeling I wasn't worthy anymore' and bringing about an inferiority complex that even Wendy believes destroyed his life.

On 1 March 1976 Don Cobain left Aberdeen and took a bachelor apartment at 410½ 6th Street, Hoquiam, less than a mile from the family home of 1967. In the separation agreement filed that month the house on East 1st Street, valued at $20,000 with $5,775 owing to the Rainier Mortgage Company, was granted to Wendy. Don was allowed a lien against the premises of $6,500 'due whenever Petitioner sells the house; remarries; or the youngest child has reached the age of majority' (it was eventually paid in August 1984). In addition, husband and wife were awarded respectively the 1965 Ford half-ton truck and the 1968 Camero.

Almost lost in the minutiae about property rights and mortgages were the arrangements for the two children. In the final settlement of 9 July 1976, after a paragraph relating to legal costs, another awarded Wendy 'care, custody and control of the minors Kurt D. Cobain and Kimberly D. Cobain', subject to reasonable rights of visitation, and ordered Don to pay $150 a month per child, which he was to have the right to claim for income tax purposes. It was perhaps unfortunate that the actual provisions for Cobain and his sister should be described as both an obligation and a burden, and doubly so as these tallied with his own self-image from then on. One of the Cobain family remembers Kurt being 'a monster' that summer, alternately lapsing into silence or violently seeking relief by banging the drum. Over the years music would become a continuous release for Cobain. For a while, it served as his most dependable ally against the rest of the world. Only later did he come to consider it a trivial activity – 'Verse Chorus Verse' – and the knowledge that it was what had made him famous drove him half-mad. He cloaked that madness in buffoonery, pushed it to one side with drugs and memorably channelled it into his bleakest, most disturbing work, but ultimately it proved no answer to the crisis set in hand in 1976.

Although Wendy was given legal custody of her son, he lived with her for only another three months. (In a book on which she collaborated this was later expanded to a year.) As well as tension with his mother's new boyfriend, there is evidence that Cobain felt betrayed by both parents ('Dad sucks' and 'Mom sucks' were the parting words he scrawled on his bedroom wall) and that he went through the normal confusion of a nine-year-old confronted with a broken home. Describing it with typical candour as 'Kurt's year in purgatory', Iris Cobain believes there was at least one thing the experience could claim to have done: 'It exposed him to some of the good qualities of his father.' A second family member agrees that 'Don's sincerity stood out in one of his fights with Wendy', where a striking sentence voices the moral compulsion on which his relations with his children were based: 'I have to believe what I tell the kids.' According to Iris, 'his father tried to teach Kurt to be happy'.

The trouble with statements like that, of course, is that they only open up more questions. Either things improve or they get worse. When Cobain moved into his father's apartment that October there was a period of genuine goodwill and conciliation. Things deteriorated when, early the next year, Don moved to a trailer home in Montesano, a lumber town fifteen miles east along Highway 12 from Aberdeen. Here some discrepancy exists between Don's version of events ('I tried to do everything to make him feel wanted, to be part of the family') and his son's ('I just fucking hated it'). The chief difficulty seems to have been Cobain's burning desire to return to his mother, who, as Don puts it, 'didn't want him'; his father's job at a lumber company, where, as a bonding exercise, Cobain would be invited to 'sit in [Don's] office while he went and counted logs'; and the infrequent hunting expeditions, during which Cobain would express silent displeasure by refusing to leave the car.

It is not difficult to feel sympathy for Don Cobain. Even members of Wendy's family agree that he went out of his way to accommodate his son. An expensive minibike was bought; weekends were spent camping or at the beach. Some semblance of family life, in the form of dinners at East 1st Street, remained. There was a new drum kit and other luxuries, none of which seemed visibly to please Cobain. As one of his cousins says, 'all the gifts have to be measured against Kurt's anger' and were thus 'nothing but a spit in the ocean'. There was something wilful about the way the boy – pampered beyond the dreams of most children's avarice – rejected his father's advances, played one parent against the other and came to believe, because they weren't artistic and he was, that he was adopted. In later years Cobain would raise protest against goodwill, generosity and acceptance into a crusade, his voice rising as the actual target of his anger receded. Once, towards the end of his life, he was asked by Azerrad to explain the basis of his quarrel with his father. 'I don't even know,' said Cobain.

At school he suffered from a deepening sense of frustration. Shortly after the divorce Cobain transferred to Beacon Elementary in Montesano, where a fourth grade teacher named Sheryl Nelson remembers him as a 'confused little boy'. According to Nelson, 'Kurt didn't want to be in my class. He didn't want to be in Montesano. I think he wanted things back the way they were.' Here Don and Wendy came together in like-minded alliance to ensure their son stayed in the local system. At the nearby high school building Cobain could be seen trudging up Wheeler Street to the redbrick classroom opposite the school emblem in the shape of a bulldog. 'He hated that sign above anything else,' one of his classmates remembers. Celebrating as it did the school football team, 'it pushed all the wrong buttons for Kurt', who was 'forever cursing it or making elaborate schemes to blow it up'. Cobain's attention was also drawn to the trophy cabinet immediately inside the school's swing doors. 'The most obscene thing in the world,' he once told a friend, rich endorsement from one so unsparing of criticism. At the Bee Hive restaurant, a 1950s diner stranded on Main Street, they remember Cobain well. 'He came in after school and spent an hour sitting alone over a glass of water. He wasn't like other kids.'

Fury entered his voice when he was asked to play football, go running or join in any organized activity. A contemporary named Scott Cokeley remembers Cobain as moody and sarcastic and 'aware, to put it mildly' that he was different from other Montesano students. Yet another classmate says he was 'brilliant in the way he always got out of things, like claiming he had stomach ache or a doctor's note he never seemed actually to produce'. At Don's insistence he did, briefly, join the junior wrestling team, an experience he unsurprisingly hated and that ended when Cobain fell limp to the ground at an opponent's feet to register protest. The *Puppy Press*, a mimeographed student newsletter, gives his favourite class as Music and records him as playing snare drum in the school band.

The exporting of the 'punk ethic', in which musicality was reduced to an option, began in earnest in 1977. As well as the new wave of British groups, the first glimmerings of a local alternative to the world of Pink Floyd and Yes could be seen in Seattle, where a club named the Bird opened its doors to 'Heavy/light punk, WEIRDNESS, droogs, derelicts' and all-comers of every description. It was the major stroke of luck, in a life not untouched by coincidence, that Cobain's own protest grew at the very moment a cause formed to shape it. The event had a specific date: 5 March 1977, the night the Ramones played Aberdeen and an unknown enthusiast spray-painted the Skookum trailer park with what Cobain called the 'simple but effective' PUNK RULES OK. It would be stretching belief to claim his own conversion from mainstream pop took place overnight or that Cobain did more than absorb the press reports of the concert, but with the arrival of punk his motive to be different met with opportunity. Musicologists cite the growth of new wave and the 'de-mystifying' of the recording process as key factors making it easier to break into the business. Punk could be grasped by almost anyone with a will to do so. It was inevitable that, in time, its influence would spread to those, like Cobain, who might otherwise never have seen the inside of a studio. By the end of 1977 a mainstream-music generation was still – just – running the show; an alternative-music generation was coming up behind, impatiently.

Cobain's claim to have owned the Sex Pistols' *Never Mind the Bollocks* in 1977 is hard to prove since Don has no recollection of the title, but the idea that he was a full-fledged convert to punk as early as his eleventh birthday is absurd. If he was even aware of new wave it could have been only as a result of magazine articles and graffiti. Cobain's favourite albums at the time were Queen's *News of the World* and the Jimi Hendrix, Led Zeppelin and Boston hits that arrived monthly in Montesano from the Columbia House record and tape club. He discovered Kiss, whose cartoon-hero stage act, says Cokeley, 'knocked Kurt out', and dabbled with the likes of Genesis and King Crimson while maintaining his first allegiance to the Beatles. According to a classmate, he was 'pretty conservative', preferring the melodious side of rock to anything avant-garde or subversive. In a student profile in *Puppy Press* Cobain said his favourite song was 'Don't Bring Me Down' by ELO, and that Meatloaf was a 'cool group'.

The markedly polite, if morose, student noted by teachers

and classmates should give pause for thought to anyone who believes Cobain was already set on an irreversible downward path. After the initial shock of readjustment, Don insists there was a period of reconciliation between father and son. Iris Cobain, too, believes that, whatever the later legend, 'Kurt was quite happy for long stretches'. A teacher at Montesano agrees that 'he was okay most of the time', although with 'a strong fatalistic streak that everything would turn out for the worst'. It was a recurrent irony of Cobain's life that, just when things seemed to improve, he suffered a disappointment. When in February 1978 Don re-married and inherited two young stepchildren, Cobain experienced a shock something like that of the divorce. Where once he was shy now he became morbidly withdrawn. 'Kurt just retreated into his own private world,' says his grandmother. Don would later tell Azerrad: 'He never came out and said anything about what was really bothering him. He's like me – don't say anything and maybe it'll disappear. And don't explain. You just bottle it all up and it all comes out at one time.' 'I was one of the last things on his list,' claimed his son.

Here, then, were the characteristics Cobain would take into adolescence: sensitivity, moodiness, a feeling of being apart or aloof, mated to paranoia, the sense of being unwanted and the unshakeable belief that he was either much better or worse than people thought. He regarded the betrayal of his parents in the most scathing light. 'It seems to me,' he wrote to a classmate in 1980, 'that I'm about as wanted round here as shit.' Avoiding chores had made Cobain famous in Montesano, and from his early teens he conceived of his mission as a negative one: he was the dissenter, the voice of protest against sport, school, religion, family and convention. The key to Cobain was his dislike of 'conformity' in relationships. People, he believed, were unreliable; the idea that an attachment might exist with his parents, much less a friend, struck him as laughable. The very best he either gave or hoped for were brief moments of relief – lunch alone with Don, a card containing money from his mother – from his otherwise ruthless self-containment and his credo that 'people stink'. A friend in Montesano remembers Cobain as 'someone who made it a religion not to join in . . . Always the one who got out of football practice or sat alone in the café over lunch.' Not surprisingly, tension existed between Cobain and his step-mother, who, Don insists, 'treated him perfect' despite the fact 'he was screwing up the whole family'. A source close to the children adds that Cobain viciously bullied his young stepbrother and stepsister.

What Cobain plainly wanted was to preserve his self-image as a loner, even if this meant beating a tactical retreat from the support offered by his family. As a reaction to the collected blows of his childhood, it can easily be understood. There is something inevitable about the endless invocation of words like 'hurt', 'bitter' and 'disappointed' his friends use to describe him. But, considering the circumstances in which Cobain found himself, there may have been a hint of exaggeration about the violence of his protest. Living conditions at Montesano, though not lavish, were never deprived. Cobain had his own room, use of a motorbike, a stereo, his father's record club subscription, ample pocket money and a stepmother who, even a member of Wendy's family believes, adored him. None of this may have lessened the cumulative shock Cobain had felt since 1976, but in striking out indiscriminately at children or at the short-comings of his stepmother's cooking, he risked raising the volume to the point where his voice began to distort. Until 1992, when Cobain underwent his tardy but opportune con-version to family life, there was hardly an aunt, uncle, cousin or grandparent who failed at some time to win his scorn. His writings are dotted with stark references to 'rednecks', 'scum' and 'trash', yet it is possible to sympathize with Beverley's view that 'half the time he was faking it', or with a friend who believes 'Kurt never had a relationship without a pathological desire to test it'.

The sense that his protest might be more put-on than real was lent weight by events at school. As he grew older Cobain's opposition to organized sport lessened and he embraced some of its routine. A fellow student who chooses anonymity remembers him jogging merrily around the school gym, then begging that this lapse not be revealed to the 'stoner kids' for whom Cobain was a kind of hero. The same friend saw him train, 'wearing a cute, little girl's outfit' for the Babe Ruth League baseball team. The 'James Dean side' of Cobain's personality is something widely remarked on by his family. 'He wasn't a tenth as rebellious as everyone thought,' says his cousin Ernest. 'Because he couldn't deal with relationships, Kurt withdrew into himself. He could be terribly quiet. People mistook that for anger.'

On 14 June 1979 Don petitioned the Grays Harbor Superior Court for custody of his son. No objection was heard from Wendy, who, the legal settlement noted, had lost 'actual physical care' of the boy nearly three years before. Although not celebrated for his intellectual abilities Don was notable for a sharp intuitive sense of logic ('If something needed fixing,' says his mother, 'he did it') and a fiercely protective attitude toward his family, accentuated, one relative believes, by the fact that one of his own brothers had died in childhood. According to Toni Cobain: 'He took custody of Kurt because it struck Don as bizarre he was still technically living with Wendy. He wanted him to know he cared.' Don 'loved the thrill of a generous emotion', says a family friend; there was a 'showboating side to him', which came out when he argued in court. Both parties agree, however, that Don was genuinely concerned about his son and, in Toni's words, that 'he wanted to show Kurt someone was there for him'. 'I did it to make him feel a part of the family,' says Don.

It had just the opposite effect. Cobain's reaction to the court decision was a violent rejection of his father and a period of five years in which he lived with three separate sets of aunts and uncles, as well as his paternal grandparents. Here, again, some disparity exists between the image of the sullen, eternally cursed youth portrayed by classmates and the intelligent and sensitive teenager recalled by his family. Iris Cobain, for one, thinks it astonishing that her grandson turned out so well despite the emotional problems experienced by the children of ever-squabbling parents. 'The best thing Don ever did for Kurt was to take him in,' she says. On the other hand, an Aberdeen neighbour remembers a 'broken kid' whose parents 'simply tore into one another' whenever they met to discuss their son's future. On one occasion Don's pleasure in accepting a ride with Wendy in the Camero vanished as she pulled into the entrance of the Community Hospital with the demand that her ex-husband seek psychiatric help. 'Those two were constantly at each other's throats,' says a member of Don's family. 'There was a lot of screaming and fighting, and there was a succession of foster parents for Kurt. In the middle of all this he was just a sullen, sulky kid who thought of himself as a reject. Who wouldn't have, under the circumstances?' The same source says Cobain 'virtually lived' on the Route 40 bus as he shuttled between relatives in Aberdeen and Montesano and that his two favourite places were the Timberland Library – the reference clerk says he 'took root in the music books section' there – and the Aberdeen Animal Hospital, where he once volunteered to look after 'anything that doesn't have a home'.

It was an almost friendless existence, Cobain's family admit. Don may feel understandably guilty, as one of his brothers says, but his guilt exposes the cruel paradox facing his son in 1980. The more often he changed homes and schools the less opportunity he had for finding the roots he craved. When in the eighth grade, Cobain transferred to Miller Junior High School, and a classmate, Lee Hansmann, remembers him 'off in the corner' at band practice, while a second contemporary graphically describes him drowning in a tidal wave of self-hate. Cobain's only human companion, an Elma resident called Ryan Agnew, would later be brutally dropped, proof of what he calls 'Kurt's tendency to see friendship as a milestone down the road to having a fight'.

Early in the new decade Cobain was taken to a child psychiatrist, who urged him to 'fit in more'. Whatever its already limited chance of acceptance, the doctor's advice was swiftly neutralized by Wendy, who, even as she drove her son to the familiar entrance to the hospital, was insisting she still wanted him to 'express himself'. Self-expression, to the Fradenburgs, had long stopped being synonymous with an antisocial lack of control. As Wendy says, 'the last thing I wanted was for Kurt to conform, to fit in'. From a strategic standpoint, Wendy was worse than wrong, she was inconsistent. The already muddled thirteen-year-old was torn by a mother who, compensating for the singular circumstances of her son's upbringing, concentrated on creating as loose an environment as possible, and a father who lobbied strongly for some kind of disciplined approach. 'It's hardly surprising he was screwy,' says Ernest Cobain. According to Ernest's ex-wife Toni: 'Kurt had a very delicate, haunted quality. Although he was mixed up, there was something unwittingly tender about him. He couldn't have been kinder to me when I married into the family. And I always remember the party when a gawky boy of six or seven was sitting by himself in the corner, looking miserable. Kurt went over and spent the whole evening talking to him. He had a genuine empathy with outcasts.'

It was predictable that in time Cobain's path would lead him to his uncle Chuck Fradenburg, drummer with the Aberdeen bar band Fat Chance. Fradenburg – who, along with Iris Cobain, emerges as what his cousin calls 'one of two people Kurt revered' – in turn introduced him to the group's guitarist, Warren Mason. 'He wasn't the guy you read about,' says Mason. 'Kurt was a quiet, but responsive kid who came alive around music.' In February 1981 Fradenburg offered to buy his nephew a guitar; Mason obtained a used six-string Lindell from a local electrician named Jeff Sanford, who remembers it as 'a piece of crap'. The instrument was restrung and painted by Mason, who sold it for $125 to Fradenburg, who presented it to Cobain. 'He was knocked out,' says Cobain's grandmother, who recalls deafening rehearsals taking place in her upstairs room that spring. 'Kurt was spellbound,' Mason confirms. 'Although the guitar was a piece of junk, it looked great' (sunburst red with a silver scratch-plate and chrome pick-ups), 'and he could already spray notes around like Jimmy Page. I was impressed, and apparently so was Chuck. He asked me to give Kurt lessons.'

According to Mason, Cobain's main goal was to learn 'Stairway To Heaven', the then ubiquitous Led Zeppelin anthem. Although he never mastered the song, Mason remembers his student as playing at dazzling speed, with real flair for the dynamics of rock guitar. 'He wasn't the most technically gifted kid in the world, but he had a genuine feel for timing and phrasing. Kurt knew that the gaps between the notes are as important as the music. He had an intuitive grasp of what would, and wouldn't work in a given song.' Significantly, Mason also describes Cobain as a 'good listener' whose pinched, introverted personality may have been a musical bonus ('the guitar became his best and only friend') and dedicated to the point that he persisted in playing left-handed, despite the technical problems this raised and the fact that 'Don still looked on it as a kind of perversion'.

Cobain cautiously and only sporadically scanned the respectable music press like *Rolling Stone* and *Creem*, but he listened avidly to the downmarket local radio stations. Strangely, therefore, he knew as much about country and western, hillbilly, bluegrass, folk and blues music as he did about rock and punk. 'That was a major factor,' says Mason. 'Because he listened to every kind of music, and he was young enough to be influenced in the heart rather than the head, all of those styles came out in later years. There was a strong undertow of folk and blues under the punk and speed metal ... Part of Kurt's problem was being painted into a heavy rock corner that wasn't his natural habitat.'

'It was definitely a good release,' Cobain would say of his early music. 'I thought of it as a job. It was my mission ... As soon as I got [the Lindell], I just became obsessed with it.' Toni Cobain believes 'Kurt's eyes would light up' around the guitar; 'he was at his obstreperous best when he was playing it,' says Sanford. With few friends of anywhere near his own age, it is not stretching belief to say that music filled the gap for Cobain caused by the damaging combination of neglect and stifling possessiveness with which he grew up. Even at this stage, one parent would periodically intervene in his life specifically to contradict the other. Although Don was quite happy for Cobain to continue guitar lessons, Wendy abruptly ended them in May 1981 after reading her son's eighth-grade report card. 'It really hurt him,' says Cobain's friend Jeannie Richards. 'That [guitar] was the only way he expressed himself.' 'It was, as Kurt saw it, yet another ritual humiliation,' adds a neighbour.

This was the period, between fourteen and sixteen, when Cobain's image of himself began to take shape. As in his childhood, it was the image of an outsider, but the special character it acquired and in the light of which Cobain continued to see himself throughout his life, was that of a creative genius, able to absorb styles faster than other teenagers and held back only by the negative pressure of his parents. Although his formal training lasted a mere three months, the die of Cobain's career had been unerringly cast. Witness after witness confirm both Wendy's misgivings and Cobain's reaction to them: he bitterly resented his mother's interference, but it did not break his spirit. Compensation came in the form of his uncle, of Mason, and in his discovery of Rosevear's Music Store, whose present manager Les Blue says, 'Kurt practically moved into the rehearsal room upstairs.' All parties agree that, even though Cobain's guitar lessons stopped dead that summer, the instrument was already part of his nervous system, a symbol of his incapacity for any other kind of disciplined effort.

Cobain seized every opportunity to expand his repertoire. By his fifteenth birthday he could play AC/DC's 'Back In Black', The Cars' 'My Best Friend's Girl', Led Zeppelin's 'Communication Breakdown' and the inevitable 'Louie, Louie'. According to Mason, Cobain's tastes ran heavily to those groups and to 'screamers like Ozzy Osbourne', as well as to old Hendrix, Beatles and Carpenters numbers, on whose tunefulness and sharpness of melody he commented to Chuck Fradenburg. Cobain later tried to deny these influences, only to revive them again at the end of his life. His self-portrayal in the 1980s as a 'stone punk' would consciously ignore what Mason calls the '50 per cent shareholding' enjoyed by mainstream influences like country and pop. 'The idea that he was a purist is nonsense,' says Toni Cobain. 'It was the whole idea of music, rather than one particular style, that appealed. When Kurt was upstairs in his room the guitar was his ally, the one thing he related to. It reached the point where he didn't mind being

41

"grounded" by Don or Wendy. It just meant he got to be alone with his best friend.'

When Cobain had appeared in his little girl's tunic for the Babe Ruth baseball team he met a teenage musician named Matt Lukin. Lukin played bass in the Melvins, an Aberdeen band then relying on Led Zeppelin and Hendrix covers, later to emerge in the vanguard of what became known as 'grunge' – the meeting-point between punk and heavy metal. Cobain also met the Melvins' singer Buzz Osborne, two years older but already several miles further down the road to anarchy. Osborne, who knew something of Tacoma and Seattle, was the first to expose Cobain to contemporary new wave – bands like Flipper, MDC and the engagingly named Butthole Surfers – as well as aspects of the punk lifestyle. 'There was a *big* change in Kurt in 1982,' says his cousin. 'He went from being a mixed-up but quiet boy to this *angry* young man. It seemed like he finally had a cause he could identify with.'

The Melvins met Cobain's fascination with friendship. Lukin and Osborne accelerated his interest in the Sex Pistols, then, retracing punk's steps, in figures like Richard Hell, Patti Smith, the New York Dolls and the Velvet Underground. He learnt something of the Standells and the Shadows of Knight. The effect on Cobain was electric. Whereas since 1976 his energy had been devoted not to exploiting, but to concealing his personality – causing some to conclude he lacked ambition or drive – now he displayed a lack of restraint and extravagance of style that made it difficult for others to take him seriously. He bought a new guitar and an amplifier. He experimented with clothes and haircuts, abandoning the fluffy sweaters and feathered David Cassidy look imposed by Wendy. In Rosevear's Cobain now gave it as his ambition to 'get stoned and worship Satan'.'' He routinely achieved the first, travelling in to Aberdeen with what Megan Kern calls 'a ton of grass' zippered into his quilted jacket. (Cobain still sang in the church choir, where his voice attracted attention.) As at other times in his life, there was a sense in which his transformation betrayed a grain of self-consciousness. 'Impressive as it was,' says Kern, there was something 'hugely contrived' about Cobain's reincarnation. Members of the family believe he clung to Lukin and Osborne as surrogate father-figures rather than (in his cousin's words) 'buying the punk message', while Warren Mason notes 'he still listened to mainstream radio and to groups like Cheap Trick', whom he admired because of the 'ironic detachment' of the lyrics.

He began to practise with other musicians, members of the Melvins or the 'stoner metalhead kids' he gravitated to at school. Cobain's report for his final year at Montesano ('Restless, bored and uncooperative') reflected his growing attachment to those, like Lukin, for whom compulsory education was 'unfocused bedlam', and his increased reliance on his new policy of self-improvement. At Timberland Library he discovered S.E. Hinton and William Burroughs, whose work would have an increasing influence on Cobain's life; he read Burgess admiringly and J.D. Salinger without complaint. Cobain hated Scott Fitzgerald, whose critical resurgence was in decline, neither liked nor understood Faulkner and couldn't talk about Hemingway without losing his temper. He began to develop a romantic association with poets like Rupert Brooke and Siegfried Sassoon, and once startled his neighbour by announcing: 'War means everything to a writer.' 'He got that idea from a book, too,' says Kern.

The final chapter of Cobain's formal education began in 1983 when he transferred to Aberdeen High School. The sprawling, turn-of-the-century complex, spread over four blocks centred on North I Street, brought Cobain into closer contact with Wendy, still living in the family home less than half a mile to the east. The coincidence served only to revive the old conflict between mother and son. 'He didn't want to be part of the family,' Wendy told Azerrad, 'but he wanted to live in the family house. He complained about everything I asked him to do, which was very minimal.' Both his mother and stepmother made various efforts to coax Cobain to think seriously about his future, including arranging part-time jobs for him and taking him to interviews. Neither woman made the slightest impact. 'Kurt was just a *pest*,' says a family member. 'Lewd, dirty, self-centred and still manipulating Don and Wendy by playing one off the other.' The tendency was also at work in Cobain's social life. 'There was a party at my place that winter,' says a local man named Larry Fancher. 'Buzz [Osborne], who was invited, showed up with Kurt, who wasn't. First Cobain was showing off, pulling faces behind people's backs, which he thought was totally hilarious. Then he sat for an hour smoking, really stoned and aggressive – he had that evil "don't fuck with me" expression of his, glaring up and down. Finally he went upstairs, shat all over the bathroom floor and put raw eggs in my bed. After that I didn't invite Osborne to any more parties.' Not surprisingly, Cobain did badly at school, ignoring other students and taking exception to the 'apocalyptic racist' views of his teachers. 'He was an absolute smart-ass,' says a man then on the school faculty. 'If you didn't buy that "sensitive artist" crap, all you were left with was a narcissist with about two friends in the whole town.' Among them was a displaced Croatian, two years older and eight or more inches taller than Cobain, named Chris Novoselic.

Novoselic was born in California on 16 May 1965. His parents Krist and Maria had emigrated in 1963, and settled on the west coast for sixteen years before moving with their two sons to Aberdeen – home to a large Croatian community – where Mr Novoselic took a job as a machinist. With his distinctive appearance (6 feet 7 inches tall by the time he graduated, and with a jutting Cro-Magnon jaw) and attitude to school ('They were assholes') it was inevitable that Chris Novoselic and Kurt Cobain would meet. The legend is that the two gravitated separately to the Melvins' practice room, where they discovered a mutual love of punk and situationist behaviour, although the assistant at Rosevear's is adamant: 'Chris introduced himself to Kurt right here, with the words "How about a smoke?"' Whatever the truth, it is certain they knew each other in 1983, that they shared a hatred of authority – not so much in principle as in its exercise over them by others – and saw music as the escape from a dead-end existence in Aberdeen.

The following May Wendy Cobain married a longshoreman, Pat O'Connor, who fiercely opposed taking in his new stepson. O'Connor does not make a sympathetic figure. He was hard-living and boorish, showing little concern for the feelings of his younger wife and less understanding of her children. The sense Cobain had of being isolated in a hostile world deepened as he was passed weekly, sometimes daily, between relatives in Aberdeen, Montesano and Hoquiam. It took Cobain 'months' to change his mother's and O'Connor's minds, crying on the telephone and, according to a relative, frequently threatening to kill himself. This 'adolescent identity crisis', as his cousin calls it, was partly resolved when, in a controlled experiment, Cobain was allowed to visit his mother, sister and stepfather in the East 1st Street home that summer. An attempt to live together as a family, however, proved disastrous. Cobain and any adult were incompatible, and he bitterly resented the way O'Connor treated his mother. For the rest of his life Cobain was an enthusiastic teller of stepfather stories, and the author Jonathan Raban saw how 'frantic hate' and 'implacable jealousy' had left a legacy of bewilderment, anger and rage, which 'Kurt played up to' in later years. In one famous incident a family dispute was settled by Wendy seizing as many of her husband's guns (there were dozens) as she could carry and hurling them in the Wishkah River. Later that night Cobain dredged the weapons from the water and sold them to buy musical equipment and drugs – a symbolic act, his cousin believes, in which 'Kurt turned, if not swords into plough-shares, then at least guns into guitars'.

In his junior year at high school Cobain met a would-be artist and Led Zeppelin fan named Myer Loftin. Loftin remembers him as 'unusually quiet' and 'only interested in music', although with a redeeming fondness for marijuana and LSD. 'There were some nights at [Wendy's] where Kurt would get stoned and start babbling about being a rock star,' says Loftin. 'I remember him playing these Zeppelin riffs and telling me I ought to take up guitar. Kurt's basic vibe was that making music was the greatest thing in the world, and that if I didn't want to join in, my role was to feed his ego and tell him how brilliant he was.'

More importantly, as a member of what he terms the 'so-called gay community', Loftin again brought to the surface all his friend's anxieties about sex. Cobain had known one other homosexual, an Aberdeen man called John Phalen who raised eyebrows by once appearing in the Pourhouse Tavern with what a local describes as 'faggot pants'. Cobain had always been polite to Phalen, the more easily since there was nearly twenty years age difference between them. But Loftin was his contemporary, born in the same year. To his cheerfully admitted lifestyle and reputation as a debauchee, Loftin was now adding fame as 'Kurt's fancy-boy' and eventually as the 'buttfucker' befriended by the school reject. For a man nagged by self-doubt like Cobain, Loftin's friend-ship quickly brought yet another crisis in his fragile self-confidence.

Nothing suggests that Cobain had started an active sex

life by 1984. There was a 'stoner girl', recalled only as Jackie, with whom he saw *Spinal Tap* in Aberdeen: another teenager in Westport briefly enjoyed the fame of having been 'finger-fucked by Kurt' during a different film. But in so far as he had any interest at all, Cobain was a sexual hobbyist, a keen collector of soft pornography and prone to wild speculation about the 'big-titted bitches' (both sexes in that part of Washington tend to a muscular physique) invited by Wendy to East 1st Street or seen walking outside Tolson's Country Mart. His reaction to Loftin showed the same convergence of naïvety and schoolboy prurience. For a period the two were inseparable, walking arm in arm from the high school to Wendy's house, or deliberately enraging Cobain's stepfather by gazing into each other's eyes at the dinner table. Homosexuality, to Cobain, never carried its local aura of criminality and dissipation; rather, it appealed to the twin tenets of his worldview, to be as different as possible and to offend mainstream Aberdeen as often as possible. 'After that,' Cobain told Azerrad, 'I started being proud of the fact I was gay, even though I wasn't. I really enjoyed the conflict.'

Cobain's break with Loftin, the boldness with which he took up his friend's cause and then turned it against him, showed how fickle he was. His suddenness in dropping both people and causes was part of a lifelong pattern of reversing himself on key issues. According to Loftin, Cobain 'simply appeared one day and said he was getting too much grief for being the friend of a faggot. He used the word faggot. Then he gave me a stiff little hug, turned on his heel and walked away. That was the last I saw of him for three years.'

When in the 1990s Cobain became known as a heroin user, immense effort went into downplaying his habit. Words like 'brief', 'casual' and 'non-addictive' were used to explain his dependence, and he described himself as having 'dabbled' with drugs for only a year. One of his friends, Dana James Bong, would tell the Seattle *Times* he was convinced 'Kurt was the only kid I knew who didn't smoke, didn't drink beer and didn't smoke pot.' Yet Megan Kern and others were aware of Cobain's reputation as a drug user as early as 1982. Loftin, too, believes 'Kurt dabbled with dope', although dabbled underestimates a habit that included, at minimum, marijuana, amyl nitrate, LSD and a taste for the local hallucinogenic mushrooms. By 1986 Cobain was addicted to Percodans, an opiate-based painkiller, and injected himself with heroin for the first time that summer. When he took a job as a janitor in a dentist's surgery it was as much for the availability of nitrous oxide as for work experience. It will be remembered that, as a child, Cobain had been prescribed amphetamines and sedatives, thus setting up a pattern of relying on drugs to offset his boredom or exhaustion, but at the cumulative cost of ruining his health. It was understandable that, at the end of his life, Cobain would seek to deny his long history with heroin, for the same reason he tried to reverse his positions on homosexuals and women. By then the Aberdeen misfit had become a rich and famous rock star, jetting between his homes in Los Angeles and Seattle, and some form of reinvention appeared necessary, if not essential. Even so the evidence of a man like Loftin bears conviction, as does the memory of Les Blue, who, even at the drive-in theatre he managed before Rosevear's, recalls 'Kurt graffitiing the hell out of my bathroom' by scrawling HEROIN next to the words SID AND NANCY and a picture of a syringe.

'Kurt's last year in school was hell,' says Toni Cobain. With the arrival of punk 'he went from being remote to being in a different world', an impression confirmed by Cobain's childhood friend Cameron Ross: 'He stood out like a turd in a punch bowl.' In his teachers' eyes he was a lost cause, someone struggling to find himself interesting, and with a love of confrontation – 'It was fun to fuck with people all the time,' Cobain would admit – much rued by his family. His constituency was the small but growing number of fans gravitating to the Melvins, a fellow new-waver named Dale Crover (who joined the group on drums) and Novoselic. Cobain himself auditioned to become a Melvin, but, in his own words, 'was so nervous that I forgot all the songs'. The relationship, still that of a fan to his idols, survived; Osborne and Lukin persevered with Cobain and took him with them to concerts in Tacoma and Seattle. To such unheard-of friendship he responded by becoming a 'cling-on' – being weak, Cobain's tendency was to follow the lead of strong characters around him – and for a year he and Osborne were inseparable. In August 1984 the two saw Black Flag play at Seattle's Mountaineer Club, a pivotal moment in that it completed Cobain's conversion from the heavy-rock fan he was to the self-professed punk he became. (In one version Cobain even sold his previously sacred Aerosmith and Kiss LPs in order to raise money for a ticket.) According to a third party present that night, 'Kurt heard a lot of music at about the same time: Psychedelic Furs and the Cars were both in town that week. So was Chuck Berry. Cobain went to all of those shows. I think what got to him was the excitement of live gigs, and the possibilities they opened up for him of making it. He always had a major ambitious streak. He loved Black Flag, no question, but there was also a sense of, "If some last-ditch has-been like Berry can do it, so can I".' That left the question of a market. Here, again, Cobain's timing, as it would throughout his life, proved flawless. The very day of the Black Flag concert happened to be the day MTV – with a rights document promising 'coverage of new wave and new talent every-where' – went on to the stock exchange. The coincidence was exquisite, Cobain completing his musical education with the desire to go professional at the exact moment a vehicle sprang up to accommodate him.

Cobain spent the winter of 1984–5 listening to and playing every kind of music he could get his hands on. To subversives like Scratch Acid and Flipper he added his liking for old-fashioned Deep Purple and Black Sabbath, and a lingering admiration for the Beatles. All this noise – from the melodic precision of a McCartney to the hysterical squall of the Melvins and Butthole Surfers – began to congeal in Cobain's mind, setting up what Warren Mason calls 'an encyclopedic grasp of pop, from Robert Johnson to Johnny Rotten'. According to Myer Loftin, 'he listened to every type of music, but particularly the old-fashioned stuff you could actually hum'.

This makes little sense when done in the name of purism; it may make more sense in the name of commercialism. However atonal and free-form punk might sound, it can be practised successfully only by people who believe single-mindedly in its mission to tear down the dinosaurs of rock, to shun the pretensions of arenas and concept albums and, above all, to keep it simple. Cobain's personality could not have been more remote from this world of duty, vocation, commitment and self-sacrifice. As Mason says, he studied music not out of revolutionary zeal, but with an eye firmly on the mainstream horizon. For someone who slouched through most of his schooldays, Cobain came startlingly alive when a Billy Joel or Meatloaf record appeared on campus. Bob Hunter remembers 'Kurt [being] jolted from the slumbers of class' by listening to the Top Twenty on radio, each song of which he would critique for its structure and melody. 'Even at seventeen, he was less of an idealist and more of a pragmatist than people thought.'

Hunter taught Cobain for his last year at Aberdeen High. By then he was spending as much time practising or talking about music as he was in school, although he could still be seen in the smokers' shed at the rear of the main building, where a fellow student remembers him having 'the biggest joint, the most pills and the weirdest kinks', one of which was his preference for wearing tight-cut women's underwear. Elsewhere in Aberdeen, where memories remained of Cobain's attachment to Loftin, it was rumoured that he sold his body to the deadbeats on Heron Street or at least engaged in a drugs-for-sex traffic in order to support his habits. Looking back from a perspective of ten years Hunter himself remembers:

> A quiet brooding kid, who I doubt was as interested in sex as much as art or music. Even in those days Kurt had a flair for adapting old songs to make them sound new. And he showed positive genius for dissecting someone else's tune and rearranging it ... There was also a large streak of hostility and anger which I, for one, tried to respect. Although he was intense about music, Kurt seemed to shut off completely from everything else. I've never in my life known someone as out of sorts with his surroundings as he was. Cobain's problem was that he was a New York or Los Angeles sort of person stranded in Aberdeen.

A mountain of effort was devoted to ensuring that Cobain graduated from high school. Hunter believes that Cobain's problem was not lack of intelligence but an attitude of mind. This attitude was said by Don to lack both discipline and self-restraint. On the other hand, if like Wendy you did not want Cobain restrained, the problem was that the school wanted him to conform. While his parents continued to argue, Cobain went about his life, smoking, swallowing pills and practising the guitar, reviving what Hunter, like

Cobain's family, calls the 'James Dean tradition' of setting oneself up as irrevocably odd, maintaining a silent vigil against routine and convention and shunning all friends except fellow loners and small children.

Early in 1985 Wendy and Pat O'Connor, finally tiring of Cobain's behaviour, again returned him to his father in Montesano. The experiment of living together as a family had proved a failure. Don's first act was to insist that Cobain pawn his guitar – it was redeemed a week later – then that he sit the Navy entrance exam. According to a member of Don's family: 'It was offered as a last chance for Kurt to pull himself together, and to find a job that would get him out of Aberdeen.' Another relative believes that 'both Don's kids had become increasingly anti-social and remote from the people who housed them and paid their bills'. Nowhere was this truer than with Cobain, whose defiance swelled in response to parental complaints about excessive spending, poor grades and a lack of ambition. In spring 1985 he turned down the Navy, then to no one's surprise dropped out of school before again returning to Wendy. It would be seven years before he next saw his father.

The move displeased the O'Connors immeasurably. Wendy was pregnant again and admitted thinking, 'I've screwed up my first kid, what am I doing having another one?' O'Connor's views are unknown, but as a hard-drinking longshoreman with a distaste for 'fags' and 'longhairs' it can be assumed that he, too, had doubts. In fact Cobain's occupancy at East 1st Street lasted barely a month until, returning from a day in the Melvins' practice room, he found all his belongings packed in boxes stacked outside the front door. It was the first application of the 'tough love' regime that his mother and later his wife would impose on Cobain in an attempt to, as a relative puts it, 'have the iron enter his soul'. Wendy may have been inconsistent over discipline and parental control, but this was incidental to her main concern. Never much troubled about wanting Kurt to conform, she had always been more deeply interested in ensuring he made a living. O'Connor's salary and her own job as a clerk in a department store barely covered expenses for the family, and with a new baby due Wendy was in no mood to support her unemployed adult son. In the last of a long line of unhappy departures Cobain left East 1st Street in July 1985, trailing his cardboard boxes a few doors away to a one-room apartment he shared with his friend Jesse Reed.

Cobain had lived with Reed's family earlier in the year during a period of mutual antipathy with Don and Wendy. Dave Reed, himself a singer in a local surf band, would recall being struck by some of Cobain's behaviour, a view that was mild compared with his wife's. (Mrs Reed's comments were of a part with a growing consensus on Cobain by his contemporaries' parents. His friend Greg Hokanson's mother describes entertaining him as 'like living with the devil', while Maria Novoselic's first thoughts were, 'Oh, my God, who's this?') The family nonetheless fed and housed Cobain for weeks, insisting only that he pay 'scant attention' to his appearance and respect their Christian beliefs, both requests he would later satirize in 'Lithium'. One of the Reeds adds merely that 'Kurt was always on the side of Kurt' and that he was a negative influence whose effect he sees at work even today on Jesse, currently enrolled in a drug rehabilitation programme for addiction to amphetamines.

A woman named Donna Kessler was intrigued to see a notice in the Polish Club Tavern that summer asking for volunteers 'for the pleasure of cleaning for 2 dedicated partyers, payment all the ab [affybud, marijuana] you can toke'. Kessler entered the apartment to be 'physically disgusted by the sight . . . there was rotting food and old beer bottles all over, dirty underpants thrown around and that terrible smell, as if someone had died.' As Cobain himself later put it:

I had the apartment decorated in typical punk rock fashion with baby dolls hanging by their necks with blood all over them. There was beer and puke and blood all over the carpet, garbage stacked up for months. I never did do the dishes. Jesse and I cooked food for about a week and then put all our greasy hamburger dishes in the sink and filled it up full of water and it sat there for the entire five months I was there.

While Cobain had attended school and lived with one or other of his parents, at least some sort of check had remained on his behaviour. Now no such curb existed. In the space of that summer and autumn his drug habit worsened, he added practical experience to his interest in sex (keeping up an active life, according to Kessler, as a voyeur; his 'special thing' was to take polaroids of the woman while she masturbated, pictures he then left lying openly around the room). As to showers, he seemed not to overdo them. Cobain, had he but known it, was on his way to virtually inventing what became the grunge lifestyle: an underachieving, underemployed existence, heavily dependent on indulgent and, if divorced, guilt-ridden parents, frequently sustained by a fierce intelligence and the determination to grasp complex issues such as health care and the environment over short-term problems like finding a job. Added to Cobain's natural inclinations for drugs and music, and his love of macabre artwork like the dolls, it was possible to see how the apartment struck Kessler as 'some kind of life-slice exhibit' or why Maria Novoselic believed 'Kurt was changing right before our eyes'.

Novoselic had a point. The empty space above her beauty shop on South M Street became the rehearsal room for a series of Melvins spin-off groups including her son, Osborne, Lukin, Crover and, reverting to his childhood passion, Cobain on drums. The Stiff Woodies and an ersatz country-rock group, the Sellouts, gave way to Fecal Matter, famous not only for having caused a riot at the Spot Tavern, a beach bar north of Aberdeen, but for providing a first outlet for Cobain's own material. The rough tape recorded by Mary Fradenburg suggests a talent based on substantially more than mere anger; Cobain took it upon himself to deliver the vocals in an unremarkable but surprisingly competent English warble and the record crackles with something that appears to be *Nevermind*'s elder brother: all histrionic drums and heavy-riffing guitar, tempered by a reassuring ear for the hook. Although Novoselic avoided Fecal Matter and the faster numbers deteriorated into thrashing, with its mud-dark sound and poison-pen lyrics the group represented Cobain's arrival as a bold, gifted songwriter and a raucous but immensely controlled singer who was exhilarating to behold.

Unemployed and owing four of his five months' tenancy in rent, Cobain moved out of his apartment in December 1985. For the rest of the year he spent his time in the Timberland Library, living with Novoselic or sleeping rough. This was the origin of one powerful Cobain legend: that for an extended period, hovering between the worlds of Don and Wendy and punk rock, his only home had been the shelter of the North Aberdeen Bridge, a bleak wood and concrete structure crossing the Wishkah River between two zones of run-down shacks, and surviving on a diet of fish, blackberries and smuggled-in drugs.* In fact, Cobain lived outdoors for less than a week. A man who visited him remembers 'Kurt hunkered down among the pilings and holly bushes, with a fire going and the continuous joints and cheap wine' without which he was unable to function, while a local teenager,

* Cobain's own version would appear on *Nevermind*'s 'Something In The Way'.

Amy Griggs, recalls the 'romantic, Tom Sawyer feel' of the place, where Cobain once told her he was spending 'a couple of nights' before moving in with friends (Novoselic and Crover) in Aberdeen.

He was rescued, first by these two, then by an English teacher at Aberdeen High named Lamont Shillinger. Shillinger and his wife ran what was almost a safe-house for displaced youth. With six children of their own, as they put it, 'one more mouth to feed wasn't a big deal'.

Like Bob Hunter, Shillinger saw a 'rebellious-but-shy, Jimmy Dean' streak in Cobain:

> He was a quiet kid who was constantly drawing or scribbling in notebooks, rather than actually playing an instrument. Kurt hated Aberdeen, mainly because it wasn't 'artistic' enough for someone of his sensibilities. I told him if he spent all his time in bars and greasy diners, it wasn't surprising the only people he met were rednecks and truck-drivers . . . He also had a special place in his heart for Don and Wendy. Kurt hated them. Neither of his parents contacted us once the whole eight months he was here.

When Cobain had broken with Ryan Agnew and Myer Loftin he spoke of loathing other people and of being shut off from friendly feelings altogether. Even James Dean never said that. Yet this was a person with genuine sympathy for the loner and outcast, who wrote poetry and drew birthday cards, and sat for hours with the children in North End Park, one of whom remembers him as 'the Saint Sebastian of Aberdeen'. That Cobain was troubled is certain – only people's defects interested him, and he played more naturally on their weaknesses rather than appealing to their strengths, thus making a habit of, as Hunter puts it, 'expressing self-hate by cruelty towards others'. The Sellouts had disbanded after Cobain physically attacked the bass player, Steve Newman, by hitting him wildly over the head with a plank, and his friendship with the Shillingers ended violently when Cobain punched and kicked one of his hosts' sons unconscious in a misunderstanding about a pizza. He moved out the next morning, staying alternately with Crover and Novoselic and returning the Shillingers' kindness – Cobain never paid rent – by pelting another of their children with a fusillade of full beer cans and pointedly referring to them around Aberdeen as 'jerks'.*

Cobain has inevitably attracted the interest of psychologists, one of whom has written that his anger was the result of conflict with his father, first because Don 'never understood' his son, and second because of some Oedipal rivalry over Wendy. A more likely explanation is that Don personified an unwelcome reminder of the real world of jobs and responsibility, and that his mother's at first obsessive love encouraged a sense of his own uniqueness and his certainty that others owed him a living.

This was the image that Cobain set up of himself during his final months in Aberdeen: a moody, highly strung individual whose brain seethed, shunned by his family, forced to scrounge an existence off the land and absorbing his parents' hostility by a hardness of heart quite unlike the affection he showed 'real people'. Among the last were Osborne and Novoselic, with whom Cobain formed a sort of assault party on establishment Aberdeen. There was an incident at the Pourhouse Tavern; another night they set fire to a house; and a graffiti raid for which (after the words GOD IS GAY were spray-painted on a church) Cobain

---

* Cobain would adopt a more conciliatory attitude by 1993, when he included an acknowledgement to the Shillinger family on *In Utero*.

received a $180 fine and a thirty-day suspended sentence. This was a period when, shuttling between his new friends, briefly returning to the bridge and not unknown at the Aberdeen Juvenile Facility, Cobain clung to Novoselic as a father-figure. Those who knew him and recalled his tendency to bond to strong characters were unsurprised by what an uncle calls 'Kurt's infatuation' for the likeable, plain-spoken Novoselic or by his renewed demand that the two form a group. (Cobain's first official live performance had been in Olympia, fifty miles east of Aberdeen, with Crover and Osborne; the review of the concert panned the trio for 'coming on like retards'.) After a long campaign to persuade Novoselic to listen to the Fecal Matter tape, Cobain finally succeeded in arranging rehearsals with his friend on bass and a man named Bob McFadden on drums, first in a garage, then returning to the empty room over the beauty parlour. When Novoselic brought his new colleague downstairs for lunch Cobain dropped a heavy glass to the floor, causing Maria to flinch. Cobain, with his acne, nervous tic and cigarette ash must have been among the very last house-guests she would have chosen.

With a loan from his father and $40's worth of food stamps a month Cobain was able to ape the manners of blue-collar Aberdeen and develop a taste for generous meals, outsize drinks and loud cars. He was not, of course, the first rock musician who could claim humble origins nor the first to exploit them, but few have been able to distance themselves so completely from their roots while maintaining so many of their childhood traits. As well as Cobain the radical nonconformist, there was a Cobain who had an inbred feeling for small-town America and a nostalgic reverence for the working-man's values. 'Anyone,' says Lamont Shillinger, 'who thinks Kurt deliberately withdrew from society, waiting for his fans to call him, has a very narrow view of Kurt. He was always calculating and planning ahead . . . The two things people overlook in Cobain are his ambition and the fact that, much as he loathed it, there was a large chunk of Aberdeen in him.' Bob Hunter agrees: 'There was a conventional side to Kurt he hated, and above all a willingness to compromise to make a living.' Even as Cobain brooded over his poetry or practised the guitar, he took a series of jobs that suggest a person, still short of his twentieth birthday, with curiously old-fashioned values and a tolerance for hard work: over the course of two summers he was first a janitor, then a YMCA youth counsellor, and finally a maintenance-man at the Polynesian Ocean Front Hotel, where the house-keeper who hired him, Betty Kalles, recalls

> A young man who kept to himself and never smiled much ... Though Kurt was quiet, he was always well-dressed and clean-cut and, once he got to know you, friendly.
>
> Although he was never able to work on Fridays and Saturdays because his band would go out and practise on those days, he would always make it to work Sunday morning on time. It was as if he was living half in one world and half in another ... Kurt was a model worker, but when he quit his job he told me the chemicals he was using to wash the windows were making his fingernails soft and he was unable to play guitar.

That Cobain 'kept to himself' and 'never smiled much' comes as no surprise. No one expected him to be easy and affable when he imagined himself fighting in a death-struggle not only with his family, but with many of his own contemporaries. Too little weight, though, has been given to the idea that Cobain's war was as much with himself as with others. One side of him, even in 1986, was rooted in the conservative Aberdeen world, and the fact that he strove so consciously to be a rebel is the best evidence that by instinct he wasn't. As well as appearing 'well-dressed and clean-cut' at work, Cobain still irregularly attended church. He applied for and received a Social Security number. He took out a Prudential life insurance policy. And, according to one of his ex-classmates, he even re-considered joining the Navy – going so far as to submit an application – thus persuading a colleague that, to Cobain, 'rock music wasn't a philosophy, but a career choice. At bottom, all Kurt wanted to do was make a living.'

Late that year Cobain's mother put down $100 deposit on an abandoned, single-storey house at 1000½ East 2nd Street, in the next block to her own home. It was among the worst addresses in Aberdeen, an area of boarded-up slums and unkempt lawns filled with furniture and household appliances, and a beauty shop in which a homicide once took place in a dispute about a tip. Cobain and Matt Lukin moved in that Christmas. Something of the atmosphere of his former apartment returned. As well as the piled dishes and festering laundry, Cobain now installed a tankful of turtles. It was, he admitted, 'a very smelly, very odorous place', although he admired the reptiles' '"fuck you" attitude' and their tendency to retreat when threatened.

Michael Schepp, a delivery boy for the *Daily World*, once called at East 2nd Street to collect payment on a bill:

> I waited, and Cobain appeared, naked and looking as though he hadn't slept for a week. The stink almost knocked me out. There were turtles crawling on the floor right in the room and dolls hanging up by their necks from the ceiling, which looked like it had been written on in blood. A naked girl was asleep on the couch . . . Someone else was in the back room laughing.

Schepp's conclusion that this was a man 'living like an experiment' was confirmed by Cobain's increasing reliance on drugs. As well as his habit for marijuana and LSD and his dependence on pain-killing Percodans, he developed a lifelong practice of adapting household items like glue, cough syrup and even shaving-cream (whose gasses could produce an oxygen-like high) to his own uses. The conviction that he could handle drugs, the more of them the better, became the Gibraltar of his life, and Cobain learned to anticipate a variety of responses from his friends and neighbours. For every person, like Kalles, for whom he was 'a down-to-earth, gentle young man' there was another, like Schepp, who avoided him like the devil. Donna Kessler says she never walked past the house on East 2nd without feeling 'a touch of evil' from inside.

For more than a year Cobain, alone or in Novoselic's safari-striped Volkswagen, had been visiting the state capital, Olympia, home of the liberal arts Evergreen College and not coincidentally a hotbed of alternative rock music. Through Buzz Osborne he met a woman named Tracy Marander, a dyed-hair exotic with a zebra-print coat and a shared fascination for artwork made of Woolworths dolls, broken furniture, piled newspapers, anatomical kits and rusty pieces of her own neighbour's broken-down Nissan van. According to a woman who knew them: 'Kurt was smitten . . . Here was a girl with fireapple-red hair who liked to party, with her own place in Olympia.' The fact that Marander had heard and enjoyed Fecal Matter was thought to be a bonus. After a few weeks the two developed a relationship, he admiring her taste in music and Olympia connections, she impressed by his blue eyes and the 'really cool' Kiss mural he drew on the side of the Melvins' bus.

Don Cobain knew that his son became a rock star – he read it in the press – but they met only twice more before the reporters arrived in 1994 looking for clues about Kurt's death. Both Don and Wendy came forward, and conceal- ment was the last thing on their minds. They and other members of the family agree that the themes of loneliness, isolation, abandonment and betrayal took root in Cobain's youth, bringing about a pattern of deliberate and often self- centred opportunism that was later so characteristic of his career. According to Beverley Cobain, 'he learnt early on not to rely on anyone but himself', while his wildly fluctuating extremes of ego and insecurity were also the direct fruit of Aberdeen.

Although success came to Cobain suddenly and at an early age, the experience of his youth stayed with him. Along with his sense of being separate and aloof, he learned something practical about drugs and guns, and had the beginnings of an enigmatic sex life. Set against the violence of his relation- ships was the softer, compassionate side he reserved for animals and small children. He could be genuinely lovable to those he trusted. Added to the self-serving view of life as the responsibility of society, not the individual, Cobain developed both drive and motivation (while looking on their results with disgust) and pursued his music with what Warren Mason calls 'Beatles-like ambition'.

Cobain himself had mixed views about Aberdeen. On one level he clearly hated it, running down its 'jocks' and 'rednecks' and telling a reporter in 1993, 'There were a lot of Beavises and Butt-heads back there. The only difference is they weren't as clever as the guys on TV.' On the other hand it was precisely in his upbringing as a small-town rebel that Cobain felt himself to be remarkable, and it was in this light that he interpreted to the world the point of his work. In other words, he relished the myth of his own suffering. Keenly aware of his role as the exemplar of the self-made man, he played the part with an intensity that gave his performance the hint of an act. The first author of the

Cobain legend and the greatest of all its propagandists was Cobain himself.

There was also a part of him that was perversely nostalgic, and that part spoke when, 'to try and remind me to stay a child', he obtained a 'K' tattoo on his forearm, or when he wrote in his suicide note: 'I need to be slightly numb in order to regain the enthusiasm I once had as a child.' He spoke affectionately about Aberdeen to Tracy Marander and the other friends he made in Olympia. Bob Hunter is only the most convincing witness to the view that 'although Kurt had problems, there was a wilful streak in him that fought unnecessary battles and railed against enemies he didn't have'. In the eight remaining years of his life his opposition to his family and childhood acquaintances softened, and he came to see them in an increasingly appreciative light. He even spoke fondly of his old schools. One of Cobain's most poignant observations (passed on by Novoselic) was that, 'We [went] all around the world, and there's a little bit of Aberdeen everywhere.'

When he died, the Cobain legend drew strength from its apparent similarity to the Christian theme of atonement and redemption. Here was a drama in which a great man shouldered the burden of a blundering and ignorant people, suffered for them and was destroyed at the height of his success. According to this version of Cobain's life, Aberdeen became a composite Bethlehem-wilderness, somewhere he was unwanted, and then survived only to be tormented. Such images have been proved wrong in other cases (like that of James Dean) and begin to look suspect again. Cobain faced the perennial challenge of any sensitive child in a backwoods community. At the same time, until his late teens he was never without a sympathetic relative and others, like the Shillingers, who made him welcome. Even under the fiercest provocation, neither Don nor Wendy ever fully withdrew their support. He was never materially deprived. When

Cobain eventually left home it was because others had encouraged the playing and songwriting that served as his entrée to Olympia.

Tony Groves, one of the few to remain friendly with Cobain in both Montesano and Aberdeen, is among those who believe 'he was really living out the cartoon version of being a rebel. Things in Aberdeen were never *that* bad, not like being down-and-out in L.A. or New York. With enough ambition and a tankful of gas there was always Highway 12 to Seattle. That's still how I remember Kurt, stopping in the big Chevy and asking if I wanted a ride out of town. When I turned him down he just laughed and gunned the accelerator.'

Tension and Release

From then on ambition replaced anger as the main drive of Cobain's life. In Olympia he discovered a haven for misfits and bohemians, a thriving college radio station and magazine publishers, and no fewer than two independent record labels, K and Kill Rock Stars. Although he later dismissed the town as 'fucked-up' and 'dead', it is certain that, for at least a year, according to his neighbour Slim Moon, 'Kurt looked on Olympia like a kid in a toy store'. What Moon calls the 'brutal, materialistic society' that emerged in the Reagan years produced a backlash among culturally ambitious students, who found themselves unable to participate in the yuppie lifestyle or to accept mainstream rock music. Evergreen College was among those that not only tolerated but actively encouraged punk and new wave, setting up a campus of alternative record stores, clubs, stages, studios, and heavily populated conceptual art galleries, available not just to bona fide students but to anyone, like Cobain, who happened to walk in. 'Of course he was impressed,' says Moon. 'It was the first time in his life he felt a part of something.'

It must have been vexing for Cobain, having first tasted freedom in Olympia, to return to Aberdeen. For almost a year after he met Marander he was spending weekends in her apartment while still living in the house on East 2nd Street. His few remaining months there show how much Cobain resented the social and intellectual disadvantage that he felt, and how rarely he forgot a fight or backed away from confrontation. There was an incident that spring involving a fist-fight in the Polish Club Tavern, and another in which a vacant house was vandalized. A neighbour once called at East 2nd Street armed with a baseball bat. But Cobain also knew how to turn Aberdeen's misgivings about him to his advantage. Many of the lyrics written in his last days on East 2nd dealt with his childhood foes, and a repertoire swiftly developed of songs about lumberjacks, barbers, authority figures, rednecks and dysfunctional parents.

The other thing which Cobain was able to turn to his advantage was his ambition and his experience in Olympia of seeing punk groups in action. An important result of that experience was his renewed faith in practice and rehearsal. When a new drummer, Aaron Burckhard, joined Cobain and Novoselic in 1987 he found 'they wanted to practice *every* night', and Cobain himself told a journalist, 'We would play the set and then I'd start playing the songs again without even looking up to see if those guys wanted to play them ... I'd just whip them into shape.' The contrast between the lethargic, unkempt drop-out who shared his living-space with turtles and the man who organized rehearsals like a drill-sergeant was also commented on by Burckhard: 'Kurt could be a *tyrant*.'

As well as practising in East 2nd Street or the room above the beauty shop, driving to Olympia and rotationally bedding Marander and a woman named Terri Buell, Cobain continued to concentrate on his singing and songwriting. He was particularly concerned with finding a voice. Cobain derived a perversely satisfying inspiration from insulting and rebuffing those who helped him, so it comes as no surprise that, while later berating the British as 'the most snooty, cocksure, anal people [for whom] I have absolutely no respect,' he started his career singing in a marked English accent.

Burckhard, with his biker's moustache and disdain for

'punk shit', was always a short-term proposition. Novoselic, too, then going through a belated hippie phase, admits to doubts about Cobain's fanatical insistence on practice. According to a fourth person involved with the group, 'What was a sort of hobby for Chris and Aaron was taken by Kurt to such extremes that its very nature changed . . . Differences in degree grew into differences of kind.' What distinguished Cobain from the other two and what constantly took them by surprise, was how ambitious he really was. 'Kurt would have gone through a wall in order to be famous.'

The same party was present when Cobain began strumming the arrangement of what would become Nirvana's debut single, a cover of Shocking Blue's 'Love Buzz', and at the group's first scheduled concert, a house-party closed down by the police before the musicians themselves arrived. The first actual performance was at the GESCO Hall in Olympia, a predictable mix of originals ('Floyd The Barber', 'Aero Zeppelin' and 'Spank Thru') and obscure covers like 'Love Buzz' and Cher's 'Gypsies, Tramps and Thieves'. Tim Arnold was one of 'twenty or so freaks' present in the audience: 'Cobain was hilarious in a floral shirt, built-up shoes and make-up. He was deep into glam-rock, as well as sounding uncannily like David Bowie. If that seventies scene was a parody, no one had told Kurt. He really meant it.'

In April 1987 the trio played a live set on Radio KAOS, the college station in Olympia, which Arnold remembers as a 'stratospheric improvement' on the GESCO show. In the course of nine songs Cobain went through half-a-dozen voices; as well as what Arnold calls his 'camp, Anthony Newley bit', there was an Ozzy Osbourne scream and a parody of a southern drawl. On the rare occasions when he was not being someone else, Cobain sang in an unexpectedly soft west coast accent with the odd New York overlay. His voice had a lazy, almost drunken quality, and even on the slower numbers he seemed to be a half-phrase behind the beat, while the lyrics that would later be simultaneously self-lacerating, spiteful and trembling with fury were nowhere to be heard.

When Cobain, Novoselic and Burckhard appeared at a theatre in Tacoma, the group instinctively came up with the name Skid Row (the area of Seattle where in the early part of the century, logs would be skidded downhill onto barges). Another night they played as Ted Ed Fred, and on others still as Bliss, Pen Cap Chew, Throat Oyster and Windowpane. Finally Cobain settled on Nirvana. Even then his mainstream sensibilities and lifelong love of 'straight pop' overcame the apocalypse of his conversion to new wave: 'I wanted a name that was beautiful and nice and pretty instead of a mean, raunchy punk rock name like the Angry Samoans,' he told Azerrad. 'I wanted something different.' By 1992 Cobain would change his mind about the name, after two other Nirvanas were paid $50,000 and $100,000 in order to settle copyright suits.

In the final days in the house on East 2nd Street living conditions touched bottom. The electricity and water supply had long been cut off. Cobain could not wash or pull the lavatory chain, and the summer smell of the turtles reached unprecedented levels. His diet consisted of hamburger meat and eggs, which he pilfered from his mother's house, and stale bread scavenged from the garbage container behind Tolson's Country Mart. As far as he had a job it lay in rehearsing, singing, songwriting and in scrawling poems, which, if dissatisfied, he would set alight and leave burning on the porch of the Open Bible Church. It was after the destruction of not only a wooden notice-board but an expensive crucifix and other artefacts that the police called at East 2nd with the suggestion that Cobain's presence in Aberdeen would be more sparingly required in future. Overnight, the local misfit had been transformed into an outlaw, heretic and fire hazard. Now Cobain was finally ready to leave town.

In September 1987 Cobain moved into Marander's apartment at 114 North Pear Street in Olympia, a neighbourhood barely more distinguished than the one he had just left. The building itself was decrepit, a wood-sided house in peeling yellow with plastic tarpaulins for windows, screened from the road by a row of sycamores and a small hill, and an overgrown front yard. Cobain's neighbours were the Washington State Lottery building, Jackpot Food Mart and an old church converted into a recording studio. The rent, paid exclusively by Marander, was $137 a month. Although unemployed and destitute, Cobain pursued both his music and his art, and according to Moon 'used to invite people in to see his work-in-progress, and also to hear about new projects'. Cobain took 'impersonal pride in his work, and used to show pieces off as though they were the view'. There was no view.

Moon had been present when Cobain, Crover and Osborne, posing as Brown Towel, had played together in Olympia the year before. 'I knew Kurt as this ragged-ass kid who hung out with the Melvins,' he says. 'I couldn't have been less impressed when he came on; it was like the school nerd getting to do his bit on speech day.' An hour later Moon was converted. To his amazement, 'Kurt had real talent – not only singing and playing, but in the way he put a song across. He had presence.' Moon and his friend Dylan Carlson, next-door neighbours of Marander, both spread the word about the other-worldly new arrival. 'Although Kurt was highly motivated,' says Moon, 'he was a recluse his first winter in Olympia.' It is a fair bet that for several months Cobain himself, whose drug habit increased dramatically, had only a vague idea of this interest in his talent. Like many small-town exiles before him, he became a hostage to the ambitions of his patrons.

Moon describes the apartment on North Pear Street as 'Dickensian'. As well as the thrift purchases from Jackpot and Woolworths, there were lurid posters of Queen and the Rolling Stones, paintings by Cobain, huge collages torn from *People* and the *National Enquirer*, pet cats, rabbits, turtles and rats, a plastic monkey named Chim Chim and an arresting photograph – glued to the refrigerator door – of a diseased vagina.

Cobain's devotion to conceptual art, and particularly to his technique of oven-baking dolls, was surprising for someone who had never developed academic discipline. He spent days at a time searching for the right type of clay, moulding it into human form and scorching it until it turned skeletal white, then hanging the result by its neck from the ceiling or piercing it with a knife to the wall. Cobain's painting, according to Moon, was 'violent, semifigurative work. It generally portrayed a foetus lying in a gutter, or some gynaecological rendering. He had a positive fetish for the birth process.'

Cobain also had a talent for forging strange combinations ('Complete shit, souvenirs of the Old West, plastic ashtrays, Woolworths prints and tin apes that played the drums, all arranged into a legitimate sculpture,' according to a friend) and a flair for using household items like a milk carton or soap dish to 'activate the space'. His diorama in toothpaste and ink, four feet square and placed outside the turtles' aquarium, was the product of one of the dizzier flights of Cobain's imagination. 'Someone should have sat down with him at an early age and told him he was no artist,' says Charles Peterson. 'There were delusions of grandeur,' admits his friend.

By now Cobain was not only proficient at rock guitar, he was improvising and writing, stumbling on melodies by means he himself didn't fully understand. He mastered the instrument by ear and intuition. A visitor to North Pear Street was startled to hear Cobain 'play a dozen different styles – Angus Young, Rick Nielsen, Eric Clapton', then explain patiently how each musician achieved his desired effect. Moon agrees that 'one of his great strengths was having a repertoire. He could play old blues licks as well as punk.' Even Chuck Berry, not one to overpraise other musicians, believes 'he had a touch most guitarists would kill for'. With an almost monastic seclusion from Olympia life ('he was like a hermit in a cave', says Moon) and a fixation on practice and rehearsal, it was inevitable that Cobain would improve as a musician: the joining together of talent, ambition and a selfless girlfriend who provided for him made an irresistible combination.

From being a spoilt child Cobain followed a well-beaten path to self-indulgence as an adult. It may seem unfair to describe his years in Aberdeen as spoilt, but despite falling out with most of his family and all of his friends, he was never without at least one sympathetic and financially supportive backer. Don, Wendy, his aunt and uncle, friends like Novoselic and Crover and, later, the Shillingers had all come forward at moments of crisis, cumulatively leading to what his cousin calls 'a tentative grasp of reality'. Now Marander herself discovered that Cobain's commitment to the relationship fell short of entering into an equal partnership. Despite earning money at occasional concerts in Olympia, and $600 for a single performance in Seattle, Cobain made no contribution to the upkeep of North Pear Street. He responded to her requests to find a job by offering to move out and live in his car. Psychologically, of course, Cobain was chronically unsuited to the demands of earning a living. Still shy, still far from articulate, he was anything but a businesslike personality: he dreaded both manual and clerical labour, with their threats of effort and routine, he was addicted to his own company, and unable to compromise. It took a 'screaming ultimatum' from Marander before

Cobain finally took a job at a janitorial company, spending his nights scrubbing floors for doctors and dentists, and in turn pocketing whatever pills he could get hold of.

When Cobain had recorded his tape at Mary Fradenburg's home, most of the self-written songs had been snapshots of Aberdeen. The new material he wrote in Olympia mixed poses of scornful superiority and self-flagellating wit with a confirmed emphasis on melody and mainstream hard rock guitar. When Novoselic and Burckhard joined him in the tiny rehearsal room they sounded, says Moon, 'like a cross between Blue Oyster Cult and the Beatles'. This was the one ever-present quality of Cobain's music: while he knew something of the world of Black Flag and Flipper, his own compositions were solidly in the most conservative verse-chorus tradition. Cobain's shifting roles of rock superstar and new wave proselyte would obsess him until the end of his life. 'He never resolved it,' says a friend. 'Kurt was always trying to touch one last base, with the inevitable result that he ended up confusing himself.' Cobain's lifelong objective, Tim Arnold agrees, was to adapt out-and-out punk to the mass market, and still retain his credibility. For all his vaunted purity and aesthete's sense of reserve, the clear motivating force of Cobain's life was ambition. Late in 1987 he began saving money to record a professional tape, while one of the few visitors to get past his door in Olympia was a disc jockey and journalist named Bruce Pavitt, later head of Nirvana's first label.

A deep sense of isolation and a cramped capacity for personal communication stunted Cobain's emotional life. There was also the fact – he singled this out himself – that he was physically ill. As a child Cobain suffered from chronic bronchitis. In his teens he was diagnosed with scoliosis, a curvature of the spine in time worsened by the weight of his guitar. Now, in Olympia, Cobain first experienced the crippling stomach pain that 'made me want to kill myself every day'. The condition dominated Cobain's life, and baffled the most distinguished doctors, causing him to self-medicate with heroin and other drugs (including opiates, which he injected directly into his stomach) until 1993, when a surgeon diagnosed a pinched nerve in his spine, brought on by the scoliosis. While it was possible to sympathize with Cobain – and his episodes of gastric pain were real enough – it was also true that, in preferring to numb himself rather than seeking a cure, he conformed to the pattern created when, as a seven-year-old, he was prescribed amphetamines and sedatives. 'Every difficulty in life could be solved with a pill,' had been his teacher's report of his tendency to console himself with drugs. The result, according to his cousin, 'became two increasingly incompatible things – Kurt's happiness and his addiction'. Heroin did not conspicuously improve Cobain's temper. His stomach ache might have made him 'the single most miserable person in the world' but after years of listening to him complain about the problem, his friends could have made a strong bid for second place. In the period from 1988 to 1993 Cobain believed he spent 500 days – *500* – incapacitated by pain, or by his efforts to treat it. He may have seen a doctor a dozen times. As well as the mystery of the illness itself, there was a still more puzzling question. Cobain had an adequate brain; why did he switch it off when his health was concerned? He knew, of course, over the years, that injecting himself with Buprenex or heroin merely exacerbated a craving for more drugs, and that by dulling the nervous system he did nothing for his creative faculties. The only answer was that Cobain took medicine out of a sort of inertia, and that in dosing himself with whatever pain-killer he could get his hands on, he followed the precedent set up when, as a boy, he drank an entire bottle of cough syrup or swallowed thirty aspirin in a sitting. 'His addictive side came about then,' says Beverley Cobain. 'From early childhood it was a religion for Kurt that everything could be cured by drugs.'

When Burckhard left, abandoning rock to concentrate on his burgeoning career as production manager at Burger King, Cobain and Novoselic asked Dale Crover to return on drums. With money saved from Cobain's janitorial job, and a loan from Marander, the group paid to record six hours' material at Reciprocal Studios in Seattle. Three of the ten numbers appeared on Nirvana's first LP; four others can be found on the retrospective *Incesticide*. The session on 23 January 1988 is important in that it shows Nirvana's songs to have been already steeped in Cobain's beliefs that the world would be as anxious as he was to dwell on his personal miseries, and that the most intense lyrics could still be set to loud, electric rock and roll. It was also significant in that it brought Nirvana together with Jack Endino. This agreeably old-fashioned Navy veteran was a seminal – arguably *the* seminal – figure in establishing a Seattle Sound. At a time when other producers were concentrating on effects and studio technique, Endino's aim was to record a group exactly as it sounded on stage. In person Endino managed the rare feat of combining humour and melancholy in roughly equal parts, with consistently engaging results. As a producer he achieved something similar, helping to weave Beatles-influenced melodies around a post-R.E.M., new wave framework and, above all, keeping it basic. According to Grant Alden, a Seattle journalist who knew Endino well, 'Jack had a classic punk attitude in that he believed anyone should have access to the studio. He also knew how to record a band quickly and economically . . . While [Cobain] seemed to lose touch with the original source of his work the more famous he got, those songs he did at Reciprocal were some of the greatest music of the eighties.'

Endino was impressed by Cobain. Although the tone of his lyrics was reflective and introverted, the songs avoided dramatic excess. And when Cobain tore himself away from the subject of himself he could be genuinely funny: 'Floyd The Barber' mixes commentary on small-town America with a Sweeney Todd nightmare of being tied down and cut with a razor. 'Paper Cuts' is a sort of Addams Family horror. Crammed with ironic references, barnstorming guitars and an almost inebriated sense of rhythm, Cobain's songs showed astonishing maturity for someone only recently weaned from Aerosmith and Black Sabbath. 'The one thing I taught Kurt,' says Warren Mason, 'is that good music is about tension and release. You can hear that in the first songs he wrote, the way he mingled heavy rock with other influences. Whatever else you say about Kurt, he had ears.'

The other thing that Cobain had was a voice. Bearing in mind that all of the equipment used in modern studios to prop mediocre singers was missing at Reciprocal, and that the musicians were lucky if more than one microphone was working, Cobain showed outstanding skill in imbuing the vocals with personality, as well as raw power. On the slower songs he showed a grasp of nuance and timing; in the thrashes his screams broke into raspy, pubescent climaxes. Endino himself thought Cobain's voice was the group's secret weapon: 'I didn't know whether to laugh or cry at the band, but the vocals could raise your hair up.' Gone was the strangulated British twang, replaced by a blues-like snarl with which Cobain belted the songs. If Nirvana benefited from a carefully planned division of labour – Novoselic at this stage acting as group spokesman and wit and Crover dealing with bookings and logistics – then Cobain was free to concentrate on his singing and songwriting, both of which showed an extraordinary advance from the level of a year before.

Groups, especially punk groups, need to be seen acting in type and not caring about the business ends of their careers. Cobain, in 1988, did just the opposite. He was a master of self-promotion and loved the attention he won so quickly in Seattle. A reporter, Dana Skene, remembers an interview with him that spring when Cobain tried to persuade her to write an article not on local groups but 'a whole big profile on just him alone'. He was thrilled when a second journalist ventured in print that 'with enough practice, Nirvana could become better than the Melvins'. As his cousin observes, 'in the two years after he left [Aberdeen] he was fiercely ambitious and eager to be unique, special, someone people would notice and admire'; intoxicated, rather than intimidated by success. As soon as he left Reciprocal, Cobain dubbed copies of the tape and sent them to every record label he could think of, always accompanied by letters, small gifts, and the request that the recipient contact him at North Pear Street. While the hoped-for call from Chicago or New York never materialized, Cobain did meet Daniel House, head of the independent C/Z label in Seattle, who offered Nirvana a place on his *Teriyaki Asthma* EP the following year.

Cobain also met Jonathan Poneman, like Bruce Pavitt a former disc jockey and record hustler with dreams of running a label. Poneman had been alerted to Nirvana by Endino, who remembers lauding Cobain as 'a backwoods guy who looked like an auto mechanic'. The actual introduction came in Seattle's Café Roma, a room furnished with paintings of cadaverous nudes and a clientele of pickpockets with lupine dogs. Even in this unprepossessing place, the depth of Cobain's ambition registered strongly on Poneman. The wasted years, as he described Aberdeen, intensified his 'manic determination' to leave his mark. At the end of the meeting – in which Cobain spoke with 'firmness, hope and self-assurance' while Novoselic sat drunk and Crover failed to appear – Poneman joined the list of those asked to call 352-0992 in Olympia.

Cobain was back in Seattle a month later for an interview with this writer.

After you adapted to Cobain – the fact that he wore a heavy overcoat even indoors, spoke in a strangely disjointed, lisping voice and avoided all eye contact – it was possible to warm to him. He was surprisingly placid for a rock musician. The six or seven cigarettes he smoked in an hour were the only sign of self-indulgence. Cobain sipped water and stared through the window at the rain for minutes on end. After a while he volunteered that 'I don't want to talk about music. The more I talk about it, the worse it gets.'

'Are you happy with the [Reciprocal] stuff?'

'Happy, yeah. I just get real mad at this vicious shit . . . [a Seattle reviewer] writes all this shit. Why can't he say we're the best fucking band since the Beatles?'

'Is that what you think?'

'I *know* we're the best.'

'The strange thing about the Beatles is that they started out as rockers and ended up as a kind of variety act.'

'There's always that danger,' said Cobain.

Comparing himself to the Beatles and insisting, 'I'm not interested in the public's image of me. I don't know what they expect of me,' took considerable sang-froid for someone who had never released a record. All the same, there was a sort of inner nerve to Cobain that was not entirely unattractive. His knowledge of the business and the powerful Seattle music industry had grown dramatically in a few weeks. Nothing he had seen or heard gave him cause to doubt his own prospects. Although he admired Soundgarden's *Screaming Life* he savagely criticized a second group whose vocalist 'couldn't sing worth shit' and a Seattle cult-figure as 'a sick boy'. Cobain knew that burning ambition and a lofty disregard for the competition were not the only means by which his career progressed. He intended to 'work like a nigger', too. But merely recording the songs and leaving his success to chance was not enough for him. He needed to have the best coverage, to be among the most famous, to be revered rather than respected. 'If ever there was a case of unbounded ego,' says his cousin, 'it was Kurt.'

The intensity of his plans concealed a haphazard private life. Cobain retained his job as a night janitor. As well as making a token contribution to his own upkeep, his wages went on LSD and heroin, although he avoided cocaine because of its dangerous tendency to make him 'too sociable'. Cobain and Marander both smoked marijuana incessantly, and the apartment on North Pear Street became a madhouse. Even Slim Moon, himself one of the most freethinking characters in Olympia, reports it was 'a mess'. Cobain was the worst housekeeper ever, and as a result the police called in response to complaints about public health violations. A citizens' deputation from State Avenue was met with a barrage of dirt and rocks. To communicate with the neighbours Cobain fixed an old Buick horn to the ledge of his window, and frequently gave it a toot. On another occasion he, Novoselic and Dylan Carlson frenziedly attacked a parked car with some lawn chairs. The interesting thing was that Cobain in private agreed with the complaints and remonstrances of his neighbours, and accepted them as sound. There was a large part of his behaviour he hated, not because it reminded him of the smashing-TVs-in-hotel-rooms school of rock star charm, but, on the contrary, because he feared it might jeopardize his chances. A local man named Dale Poore remembers 'a very sheepish Kurt apologizing for some damage and asking me not to report him to the cops, for fear his [record label] would hear about it'. A friend agrees that 'he was prepared to do anything not to screw up his career'. A radio station in San Francisco was sent a letter asking if any of the lyrics from the Reciprocal tape were unnecessarily crude; a second organization in Chicago received a 'touching' note from Cobain reminding them of his existence. According to the programme director at KCMU in Seattle, 'Kurt was almost slavingly grateful' when that station first played 'Floyd The Barber'.

In 1988 motive met with opportunity.

From the start of his career, Cobain had cultivated an image as an outsider, someone whose work ran ahead of both the public and the corporate music scene. 'I always thought I was an alien,' he told Tim Arnold. The truth is that in Seattle Cobain found himself in the right place at the right time, and when his chance came he seized it with what Arnold calls 'a flair to win approval, gain favour, and bend others to his will'. 'Rest and relaxation seemed to be painful to Kurt,' another friend says. 'At least where his career was concerned, he was anxious to plug into as many circuits as possible,' constantly 'running off tapes and mailing them', along with 'feverishly scratched letters and notes . . . followed by a flow of phone calls.' There was always a part of him, inside and out of reach, that was quite complex – easily complex enough to know the value of his own simplicity – a side that Skene calls 'graspingly ambitious under the skin'.

The music business is geared up to perpetuate new groups in order to perpetuate itself. The talent-spotting system is so sophisticated that, as Bruce Pavitt says, 'the second a band with any promise as much as stirs, they're surrounded'. It was inevitable that, in a relatively small market like Seattle, two ambitious souls like Pavitt and Cobain would meet, and that the former would be impressed by 'Kurt's not only knowing how to look and act, but [how to] deliver live'. In the whole history of these relationships, few have been as symbiotic as that between Nirvana and Sub Pop Ltd: the one with their genuine technical ability and ambition, the other with their flair for hype, undoubted enthusiasm and unrivalled grasp of the market. According to Patrick Mac-Donald, veteran correspondent of the Seattle *Times*: 'Bruce and Jon Poneman both have great ears, and after years of working on radio were naturals to run a label. Plus they had business sense that was more Chicago than Seattle.' (Pavitt and Poneman were from Illinois and Ohio, respectively.) Grant Alden agrees that 'Sub Pop used the so-called Seattle scene as a marketing tool. Part of their skill lay in having studied the ups and downs of previous indies and learning from them. They both knew exactly what they wanted.' As well as a shrewd understanding of the market – it was Pavitt who sold T-shirts proudly proclaiming 'LOSER' at the height of the media obsession with yuppies – Sub Pop shared Cobain's own faculty for marrying hardcore rock with an old-fashioned pop sensibility. It is not the least significant part of his career that Pavitt worked for years at Yesco, a company that specialized in programming background music tapes, later known as Muzak.

Sub Pop unquestionably made conscious efforts to learn about and profit from the new wave of groups emerging around Seattle. It was an article of faith in the late 1980s that any musician could have access to a studio: Pavitt formed a pact with Jack Endino to record, in a year, upwards of a hundred sessions, and the resulting thousands of spools of tape – some good, some not so admirable – are evidence of what Alden calls 'the mutual advantage society between Sub Pop and Reciprocal'. The label's other selling-point lay in styling and marketing. Poneman hired Charles Peterson to take the all-important photographs – grainy, action-packed shots combining strobe and ambient lighting – to sell an image of, as Peterson puts it, 'the bands' hairy, sweaty, Neanderthal sides' the world over.

Sub Pop gave the burgeoning Seattle underground a kind

of cohesion. Suddenly there was an outlet for groups like Soundgarden, Mudhoney, TAD or Nirvana, all of whom, to varying degrees, now had the potential of releasing hit singles while retaining their crucial punk credentials. No one benefited from this prospect more than Cobain. His discovery by Poneman in 1988 encouraged a belief among industry insiders that he was a rising star of Northwest rock. In the first six months of the year, articles in *Backlash* and the *Rocket*, two specialist music titles, described him as a prodigy, a standout of the 'new mainstream'. A fellow song-writer described him as the most original talent Seattle had seen in twenty years. One well-respected New York maga-zine dubbed him a 'man of destiny', while KCMU Radio described him as 'just about the hottest talent in the North-west', a certain success, if he wanted to be, and a leading candidate for superstardom in 1989 or 1990. Since Cobain had left Aberdeen, the *World* pointed out, 'the whole Seattle scene' had been enriched and 'young Aberdonians are being named Kurt, proof positive that his influence has already passed into another generation'.

The *World*, for once, was being ironic, but it was right to identify a 'Seattle scene', which Cobain had now entered. At the heart of that scene lay the factors underlying the Pacific Northwest, which made it uniquely susceptible to the coming grunge revolution.

The Northwest, dominated for a century by logging and fishing, has an aggressive blue-collar tradition. Radical groups used to congregate there, and sometimes in down-town Seattle old anarchists can still be found singing their ballads of longshoremen's revolts. The place has been called 'the hideout capital of the USA', a far-flung outpost of a town where generations of the nation's wretched and washed-up have gone to disappear. Seattle also has a sub-stantial college-educated population, and a reputation for being a trendsetter in new art, theatre and music. It was to this constituency that the groups emerging in the late 1980s spoke.

Seattle is physically remote – closer to Russia than it is to New York – and, for all its recent progress, a quintessential small town; where San Francisco has Oakland and Berkeley, Seattle's suburbs fade into interminable hills and valleys pummelled by rain and offering a continual diet of clapboard houses, timber yards and commercial neon. For both these reasons, size and geography, it is possible to think of the region communally, and to speak of cults, scenes and fads as peculiar to the Northwest.

Seattle is America's Most Liveable City, known for informality, anonymity, general lack of hidebound tradition, and the almost unnatural niceness of its inhabitants: the 'happy face' logo is a local creation. 'Have a nice day' is still mouthed unblushingly on the streets. The untrained eye might strain to see anything new in all this. After all, California, with its near-identical values, was fashionable a long time ago. Nearly thirty years have passed since the Grateful Dead kick-started the San Francisco hippie era. The difference lies in Seattle's unique position as an end-of-the-line frontier town, a spring for every nostalgic or revivalist trend in America, and consequently a target for lifestyle commentators the world over. By the mid-1980s food writers were extolling the locally brewed beer and coffee; sports correspondents were talking up the area's skiing and boating facilities, while the fashion columns wrote about the 'Northwest look' of jeans, heavy boots, flannel shirts and long underwear. A dry and notably whimsical sense of humour (epitomized by the Seattle cartoonist Gary Larson) and the wisdom that politicians were not to be taken seriously – three of the area's elected officials were Messrs Dicks, Beaver and Bonker – merged with the belief that, for all its vaunted charm and quality of life, the Northwest was the 'freak capital of America', a refuge for malcontents and felons, and by extension a den of illegal drugs.

Seattle is a clean, well-organized place surrounded by water and mountains and where almost everybody seems vaguely happy, except, as Larson puts it, 'the ones who know in their hearts something's missing'. As Gillian Gaar wrote in *Goldmine*: 'The Northwest's perenially grey skies and drizzly weather are said to be a contributing factor to the higher than average suicide rate in the region.' Alcoholism is rampant, and 'crime writers have long noted the preponderance of serial killers who have resided in the Northwest, such as Ted Bundy, a University of Washington graduate who dumped the bodies of his victims in the dank, tree-lined hills around North Bend and Snoqualmie, the setting for David Lynch's dark soap opera *Twin Peaks*.' In 1971 a man posing as D.B. Cooper hijacked a jet and parachuted into the forests below Mount St Helens, itself much in the news in 1980. One of the most violent mass-murders in American history took place in Seattle, in 1983, when one Chinese gang exterminated another. Four years later two local girls, aged fifteen and seventeen, were taken at gunpoint, tied up, tortured with a blow-torch and raped, an event remembered by Cobain in 'Polly'. The Green River Killer, still at large today, is thought to have murdered forty-six women in and around Seattle. Alongside its reputation for progressiveness and sociability, the Northwest harbours a streak of what Grant Alden calls 'rain-drummed Scandinavian *noir*', and a sense of latent menace, barbarism and violence.

Some of this barbarism and violence was at work in Seattle's music. As early as the 1950s the area was synonymous with the raucous, guitar-driven sound pioneered by the Sonics, the Wailers and the Kingsmen, the last of whom recorded the classic three-chord rock and roll anthem 'Louie, Louie'. What Patrick MacDonald terms the 'free-form, crazy and abandoned' tradition of Northwest rock progressed directly, via the local disc jockey Pat O'Day, into a 1970s obsession with heavy metal and groups like Kiss and Led Zeppelin. To Cobain, and most of his fellow Aberdonians, this kind of music had much to commend it. Above all, it represented an opportunity to offend their parents. A heavy metal record promised the chance to convert brooms and baseball bats into guitars, and to mouth lyrics that a substantial part of the adult population thought to be devoted to devil worship. Jimmy Page and Gene Simmons were never the dark artists their more credulous fans believed, but to Cobain they became role models, whose influence he never fully broke and who raised what he described later as endlessly varied questions on the single topic: 'How can I make it?'

The other influence on Cobain, of course, was Jimi Hendrix. As everyone involved in Seattle music knows to this day, identifying with Hendrix was an obvious strategy to gain attention. There are compelling similarities – and appreciable differences – between the two careers and older fans admitted to *déjà vu* when, in 1994, the left-handed Seattle singer, songwriter and guitarist, just four albums into a dazzling career, was found dead at twenty-seven. Like Hendrix before him, Cobain was a profoundly shy man, ill-educated, oversensitive and driven by strange furies. Unlike Cobain, Hendrix took no responsibility for radical ideals and was resigned, if never fully reconciled, to his fame.

With that major distinction, Hendrix's career can be seen to anticipate Cobain's in critical ways. 'No doubt Jimi became Kurt's surrogate father,' one Nirvana chronicler has written; while another notes, 'Cobain kept a photograph of Hendrix wherever he went', a fact for which 'psychological explanation' would be available. According to Dana Skene, 'Almost every twist and turn of one's career was shadowed by the other . . . It was as though the qualities of Jimi's life moved [Cobain] to special efforts to match him.'

The facts of Hendrix's life are that he was born in Seattle

on 27 November 1942; like Cobain he had a troubled childhood – his mother was one of the heaviest drinkers in King County – and like Cobain his parents divorced when he was nine. Hendrix's father, Al, fulfilled roughly the same role as Wendy Cobain, a forceful and at times overbearing personality who nonetheless devoted himself to his son's welfare. (Hendrix's mother Lucille died in hospital in 1958.) The seminal moment of Hendrix's adolescence came on 1 September 1957 when, along with 15,000 other fans, he saw Elvis Presley perform in Seattle. According to Noel Tyler, who sat next to him, 'Jimi was overwhelmed with excitement, not just at seeing Elvis, but at the thought that he, too, could make it' – an exact harbinger of Cobain's own emotion when, in 1984, he saw Black Flag in the same city. By the time he was sixteen Cobain had what Warren Mason calls 'an encyclopedic grasp of pop', compensating for a mediocre schooling and wretched home life by endlessly copying not only Scratch Acid and Flipper but mainstream groups like The Who on his guitar. At the same age Hendrix was listening to Elvis and Big Bill Broonzy and practising, as his aunt puts it, 'with a kind of nose-to-the-grindstone devotion' on a Supro Ozark bought by his father. When he was eighteen Hendrix met the bass guitarist Billy Cox, thus beginning a nine-year liaison comparable to that between Cobain and Novoselic – the man of genius yoked with the man of talent, relationships that not only served all parties concerned but also rested on genuine affection and regard. In 1985 Cobain began playing semi-professionally in and around Aberdeen while intensifying his career as a petty thief and graffitist. Hendrix, too, was performing for money while stealing clothes from the second-hand stores around Seattle, eventually graduating to car theft, arrest and a two-year suspended sentence.

There the stories part, for at the age at which Cobain moved to Olympia and Seattle, Hendrix left the area to join the army. Circumstances put off his musical career until he was discharged for 'medical unsuitability', thus establishing a pattern of mysterious stomach and back ailments that came to rival Cobain's.

Although adolescence proved a stormy period for Hendrix as well as for Cobain, their defiance took quite different forms. Those who knew Hendrix in Seattle recall a lively, outgoing boy, almost unnaturally polite, who spent as much time as possible illicitly listening to records stolen from a lending library downtown. He was never trying to change or revolutionize anything, except, as his father says, 'his own place in life'. Much in Cobain's first years – his exaggerated need for attention and sympathy, his flouting of authority and problems at school, his mixture of ego. and insecurity – leaves the impression of a troubled child struggling with bewildering inner demons. In one form or another, as his adult behaviour later showed, Cobain's childhood difficulties dogged him all his life. By comparison, what seems most striking about Hendrix is the extent to which he identified with, and drew strength from, his father and managed to convert his problems into effective means of accomplishing his goals and sustaining a stable private life.

Both Hendrix and Cobain rebelled against what they saw as the petty, small-town restrictions of their childhoods. Neither showed any aptitude for business or sport, and it is difficult to imagine either being successful in the world into which they were born. Their careers were possible only in the new order created by the pop revolution of the early 1960s. Both relied on the support of the disc jockeys, journalists and record-pluggers whom (at least in Cobain's case) they claimed to despise, and both benefited from the patronage of the same man in London: John Peel was an early champion of Hendrix and did more than anyone to enhance Nirvana's reputation overseas. He remembers Hendrix as 'just relieved to have left Seattle' and even in London playing on flamboyance and a gift for showmanship in order to be noticed; Cobain 'merely needed to turn up'. Even this is superficial compared with the key difference in the two men's lives. Cobain's protest took the form of a romantic association with the loner and outcast, and throughout his life he struggled with the worry that success had come easily and at too early an age. Hendrix was genuinely disadvantaged. One man knew actual prejudice, and reacted by a flair for stagecraft, by working twice as hard as he needed, and so converting his critics. Hendrix, a friend believes, was in the tradition of the old plantation workers who sang with a fixed smile and 'an ingratiating sense of servility' at the white man's feet. Cobain's belief that music and radical ideals could be combined – and that compromise was unthinkable – was justified by the sea-change that occurred between 1970 and 1990. In forming his own group, Cobain was spared the contortions to which Hendrix had to resort in order to sway his enemies. Both locally, via Sub Pop, and globally, through a new breed of record executive and rock writer, Cobain was a success virtually the instant he emerged; the music media went wild, with blanket coverage, as well as radio and MTV dancing attendance. As Peel says, 'Once he was in the saddle and working, Kurt had it made. Rock had been waiting to be recycled.' To the flawless timing Cobain showed throughout, he added a driving ambition, a combination of delusions of grandeur along with the conviction he was a victim, an excessive suspiciousness and the working of paranoid delusions into a logical pattern capable of endless adjustment to protect itself. 'Why, when he had so much,' asks Peel, 'was he so miserable?' To another man who knew them well, it seemed that 'Jimi worked hard for success and embraced it', whereas Cobain 'struck a home run and then stood there petrified, unable to move'.

In Hendrix's day rock was diagnosed as a sickening child

and was going to die young. By 1988 popular music had become big but fickle business. Sub Pop was one of a dozen labels springing up at the same time in protest against artists like Bon Jovi, Van Halen and Poison – what Lou Reed calls the 'hair farmer' bands – and offering Reciprocal time (the pun was intentional) to fresh talent. Pavitt and Poneman spent the best part of a year investigating local groups, featuring such acts as producer/musician Steve Fisk and the U-Men, before releasing a five-track EP by Seattle's Green River, *Dry As A Bone*. *Screaming Life* followed in October 1987. From the start, Sub Pop aimed itself at collectors, striking a firm corporate identity with its Singles Club, selling limited-edition releases on subscription, and setting up an elite of like-minded individuals recruited around an idea. As was said, once in the clique it was possible to share a feeling of moral superiority, a sense of mission and a contagious certainty that anyone outside was culturally beyond the pale. 'That was where Bruce pulled his coup,' says Patrick MacDonald. 'Forming a club was a master-stroke in that it gave a collector's sense of elitism, reinforced by a powerful brand identity.' Charles Peterson agrees that 'In the way it showcased a certain type of band, and a particular city, it was almost like Motown.' Eventually the success of Soundgarden and the rest sent a swarm of A&R men rushing to Seattle in search of major-label signings, but for at least a year Sub Pop was a well-kept secret, grooming, recording and bankrolling new talent, and creating what Peterson calls 'one of the few distinctive noises in rock' before boredom and self-parody set in.

A year or so after Cobain moved to Olympia he was seen by Bob Hunter, sitting on the stoop of Capitol City Studios and eating a bowl of rice. On the twin grounds of 'looking very well' and 'speaking in a subdued voice' Cobain struck his former teacher as 'turning into a well-mannered man'.

Lamont Shillinger, who saw him a month or two later, had the same impression. His high standing with his teachers rested partly on Cobain's persistent efforts to ingratiate himself with the men and women who were judging him. With a few notable exceptions, he took special pains to flatter his elders, invariably agreeing with them and striking one Olympia figure as 'obsequious'.

Cobain's contemporaries reacted differently. Myer Loftin, violently rejected by his schoolfriend in 1984, was struck by the 'punk depravity' of Cobain's lifestyle when they met by chance three years later. According to Loftin, 'the house was a found-art museum, with dolls and figurines smeared with shit, weird pop culture artefacts, and a statue of the Virgin Mary with its head cut off.' A second acquaintance agrees that 'Kurt's demented side came out in Olympia. After Aberdeen, it was like turning a wild animal out of a cage.'

Cobain was to say later that he could not remember a time when he was sexually normal. As a teenager he used to proclaim his sympathy for homosexuals while, as Loftin puts it, 'not wanting to get involved with one'. He was a voyeur and collector of pornography, particularly the titles in which 'big-titted bitches' posed in combinations with farm animals, men and each other. In later life Cobain's loathing of rape and stereotyped male behaviour became proverbial, a continual theme in his songs and interviews: 'Polly' was a reference to the 1987 incident when two girls were kidnapped and tortured; 'Been A Son' spoke disparagingly of the preference for infant boys over girls; 'Rape Me' was a straightforward protest, as well as commenting on the singer's own miseries. While no one doubted the sincerity of Cobain's lyrics there were some, like Loftin, who wondered if he 'protested too much' in constantly professing his support for women. A friend in Olympia believes that 'Kurt became obsessed with rape and macho-type behaviour.

It was as though he was apologizing for being male.'

A woman named Marcy Drew (for the purpose of this book) knew Cobain in Seattle in 1988. According to her, his public attitude to women was a pose and songs like 'Rape Me' sprang out of personal guilt. Drew recalls an incident in which, organized by Cobain and another musician now working successfully in Seattle, a group met in the adults-only Apple Theatre. After a film she remembers only as 'some kind of gynaecologist's office fantasy', the four were driven by taxi to a club in Pioneer Square. Once Cobain began drinking he expounded loudly every weakness of 'bitches' like Marander, and seethed when asked by the female bartender for proof of his age (in truth, only weeks over the legal limit for buying a drink). Things deteriorated when a man holding a pool cue taunted Cobain as a 'faggot' and made an invitation for the women to join him.

All this, says Drew, contributed to a hot-headed and vol-atile atmosphere. When the party stepped outside into the dark alley behind the square, there was a moment when she and Cobain were alone. 'I want you and I'm going to have you,' is her recollection of the exact words which he hissed to her. Then

> Kurt rammed his hand hard between my legs. It was terrifying . . . He was panting like a dog, and there was a froth of spit around his lips. I yelled at him to stop and he laughed at me. With one hand he backed me up against the wall and the other he pushed into me.

When Cobain was with punk musicians he was the epit-ome of punk, just as when he was with Hunter or Shillinger he was the picture of docile youth. Cobain took his identity from the company he kept, many of whom saw only the image they projected on to him and he reflected back to them. So far as there was ever a consensus reached, it was that, in Azerrad's words, 'Kurt [was] a very sensitive person, sweet and bright' and an admiring disciple of women. This woman's testimony is striking because it shows a part of Cobain that fits poorly with the stereotype. According to her, he was 'berserk', 'a brute', someone who was guilty of sexual battery and assault. 'If [the other couple] hadn't come back when they did, he would have raped me,' she says. 'As far as I'm concerned, all the stories about Kurt-the-feminist are a sick joke. He *hated* women. No one who does what he did has a right to any respect.'

In early 1988 Crover left Nirvana and was replaced by Dave Foster. Foster, with his jazz background and self-confessed stable personality, was immediately at odds with Cobain, who struck him as 'trying to flex his punk muscle'. Charles Peterson, too, believes 'part of Kurt's personality was the result of revenge for the years in Aberdeen'. There may be no such thing as a saturation point in such compensations, but Cobain went about the business of reinventing himself in Olympia and Seattle with a single-mindedness Foster found 'scary'. He took drugs and, for the first time in his life, began drinking heavily; he spoke of himself, on the basis of the dolls and figurines, as an 'artist'; above all he rehearsed and practised continually, lobbying Poneman for work on the lucrative club circuit. That winter Nirvana made their Seattle debut at the Vogue, a room with a long bar and a small stage catering to an eclectic cross-section with only their pierced extremities and body rings in common. Cobain came in carrying his guitar and sat down at the edge of the counter. 'Why do you think some people are so afraid of us?' he asked. 'I mean, *hate* us?'

When Cobain said that he actually looked around the room nervously.

'Do you think they're frightened of you?'

'Ooh, *yeah*.' Here Cobain gave a dazzling boyish grin. 'Illiterate-backwoods-hicks infiltrate grabola mainstream. They're fucking *terrified* of me.'

'You call this the mainstream?'

'I'm not sure I've got that relentless, ruthless ambition any more,' said Cobain, whose talent for ignoring points made at his expense would have qualified him for a career as a lawyer. 'I mean, to perform. Writing takes up so much time.'

'I liked the one about the barber.'

It was the correct response. Cobain was delighted. 'Of course you loved it,' he roared. 'I wrote it.'

The performance that followed was a disaster. Charles Peterson was so unimpressed he never used his camera. 'The band had virtually no presence,' he says. 'Kurt may have been a hit in his own mind, but as far as I was concerned he stank.' Poneman, too, remembers Nirvana as 'not particularly engaging'. Apart from a malfunctioning sound system, later destroyed by Foster, the main problem was Cobain himself. Some of his posturing and self-obsession were as unengaging on stage as in person. Each song was illustrated by a sort of spastic jig, Cobain pumping his fist in the air, a performance that failed to animate the sparse, Sunday-night crowd. 'At the beginning Kurt was a shambles,' says a friend. 'Because he was over-excited and had a strange view of himself, he came across like a parody of Mick Jagger. It took him months to get over that.' As late as June 1989 the journalist Johnny Renton noted that Cobain spent large parts of a performance 'writhing on the floor at the drop of a hat', while that same summer Steve Fisk said, 'I hated them ... Kurt had broken a string and was really upset and stood in the corner trying to change his guitar string. They were just clowning off', a view corresponding to Pavitt's own assessment of Cobain's stage act: 'He totally sucked.'

* * *

One of the most striking things about Cobain was his urgent need to achieve a sense of belonging by attaching himself to a movement, a crusade, an elitist culture. It may seem odd to describe punk rock as elitist, but in the way Cobain practised it, constantly stressing the need for 'purity' and raging at those who were 'in it for the money', he impressed Tim Arnold with his missionary zeal. More than anything else it was his attitude toward the punk ethic that shaped Cobain's personality in Olympia and brought him into conflict with those who saw music as a hobby. Sooner or later it was inevitable that he would fall out with Foster. When the drummer was involved in a brawl in Aberdeen, Cobain used this 'typically redneck' incident to re-recruit Aaron Burckhard to the group. Burckhard himself was replaced, by way of an advertisement in the *Rocket* ('Heavy, light punk rock band seeks drummer') by Chad Channing, travelling in to Seattle with his instrument on the ferry and striking even Cobain as 'one of the nicest people I've ever met'.

With Channing Nirvana took a step back into the mainstream. His own influences included Aerosmith and Vanilla Fudge, and some of those groups' brute power was added to the art-noise experiments of Cobain's songs. According to Peterson, 'Kurt was going back to his roots and discovering bands like the Sonics and the Wailers ... [1988] was the year he put together the elements for his own sound.' For the final ingredient Cobain reverted to the blues-folk tradition of Huddie Ledbetter, whose mingling of deceptively wry lyrics with inimitable r&b-type rhythms became Nirvana's own trademark; for both artists, the music energized the message. Slim Moon remembers lending Cobain *Leadbelly's Last Sessions* and hearing 'Kurt play it over and again in Olympia ... He was so struck by the combination of words and melody.' Cobain himself told a journalist in 1993, 'Leadbelly is one of the most important things in my life. I'm totally obsessed with him.'

In cold terms Cobain was a musicologist who, beneath a surface purity, harboured a driving ambition and a pragmatic view of his own prospects. 'I've never in my life met someone as single-minded,' says Arnold. Cobain had strong commercial instincts. There were deep ambiguities in his thinking – his cousin agrees that 'he hated the idea that he was selling out' – but in private he was a stickler for practice (the reverse of the laissez-faire punk ideal) and spoke without irony of becoming 'bigger than the Beatles'. To say that Cobain's taking up music was governed by a rejection of 'dumb-ass morals' is not to say that he had no principles of his own. His career flowed from his belief in his exceptional talent and his willingness to do anything needed to succeed. That spring he built a rehearsal studio in Novoselic's basement, putting his sculptor's affinity for broken furniture, old boxes and scraps of carpet to good use and appearing there with what a friend calls 'commuter-like regularity'. He also practised new material at Naked Zoo studios in Tacoma, greeting a man called Jack Daugherty at the door with a 'businessman's handshake' before beginning eight solid hours' work.

When Cobain 'came across like a parody of Mick Jagger' one of his set-pieces was 'Love Buzz', a straightforward pop song with a histrionic guitar solo. It was significant that he chose this, rather than an original number, to be Nirvana's first single. Although Azerrad believed 'they liked the idea of recording a new track instead of re-recording something off the [January 1988] demo', an engineer at Reciprocal remembers 'Poneman telling Kurt to put out a commercial single, and Kurt agreeing'. Along with 'Love Buzz' the group recorded Cobain's own 'Big Cheese' and returned to two other songs from the January session. A telling example of Poneman's role as *de facto* manager – there was no actual contract – came when he ordered Cobain back to Reciprocal to re-record his vocals. 'There was a lot of bitching,' says the same source, 'but also a realization by Kurt that Jon knew what he was doing. Cobain would have followed him to the ends of the earth to score a hit.' Peterson also believes that 'Kurt relied on Jonathan to get a song in the charts.' The 'Big Cheese' referred to in the title was Poneman himself.

It used to be the case that McCartney or Bowie or Townshend personally supervised every aspect of their careers, taking advice only on the most esoteric or technical details of recording. Cobain's ego was such that he put himself forward as Nirvana's singer-songwriter and leader while actually relying on Poneman, Pavitt and, for the music, Endino and Novoselic. According to Reciprocal's engineer, 'Kurt was lost without Jack to steer him'. He was seen as an admittedly gifted but temperamental child who threw tantrums in the studio and was sarcastically dubbed 'the cotton-wool kid' because Poneman shielded him from the media. When an interview was arranged with Cobain that summer he appeared halfway through the allotted hour, a twitchy dwarf in black leather, and greeted the writer with a volcanically aggressive 'Fug yew'. He didn't get any nicer. On the other hand, Cobain could be deadly serious when promoting his career, avoiding the arch and anti-sincere gestures of British punk – taking care to measure the distance between himself and the 'pantomime villain figure' of Johnny Rotten – talking for hours about his 'art', which he saw as springing from the old folk tradition of protest and dissent, and publicizing himself with an intensity Freddie Mercury would have found embarrassing. In a handwritten biography of Nirvana he sent out that summer, Cobain spoke of having 'struggled with too many undedicated drummers', of his willingness to 'compromise on material' and 'tour any time forever' before neatly closing with Marander's address and phone number in Olympia.

In the end, haggling about costs meant that five months passed between the recording of 'Love Buzz' and its release. By the time Nirvana's first single reached Sub Pop's subscribers the group had gained a substantial west coast following, helped transform the hardcore fringes of punk into the mainstream and, along with R.E.M. and Sonic Youth, increased the specific gravity of rock virtually overnight. 'Love Buzz' was a dramatic improvement on the material recorded only six months before. Some of the later Nirvana formula, the hard rock drums and insinuating guitar, was already present, as was Cobain's experimenting with tempo by way of steady upbeat progression. Warren Mason's lesson about 'tension and release' had been well learned; Mason himself calls 'Love Buzz' 'an inspired piece of pacing', while to Peterson the song showed incredible progress over the standards set at the Vogue. 'For a band which liked "Let It Be" as much as "Revolution",' he says, '"Love Buzz" had all the ingredients: the tune wooed the Zeppelin or Stones vote, while the dirty mix raised interest in new wavers.' 'It was the way Kurt mingled lethargy and aggression,' says Grant Alden. 'That and the screaming were what made Nirvana.'

When KCMU first played 'Floyd The Barber', Cobain, in what was to become a career pattern, had been 'slavingly grateful' for the exposure. Nine months later when he and Marander were driving back to Olympia from Seattle, they listened to the same station for 'Love Buzz'. According to Azerrad: 'Kurt made Tracy stop the car at a telephone booth, where he called the station and requested the song. They couldn't drive any further or they'd lose the signal, so they waited twenty minutes until they played the single . . . Kurt was excited.' When the press agent Phillip Quinn looked at pictures of Nirvana that autumn and saw Cobain was always in the middle he began to think he had 'really met an operator'. Charles Peterson believes 'Kurt thrust himself forward, though under Jon's general guidance'. In Poneman, Cobain had a brilliant publicist with personal radio experience who could encourage and support his ambitions. He also bolstered Cobain's punk credentials: an early backer of Mudhoney and Soundgarden, Poneman signalled that Nirvana were sincere about 'bringing music back to the street'. In an interview in a Seattle club that winter, Cobain spoke of 'the half of me that wants to make money' as opposed to the half 'jivey enough to want [society] fragmented', his very awareness of his options suggesting which one would prevail. Almost everyone who knew Cobain agreed that he possessed a strong, self-centred streak. He was a diffident, yet aggressive personality who struggled with demons that drove and tormented him. He had to be the best, outshine all the competition and win at almost any cost. However small or large the stakes – whether begging a journalist for coverage, plugging his own song on the radio or, later, arguing with his colleagues over royalties – the premium was on winning by any means. He balanced his actions against the knowledge that other rock stars did similar things. Indeed, he could never have carried off his tainted musical and financial gains in an atmosphere of pre-Beatles naïvety. To describe Cobain as self-seeking might sound extreme, but it is wishful thinking to suppose that personal motivation and a supposedly egalitarian art-form like punk are incompatible. As a man of some intelligence and insight into others, Cobain must have occasionally puzzled over his own private war – his incessant reach for dominance and fame. Yet it was never enough to hold him back. As early as 1988 he acknowledged in private to a grasping need for 'Madonna status', while in his last major interview he told *Rolling Stone*: 'I have to admit I've found myself doing the same things that a lot of other rock stars do.' As Charles

Peterson says, 'Kurt's career proceeded more conventionally than people thought . . . You don't get to be that famous by accident.'

When the last wave of modern punk broke in 1980 it was followed by a 'hardcore' movement in which groups played wildly distorted electric guitars over lyrics that tried to be meaningful. Names like Gone, Dinosaur Jr and the Meat Puppets were among the first to merge the garage-band tradition with serious-minded morals, including, in some cases, a disdain for drink, drugs and sex, thus reversing the entire premise on which punk had originally been founded. While Tim Yohannan believes that 'by 1981–2, a new crew of kids came along, saw the bullshit for what it was, and began a whole new period of mainline punk,' Grant Alden is more specific: 'Like all worthwhile rock, hardcore formed in protest to political oppression. Under Nixon you had *Sticky Fingers* and *Blood on the Tracks*, with Carter you got the Bee Gees. When Reagan came in in early '81 there was an immediate gathering of musicians, writers and poets appalled that the country was being run by a 70-year-old Nazi. *That* was the starting-point of hardcore.'

In Seattle the movement threw up its share of enthusiastic young activists, some of whom not only formed groups but created record labels like C/Z, PopLlama and, in time, Sub Pop. C/Z's 1985 compilation *Deep Six*, though not featuring Cobain, was the first coming together of a recognizable 'Seattle sound' and a primer for what became known as grunge. While no one now remembers the Shemps, Uncle Bonsai, the Fucks or Throat Oyster, these were the groups that eventually coalesced into Soundgarden, Alice In Chains and Nirvana, and that led a media-driven frenzy to the Pacific Northwest. Other than personality in the performers, parody in the costumes and energy and speed in the music, there may have been less in common among the bands than outside journalists thought. There was deliberate playing-up to the Seattle image by some who, as Alden says, 'came on like trained bears in the zoo'. Even Cobain once calmly took a knife to a T-shirt just before performing and ripped the fabric by an inch. That inch was rebellion superbly controlled. 'A lot of Kurt,' his engineer insists, 'was hamming up to the myth. Even in the early days he affected a look so he'd appear in all the spreads in *Melody Maker* and *Sounds*.' Having devoted himself to punk in the abstract, now he was part of an actual movement.

What kind of movement? Between the eruption of hard-core in 1981–2 and the ready availability of studios like Reciprocal five years later, Cobain was able to ply his trade on the booming Seattle club circuit. By the mid-1980s the Vogue, the Central, Skid Row, the Off Ramp and the Canterbury, as well as a growing number of rented rooms and halls, all featured twice-weekly 'pop/punk nights' primarily to showcase new talent and deliberately blurring the traditionally set distance between audience and performers, many of whom would casually climb onstage from a place on the floor. A friend believes these 'killing fields', in which men like Cobain learned in a few nights how to engage a crowd, were themselves a result of political activism. The 'brutal, materialistic society' that emerged under Reagan produced, he says, a backlash among the educated middle-class and a feeling, absent in the 1970s, that alienated, home-less intellectuals should unite in self-protective alliance. The upshot was the explosion of a network of clubs and meeting places in which performance art, poetry, music and deviant dress offered an interstice in mainstream life. The irony was that the new entrepreneurs embraced not only laissez-faire morals, but extreme – even Reaganite – economic conserva-tism. 'The people who ran those places tended to be sharp, no-bullshit businessmen,' Cobain's friend admits. 'They needed to be, to avoid the drop-dead, cocaine mentality of the seventies. It's a myth that the so-called punk and grunge revolution came about by chance. It was *incredibly* well organized. There was a lot of meticulous planning, within a general framework of political dissent.'

A more prosaic explanation is made by Patrick Mac-Donald, who believes the inspiration behind grunge to have been neither principle nor protest, but expediency. On this reading, the sudden boom in Seattle clubland was partly in response to the sheer volume of groups emerging in the eighties and partly a reaction to the state's archaic licensing laws. 'Rock music and bars tended not to mix,' he notes, 'mainly because it's still illegal to so much as sniff a drink under 21. When the new bands formed they worked outside the system, hiring all-ages venues like lodges and old churches where they could make as much noise as they wanted and generally raise Cain. Strange as it is, the Liquor Control Board was as responsible as anyone for the Seattle Scene. Those old halls were the manger in which grunge was born.'

Its disciples would be Generation X, also dubbed twenty-somethings or later slackers, and stigmatized by Douglas Coupland as '42 million gripers' so dismayed with life and the prospects for self-improvement that they grew angry and disaffected. According to Coupland, 'their anthem was dark rock from Seattle' and their uniform a dismal costume of plaid flannel shirts and ripped jeans. Thousands of slackers pierced their bodies as a destructive symbol of disaffection: belligerently anti-social and anti-society. Their heroes were Cobain and River Phoenix, both of whom died tragically young, unable, apparently, to cope.

A vast majority of slackers are children of divorce. As a result of the liberation movement of the 1960s, says Myron Magnet, 'mainstream culture began to be intoxicated with its own sexual liberation ... if marriages broke up, as increasingly they did, that was OK, because individual, personal fulfilment was more important than family stability.' There was no need to stay together for the sake of the children. That was unjustifiable restraint, and 'kids', as Cobain's own relative says, 'are resilient'. This view, which Baby Boomers fancied to have weight and importance and which actually had some influence, was not only based on a generalization but also overlooked the new realities – financial recession, a crippling lack of jobs and the fact that they spent their sexual prime in the shadow of AIDS – dogging the children of divorce. Cobain himself was suitably unspecific as a spokesman for Generation X. Other than vague support for feminists and homosexuals, he was notably shy of political sayings. Despite an occasional insight and some ingratiating flashes of self-revelation, he was always more interested in his own career than in advancing his views on society. So far from being a slacker Cobain worked at a pace Peterson calls 'manic' and met his end while living the yuppie dream in a $1.5 million mansion. His protest, in a word, did not always cut very deep. But Cobain represented something that a great many twentysomethings valued. What made him great, according to his father, was that he understood the 'psychology of the underdog'. Many so-called slackers, actually well-educated college graduates, would have claimed added commonsense and a greater grip on reality than their parents, plus what Peterson calls 'a need for success on their own terms.' A friend agrees that 'in touching on universal themes in his music and acting as a kind of figurehead' Cobain gave hope to those 'rightly concerned at finding the guardrails that define society'. A twentysomething today has grown up to see an ideology evolve in which no-father homes are just as good as any other, where, according to American Labor Department statistics, one-third of all college graduates will become immediately jobless, and in which teenagers routinely carry deadlier firearms than the police. To speak of such things with concern is not just whining.

Slackers have less money, more time and are more analytical than their parents, many of whom (like Don Cobain) they despise for 'not having worked it out'. The label itself can be affectionate as well as derogatory. Cobain used 'slacker' to describe someone as being pragmatic and resourceful in the face of adversity. In a 1989 interview with this writer he defined 'the best qualities of the under-thirty-twos' – the age Cobain always chose to denote middle age – as a caring outlook, tolerance of diversity and deviant sub-cultures, self-awareness, and a willingness to tackle big issues like world hunger and poverty. Cobain had a firm grasp of the hopes and dreams of his constituency. With his uncanny instinct for the non-ambitious, hedonistically slack (while all the time climbing his own personal corporate tree) he articulated their views in a string of plausible quips and homilies. As an example of the deadbeat, forlorn, under-achieving sub-class portrayed on the covers of *Time* and *Newsweek*, Cobain left a lot to be desired. As a symbol of his times he was perfect.

When journalists sought to shepherd twentysomethings – particularly those with an affinity for the same kind of dress and music – into easy-to-target pigeonholes, they came up with the name grunge. The actual origins of the word are obscure. Some think Poneman (in what Cobain called a 'typically twisted joke') coined it: others insist it was an invention of the British writers who discovered Seattle in late 1988, specifically Everett True of *Melody Maker*. By Christmas of that year the musical elements of grunge – distortion, extreme volume, and an emphasis on the rhythm section over the vocals and guitar hooks – had been noted in *Sounds*. The fashion for flannel shirts and turned-around baseball caps was featured in *Harper's*, while the 'grunge ethic' had been explained in the *New York Times* as 'what happens when children of divorce get their hands on guitars'.

As with the slacker community from which it came, grunge covered a wide territory, full of contradictions and ironies. Despite the studiousness of their pose and their attempts to offend in their song lyrics and slogans, many of grunge's exponents were shockingly normal. There was even an old-fashioned and reassuring feel to their vocabulary, which bristled with words like 'cool' and 'cute' and 'bummer', while their clothes were rooted in the most conservative tradition of longshoremen and lumberjacks. Few of them were idle or stupid. If such a thing as a grunge stereotype existed it was a man or woman – feminism was an important part of the premise – articulate, well-educated, lacking faith in institutions but harbouring a personal optimism and seeking, above all, to prolong a non-adult innocence into maturity. As Grant Alden says, 'It's hard to understand now how grunge was considered a threat. The protest was always a pretty mild one and so far as there was a philosophy it was the old flower-power trip, with added social awareness. Anyone relying on grunge for his power-base didn't have much hope.' 'Kurt knew it and in the end it killed him,' says a friend.

In November 1988 Sub Pop released 'Love Buzz' – promoted as 'heavy pop sludge from these untamed Olympia drop-ins' – as their first Single of the Month, a marketing ploy that allowed Pavitt and Poneman to charge astronomic prices for a limited-edition release.* It was followed by *Sub Pop 200*, a collection featuring tracks by, among others, Soundgarden, TAD and Mudhoney. Nirvana's contribution was 'Spank Thru', a bludgeoning vocal *tour de force* and

* *Record Collector* values a mint-condition copy of the single at £200.

guitar thrash that never scaled the evolutionary ladder to songhood. John Peel wrote up the compilation in the *Observer* as 'the set of recordings by which all others (will be) judged' and noted the Motown comparison also made by Peterson. Today Peel adds that 'the band that really impressed me was Mudhoney' (whose *Superfuzz Bigmuff* was in the UK alternative charts for a year), 'whereas some of the others sank into headbanging. Nirvana didn't register at all.'

British involvement in building and preserving the grunge myth was remarkable for both its intensity and its naïvety. While still actively courting outside groups like Sonic Youth, Sub Pop was shrewd enough to market itself as a one-town label. As Pavitt said: 'The reason [the British] picked it up was there was a regional identity and flavour to what we were doing.' This view was echoed by Peterson: 'We deliberately sold it as a "scene", which made it easier for someone to pinpoint from abroad.' At one end there were experienced pundits like Peel and his colleague Jeff Griffin, while at the other were British slackers like Sheridan Mortimer, an unemployed history of art graduate, who 'latched onto grunge as the perfect anti-yuppie protest'. Everything from the look to the music to the 'sexually charged album titles'* was seized on to form what Griffin calls 'an off-the-peg lifestyle', playing on the eternal British adolescents' fixation with America and giving Peel a sense of *déjà vu* 'in the way we embraced Sub Pop twenty years after Hendrix.'

Nirvana and the new fauna of Seattle rock shared a number of attitudes and tastes, including a form of exoticism centred on punk, a public display of apathy, a disinterest in work, the cult of feminism, and the subversion of traditional

* Both Superfuzz and Bigmuff were the names of guitar distortion pedals.

values via music. It was inevitable, given Pavitt's and Poneman's promotion, that sooner or later British journalists would discover the phenomenon. When, towards the end of 1988 and the beginning of 1989, Seattle was invaded by sociologists and trend-spotters and drew to its clubs all those who found an answer, a sympathetic aesthetic, or simply an agreeable paid holiday, the press wasted no time in dubbing the cellars 'the new Caverns' and falling over themselves to explain grunge. There were some curious delusions. According to Brad Morrell, 'it [was] easy to find in Seattle the last outpost of pre-civilization . . . a more innocent, primeval society, excluded from the cultural breezes that fuel the rest of the nation.' Frontier metaphors were clutched at in order to capture the 'grunge *zeitgeist*' (*Sounds*) of the area. In a piece still widely enjoyed in Seattle today, the arts correspondent of one national had 'real-life Indians' whooping in the streets, while *The Times* found symbolic value in the 'Bonnie and Clyde ambience' of Pioneer Square. 'Laughable as much of it was,' says Peterson, 'it was still a master-stroke to invite, and in some cases pay for the Brits to fly in. It gave the whole thing a cohesion and credibility and definitely kick-started a number of bands. There's nothing like being called a scene to make you feel you're in one.'

'Kurt always knew he was going to succeed,' says his cousin. But that did not stop him from dramatizing the possibility of his failure – to the extent that he told two friends in Olympia that he would rather kill himself than find a job. Those close to Cobain observed his ambition from different angles. Some, like Slim Moon, believed he wanted to make good in a punk context. Others agreed with Skene that 'Kurt's ego was a meter that never stopped ticking.' Significantly, in order to rehearse with Novoselic and Channing, Cobain even agreed to return to Aberdeen, practising again in the room over the hair salon and interrupting nine or ten hours' work only by a meal break at midnight. On 21 December 1988 Nirvana played a concert at the Hoquiam Eagles Lodge. Dana James Bong, who made a video of the night, talks of 'the gig's near-mythic status in Aberdeen'. Novoselic played the entire set in his underpants, while Cobain arrived on stage with his neck painted bright red. After the performance the two native sons made an unscheduled appearance at the Pourhouse, playing old Beatles hits and inviting 'stoner chicks' onto the stage to dance. When their set was over, they passed the hat and collected a total of $11. Thrilled at his success, Cobain grabbed one of the girls, emptied a pitcher of beer on her, then started to pull off her dress. 'He already had the straps over her shoulders,' says Linda Fetz, present behind the bar, 'when a 200-pound jock-type took offence. The last I saw of Kurt was him running to the car screaming "Don't hit me! Don't hit me!" and giggling like a woman.'

What Nirvana were doing in the room over Maria's Hair Design and occasionally in Novoselic's basement was rehearsing material for their first album. Over the New Year holiday they recorded at Reciprocal for thirty hours, all of it billed to the group rather than the label. The ticking of the studio clock brought with it an incentive to work at top speed, causing Cobain to gabble the lyrics breathlessly and everyone else to pound and thrash their instruments towards the same quick conclusion. Another Sub Pop artist, the Seattle poet Jesse Bernstein, would that winter praise Nirvana for 'their freeze-dried vocals', but even he may have confused necessity for invention. As well as sheer pressure of time, Cobain faced a second challenge while at Reciprocal. According to Endino's engineer: 'Kurt turned up every day high on codeine syrup or Dramamine. I saw him spray antiperspirant down his throat. He had a positive genius for misusing toiletries.'

Even this underestimates the drug habit that filled out Cobain's time between one session and the next. A second source at Reciprocal remembers Cobain and Marander, both dressed in black, 'jumping down from a ledge like a pair of bats', then registering their presence by pouring beer onto the mixing-desk. After that exertion Cobain lay on the floor and demanded an assistant send out for Chinese food, which he found he could only manage by using his fingers. After smearing most of the meal on his face he started to belch in counterpoint to the playback booming from the studio speakers. Finally Cobain began striking and dropping lit matches on the floor, the desk and eventually himself, including one in his open mouth. He followed that by a swig of cough syrup and a fistful of white pills which he took from a jar in his pocket. A microphone had to be lowered to floor-level in order for him to sing 'Floyd', which the engineer remembers as 'consisting largely of grunts, groans and belches', culminating in 'one titanic, rasping fart'. Unsurprisingly, the original version of the song, recorded a year earlier, was chosen for the album.

When Cobain arrived at Recriprocal he usually carried a small black satchel. As well as his supply of codeine syrup and pills, the bag held a virtual pharmacy of drugs and devices that could only have been there for sexual use: a cork on a long string attached to a hot-water bottle, a set of rubber underwear and Cobain's pornography collection, mainly polaroids of healthy or diseased vaginas, and a curiously innocuous book of Victorian erotica. Apart from his sex-life with Marander, it was clear Cobain enjoyed a secondary career as a voyeur and fetishist. He travelled everywhere with the polaroids and used to scour medical suppliers for reference-books on gynaecology and obstetrics. By no means the feminist and minority activist he became later, he could be crude in his treatment of women and homosexuals, manhandling the one and greeting John Phalen in Aberdeen by dropping an ironic and extravagant curtsey, and moving swiftly on.

Cobain could afford to indulge himself, even when the meter was running at Reciprocal, because he had the most plausible reasons to believe that what he was doing would work to a final good. The press had taken him up by the end of 1988, and as a result of Peel's patronage and favourable reviews for 'Love Buzz' he saw himself as a coming man. Peterson confirms that 'Kurt's confidence seemed to double in six months,' while Skene also believes 'he stood on the pedestal of his own self-worth'. The other reason Cobain could run up costs in the studio was that someone else was paying. A friend of Channing's, Jason Everman, had been introduced to Nirvana that winter. Early in 1989 he joined the group for six months before being fired by Cobain. More importantly, he donated the $600 needed to book studio time at Reciprocal. Although he was repaid with a credit on the album, Everman was never refunded. 'It wasn't a big thing,' Skene insists today. 'Kurt was generous whenever he could afford it.' Nor, however, was it a small thing, part of a lifelong habit to have others support him. Don and Wendy, friends like the Shillingers and, more recently, Marander had all been victims of Cobain's policy on money. It was true, as he pointed out, that as late as 1991 he was 'totally broke', his bills were 'mountainous' and the phone was in danger of being cut off for non-payment. It took the success of *Nevermind* to bring him what he called a 'minimum wage'. Even so, he took a notably cavalier approach towards his debts. A woman in Aberdeen died in 1993 without ever being repaid the $100 she lent Cobain a decade earlier. Lamont Shillinger notes that 'while Kurt did certain chores, he never once paid rent in the eight months he was here'. Cobain himself told Azerrad that the $600 loan from Everman was being held for 'mental damages'.

In February 1989 Nirvana began a west coast tour, travelling as far as Los Angeles in Novoselic's van and developing their stage-act to something approaching the ingeniously melodic but sweatily incarnated riot it later became. If their time at Reciprocal had improved the group on vinyl, their working of the clubs and bars along the I-5 corridor taught the basics of performing live. As early as October 1988 Cobain had ended a concert by smashing his favourite Fender Mustang into firewood. Auto-destruction became a ritual climax to the group's appearances. While some, like the San Francisco *Chronicle*, admired 'the true spirit of punk' summoned up in the violence, others detected touches of self-parody, play-acting and ultimately madness when, in later years, Cobain would appear alone, rolling around with his guitar and screaming uncontrollably while he wrestled the instrument and thrashed the stage. 'It took over,' says a friend. 'At the end there was something demented about it, but in '89 it was all part of an act.' At a homecoming concert in Seattle Cobain jumped into the crowd and was passed fastidiously over the audience's heads, an honour previously reserved for Mark Arm of Mudhoney.

Nirvana's learning curve was not always painless. A woman in the crowd in San Francisco pulled a convincing toy gun on Cobain, and a man who 'heard voices' attempted suicide because of him. On another occasion, a heroin deal in Seattle turned violent, whereupon, terrified of being beaten, Cobain ran for the car, leaving Channing and Everman to negotiate for him. 'Kurt was as much a voyeur as a user,' says Arnold. 'It always struck me how he got the title for his album from a needle-bleaching slogan.' 'He was fascinated with the ritual of dope,' adds Skene. 'Having said that, he didn't necessarily want to get involved. Kurt would put himself in a front-line situation, and if having done so he sensed danger, he got out fast, ignoring the consequences.'

Bigger Than the Beatles

According to some, 'the astonishing, the amazing, the astounding, the almost unbelievable' (others said the patronizing) *Melody Maker* of 18 March 1989 was the beginning of the Cobain myth.

British interest in the Northwest, and in Sub Pop specifically, had begun with John Peel's article in the *Observer*. The word zigzagged a meander through the Style and Travel pages before a second wave of writers, some financed by Sub Pop, arrived in Seattle in late 1988. Two London journalists took up residence in the Camlin Hotel, where they sat, in Cobain's own words, 'like a pair of monks at a holy writ', diligently recording the 'meaning' of grunge and promising 'front-page treatment' on their return to Fleet Street. In the end it was Everett True whose splash in *Melody Maker* ('Seattle's New Generation Of Thrash Metal Merchants') gave form to an idea and turned Cobain into a minor international star overnight. After praising Mudhoney and touching on groups like Run, Swallow, Green River and Beat Happening, True turned to Nirvana:

> Basically, this is the real thing. No rock star contrivance, no intellectual perspective, no master plan for world domination. You're talking about four guys in their early twenties from rural Washington who wanna rock, who, if they weren't doing this, would be working in a supermarket or lumber yard, or fixing cars. Kurdt Kobain [*sic*] is a great tunesmith, although

still a relatively young songwriter. He wields a riff with *passion*.

The article, followed by features in *New Musical Express* and *Sounds*, created an immediate demand for Sub Pop groups and cemented Cobain's place at the centre of a movement. Each paper had something to say on the wildness of the phenomenon, the grungy, backwoods ambience and the uncouth musicians who peopled it. From then on, Cobain's name, whether alone or alongside those of his peers, was relentlessly hammered into the mind of the public. 'Grunge? We don't know what that is,' Nirvana had insisted in a biography only four months before. But in June 1989, overwhelmed by both the press and the public that had appropriated the term, Cobain himself used it, giving in to what, by then, had clearly become a fad. The word began to represent, haphazardly, a philosophical current, a way of life, a 'happening', a vast category that could accommodate anything society had previously rejected as deviant, marginal or anarchic. It also imposed an image on Cobain he bitterly resented.

When Sub Pop had released 'Love Buzz' it was marketed as 'sludge' from 'untamed Olympia drop-ins'. The label's promotion of the group as (in his own words) 'illiterate redneck kids' deeply displeased Cobain. In August 1988 a Seattle photographer named Alice Wheeler had taken shots of Nirvana posing under the Tacoma Narrows Bridge to publicize their first single. 'Everyone was nervous,' she says, except the 'Czar-like figure' of Pavitt, who wanted 'as grainy and ugly' a look as possible. Six months later Wheeler took a series of suitably stark, unflattering portraits of the group under fluorescent lighting backstage after a show. 'This time,' she says, 'a major fight broke out between Kurt and Bruce. Pavitt loved the shots because they captured the Neanderthal look he wanted, whereas Kurt loathed them.

He was worried you could see his acne.' A friend agrees that 'Kurt's ego was hurt that Bruce and Jon wanted to market him as exactly what he tried not to be – a redneck.' Cobain himself told a journalist, 'To be thought of as this stump-dumb rocker dude from Aberdeen who just blindly found his way up to Seattle . . . felt degrading.' A photograph taken by Marander – for which she was never paid – would eventually be used on the cover of *Bleach*.

More importantly, Cobain saw Sub Pop's hand at work on the music. The songs on *Bleach* were deliberately bleak, claustrophobic and lyrically sparse, with none of the manic derangement or sense of release of the live performance. 'We purposely made that record one-dimensional, more "rock" than it should have been,' Cobain admitted. 'There was pressure from Sub Pop to strip it down and make it sound like Aerosmith.' It was ironic that Cobain began his career by repressing his pop-melodic tendencies in order to conform to an image, and ended it worrying about having 'sold myself' by releasing a commercial record. Wheeler's story is enlightening not only about Cobain's egotism and self-image, which was more elevated than his brief career fully warranted. What is revealing is that, even in 1989, Cobain sought to present a more polished and urbane side of himself than Sub Pop wanted, and that he was never happy as the 'prince of grunge' or auto-mechanic *manqué* depicted in the press. When the style pundits noted Cobain's 'patent lumberjack shirts and ugly fifties geometric-patterned jerseys', seeing an example of 'low-couture chic' they missed the point that flannel shirts and sweaters were everyday dress in the marine climate of the Northwest. As the grunge look became a fashion rage, ending up in K-mart, Cobain took note of the irony that that was where the style had begun. 'I was never trying to start anything,' he said, 'or act as a role model for some idiot-savant lifestyle. The [plaid shirts] weren't a statement. They were my clothes.'

Cobain's territory, during his visits to Seattle from Olympia, was reduced to a triangle: Reciprocal, the university district where he bought drugs, and the midtown clubs like the Vogue, the Off Ramp, and later the Crocodile Café. The move from country to city was neatly made by his helping decorate the Crocodile in the style of a rustic diner: over the ugly green and white check floor and plate glass windows hung furry dice, lanterns, and warped thrift-store art he assembled in North Pear Street. The music area of this old taverna looked like the lounge of a bad Aberdeen café. Two bare-floored rooms, each with a low stage lit by garish purple and blue spots and furnished with black plastic couches joined onto the central restaurant. Of this, Patrick MacDonald says 'the food was surprisingly good'. The tall windows along Blanchard Street had been daubed amateurishly with graffiti and posters spelling out the names of the local bands: Blood Circus, Girl Trouble, Thrown Ups, Cat Butt, Nirvana. When a group decided they were ready to take the stage, they were liable to stroll on from the restaurant, in Cobain's case once with a bowl of rice and beans still in his hand.

Three figures dressed identically would then plug in their equipment, light cigarettes and tear into 'Love Buzz' with such ferocity that the noise seemed to detonate, exploding off the damp back wall. It was a sound Cobain described as 'low-fidelity'. But Nirvana's songs often took the high road, with Cobain's voice wrapping melodies around lyrics about high school, divorce and absent parents. The assault would shift seamlessly into an acoustic ballad, Cobain almost crooning 'About a Girl', before returning to a medley of rock, blues and pop standards, all amplified to the threshold of pain. Once he had put a few songs under his belt Cobain would start to loosen up. This was the moment he might jump into the crowd or demolish his guitar. One night at the Paramount he interrupted 'Spank Thru' to hurl a bottle into the stalls, shouting, 'I only play for money. I don't give a shit about the fans.' Then he played a guitar solo with his teeth.

Anyone present at the Crocodile, the Vogue or the other new Caverns could expect a punk-rock hybrid of music, noise and situationist behaviour, as when Cobain stared straight at the crowd and asked, 'What are *you* for?' As Wheeler says, he was 'the forerunner and leader in challenging his audience'. A Nirvana concert might be abrasive, exhilarating, violent, confrontational: it was never comfortable. The part of Cobain that admired structure and musicality hated the 'grabola free-for-all' his antics provoked. But the side of him that admired spontaneity and playfulness looked kindly on the 'thrash metal revolution' identified in *Melody Maker*, at the centre of whose 'redneck core' lay the elfin figure with the blue eyes and the disarmingly boyish smile.

By the summer of 1989 the uprising was well under way. 'It was always cool,' says Wheeler. 'It was always Saturday night.' Seattle had already been discovered. Sub Pop had already become the most talked-about phenomenon in the area. *Rolling Stone* was writing about Soundgarden and Mother Love Bone as well as Dire Straits and Eric Clapton, and the 'grunge look' began to be copied in San Francisco and Los Angeles. Nothing better illustrated how the ancient rites of rock had dissolved under pressure both from without and within. Even Mick Jagger could be seen sporting a flannel shirt and vest, while magazines like *Q* and *Vogue* teemed with stories about drugs, drizzle and Northwest *noir*. The Seattle scene swung to its zenith that summer as twentysomethings buttoned up in Value Village jeans sat hunched over their *latte* and cigarettes or lurched through Pioneer Square, closely followed by photographers from *Time* in search of data about grunge. According to a friend, there was a convergence of factors, crucial among them 'outlets for new bands' that, with notable exceptions, 'weren't in it for the money ... No one had an agenda except to have a good time and scare up old farts like Jagger. In that sense it *was* a revolution.'

'A coming together of freaks and losers' is one description of the phenomenon. So far as grunge had non-musical principles they were negative: disapproval of the state's anti-homosexual bills, opposition to the Omnibus Drug Law and a mélange of Utopian-socialist mumblings, of which strident feminism was the cornerstone. The image of an anti-social but informed generation combining in self-protective union was sociologically attractive, and soon even local politicians were preaching on grunge's text. A lecture on the New Hedonism drew 2,000 to a suburban Seattle meeting-hall. The City Council began to print the locations of Sub Pop and the Crocodile on their tour maps. Pavitt and Poneman were recognized in public. The grunge sub-culture brought with it an eruption of clubs, cafés and bric-à-brac stalls purveying kitsch and conceptual art of the kind practised in North Pear Street. It says much for Cobain's lugubrious view of life that, even as a whole world opened up to accommodate him, he remained an outsider. 'I found Seattle incestuously small and cliquey and everyone knew one another and they just seemed so stuck up and they'd seen it all,' he told his biographer. A musician who played with Cobain that summer agrees he was 'worried about being taken up by cultural elitists' for their own ends. 'He felt he was being patronized,' says Wheeler.

With the recent spate of interviews, profiles and full-length features in the British press, it was easy to forget that Nirvana had only ever released three songs. Immense effort went into pushing the group's name before the public. Pavitt and Poneman realized that a period of image-building and spinning what Peterson calls the 'mountain-man myth' of the band would inevitably lead to a demand for product.

They also realized that, in order to benefit from the strategy, Nirvana would sooner or later have to deliver an album.

Bleach was released on 15 June 1989. Despite the eccentric mix and Cobain's unshaken belief that the world would be as eager as he was to avenge itself on Aberdeen, there were endearingly familiar landmarks: the dentist's-drill guitar and punchy rhythm would both have suited a Cheap Trick album, while Cobain's voice, albeit buried near the bottom of a deep, echoing well, recalled *Rubber Soul*-era Beatles. There were some specific references: the guitar part on 'Love Buzz' was lifted from Sparks' *Kimono My House*, while the drum on 'Floyd' reminded some of the Stones' 'My Obsession'. On 'Paper Cuts' Cobain's vocals rose almost to Robert Plant register. Whereas Sparks, the Stones or Led Zeppelin were a shameless study in commercial rock, *Bleach* used much the same ingredients to cast a darker spell. The wildly distorted guitars and muddy rhythm created an effect one critic described as 'retro-punk.' The deliberately stark design and crude photograph also gave the same vicarious thrill once experienced through the Sex Pistols.

Bleach, says Grant Alden, was a 'perfect documentary of Nirvana live'. While Cobain later tended to disclaim the album, even he agreed that Endino caught the complex mix of studio and stage. Although the songs progressed at breakneck speed, they still sounded completely unhurried. 'The sheer *structure* of the writing was what got me,' says Peel. 'The songs evolved, rather than just announcing their intentions and fulfilling them.' Alden also calls it 'a classic example of an album that gets better with time.' According to Slim Moon, '*Nevermind* seemed dated almost as soon as Kurt made it. *Bleach* sounds hot today.'

The album's enduring moments were 'School', only four lines long but memorable for the chorus that served as the rip; 'Scoff', a parting salvo at Don and Wendy; and 'Negative Creep', whose subject was the singer himself. On 'About

A Girl' Cobain managed the rare trick of combining tenderness and anger in roughly equal parts, with a consistently winning result. The line 'I can't see you every night for free' was a direct observation on Marander's request that Cobain find a job, as was the reference to his being 'hung out to dry'. If the lyric struck a lachrymose note it was balanced by a melody that veered on the commercial side of blues-rock and dashed Nirvana's art-noise credentials. It was also the first song on which Cobain showed true pop star potential.

At the other end of the scale, 'Paper Cuts' carried the folk-influenced melody and ponderous rhythm of an early Led Zeppelin number; 'Mr. Moustache' addressed itself to Nirvana's male fans; 'Downer' showed the same exceptional contempt for the group's audience. These three, along with 'Big Cheese' and 'Blew', were Nirvana's signature sound, a sepulchral downbeat tempo welded to headbanging guitar under which three-minute pop songs signalled wildly to be let out. The vague avant-garde pretensions were matched by Top Forty contenders like 'Love Buzz'.

Although *Bleach* grazed the lower reaches of the alternative chart, it failed commercially. The critics tended to divide along party lines. To the Seattle *Rocket*, cultivating a niche as the bulletin-board of grunge, it 'carried an undeniable power that should reach even those too timid to turn the volume on their stereos up past "two".' Grant Alden saw it as 'a wake-up call' and 'an incredible jump in only a year'. KCMU began plugging *Bleach* immediately, as did Peel and Charlie Gillett in London. On the other hand, *Rolling Stone* ignored the album for months, before dismissing it as 'undistinguished' and 'relying on warmed-over 70s metal riffs'. The *Conflict* review consisted of the advice, 'If you're going to be a simpleton rock band, then at least be more entertaining than this shit.' Patrick MacDonald says *Bleach* struck him as 'just another thrash for Sub Pop'. The notice in *Playboy* was all too obviously an attempt to place the group at the head of a movement, 'the harnessing of hardcore punk to its subversive potential'. It was always the anarchic side of Nirvana that Sub Pop pushed to the press. In Pavitt's scheme there was a conscious effort to market the 'un-L.A. look' and 'acne and stubble' image of the band. 'On one level,' says Alden, 'Kurt really *was* lewd, uneducated and dumb.' On another, there were mocking intimations of wit, intelligence, even of intellect, and the quietly expressed conviction that '*Bleach* [would] sooner or later be discovered as a classic'.

Uncertainty as to who Cobain really was led to some curious scenes. A Seattle artist named Lisa Orth, commissioned to design the cover for 'Love Buzz', remembers him as 'a chameleon . . . someone you wouldn't recognize the day after you met him'. Wheeler notes that *Bleach*'s 'Status Quo cover', as well as a reversal of her own 'acne and stubble' portraits, physically obscured Cobain from the public. There was a conscious effort to play up to the enigma. When Alden arranged to interview Nirvana that summer he was greeted by Novoselic and Channing, 'and the cryptic apology that Cobain was at home building guitars'. Finally, both on 'Love Buzz' and *Bleach* the singer was credited as 'Kurdt Kobain', the first in a series of variations originally blamed on a simple typesetting error but actually, says Skene, 'a carefully planned effort to tease the public and seem mysterious'.

Friends of Marander note that the tension hinted at in 'About A Girl' was all too real. According to Wheeler: 'Tracy got tired of being the provider' and 'cared for Kurt more than he seemed to care for her.' Towards the end of 1989 Cobain met a woman named Julia Levy, a painter with short-cropped hair, a small, waif-like figure and a face not unlike Marander's. She had recently moved to Olympia to 'find life', and her discovery came to be fulfilled by Cobain.

'Why he picked on me, I don't know. Perhaps because I had a great record collection; or because I was one of the greatest lays of all time.'

In 1990 Cobain would take up with Tobi Vail, a musician and journalist responsible for forming the Riot Grrl movement, a feminist sub-division of punk. According to Wheeler, 'Women like Tobi and Kathleen Hanna [of Bikini Kill] were responsible for developing the feminist, politically correct side of Kurt. When he came to Olympia he was still socially retarded. Tracy used to say that he was a typical Aberdeen product.'

Nirvana's pro-feminist effusions and Riot Grrls' occasional pro-Cobain displays of unity are generally better known than the 'retarded' side he showed periodically in private and not at all in public. When Cobain was drunk, on drugs or in the company of his male friends he still contemptuously referred to women as bitches. He still collected pornography and erotica. As someone whose protest lay chiefly in drugs and punk rather than sex and alcohol, it was true that Cobain was almost blushingly monogamous compared to other rock stars. His shyness was real, as was his modesty. According to Azerrad, 'he slept with a total of two women on all of Nirvana's tours'. That Cobain enjoyed the ritual side of sex is, however, certain and Levy reports 'an almost gynaecological interest in the body'. 'He got gentler and nicer as the years went by,' says Wheeler, 'but it was a struggle with Tracy. Kurt still had strange views in those days.'

In February 1989 Nirvana were a band from the American northwest which had been loosely together for three years with little to show for it but a local following and two independent-label releases. Six months later they were the next-big-thing. They were taken up by opinion-formers in London and New York, had their album played on the radio and enjoyed the significant status of a cult. Later in the year Poneman would insist only half-facetiously to a record producer, 'These guys are going to be bigger than the Beatles.' It was a prediction roundly endorsed by Cobain. When he returned to Aberdeen now, either to rehearse or to visit his half-sister, he struck Tony Groves as 'driven' and having 'put clear water between the old Kurt and the new'. In an interview that summer Cobain spoke of his admiration of two men, John Lennon and Iggy Pop, both of whose 'breaking for light from the underground' he meant to emulate. A woman who met him in Wendy's home on East 1st Street remembers his 'politician's itch for success', one still tempered by Cobain's 'personal niceness' in dealing with old friends. 'That's just the way he was – concerned and interested in other people.' Another woman remembers, 'To the people in Aberdeen, he was the man among men . . . just kind and extremely considerate of everyone.' It was not the least of Cobain's qualities that he could conceal personal ambition under a generally benign, laidback façade and give his cousin the uneasy impression that 'there was one Kurt for public view and another in private'.

A sign of Cobain's growing self-confidence was his insistence that the verbal understanding with Sub Pop be replaced by a contract. Although Nirvana had been agitating for a written agreement since 'Love Buzz', it was only when Cobain 'bellowed at Bruce' for a royalty statement that a document was drawn up. Again, according to Peterson, 'it was typical that while Chris usually did the business, the impetus was Kurt's'. Although the deal proceeded in authentic punk fashion – Novoselic snarling 'You fuckers, we want a contract,' while banging drunkenly on Pavitt's window – it varied only slightly from the terms and conditions of a standard agreement. (Poneman had recently been reading *This Business of Music*, and according to a witness to the deal brought microscopic detail to the proceedings.) 'There was a sense of mutual wariness,' says Wheeler. '[The contract] fuelled Kurt's fears he was going to be exploited.' In the Sub Pop catalogue that summer *Bleach* was described as 'hypnotic and righteous heaviness from these Olympia pop stars. They're young, they own their own van and they're going to make us rich.'

By identifying themselves with Cobain, Pavitt and Poneman were able in time to claim a share in the pull of his name, and his earnings, and so find a vehicle for their own self-promotion. Pavitt had a flair for image-making and later admitted to playing on the myth of 'Kurt the trailer-trash kid', with himself and Poneman posing in suits and ties, adding a little theatre. But Sub Pop did more than just add theatre. They actively talked up the label, first in Britain, then at home, as the kind of latter-day Motown noted by Peel. They gave a series of hyperbolic interviews describing themselves as 'starmakers' and 'moguls'. They began to encourage the attention of outside labels – Island was one contender to buy Sub Pop in 1989 – while stressing their 'independent' and 'alternative' credentials, mainly through the brilliantly simple artifice of the Singles Club. Alice Wheeler says that 'Bruce and Jon had an intuitive sense of how to pitch not only Nirvana but themselves,' while Lisa Orth remembers 'Pavitt's influence extending down to the minutest detail of ['Love Buzz's] design.' 'They brought a kind of East Coast savvy to Seattle,' agrees Alden, portraying Pavitt as 'passive-aggressive rather than sharp'. It was no accident that Sub Pop began to attract global attention as America re-elected a Republican president, Alden believes. Poneman had always thought it was 'conservatism in one form or another' that fired subversive rock and gave cohesion to an under-class united by their 'gloomy, vengeful' outlook and 'rejection of the mainstream'. Where Sub Pop made their breakthrough was in their appeal to the large number of disaffected slackers alienated by the prospect of a Bush administration, and prone to the hype of a club that existed in large part to enrich its owners.

Sub Pop in those days occupied an attic room in the Terminal Sales Building in downtown Seattle, south of the Crocodile and opposite the Midtown Theatre, of whose pornography Cobain was a well-known patron. The office, according to Orth, existed in 'Bedlam – no filing system and records stacked up in the bathroom', though even then Poneman's and Pavitt's commercial instincts were at work. A second designer involved with the label in 1989 believes 'greedy outside investors saw Sub Pop as equally greedy' and recalls immense effort going into the label's selling point of 'anarchy tethered to the unspoken ambitions of the two principals'. 'Under the surface chaos,' Orth agrees, 'Jon and Bruce were personally ruthless . . . Not only were they permanently broke, they regularly hit on suppliers like me for loans.' The figure of Pavitt, in particular, emerges as partly attractive, partly the reverse, and Orth emphasizes his paradoxical character. If her comments end with the tentative suggestion that he may come to be seen as the 'Berry Gordy of Seattle', much of her memory is less flattering. Pavitt was a man who, according to his neighbour, avoided most concerts because 'he couldn't be fucked'. He used to spend hours going over Sub Pop's books while simulating an artistic disdain for money. He struck even a member of the Asia Pacific Chamber of Commerce, located in Sub Pop's building, as 'someone whose reputation for being laid-back was as inflated as his ego'. Though few openly said it, Sub Pop in the late 1980s was also at the centre of a flourishing drug trade. The daily heroin consumption, according to their neighbour, was famous around the building, where 'figures stumbled about, dazed and asking for the john'. According to Patrick MacDonald: 'When an out-of-state band auditioned for Sub Pop, they were staggered at the amount of dope being passed around.' Orth, too, believes

'Drugs were a big part of dealing with the label.' Looking at Cobain's life as a whole it is possible to see a kind of weakness of which his susceptibility to pressure was symptomatic. Just before his death he compared Pavitt and Poneman to his mother: '[They] had the same mean streak and the same killer instinct when it suited them.' Here was the most powerful male influence Cobain had yet seen in action, and Sub Pop – with its mix of loose morals and economic conservatism, its tolerance of drugs and thrusting for the mainstream – affected and haunted him throughout his life.

The mortal break in Sub Pop's ranks came when Soundgarden, the first group to send a swarm of talent-spotters to Seattle in search of new blood, signed with A&M. Suddenly the exponents of what Morrell calls 'the punk/Sabbath crossover' found themselves recording pop songs for a label co-owned by Herb Alpert. The effect on Cobain was dramatic. Almost as soon as the ink had dried on Nirvana's own contract, he was agitating to break it. From the summer of 1989 his career became a modern variation on the more primitive log-cabin-to-White-House theme, as a friend says 'a series of steady progressions, ending in *Sunset Boulevard* seclusion in the lakeside mansion'. That June, in yet another self-penned biography, Cobain listed the Bay City Rollers and the Beatles among Nirvana's influences; approvingly described the 'underground scene [as] becoming more accessible towards commercial major label interests'; compared Pavitt to Henry Mancini; and again closed neatly with Marander's address and phone number.

Cobain constantly spoke of 'purity' as the decisive factor in music, but the impression of single-mindedness that he sought to convey was matched by the intensity of his ambition. 'As time goes on,' he admitted in October 1989, 'my songs are getting poppier and poppier . . . Some people might think of that as changing into something, but it's something I've always been aware of [and am] just starting to express.' Six months later he amplified on what even a close friend called the 'Paul McCartney side' of his work. 'There won't be any songs as heavy as "Paper Cuts" on the new record. That's just too boring. I'd rather have a good hook.' All the material Cobain wrote following the release of *Bleach* – the relentlessly catchy 'Stain' or the Beatlesque 'Been a Son' – was of a part with what Arnold terms 'a political thrust to the top of the charts'. Nirvana did, of course, engage in a few carefully staged demonstrations of their punk credentials. Cobain interrupted one Olympia performance to vomit into the crowd. Instrument smashing became routine. The group's rabble-rousing potential was very real; keenly aware of his role as the untamed mountain-man of Seattle rock, Cobain played the part with a consistent and convincing energy. But he was also a clever man, easily clever enough to know the value of his own simplicity, and he played up to the dim-witted myth while lobbying behind the scenes for a better contract. Early in 1990 Nirvana began hawking songs, ostensibly meant for Sub Pop, to outside labels. Cobain resumed his flirtations with MCA and Columbia. He drove to Los Angeles, wearing a velvet jacket and carrying a briefcase, to meet the entertainment lawyer Alan Mintz, whom he impressed as businesslike. All this took place behind Poneman's and Pavitt's backs. In private Cobain complained: 'We've never known how many records we've sold. We don't know how many copies of *Bleach* we sold. And we're not being promoted very well. I challenge anybody to find a *Bleach* ad.' In public he insisted that 'Everything's coming up roses at Sub Pop.'

A mark of Cobain's mounting disaffection with his label was his almost promiscuous involvement in other projects. That summer he recorded a cover of Kiss's 'Do You Love Me', issued in August 1990 on C/Z's *Hard to Believe*. He played on the single 'Bikini Twilight' by Olympia's Go

Team, released on K. In August 1989 Cobain collaborated with Screaming Trees' Mark Lanegan on two tracks, 'Where Did You Sleep Last Night' and 'Ain't it a Shame', the first of which appeared on Lanegan's *The Winding Sheet*. A visitor to North Pear Street remembers 'Kurt hunched with the guitar playing pop, blues, folk' – anything but the one-dimensional grunge redolent of Sub Pop – his strumming of which was 'a substitute for speech'. He did, however, accompany a man named Mark Lane to the Jackpot Food Mart, where 'Kurt's favourite gig was to ask the clerk to fetch him something off a high shelf and then, when his back was turned, steal a load of stuff. He thought that was real funny.' The other thing Cobain found amusing was frequenting gay bars in Seattle, where according to Lane 'he used to stand posing by the jukebox, rubbing himself and batting his eyes at the trade'. Cobain ended up in an alley behind the Sales Building one night with a friend whom Lane saw engage in the 'gay ritual of peeing over his part-ner', who 'lay on his back without moving, quietly laughing'.

On 22 June 1989 Nirvana began their first extensive US tour, the four musicians driving in a broken Dodge van and playing bars and assembly halls for $100 a night. The rock clubs of Minneapolis, Pittsburgh and Newark were about as far as one could travel from North Pear Street – bleak, half-filled outposts of original punk, where Nirvana's pop-fuelled repertoire was greeted with puzzlement, if not down-right hostility. At a concert in Chicago Cobain hailed the crowd as 'fuckers' and then proceeded to harangue them from behind a bourbon bottle. Later in the performance he screamed at a fan for the provocative remark: 'Hey, Kurt. How are you doing?' Backstage Cobain took out his frustra-tion by destroying the makeshift dressing-room, hurling his guitar through a window and pulling a female first-aid worker into the shower where a public – and unsatisfactory –

coupling took place. Later still he purchased a large crucifix, strapping it to the Dodge like a figurehead until even Novoselic protested. A fight ensued, circling like so many of Cobain's from the specific to the general and ending with his repetition of what he called the Sex Pistols test. 'However great and wonderful and amazing a show, and even if it's a great gig for Nirvana, we have to ask ourselves, "Would the Sex Pistols have dug it?" And if the answer is yes, we've blown it.'

Nirvana's first contact with the road came as something of a shock. For four weeks the van ploughed east, such shows as they had desultory affairs in Texas or Ohio, where the group, permanently hungry, compensated by drinking everything they could lay hands on. Cobain and Novoselic began a sort of rivalry to see who could appear most belligerently drunk onstage. The contest was abandoned when Cobain fell from a ten-foot high speaker stack, splitting a lip and bloodying his nose, before wading into the small crowd in order to speak directly to the 'shitheads' and others present. Nirvana were never known for their propriety, but at this stage their drunkenness, drug-taking and public lewdness were the result of a cultivated snobbery, in which, as would be expected, Cobain found himself wholly at home. According to Heidi Stern, a woman who met them in Pittsburgh, 'Kurt came across as a middle-class brat who was slumming it. Everything about [him] was a study in rock star poses.' The image became proverbial. Stopping at motels and the inevitable roadside diners meant the same ordeal for all four musicians – even quiet, mild-mannered Everman – of silent looks and open hostility. After being refused service at a bar in New Jersey Cobain retaliated by urinating on the front door and setting off in search of a 'killer rodent', which he planned to introduce into the kitchen.

On a commercial level, at least, the tour achieved its

modest objectives. Somewhere on the east coast it gradually bore in on Nirvana that they had every prospect of making it. College radio began playing songs like 'School' and 'About A Girl'. Sales of *Bleach* increased. It was a 'creeping thing', says Channing, the metamorphosis of the group from regional cult to national fixation. Studiously as he ignored them, Cobain's audience provided him with friends and a public, which he loved. After eight years of intense cramming and competition – first in Aberdeen, and then the clubs of Olympia and Seattle – Cobain at last saw the chance of infiltrating the host culture and becoming a star. Even in New York, where the tour ended on 18 July, he was staggered to see posters of the group alongside those advertising U2 and the Rolling Stones. 'We were totally poor,' he told Azerrad, 'but we were seeing the United States for the first time. And we were in a band, and we were making enough money to survive. It was awesome. It was just great. And if Jason wasn't such a prick, it would have been even better.'

As Cobain grew in fame and self-assurance he began to develop his stage-act to include elements of burlesque and parody. One evening he appeared in a flaming pink jacket and black shirt and spent the night bumping and grinding in front of the band. On another he laid down his guitar and limped onstage like a cripple, throwing the mike stand toward the floor but catching it before it hit by going into a hunched-up Quasimodo pose. Cobain took to smashing his Fender Mustang roughly every other performance, hurling the guitar to the ground and jumping on it, or burying the instrument in Channing's drum. While Novoselic praised the routine as 'rock and roll' and audiences everywhere cheered, others were less persuaded by what *Village Voice* called 'the pallid shadow of Pete Townshend'. When Nirvana hired the sound engineer Craig Montgomery, a Scot with a keen sense of thrift, he almost came to blows with his employer about the latter's 'fucking stupid auto-destruction'. After Dale Crover briefly returned to the group in 1990 he told Cobain, 'Whatever you do, do not jump into my drum set. *Do not*.' Crover also felt the increasingly formulaic stage act to be 'anticlimactic ... Kurt trying to break a guitar – it takes him fifteen minutes.' And Jeff Sanford, who supplied Cobain's first six-string Lindell in 1981, thought it both 'criminal and pathetic' that he should demolish the tools of his trade.

Cobain's reputation, both on and off stage, was burdened with rumours of dissipation on a scale shocking even to punk rock. 'I almost thought the tradition of the musician on dope was part of the myth,' he admitted. 'Everyone from Leadbelly to Iggy to Sid Vicious – these were my heroes.' But the musician on dope was but a snort away from the addict who made music. By 1989 Cobain had reversed a lifelong aversion to cocaine and become an enthusiastic user, fixer and sniffer from toilet seats. At an address in Jones Street, New York, he obtained, in Lane's words, 'a truckload of grass, amyl nitrate and high-grade Colombian', a quantity 'even Keith Richards would have found big-time'. Rush-hour commuters that night were treated to the sight of Cobain wandering distractedly around Sheridan Square, flapping his arms like a bird and stepping into the street to lecture a parking-meter. In Seattle, Pavitt and Poneman, at that time with drug problems of their own, loyally protected their investment and insisted Cobain would shortly be in 'hands-on mode' in the studio. Above all, he wanted to get his hands on more cocaine. Cobain's drug habit seems to have been born partly from weakness, partly boredom and partly from his morbid desire to find a wound that matched his bite. There was also the question of supply. Not all his friends, colleagues and the fans he met as he scurried out of the stage doors of clubs and bars were strangers themselves to drugs. Cobain's access to cocaine and heroin increased proportionately to his fame. 'Regular kids,' as he called them, began sharing their supplies with their hero. Free samples arrived from dealers whose cachet was enhanced by Cobain's patronage. The gifts bestowed on the still naïve twenty-two-year-old represented, all in all, a rather modest introduction to the snare of celebrity. In later years whole fortunes would be made striking more commercial deals to provide Cobain with heroin. But by 1989 he was already well on the path to accumulating a debt he would never quite pay off. 'It might have served Kurt better,' says Peterson, 'had someone sat down with him early on.' Cobain himself would insist, towards the end of his life, 'If there was a Rock Star 101 course, I would have liked to take it. It might have helped me.'

Nirvana returned to Seattle on 22 July 1989. In six months Cobain had developed and extended his act, formed the basis of a cult, been noticed by *Village Voice* and released an impressive if modestly selling album. He remained, said the *Weekly*, 'a half-baked figure', someone whose maturity had stopped dead in adolescence, a strange mixture of ego and reticence – he hated to have his photograph taken – above all, who always found conditions in the real world incompatible with those in his head. Cobain was convinced he was already a star. Yet even in Seattle, where Nirvana played third on a bill to Mudhoney and TAD, they were 'just one of the stable of Northwest garage-rock grunge bands' (*The Times*) or 'pure trash-a-thon' (*Taboo*). In a letter that summer Cobain spoke of himself as a sure bet for success, the next Iggy, and Nirvana as destined for a following of millions. Yet nothing happened. Sales of *Bleach* fell off and the group returned to playing for a case of beer and a few dollars a night.

Part of the problem lay in Cobain's handling of Everman. Here, at least, relations were consistent. They hated each other. While much was made of the inevitable 'musical differences' – Everman, says Novoselic, 'wanted us to be more rock and we were more punk' – there was also a simmering rivalry under the surface. Early in the American tour Cobain noticed that his second guitarist was attracting more female attention than himself. There may have been a touch of resentment when he told Azerrad: '[Everman] was like a peacock on amphetamines. He was so posey I couldn't believe it ... It was so contrived and *sexual*.' To this day Alice Wheeler believes 'part of the reason Kurt hated the original shots for *Bleach* was that Jason looked cuter than he did.' There was also what Everman calls 'a control thing', Cobain insisting that his and only his songs be covered and that outside contributions went unrewarded. Whatever the cause, the result was that in early August Everman was laid off from the group, though even then Cobain's talent for equivocation and ambiguity was at work. 'Nobody formally fired Jason,' says a friend. 'The decision wasn't reached, it arrived.' 'We were just too maladjusted to tell him to his face,' says Novoselic. Everman himself believes he resigned. There may well have been, as Nirvana insisted, compelling artistic reasons for the split, but in his high-handed treatment of Everman and the facetious tone he used to talk about him, Cobain revealed his unhappy knack of 'hurting people just to defend himself' – a trait still widely remarked on today.

That September Nirvana recorded material at Music Source Studio in Seattle. Any doubts concerning the group's future direction were removed by Cobain's first words to the producer Steve Fisk, 'We need a Top Forty drum sound,' and his muttered aside to Novoselic, 'Goddamnit, I want something I can *hum*.' Of the five songs covered, 'Stain' and 'Been A Son' again showed the pop sensibility vying with the punk affectations; these and two tracks reprised from *Bleach* were issued as *Blew*. A final (unreleased) song dealt with the 1987 rape of two teenage girls in Tacoma, with a lyric that was anger unleashed. When in New York Bob Dylan first heard 'Polly', even he remarked 'the kid has heart' and the band possessed 'guts'. Nirvana cast a different persona on *Blew* than previously – more sharp, less tentative, and mired in gloomy material. The distance between Cobain's lyrics and all-too-obvious pop ambitions made the songs seem oddly disjointed; time and again the message was diluted by the melody. On the other hand, his ear for a hook and nail-biting perfectionism stood Cobain in good stead on a song like 'Son', where he came across as more of a songwriter than most singers and more of a singer than most writers, and avoided the bland no-man's-land in between. *Blew*, criticized for audaciously mimicking the Beatles, also showed Cobain's impressive grasp of his own roots.

They loved Nirvana in Europe. This unequivocal conclusion can be gleaned from the fact that from October to December 1989 the group played thirty-six sold-out shows in Germany, Holland, Belgium, Switzerland and Italy, packed by 'regular kids' as opposed to the writers in magazines – not to mention Britain, where *Bleach* outpaced even the Rolling Stones in the charts. Cobain himself achieved a status as a purveyor of exhilarating punk and singalong rock – what Peel calls the great average – he never fully lost. Word about him spread from Hamburg to Bordeaux. Nirvana posters began to appear in bedsitters and common-rooms the length of Britain. Cobain himself was quoted frequently, always with approval. A fan club was organized. While many of the stories about the hardships of his youth celebrated in Cobain mythology were true, it is significant that stardom came to him easily and early on. At twenty he was utterly obscure. At twenty-three he was internationally famous, renowned as the king of grunge, critically acclaimed and a fad on both sides of the Atlantic. When fans stared at Cobain he often sidled up for a friendly word because, as he said, 'It makes their day.' There was no arrogance in the assumption, just an acknowledgement of his status. For all his excesses, he could still be what Wheeler calls 'the nicest guy in the world' while writing 'the best rock songs in the world'.

Little of this was evident at Nirvana's opening concert in Newcastle. The performance itself was uneven – the group playing second on the bill to TAD – and the reviews were perfunctory. According to the *News*, the songs from *Bleach* were charmless, while another notice thought that Cobain screeched rather than sang a repertoire 'almost entirely about himself'. The next morning, noted the *Herald and Post*

> Well over 100 ecstatic youngsters gathered at Newcastle's Royal Victoria Infirmary to see their favourite pop stars launch the Radio Lollipop appeal. Among those on hand were potential megastars Big Fun and London Boys ... It was a pity other invited groups were unable to support this worthy appeal.

The press, with one or two notable exceptions, was indifferent throughout the first part of Nirvana's tour. Such interest as there was centred on the 300-pound form of Tad Doyle, the quintessential 'stump-dumb rocker dude' shunned by Cobain and, in student union circles, the ethics of 'faux-naif imported punks' (*Stop Press*) 'repudiating the possibility of a counterculture in favour of the bucks'. In fact Nirvana appeared in Britain for a fee of between £50 and £100 a night. They, TAD and three road crew travelled in a ten-seat Fiat van, ploughing the autobahns and *routes*, sleeping, or in Cobain's case, swigging cough syrup and chain-smoking, in the hours and sometimes days between concerts. According to a musician present:

After a week of guys drinking and toking in the van the windows were fogged and it stank of something worse than shit ... Everyone was in it together, sharing hash and getting high. Everyone except Kurt. He just *sat* there, drinking his [syrup] and looking like death. He was definitely a one-off, didn't join in. Not a regular guy.

On 9 November Nirvana were on hand to witness the fall of the Berlin Wall. At two o'clock in the morning, in a small courtyard on the south side of the Reichstag, a klieg light picked out Cobain and another figure lying semi-naked – the police described it as 'a gross combination' – celebrating with the aid of a bottle and a stolen Federal Republic flag. A minute later both men were racing up the East-West axis with their eyes smarting from tear gas. It had been an eventful year for Cobain, but even he must have been impressed at the distance travelled: from rehearsing over the hair salon in Aberdeen to sprinting blindly from the march of history, and pulling up his trousers.

At the next night's concert Cobain destroyed his guitar six songs into the set and walked off. Not only was he tired, dispirited and ill, living exclusively on a diet of cough linctus and pot, he suffered one of his cyclical bouts of homesickness for his girlfriend. A postcard Cobain sent to Marander repeated the words 'I love you' eight times over his signature. He even spent part of his meagre performance fee to call his mother in Aberdeen. 'I can't stand it here' (in Rome), his colleague remembers him saying. 'They can't fry a decent hamburger.' As a teenager, Cobain had seen Europe as an escape-route from what he called a life of 'ass-kissing and boredom' in the Pacific Northwest. Now that he was there he found conditions to be eccentric, alien and intimidating, 'shittier not the reverse' than Aberdeen. It was one of the peculiar paradoxes of Cobain's life that while everything got easier, he saw it as having worsened. Never had he been more successful, never did he seem more miserable. Never had he been more popular, never did he look more woebegone. In Rome Cobain commented acidly on the arrival of Poneman and Pavitt, whose choice travel arrangements he contrasted to his own 'shitola' surroundings. At the performance that night he dramatized his annoyance by climbing onto a row of speakers and suffering what Pavitt calls 'a nervous breakdown onstage'. For a quarter of an hour Cobain clambered through the rafters, clawed the curtains, swung from a chandelier and, apelike, prattled at the crowd. According to Azerrad, 'He wound up backstage, where someone from the venue was arguing with their tour manager over whether Kurt had broken some microphones. Kurt grabbed both mikes, flung them to the ground, and began stomping on them. "Now they're broken," he said.' Then Cobain announced he was leaving the group, 'shrieked like a beast' at Channing, and burst into tears. A reporter who happened to witness the scene was pushed aside by Novoselic with the words 'Fuck off, prick' and screamed at by Cobain until he, too, began to cry. Things might have gone on indefinitely but for the arrival of Poneman, beaming, in a reporter's words, 'millions of volts of synthetic charm', and assuring everyone Kurt was fine; comments that aroused Cobain to new seizures of rage and grief. When eventually he was persuaded to leave the hall he spat in the face of a man standing in the street to photograph his wife.

The nadir came in Switzerland. Under massive sedation Cobain was installed in a compartment on the Rome–Geneva express, aboard which his clothes, wallet and passport were somehow lost. It took all Pavitt's formidable powers of negotiation to persuade the authorities to admit his unshaven, whimpering and now heavily drugged protégé into the country. 'I don't think I have ever seen another human being look as absolutely miserable as Kurt Cobain did at that moment,' said Poneman. The concert that night was cancelled at a few minutes' notice, and the audience sent home with a brusqueness that turned mere disappointment into mob rage. As Cobain was driven away to eat, his car was engulfed by shaken fists and faces upside down, mouthing obscenities, until Pavitt managed to clear a way ahead.

The zenith came in London. By the final concert at the Astoria on 3 December Nirvana had honed a set that shuttled between Cobain's teenaged songs and *Bleach* in a way that eradicated the eight years in between. Played at breakneck punk-era speed, the opening numbers were marred by a sound quality that also seemed to have been taken from 1981. It was 'About A Girl', with its chiming melody and ironic chorus, before Nirvana blended as a group. When everything came together perfectly – Cobain's foghorn voice and simple-but-effective guitar soaring over the gigantic beat – it seemed at last that musical enterprise had replaced hype and overkill in the performance. During the final numbers the audience actually broke off from their fighting to listen. One woman even threw flowers to Cobain. According to Keith Cameron in *Sounds*, 'It was exhilarating and it was exciting because that was the nature of the music, but there was also an almost palpable sense of danger, that this whole thing could fall apart any second. There was never any relaxation from the first note to the last.' Poneman insists 'it [was] one of the proudest moments in my life.' *Melody Maker* thought that it was 'a good show [in which] the singer-guitarist [was] pretty graceful in a longhaired kind of way, the wound-up genetic offspring of Neil Young and Lemmy ... Call me a Tory, but Nirvana only work up momentum when there's actually a *tune* in there fighting to get out. The rest of the time they're Hüsker Dü tuning up, the Kinks with a headache.'

The generally favourable reviews pinned their colours unashamedly to the Nirvana phenomenon, rather than to anything Cobain actually said or did. It was in Britain that the 'stump-dumb rocker dude' image was most brazenly peddled. 'They're a little bit gross and a little bit awesome,' read one profile. 'What else would you be if you grew up in the backwoods redneck helltown of Aberdeen?' In pushing Nirvana as untamed exemplars of the Old West – one looked in vain for the arrow through the guitarist's temple – Pavitt and Poneman consciously followed in the footsteps of Hendrix and his manager Chas Chandler. When the former arrived in Britain at twenty-three, just a year older than Cobain, a premeditated effort began to sell a myth at odds with the bouncing-clean image of the home product. Photographs of Hendrix were chosen to make him look ugly. Chandler's already absurdly inapt portrayal of Seattle as 'a one-trick town' was seized on in the media. *Disc and Music Echo* were the first to dub Hendrix 'The Wild Man of Borneo'. *NME* headlined its profile 'The scene's wildest raver' before concluding, 'the most obvious thing about Jimi Hendrix is that he's not pretty'. After Hendrix was added to a package tour alongside the Walker Brothers, Cat Stevens and Engelbert Humperdinck, each paper had something to say on the crowd that was 'a mob rather than an audience', the 'many broken chairs', the 'twenty fainting girls', and the 'rabid frenzy' of the performance. When Hendrix not only plucked the guitar with his teeth but set the instrument on fire it was all that Chandler could do to contain himself. 'The dark side was immediately hammed up,' he says. From that time on, and much to his own lingering puzzlement, Hendrix became a public figure. His debut was remembered as the musical event of 1966. His reputation as more colourful and dramatic than anything seen before became proverbial, accepted. Probably he subconsciously played up to it. Undeniably it helped to sell Hendrix not only overseas but at home in Seattle, where the simple fact that a native son had made the cover of *Disc* was a front-page story in itself. Now, twenty-three years later, Sub Pop performed the same devastating trick with Nirvana. Hardened critics made the link between Cobain's instrument-smashing and Hendrix's ritualistic *auto-da-fé*. Those with long memories commented on the similarities of the 'untamed drop-in' and the 'wildest raver' from Seattle. 'There *was* a link,' says Peel. 'Both Jimi and Kurt were shy, unobtrusive men ruthlessly sold as dangerous and foreign. The European fame rebounded back to the US. You can call it exploitation, or you can call it playing on the British teenager's obsession with the States.'

Peel himself met Nirvana in London and invited them to record 'Love Buzz', 'Spank Thru', 'About A Girl' and 'Polly' for Radio One. His own impression was positive: 'The early songs struck me as complete. They couldn't have been improved on by adding or subtracting anything. Within the limits of what they were trying to do, they were perfect.' At the same time Peel detected a 'central volatility' in Cobain, whom he saw as 'already weakening to the ways of the business'. He was 'movie-star rude' when kept waiting for food or drink. When Nirvana left the country to fly home there was an incident on the jet when Cobain and Channing had to be prevented from throttling each other, after which each sat in scowling silence, staring out of a window.

Cobain was at the release party for *Sub Pop 200* on 28 December, and at Novoselic's wedding in Tacoma two days later. Uninvited but also present was a woman whose business was to supply amyl nitrate, cocaine and heroin. After these had been snorted, bottles of Jack Daniel's drunk and an assortment of other drugs swallowed, the bride and best man disappeared into the bathroom. Novoselic and two friends engaged in a wrestling match. It was in this heady atmosphere that Cobain barricaded himself in a bedroom with a woman with whom, for a month at least, he announced he was 'really in love'. He was not to know that for her (aged seventeen) he was the latest in a string of rock-star conquests that had already included a member of Mudhoney and a visiting British guitarist – both, like Cobain, self-professed feminists with a disdain of 'groupie bullshit'. The woman was also conducting affairs with a manager at Sub Pop and a Seattle journalist, equally fully liberated. She exonerates Cobain's attitude toward sex: 'To sleep with someone who he worked with or liked was as natural as playing the guitar, but to screw someone just for sex was out of the question.' She sees in Cobain's taste for independent women a warped reflection of his lost relationship with the mother who abandoned him. On the physical side she notes only that 'Kurt was passive, and enjoyed playing the traditional girl's role in bed'. Sex was part of a 'big production number', in which 'the chick did the work', after which Cobain was 'quite emotional' and spent 'hours' in a post-coital daze – as when he came downstairs and told the group, still waiting in the living room, that he was in love.

In the first week of the new decade a designer named Cheryl Han was standing in the Visual Concepts office in downtown Seattle. From a corner window she looked over Aurora Avenue onto a concrete underpass leading to a futuristic prank called the Space Needle, a 1960s construction sometimes mistaken for the city centre. Han watched as a 'thin, shaggy blond' in his twenties approached an individual whose leather jacket, stubble and furtiveness of eye added to the impression that this was a man cognizant of illicit trade. While this person looked edgily down the street, the blond reached up 'like a cat' and snatched out of his hand a packet of tinfoil. For a moment the man's face was turned to the sheer grey wall. His back and shoulders appeared to be heaving, his meagre body shaking as though in a transport of ecstasy or horror. Then there was the unmistakable sight of retching. When the blond turned again there was a moment when Han made contact with the piercing eyes and look of abject doom that still haunt her.

Nirvana toured America from 1 April to 17 May 1990. However tortuous the path Cobain took after stardom, reaching that state was relatively easy. By the time he was twenty-three he realized he could assimilate some of the trappings of fame by yielding to it in certain ways. He began to insist on better accommodation and travel arrangements. Promoters were encouraged to single him out in advertisements. More than one marquee read 'Welcome Kurdt Kobain . . . and Nirvana'. The group obtained the services of a full-time road manager and two assistants. The non-musical part of touring was a constant torment to Cobain. 'He hated to share,' is the memory of one ex-colleague. 'The romance-of-the-road never attracted Kurt. Didn't appeal at all.' Already, by 1990, he was cutting himself off from the 'hassle and shit' which, only months earlier, he 'tolerated in the hopes of making it'. 'There was a big change in Kurt on that second tour,' says Peterson. 'It really seemed like a star had been born.'

Peterson was present for an appearance at Ranji's Club in Los Angeles. The event yielded the shot of Cobain prostrate on Channing's drum-kit included on the CD of *Bleach*, as well as an equally enigmatic pose used to promote Nirvana's next single. The raw power of the performance was what struck Peterson:

For anyone used to the old detachment of the artist from the audience, it was a sensation. About halfway through the first number Kurt sailed headlong into the crowd, still playing the guitar. Things went on from there. My aim was to capture the crazy, free-form, anarchic sense of theatre – to blur the distance between the band and the fans.

Most of the delirious crowd (which chronicled Cobain's growing fame by way of a parade of T-shirts) would have cheered the sentiment. In an era lacking enduring musical direction of its own – a decade after original punk self-destructed into Two-Tone and the New Romantics – Nirvana thrust to stardom via a repertoire of aggressively played yet intricate pop, unrelenting rock and rabble-rousing effusions of rage and self-violence. The best example of the group's fusing of old and new stagecraft came when Cobain segued from a cover of 'Bad Moon Rising' into an explosive rendering of 'Negative Creep'. With fans screaming along and the critics dancing attendance, it was apparent that Nirvana were now one of the most potent acts in America, and that in Cobain they possessed the epitome of Peterson's 'crazy, free-form, anarchic' sense of theatre. On the strength of *Bleach* and new songs like 'Sliver' and 'Dive', he was voted 'most popular punk' – an early foretaste of the contradictory claims made on Cobain's name – by a chain of west coast fanzines. That popularity was based on universal rock and roll virtues – the tuneful melodies and flag-waving lyrics enlivened by a sense of honesty, musicality and passion at odds with the outworn vogue for detachment and arrogant superficiality. 'Kurt replaced irony with feeling,' says Peterson. 'That one achievement has been woefully unrecognized. He changed the whole nature of rock for virtually every band that followed.' Cobain himself returned the compliment, though typically moderating his praise: '[Pavitt and

Poneman] were totally manipulating in trying to put this package together. They've gotten so much credit for being these geniuses, these masterminds behind this whole thing, when it really had nothing to do with them. It really didn't. It had more to do with Charles Peterson's fuzzy pictures than it did with their attempts at making sure we appeared stupid in interviews. I always resented them for that.'

Further proof that Nirvana had impressed themselves on their public came in New York. At the Pyramid Club they played to not only a scout from Geffen Records but an admiring audience of their own peers: Kim Gordon and Thurston Moore of Sonic Youth and, bellowing encouragement from the wings, the *éminence grise* of punk, Iggy Pop. Cobain's arrival as the coming man of the nineties did little to improve his mood. A girl waiting outside the club for an autograph was treated to a 'filthy side glance' and a lecture that caused more delay than would have resulted from mere compliance. Cobain harangued a second fan for admiring 'cripple mutants like Nirvana'. About his colleagues he was particularly scathing. Towards the end of the tour Cobain began a campaign to oust Channing from the group. In private he hinted that even Novoselic's services might be less frequently required. Within weeks Cobain's simmering resentment of Sub Pop had boiled into a crisis, while in April he called Marander to tell her 'he didn't want to live together, but [he] still wanted them to be boyfriend and girlfriend'. ('He wanted me to be artistic and I didn't have the time to be artistic,' she says. 'I was supporting him.') He was filled with 'unspoken thoughts', says a friend, swallowing 'great gulps of frustration' with others.

By the time he returned to Seattle that spring, Cobain had achieved the pinnacle of his ambition: a living wage and his starting principles still intact. He told his mother he had come as far as he could, journey's end, with nowhere else to go.

5

Into the Black

Although Cobain was praised for his populist 'free-form, anarchic' stage-act, at no time in the 1990s was he an anti-materialist. He was a commercial musician, writing songs as melodic as R.E.M.'s or David Bowie's. Cobain occasionally practised his unique brand of latent ambition in full view. At other times he kept a low profile, content to operate in the shadows, rarely seen, a master of wheedling and persuasion, the bedrock on which Nirvana's whole career grew. The more his reputation spread, the more Cobain's determination not to relinquish the limelight deepened. It was thought, for instance, that he might collaborate on songs with Channing, whose embellishments had done much for the one-dimensional material on *Bleach*. Instead, Cobain redoubled his campaign to fire the drummer, as well as furtively opening negotiations to leave Sub Pop. That spring, according to Skene, 'there was muttering behind the scenes by Kurt', who nonetheless remained scrupulously polite to his managers' faces. To another friend he admitted he wanted to be the impossible: an average, 'normal', uncomplicated human being who could experience simple contentment. But since his personality was also the major source of his talent, there were no signs that his wishes were to be fulfilled. Cobain, says Charles Peterson, was someone whose professional success 'ran ahead of his happiness'.

It was typical of Cobain that he refused to approach Pavitt, Poneman or Channing direct. Apart from his adult fear of confrontation, he already saw himself as the master strategist (genius was the word he used) behind Nirvana, someone removed from the day-to-day function of 'business' (a burden taken up by Novoselic), an initiator of ideas rather than enforcer of plans. It was in this light that Cobain undoubtedly allowed fame to fan his ego, and far from becoming a mellower character in the wake of national stardom, his private persona became even more brittle, his egotism more pronounced and his attitude towards those who thwarted him increasingly spiteful.

Pavitt and Poneman found out about Cobain's plans only through rumour and hearsay. As with Everman, he refused to express his feelings to them openly. When Pavitt appeared in Olympia he left after five hours, 'beads of sweat on my forehead and everything', still under the impression that Nirvana were committed to Sub Pop. Poneman met the group in Seattle at about the same time. Here Cobain gave way to a disturbing streak that would mar his remaining professional career, namely, a marked vindictiveness towards those who helped him, as well as a growing tendency to dissemble his real feelings under what Skene calls 'a surface niceness'. Poneman, too, left with the notion that 'all was well between Kurt and Sub Pop', a delusion that made the blow delivered by Novoselic all the harder. 'I can think of very few things that have happened in my life that have hurt my feelings more,' Pavitt told Azerrad. 'It really fucked with my head for a while.'

This was perhaps the most offensive part of Cobain's character (at least until drug addiction caught at his heels), and his duplicity was widely remarked on by colleagues and friends. According to a Seattle artist who prefers anonymity, 'The two things about Kurt were that he always thought of himself as the injured party, and he *never* spoke his mind.' Cobain himself told a journalist, 'I just don't understand how you're expected to come right out and tell someone something (to their face). I suppose it's the adult thing to do, to tell someone that you don't want to have anything to do with them anymore. It's a really hard thing to do. I've always quit my jobs without any notice. I just quit one day and not show up.' Although Cobain held court in Broadway's Café Roma most afternoons, his table was never crowded. He had alienated too many people, spoken too freely of the failings both of those who trusted him and of the whole Seattle music scene. His friends, like Poneman and Pavitt, had admired him for his songwriting, his sense of theatre and his punk ambition, and still did; but by his double-dealing, conceit and raging ego they became increasingly embarrassed.

When Cobain fired Aaron Burckhard and Dave Foster, the first the drummers had heard of it was, respectively, by rumour and an announcement in the *Rocket*. Jason Everman suffered a similar fate. Cobain's next sleight of mouth came when, while praising Channing as dedicated and original, he complained in private that 'Chad won't make it onto a major label'. The job of translating Cobain's displeasure into action was left, as always, to Novoselic. After the shouting had died down, Channing, who agreed to the familiar musical differences in public, gave a single interview: 'I was really hoping to participate more and become part of what was going on . . . I wanted to get more involved in the band and feel like I was actually doing something. It was then that I realized that it really is Kurt's show and that what he says goes and that's it, no questions asked.' There were two specific factors behind Cobain's decision to drop the only colleague, bar Novoselic, he ever respected. The first was essentially the same reason he fired Everman. Cobain was suspicious, prone to manipulating people's hostilities more readily than appealing to their goodness; he could never tolerate a potential rival inside the group. As Cobain scorned the technical deficiencies of his drummer, others saw only egoism in 'the way Kurt paranoically sensed a threat'. The second reason was that Cobain felt Channing lacked both the motivation and character to be a star – the very ambition he now admitted to in the bars and rock clubs of Seattle. When a woman named Karen Pelley met Cobain in the Central that summer she was told that Channing had been 'kind of weird', 'just wasn't ready for the big time' and 'annoyed the hell' out of Cobain and Novoselic by 'ignoring one and patronizing the other'.

Channing's departure forced Nirvana to cancel a second European tour. In Britain, where the missionary work of Everett True, John Peel and Keith Cameron had led to a cult following and steady sales of *Bleach*, the occupancy of Nirvana's drum-stool was debated in the way a previous generation had argued the merits of Pete Best and Ringo Starr. The letter columns of *Melody Maker* blossomed with comments. Peel referred to the matter on the air. On 7 July *Sounds* led with the startling suggestion that

J Macsis, Dinosaur Jr's mainman, may be joining Nirvana, replacing Chad Channing on drums!
    Sources close to both Nirvana and J Macsis told *Sounds* that Mascis had definitely auditioned for the Seattle band and 'really wants to play with Nirvana'.

In fact, by the time the paper went to press Cobain had already hired Dan Peters of Mudhoney, announcing archly 'it felt good to play with someone who [was] rhythmically competent'. When Peters was unable to tour he was briefly replaced by Dale Crover. The first mumblings of dissent came when Cobain forgot himself and hurled his guitar into Crover's drum-kit, as he once had into Channing's. Crover protested at the guitarist's 'retardness'. Cobain retaliated and insisted, none too convincingly, that the instrument had slipped. An argument broke out and for a moment the two men were in sharp contention as to whose commitment to stage protocol and decorum was greater. This ended in a fist-fight, which was broken up by Novoselic. A month later Peters returned to play his one and only concert with the group, before he, too, joined the long list of ex-drummers.

Meanwhile Nirvana had recorded material at Smart Studios, Wisconsin, under the baton of TAD's producer Butch Vig, the man to whom Poneman had insisted 'these guys are going to be bigger than the Beatles'. Five of the seven songs would later appear, in similar form, on *Nevermind*, or 'Sheep' as it was then known. A self-confessed 'pop geek', Vig was the perfect translator of Cobain's growing talk of 'hooks' and 'bridges' onto vinyl. The Smart material accelerated the upward continuum from 'Love Buzz' and the more melodic tracks on *Bleach* into a shamelessly virile, hard-rock confection. It also defined the Cobain songwriting formula: a soporific first verse erupting into a whiplash chorus, the skewed emotion of the lyrics spliced to appropriately rough-and-ready rhythms and played with a verve that belied the group's inexperience in the studio. If ever there was a statement of future intent, 'Sheep' was it. Slim Moon, Cobain's neighbour in Olympia, remembers the 'glee and perpetual air of enthusiasm' with which his friend spoke of the songs. 'Kurt's great gift was his ear – that was the thing; an inborn ability to drag the fringe into the mainstream. The gift of simplification of all issues – which was the magic formula – eventually cost Cobain his personality. But it also made him a star.'

It was not merely the fact of Cobain's thrust for the top that took the breath away, although to some in Seattle that was astonishing enough. It was the fickle way he changed direction that was so continually surprising. Having started out a lover of commercial pop he reached adolescence at the very moment of the hardcore explosion of the early

1980s, of which Cobain sold himself as a disciple. Now, that claim appeared patently false, and it was clear, as he worried over the upbeat and flagrantly crowd-pleasing tunes on 'Sheep', that he no longer believed in it himself. No matter how hard he tried for 'purity' of expression, Cobain's canny sense of melody still nagged him. He wrote pop songs because, for all his occasional insight and self-revelation, the mundane part of his talent always surfaced – the meticulous way he polished his songs, the careful planning of the seemingly spontaneous arrangements. In the aura surrounding Cobain the conventional side of his character has been constantly overlooked. He had the lifelong habit of striving for effect through detail, and a repetitive 'dream of [being] a big rock star' that saw him toe the commercial line more readily than the new-wave tightrope.

Evidence of Cobain's pop ambition came in the choice of Nirvana's second single, recorded on 11 July 1990 and released that September. 'Sliver', in some views a simple rock song, in others a furious salvo at Cobain's family, was melodic yet devastatingly angry, direct action down a well-defined line of spite and revenge and, as Peel says, hummable to boot. The pressure to come up with a single had proved a problem for other Sub Pop groups, who spent most of their waking hours between concerts, and used their limited time in the studio merely to put across what Doyle calls 'the word'. No such obligation was embraced by Cobain. 'Sliver' was a characteristically spry, feel-good melody freighted with lyrics in the classic rock and roll tradition. Though, in hurling abuse at his grandparents, Cobain diligently touched the familiar teenaged bases and the gravelly, angst-ridden vocals also recalled the best of the original pop groups, there were some significant new departures: the pairing of 'Sliver' with 'Dive', from the Smart session, was a deliberate forerunner of the fat, swaying guitar sound and oblique lyrics of *Nevermind*. 'It was like a statement,' Cobain said. 'I had to write a real pop song and release it on a single to prepare people for the next sound. I wanted to write more songs like that.'

Among 'Sliver's' fans was Patrick MacDonald, who, in a tribute to Nirvana's assimilation into the mainstream, remembers it as 'the first track that had real genius – not just technical flair'. The unforgettable chorus and 'weird accessibility' of the single were 'right off the Richter scale of punk experimentalism', and it was hard to imagine 'Dive', in particular, enjoying a long shelf-life in the fringe clubs of Seattle. *Bleach*, by comparison, sounded positively rootsy. But what was even weirder was that the music, with vocals that were all camped-up yet bellowed rage, somehow made the songs life-enhancing and joyous. It was this ability to popularize an unsafe, threatening message by welding it to a safe, all too comfortable melody that exasperated the purists and thrilled Cobain's fans. The dread word 'sell-out' was first heard in *Raw*, while to MacDonald there was something 'natural and honest' about Nirvana, 'who, like the Velvet Underground, appealed to the hardcore while never forgetting they were writing pop songs'. Cobain himself made the comparison by recording the Underground's 'Here She Comes Now' for the compilation album *Heaven and Hell Vol. 1* later in the year.

Cobain had never disguised his liking for guitar-heavy rock songs. What was surprising about 'Sliver' and 'Dive' were the tightly composed arrangements that shunned histrionic riffing in favour of a Beatles-like sense of harmony. His out-and-out punk credentials, in short, did not always run very deep. Cobain admitted as much when he spoke about the Smart material: 'I'd finally [reached] the point where I was mixing pop music and the heavy side of us in the right formula. It was working really well, mostly because of the reports from our friends and other bands. Everyone was saying that it was really good. I could tell that it was definitely more advanced than *Bleach*.' The hunger for attention that had given such personality to Cobain's life in Aberdeen and Montesano now spilled over into the studios and punk clubs of America. For critics like MacDonald it was, of course, a bonus that 'one could sit somewhere like the Vogue and hear great music'. And yet there was something profoundly unsettling about a punk icon – for such, after *Bleach*, Cobain had become – swaggering about Seattle and insisting his record label of only a year 'wasn't good enough'. After the meeting with Pavitt in Olympia he began to press more aggressively for a 'grabola deal' and to soften his previous antagonism to corporate rock: 'It's not hard to keep your dignity and sign to a major label. Sonic Youth have been really smart about what they're doing. I feel we're experienced enough to deal with it now. We're changing a little bit, we've been into more accessible pop styles for the last two years . . . So we figured we may as well get on the radio and try and make money at it.'

'Kurt's ambition,' says Slim Moon, 'was still the punk ethic of making enough money to live.' Cobain himself would insist, 'I would have been comfortable playing to a thousand people. Basically our goal [was] to get up to that size of a club, to be one of the most popular alternative rock bands, like Sonic Youth.' Yet in private he railed against the limitations of both Sub Pop and Seattle. He was infuriated when his label failed to promote *Bleach* adequately. 'We felt we deserved a little bit more than we were getting,' he recalled in 1992, though even that underestimates what his cousin calls 'burning rage' at Poneman and Pavitt. To a second relative 'Kurt went nearly off his head' when complaining about his record label. Once again awareness of his own ability inflated Cobain's ego, already unbearable bexcept to those who admired or loved him. He had signed to Sub Pop with humility, glad to be being paid, but the very voltage he generated gave him a growing sense of importance. Because the Smart material was the 'right formula' he became convinced he was on the road to stardom. Though he still sought the opinion of Novoselic and even Pavitt and Poneman, he grew less willing to accept their advice. The irony and self-deprecation of his early work began to desert him, replaced by self-obsession of a titanic scale and cruel in its victimization of those in Aberdeen, Olympia and Seattle who had crossed him. As his embrace of mainstream pop grew more obvious, so Cobain's ambition and lust for revenge intensified to the point where even friends sensed a different Kurt to the self-effacing recluse of old.

Like many who have set great store in clinging to their principles, Cobain was all too versed at the art of compromise. Alice Wheeler is only the most telling witness when she speaks of the shared ethic of punk, its sense of 'nerds binding together in protest against organized rock'. According to Moon, 'in Olympia particularly, there was a feeling of holding out against the crowd', 'a siege mentality' and 'a communal idea that we were on the inside looking out'. (The house in which Marander lived before moving to North Pear Street had been called The Alamo.) Cobain, it now seemed, had gone at least halfway to meeting the outside world. Not only did the Smart material 'mix pop music and the heavy side', it appeared that Nirvana's whole career was a case-study in pandering to the mainstream. One of the group's first names had been the Sellouts. Their debut single was an accessible, if left-of-the-dial, pop song. Cobain admitted to having suppressed his melodic tendencies on *Bleach* (even then, a tidy success) because his label 'couldn't handle them'. Most of Nirvana's songs might have been in a minor key, or have had an 'edge' to the lyrics, but they were still firmly from the pop playbook. For all Cobain's fury at his family, teachers, friends and record label, it would be a mistake to take his material or the group's image at face value. Like a rock and roll inkblot test, Nirvana could mean a number of things in the eyes and ears of audiences. To the appearance-obsessed, it was the anarchic stage-act and sense of abandon of the three players. Critics keyed in on the exceptional voice and abrasive guitar of the leader. Song-lovers responded to power pop that carried the style of predecessors like the Knack and Cheap Trick to a harder rock level without forgetting its roots. There were even credulous fans who believed Nirvana were 'nerds binding together'. What all of the group's followers consistently and resolutely over-looked was that they were commercial musicians, whose songs began, ended or expired on Cobain's whim, and whose career proceeded under the same one man's exceptional control. As far as Patrick MacDonald was concerned, it was a case of 'a single genius, and two talented but passive also-rans'.

Marander moved out of the house that June, leaving Cobain free to entertain Tobi Vail and, in his cousin's words, 'the charmingly flustered young men' who filled out his time between recording and concerts. At a costume party in Olympia that summer, Cobain and an admirer arrived dressed as identical circus freaks, and neither Vail nor Julia Levy accompanied them. A local woman was 'beyond fury, beyond embarrassment' when Cobain appeared at her house holding a magazine 'with pictures of oiled-up musclemen', which he tore out and handed to her children. During one party 'he dropped his pants and did this trick with his joint . . . sliding it back and forth like a trombone'. At the end of the evening Cobain and his male friends thought nothing of mutually relieving themselves on one of the sycamores on North Pear Street. On the other hand, he spent much of the seven-date tour that August with a self-admitted 'grunge freak', Randi Edlin, whom he struck as 'a sensitive, touchy guy' with 'not much passion for sex' but, again, 'a childlike curiosity in the woman's body'.

When Cobain left the Melody Ballroom in Portland after a concert on 23 August he met a local fan named Geraldine Hope. Hope accompanied him to a diner, where 'Kurt ordered the zillion-calorie plate and drank six beers', surprising but not shocking her with his manners and belching loudly at the elderly waitress. (What was surprising was that he simulated fellatio with his beer bottle as he drank from it.) When Cobain insisted she join him in Seattle, Hope next found herself amid Nirvana – they had a flair for 'farting and double-entendres' – 'aggressively trashing their label' and 'sucking butt to Thurston [Moore, of Sonic Youth]', present for the ride. 'Kurt was *so* impressed by him, it was ridiculous. He would kind of giggle at whatever Moore said.' After the next night's performance Cobain and Hope had sex in a parked van behind the theatre, an event she recalls for only two things: the morbid interest Cobain took in the abrasive part of the act ('He said he wanted to bring on my period and then drink the blood') and, more typically, that 'the second he zipped his pants he was back to ranting about Sub Pop and how Nirvana were too good for them. Kurt was so hyper in those days. He had a definite crazy dream.'

In fact Nirvana's arrival as rock stars – 'too good' for their label – came just a month later.

The concert at the Motor Sports International and Garage on 22 September 1990 is remembered today as the high-water mark of the Seattle scene begun so unobtrusively by *Deep Six* five years before. Yet as the Derelicts, the Dwarves and the Melvins were followed onstage by Nirvana, the packed house swaying and screeching, the clenched fists raised aloft reaching to the far corners of the room, it was evident that the once tentative and ad-hoc movement had become mature and ambitious in its machinations, the embodiment rather than the opposite of mainstream rock, and the inevitable target of talent-spotters queuing in the Garage's wings to assure any musician present they 'had it made'. By the time they played 'Dive' Nirvana had turned the event into a rally and the audience into a plaid-shirted army that sang every word of the song's low-key verses and erupted into mayhem in the chorus. 'It was pandemonium,' says Charles Peterson. 'That was the ultimate gig for climbing on stage and dancing with the band. The security came later.' What Peterson calls 'the last-gasp celebration' of grunge yielded some of the best-known photographs of Nirvana ever published, including one of Cobain apparently levitating on stage. Tim Arnold recalls it as 'the night it all came together, when guys like Kurt realized they could actually fill a hall' and used that knowledge 'to start deserting the kids who put them there in the first place'. In the actual concert Cobain had displayed the schoolboyish glee he still had for performing, at one moment asking for requests from the crowd, at the next pumping his fist and effortlessly raising 'Dive' to anthem status. An hour later, across the street in a bar, a quite different Cobain was in evidence – the brooding introvert who nursed his drink and refused to sign autographs, who winced when strangers approached and even offended one of his old mentors, the Melvins, 'by laying it on the line he was a big shot now'.

The day after the Motor Sports show, Cobain, Novoselic and Peters were interviewed by Keith Cameron of *Sounds*. The tone was duly respectful, dwelling not only on Nirvana's musicianship but on their doubts about Sub Pop, and toeing the line energetically pushed by Cobain:

> With furiously catchy pop songs set to monster heavy rock riffs, Nirvana stand out. Tempers and instruments fly. They're for real. They're the beef.
>
> It's been pretty obvious for some time that if any

of the emergent US underground bands are to break through into the mainstream, Nirvana will be the ones to do so. Their label knows it ... Money, Nirvana freely admit, is the essential reason for them seeking to quit the Sub Pop nest.

Cobain's financial ambitions were one thing. Less well known was his drug habit, enigmatic sex life, his cocksure ego, tactlessness and haphazard manner of dealing with friends. As part of the *Sounds* cover story Nirvana were photographed smiling and joking with each other at Novoselic's house, while only inches away sat the man who, unknown to Peters, was being auditioned as the group's next drummer. Without further reference to Sub Pop, still officially his employer, Cobain had decided not only to replace the man he described as a 'beautiful guy and beautiful drummer' but to hawk the Smart material to an outside label. A man who knew Pavitt remembers his friend saying that in his estimation this was Cobain's lowest hour, while Cameron's assistant believes 'Kurt was desperately trying to flog himself as a punk even as he knew he was becoming a cartoon', an impression lent ironic weight by *Sounds*' placing its interview with Cobain next to a full-page profile of Johnny Rotten.

Peters's replacement was a twenty-one-year-old Virginian named David Eric Grohl. Like Cobain he was a high school dropout and, like Cobain and Novoselic, his parents were divorced. Grohl was active in community theatre as a child, discovered punk through the B-52s and later learned to play drums and guitar. By 1990 he was a veteran of half a dozen groups, had a small following as an old-fashioned, hard-hitting drummer (Grohl had John Bonham's three-circle logo tattooed on his arm) and enjoyed a mutual admiration with the Melvins. Through them he was introduced to Nirvana. What happened next is open to conjecture. In one version Grohl inadvertently insulted Tobi Vail, in another he had his offer of an apple turned down by Cobain on the grounds that 'it'll make my teeth bleed'. What is certain is that the impression left on both sides could not have been worse. It was against this background that a discreet audition took place in suburban Seattle. Possibly it was Cobain's ever-sensitive nose for a rival, or possibly his awareness of the enormity of the commercial challenge and of his need for like-minded colleagues, but on 25 September Peters was duly replaced. In his own words, 'Kurt called me up and [said], "Ahhh. Ummm. Well, ah, well . . . We got another drummer." I wasn't sure how [Nirvana] were feeling because their communication skills at that time were kind of not happening.' According to Grohl, 'I had everything in common with Kurt, right down to the childhood and the in-your-face style of music. I fit.' Grohl was right in saying that, in their all-encompassing pursuit of true grunge, men like Channing and Peters had sometimes overlooked the innovations pioneered by bands like Cream and Led Zeppelin. Time and again their drumming had fallen short of the giddy expectations generated by the melodies. Grohl, who might have doubled for Bonham or Ginger Baker, had no such failing. His beat galloped like a pantomine horse under Cobain's crop. According to Peterson, 'with Dave the last piece of the puzzle came into place. He *rocked*'.

The amended line-up – Cobain, Novoselic and Grohl – returned to Europe to promote 'Sliver', winning glowing reviews from *Melody Maker* and recording a second session, consisting entirely of covers, for John Peel. This was the generous, self-effacing side to Cobain which few of his colleagues had ever seen. His loyalty to groups like the Vaselines and the Wipers, whose off-centre tunes he recorded for Peel, was, writ large, his loyalty to punk. Other musicians might be admired for their image or, by the press, for their embodiment of a cause. But Cobain's appeal across the chasm between Nirvana and a host of lesser groups rested in large measure on the trust he inspired – a trust that he had plans for others as well as himself, that he would not promote Nirvana exclusively but the 'whole scene'. Among the many beneficiaries of Cobain's patronage were the Raincoats, whose revival in fortunes owed much to his sustained support and friendship. The Meat Puppets, a long-running but relatively obscure Phoenix band, had also been enthusiastically taken up by Cobain, and would later join Nirvana for their 1993 *Unplugged* set. To say that Cobain's approach to his career was governed by his faith in the punk ethic is not to say that he had no ambition of his own. By this stage he was already negotiating with Gold Mountain Entertainment (home of Bonnie Raitt and Belinda Carlisle) to arrange a recording deal. Cobain's endorsement of lesser groups flowed from his belief that his role was to be the leader of a broad movement. It also stemmed from the knowledge that neither the Wipers nor the Vaselines would ever pose a threat. Cobain was shrewd, confident of his own success, and could afford to be generous.

In 1989 Nirvana's tour had been a cheap progression through the cold backstage rooms of provincial British clubs. A year later they travelled as a small army, with a tour manager, two sound engineers and their own bus, complete with continually playing videos of Monty Python and *Spinal Tap*. Where previously their audiences had been a select elite, loyal but small, now they played to packed thousand-seat houses. The crowds received their money's worth. A Nirvana concert started out over-the-top, with Cobain slinging on a guitar, shrieking, then throwing himself into the arms of the crowd, and went on from there. Time was turned back with surprising enthusiasm, especially by the sound technicians who achieved an authentically dreadful Sex Pistols-era mix. With Cobain's voice as clear as a station tannoy and the rhythm amplified to the pain threshold,

Nirvana tore into 'Love Buzz' and 'School', as well as the more melodic material from 'Sheep', all strung together in one breathless opening salvo. The shouted vocals and ear-bruising guitar were everything the most recherché punk could have hoped for. Next Cobain shifted gear into the almost-whispered 'About A Girl'. Much as it was an achievement in itself to create such a switch, there was never any danger that Nirvana would succumb to a soporific, *Unplugged*-like atmosphere. Both 'Sliver' and 'Dive' were a study in focused musical aggression. Next, from the Smart session, came 'Lithium', conjuring an exquisite mix of self-loathing and vituperation and a screamed version of 'Pay To Play', later renamed 'Stay Away'. Stretched over an hour-and-a-half, the cumulative effect of so many furiously dispatched songs, fuelled either by boiling anger or dark cynicism, inevitably began to feel like a barrage. Yet, with their ear for a tune and obvious dedication to the job at hand, Nirvana never sank into headbanging. They were exhilarating rather than showy. At a time when heavy rock had all been laid to rest in favour of nonentities like Bros and Milli Vanilli, the group brought a sense of danger, rage, and thrilling insanity to the stage. They were the antithesis of music as product or entertainment; it was impossible to imagine 'Love Buzz', let alone 'Pay To Play' being used to advertise beer on television. By the end of the concert the floor of the hall was a spent, writhing jumble of bodies and Cobain, for the first time all night, would break into a smile.

As the tour faded from memory, Cobain focused his energies on breaking up with Vail. It was a protracted, ugly, emotionally draining spectacle. At the root of all Cobain's relationships was his craving for domesticity and family. 'I was definitely looking for somebody I could spend quite a few years with,' he told Azerrad. 'I wanted that security.' It was to the sense of loss of this security that his misery was a response. Vail portrayed Cobain as a man consumed by self-hate: when she tried to hand him some flattering reviews as he was leaving the house, he first screamed at her, then threw the papers out of the car as he drove away. Vail said that a recent hospital visit that Cobain attributed to fatigue was caused, instead, by a drug overdose. Like Marander before her, she was bewildered by his moods and unable to find the truth behind the 'ten or twenty masks' Cobain carried in his spacious internal wardrobe. Another version is that, at twenty, Vail was in no hurry to settle down with a man interested in casual sex or a long-term relationship, but very little in between. Her resulting defection, combined with the nostalgia he still felt for Marander, left Cobain despondent. He began to suffer renewed bouts of depression. That Christmas Grohl moved into the North Pear Street apartment he describes as 'small, cluttered, dirty, smelly', and that Wheeler, who visited it, recalls as 'full of animals and crazy'. A third person remembers 'Kurt out of his head' at first Marander's and now Vail's desertion, and 'playing Leonard Cohen songs all night on the guitar'. For relaxation he and Grohl fired BB guns at the State Lottery building across the street, or, on one occasion, removed the 'Welcome to Olympia – All-American City' sign to the sewer-hole at the foot of the hill to the south.

Cobain compensated for his lack of love-life by gradually becoming more visible around Olympia. According to Slim Moon, 'That was the last chance Kurt ever had to go out, listen to music and be part of a scene . . . I knew it wouldn't last. He was definitely on his way north.' Cobain himself admitted he was 'tired of living in Olympia with nothing to do' and that he was 'long overdue for a change'. It surprised some in Seattle that the man dubbed semi-facetiously King of the Scene still chose to haunt an obscure if Bohemian backwater, with more than a touch of Aberdeen, sixty miles to the south. Cobain continuing to live in North Pear Street was the more bizarre in light of the fact that Seattle, as *Billboard* now put it, was 'Suddenly Hot'. That November the *New York Times* profiled four groups from 'America's latest music mecca' and *Melody Maker* continued its relentless promotion of the 'slowed-down, staggering, Seattle sound', arguably more audible overseas than in the city itself. What is certain is that in Mother Love Bone, Alice In Chains, Soundgarden and Nirvana a recognizable noise – the more striking in contrast to the downtown Seattle sound, where no one honked his horn – had been latched onto by the press and rewarded by nine Grammy nominations for Northwest groups that winter. By then a local whim had become an international phenomenon, and with the arrival of London journalists and New York A&R men with cheque-books at the ready, the grunge wave had truly broken; even Pavitt was heard to mutter, 'There are no brakes on the hype at this point. It's just going through the roof.' A sign that the style had already become clichéd and formulaic was the turning of the 'grunge look' into a fashion rage, while in their playing to the 'stump-dumb rocker' myth several of Seattle's musical lights effortlessly extended their sense of irony into self-parody. Alcohol and drug abuse became routine. The community suffered its first major heroin-related loss when Andrew Wood of Mother Love Bone overdosed in March 1990. Even this was seized on by *Sounds* as evidence of grunge 'perfecting the art of self-indifference'. Yet there was nothing half-hearted about the way Cobain articulated his dreams and resolutely hammered anger to ambition. As well as his later explanation for living in Olympia ('I didn't have any extreme thing I could do to get out of it … It wasn't like all the other times when I could have a fight with somebody and get kicked out'), he was in no hurry to join an already congested clique from which he was, in important ways, artistically aloof. From the beginning of his career in Aberdeen he considered himself to be, and was accepted as, an outsider, and his tastes, manners, habits and styles were shaped accordingly. While lesser talents chased recording deals in Seattle, Cobain was content to let Gold Mountain come to him, strumming and practising in North Pear Street, smoking, and listlessly scrawling graffiti. It was one morning later that winter that Julia Levy entered the house, stepped over the crawling turtles, and saw the newly daubed message on the bedroom wall: KURT SMELLS LIKE TEEN SPIRIT.

David Geffen could hardly be called an 'arch punk scenester', as Cobain had described his ideal record executive. For one thing Geffen was friendly with decidedly non-punk figures like Cher and Barbra Streisand. His own preferred listening was to the seamless, AOR strains of the Eagles and Jackson Browne. Moreover, wealthy enough to boast he was America's top taxpayer, the head of a billion-dollar entertainment empire and the holder of an all-access White House pass, Geffen almost embodied the upper-echelon American celebrity Cobain despised. Yet the self-professed 'capitalist lackey' was always the favourite to sign Nirvana from Sub Pop, if only because the label he headed was so successful. In Cobain's mind there was no substitute for victory.

In November 1990 Nirvana formally signed with Gold Mountain, which, in turn, identified Geffen or Charisma as the labels best suited to the group's talents. Cobain could not have wished for a more agreeable month than the one that followed. On the basis of the Smart material and remorseless promotion by their management, Nirvana were bid on like a stock auction. Cobain downplayed the financial aspect of the negotiations. Gold Mountain had asked him to omit dollar figures when speaking to the press; he did their bidding, on the surface. But Julia Levy had already told journalists (off the record) that the transaction would be in the multimillion-dollar range. Asked at a press conference about a reported figure of $2 million, Cobain responded disingenuously, 'I wonder where they got that from.' When the *Alternative Press* stringer pressed the point, he replied: 'I don't know if that's right or not. I just said I don't know where it came from.' Cobain also relished the chance to be entertained by record executives in standard industry fashion. At one office he was greeted by a specially made video of his life and a bracelet engraved with his name; in another the gift was a pouch of high-quality cocaine. When Cobain entered his hotel room in Los Angeles he found two naked women sent by one hopeful label, who applied a vibrator they produced from their baggage before arranging themselves, a leash and a champagne bottle in a striking pose. It was the same story wherever the group went. Twelve months after he lay drugged and whimpering on a train in Switzerland, Cobain sat sipping wine in the Geffen board-room and flying first class to New York to interview Charisma. 'We felt like snotty hot-shit kids,' says Grohl. 'We felt like we were getting away with something.'

In the end a mutual endorsement by Sonic Youth per-suaded Nirvana and Geffen to agree terms. Mark Kates, the label's Director of Alternative Music – the very title impressed Cobain – talked up the group as having 'the potential of writing hit songs, while still coming from an edgy atmosphere', a remarkable tribute to Nirvana's feat of assimilation. From then on Kates and Gary Gersh of Geffen and Danny Goldberg and John Silva at Gold Mountain would be Cobain's link to the outside world. It is tempting to think that he recognized his volte-face as easily as he made it, but Cobain's sole comment on Geffen – 'They have an alternative, young staff. They have some credentials in the underground' – was almost satirically forced. A more reliable version is that of the Geffen executive who remembers 'all three [of Nirvana] just zooming in on the bucks'.

That night, after realizing he was paper rich and with every prospect of becoming a millionaire, Cobain sat in a room with Julia Levy and cried.

His emotion was trifling compared to Sub Pop's. Despite giving one journalist the impression the deal was settled without apparent animosity on either side, both Alice Wheeler and Lisa Orth have a different recollection. According to them, Poneman and Pavitt were 'frantic', 'woe-begone', 'distraught' and 'furious'. Their response was partially offset by the terms of Nirvana's contract with Geffen: a $290,000 advance (and uniquely generous royalty rate), along with $75,000 compensation to Sub Pop and a percentage of the group's future sales. 'Without that agreement,' says Poneman, 'Bruce and I would probably be washing dishes.' According to a friend, after the shouting had died down 'there was a rather philosophical feeling – "They had to go and they've gone".'

Others in Seattle pinned the blame for this sequence of events on Cobain, claiming that his egotism and cavalier desertion of Sub Pop nearly drove the label into bankruptcy. According to this reading, $75,000 was ridiculously low reward for having launched the group in the first place, and in the early weeks of 1991 discussions continued about an adjustment to the buy-out fee even Geffen considered minimal. That Cobain shunned these talks and repeated his conviction that Sub Pop were finished was construed by Pavitt and those who heard of it as ingratitude, even megalomania. Worse still, a few days after agreeing with Geffen, Cobain was pressing his old label for up-to-date royalty statements and, when these were delayed, physically removed armloads of records, advertising material and drugs from the stockroom as 'damages'.

Cobain undoubtedly played into the hands of the critics who believed Nirvana had sacrificed purity for profit. By the time he recorded 'Sliver' in July 1990 it was obvious that the 'left-wing stoners' he once fronted harboured distressingly centrist goals. Nirvana's UK publicist Anton Brookes recalls his first meeting with the group that autumn: 'I remember Kurt saying the album was going to go Top Ten and there were these tracks that were going to be massive as singles. You could see in his face that he totally believed that. He *knew* it.' In the years after he abandoned the Seattle demi-monde, other groups claimed the territory for their own – most notably, TAD and Mudhoney. Cobain had no regrets about having forsaken his former constituency. 'I wouldn't know how to make a punk album anymore, just as I don't know where to begin writing stuff that's going to change anything,' he admitted in 1991. Instead – and in line with Geffen's dictum that the most successful performers are best served commercially by 'crossover' releases – he followed his own interests. From then on Cobain's songs would be a grunge-rock medley with T. Rex undertones. Their appeal was their self-confidence and absolute clarity and simplicity, in which the ambiguities of *Bleach* were resolved in favour of meticulously crafted mood music and fist-pumping arena pop.

Although Cobain was the group's strongest personality, the depth and dynamics of Nirvana's music hung on intricate guitar-bass interplay and a pneumatic beat. Novoselic and Grohl were vital to the end-product. It depressed some to see how badly Cobain appeared to treat them. Away from the public eye, all three could be heard in ever more frequent and furious rows. Cobain was seen as an egomaniac, ruthlessly using his colleagues to further his own ambitions as a rock star. Tales were told of his obsession with himself, the hours he spent each day complaining about his childhood and plotting revenge. No one would have denied

Cobain his refuge in the world of rock and roll, or his chance at personal success and redemption. The unrelenting gloom of his upbringing once won him the nickname 'Hurt Kurt'. But it grated to hear Cobain speak of the 'punk ethic', when a study of his actions behind the scenes shows that his first and overpowering loyalty was to himself. 'Our differences aren't important,' Cobain later insisted. 'We never yelled at each other.' Nor, however, were they unimportant, and Levy sensed 'real resentment' at the way 'Chris had the ability to make people laugh, and Kurt didn't'. According to her, Cobain 'tore into' Novoselic for his relaxed attitude to practice and 'savaged' Grohl for the deficiencies of his drumming. A critic believes, 'In any decision about Nirvana, it was Kurt's will that prevailed.' In another man's view, 'he ran it like an army'. If anything this belittles a leadership style that eventually bordered on tyranny. At the very height of his fame Cobain would complain that 'I can't believe that people wouldn't think more highly of me', and not only colleagues like Novoselic but admirers like Lisa Orth had their work disparaged by the man who insisted in private, 'I did it all.'

He did not. Cobain was outrageous in his conceit, his egoism and his self-righteousness. He liked to dominate rather than to share. These vices he turned into qualities of greatness as a career musician. But his belittling of loyal collaborators and need to 'put himself across' did Cobain no credit. As his fame increased more and more people in Seattle came to view the winter of 1990 as the Rubicon dividing the 'old Kurt' from the egotist who used his success as a weapon against those who threatened him. Julia Levy saw an 'overnight change' in Cobain when he signed with Geffen. A member of Nirvana's road crew speaks of 'the daily fit' thrown by his employer on a tour of Europe. By 1991 Cobain ran the group as a virtual dictatorship under a veneer designed to convey the reverse, a formula he admitted to *Rolling Stone*:

Q So you call all the shots?

A Yeah. I ask their opinions about things. But ultimately, it's my decision ... It's not like they're afraid to bring up anything. I always ask their opinions, and we talk about it. And eventually, we all come to the same conclusions.

There may be no such thing as a saturation point in avenging an unhappy childhood; but if there is, Cobain, above all, should have been able to find it. Everything he did from 1990 onwards was a consistent if sometimes oblique plea for recognition. He began to brag to his neighbours in Olympia of having 'made it'. He talked up the Geffen contract in the bars and clubs of Seattle as 'the big-time'. He even returned to Aberdeen to inform the drinkers at the Pourhouse that 'they wouldn't have Kurt to kick around anymore'. Where once Cobain had been content to graffiti GOD IS GAY or HOMO LOVE RULES, now he spray-painted a wall with his own name on the grounds that 'people should get used to it'. He insisted on continual practice and rehearsal. Grohl, in particular, was surprised at the highly organized way Cobain would go about editing lyrics and reworking melodies, polishing his material to a gloss. He also remembers the silent hour-long drives from North Pear Street to Novoselic's home in Tacoma, where, according to Skene, 'Kurt would go from a rolled-up ball of indifference to a little Hitler' in an instant.

One of the projects occupying Nirvana was the Sub Pop single negotiated in the buy-out, a cover of the Vaselines' 'Molly's Lips'. Even this seemingly simple project followed in the ground-breaking mould of the Rolling Stones in causing friction between the defecting group and their label. Pavitt had hoped for an original work to do mutual justice to the split, while Cobain himself described the song as a throwaway and asked Poneman not to release it. In the end 'Molly's Lips' was issued in a limited edition of 7,500 with 4,000 on green vinyl – and the word 'Later' etched into the run-out groove.

Cobain was fully alive to the lunacy that inevitably attends American celebrity. He made a study of it. The two books he read continually that winter were biographies of Lenny Bruce and Frances Farmer (the Seattle-born actress committed to an asylum in the 1940s.) Despite his sensitivity to criticism and need of a 'Rock Star 101 course', Cobain was well aware of the advantages his place in time afforded: he caught the 'generational drama' of the nineties, he explained to an interviewer. 'Every record label was looking for a Kurt Cobain.' To say he made the most of it would be an understatement. By the second year of the decade he was being written of as 'a prophet', 'a seer', someone whose songs 'captured what people felt before they knew they felt it'. The critics at *Sounds* voted Nirvana number one on their 'most promising newcomer' list, followed by the likes of the Pixies and the Spin Doctors.

The irony was that while Cobain was the most talked-about new talent in rock, he continued to live on the breadline in Olympia. Geffen had spoken of a 'legal review' before Nirvana's new contract was drawn up. In the end, because of the usual delays, the formal signing was postponed from Christmas to Easter. Cobain spent the intervening months in North Pear Street with Grohl, living on a diet of corn dogs, wine and assorted drugs, rehearsing and continuing their target practice at the lottery building opposite. In an interview, Grohl recalled that winter as 'the worst time I'd had in years'. According to Cobain: 'I almost went insane . . . I just couldn't handle it. I was so bored and so poor. We were signed to Geffen for months and we didn't have any money.' It was entirely in character for Cobain to forget to mention that Nirvana were each being paid $1000 a month as a retainer – a living wage in Olympia – and that he would later look back on that winter as a 'golden time', a 'breathing-space' between the zealot he was and the performer he became.

Cobain began the pursuit of his future by reconciling with Marander. After his break-ups with Julia Levy and Tobi Vail he enjoyed a number of nights with his ex-lover in Tacoma and Seattle. They spent nostalgic weekends in North Pear Street, where Cobain was not always appreciated for inviting local teenagers to the loud, late-night parties he and Grohl threw.* Virtually everyone who knew her remarked that Marander seemed unhappy, quieter somehow, and certainly more exposed to drugs after rejoining Cobain. His 'total addiction' meant that, according to Levy, 'no woman was going to stay around very long'. In Moon's version, 'Kurt was so caught up in his work, it was difficult to sustain a relationship ... writing and rehearsing were what he was into.' In these last, relatively innocent weeks before fame struck, Cobain polished the Smart material into the genre-breaking *Nevermind*, recorded two songs, 'Dumb' and 'Pennyroyal Tea', which would appear on *In Utero*, and wrote at least one set of lyrics, 'Opinions', which made it clear that, wherever else he moved, it would be impossible to go back to Aberdeen.

By Christmas Cobain had graduated from a frequent and ingenious abuse of household items, like cough syrup and glue, to a reliance on pain-killers and, eventually, heroin. He told Marander that the drug made him feel social: 'he felt like he could go out and have a good time and talk to people and not feel uncomfortable.' According to a friend

* According to one long-suffering neighbour, 'there were two albums (Cobain) played over and over until you were sick of them': *Led Zeppelin 2* and Captain Beefheart's *Trout Mask Replica*.

in Olympia, 'Kurt did [heroin] seven days a week all winter. His thinking was that it made him less of a hermit.'

In fact, Cobain became something worse, first a user and then an addict, alienating both Marander and his colleagues in Nirvana. From a distance of five years, Arnold believes this was the moment 'the dice rolled for Kurt'. According to Novoselic: 'It bummed me out. It was shocking . . . I told him so.' His friends' protests did nothing, of course, to curb Cobain's habit. As they complained, so he retreated ever further into a show of defiance. The excesses of his addiction are well documented, and in the months following his death a reaction set in that portrayed Cobain as little more than, in one critic's words, 'a sick child'. That was an inadequate picture of the man. Cobain's reasons for taking drugs were mature and sophisticated in their ingenuity, shrewdly argued, and revealing all the psychotic delusions repressed in more orderly minds.

Cobain would later say that he 'discovered' heroin in 1990, and that thereafter he dabbled with it once or twice a year until the birth of his daughter in 1992. Yet it is certain that he began his drug use in Aberdeen and continued it up until the moment of his death. Cobain saw addiction as a fault of society, not of the individual. Time and again he denied responsibility for seeking merely to 'neutralize' his existence. He blamed 'unscrupulous dealers' for supplying him in the first place. When a doctor once prescribed anti-biotics Cobain threatened to sue him for 'failing to warn me not to take smack'. The woman he married would describe heroin in Seattle as 'like apples in the orchard'. Amazed by the ease with which the drug could be bought around the city, she complained, 'The police won't do any-thing about it. I asked them, "Don't you get embarrassed when you hear that Seattle is famous for grunge, cappuccino and heroin?"'

One of the reasons Seattle was known for music and drugs

was, of course, Kurt Cobain. That he spoke of heroin as an antidote to his stomach pain was only his latest attempt to rationalize his habit. In so far as the drug dulls the central nervous system and the intestine (killing appetite dead), there may have been truth to Cobain's claim that he 'took it for its analgesic property', even if there was a different, hedonistic motive. That left the question of dependency. By late 1991 Cobain was demanding twice-daily injections from his girlfriend, setting up a cycle of romantic interludes and violent scenes. In one, Cobain kicked open the door of an apartment and demanded 'Smack – *now*' from the startled woman who referred him to her younger next-door neighbour. He was physically ejected from a second home for illustrating his locally popular nickname of 'Hurler' by throwing up into his dinner. His own dealer was roused into giving him mouth-to-mouth resuscitation when, in the middle of a transaction, Cobain turned blue and collapsed. A profile in *BAM* magazine that winter noted: 'Kurt . . . was nodding off in mid-sentence,' and that 'the pinned pupils, sunken cheeks, and scabbed, sallow skin suggest something more serious than fatigue.' In a muttered aside he admitted that he was terrified of being 'pulled over, recognized and made to go cold turkey in jail'. The feeling in Seattle was that Cobain was already imprisoned by the drugs that shaped his life more than anything else. Percodan, cocaine and heroin had become his constant companions, his most dependable friends. Sometimes, in a club or bar, he would take his bottles and phials out of his bag, count them, and talk to them like humans.

Along with his self-professed 'bitchy side' and 'ugliness' on drugs came infusions of love for his colleagues, his music and even the women who filled in his time between rehearsals. According to one of them, 'When everything came together, Kurt was the greatest guy in the world. When it didn't, he was a shit. In my opinion there was something wrong with that boy.' In contrast, another lover insists that 'even the dope didn't alter the fact that he was a shy, genuinely kind man. He was real.'

Although Cobain later offered to warn people of the misery of his own ordeal, his services as a drug counsellor were not to be required. Instead it was he himself who would be driven into treatment, vainly seeking to reverse a dependency which began in 1974, when he was seven. Addiction did not sweeten his disposition. During the two years he was with Nirvana, Chad Channing had suffered near-nightly attacks by Cobain, both verbal and physical, as comments about technical defects had been demonstrated by a thrown guitar, or Cobain himself sailing into the drum-kit. By 1990, no Nirvana concert was complete without a ritual display of violence and a black eye for Channing. In-fighting became part of the performance. Among a certain stratum of the punk-rock audience, therefore, Cobain's bullying of his drummer produced neither shock nor outrage, only ecstatic mob scenes and a mass-baying for bloodshed. 'You have to remember the times,' says Julia Levy. 'Back then Kurt was considered a pioneer of situationist behaviour. So naturally everyone cheered.'

In contrast, various friends of the soft-spoken Channing were extremely distressed. They did not regard Cobain's antics and increasingly manic kamikaze attacks as an illuminating commentary on the paradoxes of preserving the punk ethic in the context of a traditional stage performance. They regarded the sight of a battered, bruised Channing, soaked in blood and Cobain's spittle as prima facie evidence that 'Kurt was sick'. Channing and others were only the latest victims of his lifelong need of aggressive revenge. Added to a dependency on mood-altering drugs (exacerbating rather than improving Cobain's problem), it was possible to see why his behaviour would repel as much as attract, although virtually no one knew the full extent of Cobain's madness.

Barely a week after he returned to Olympia, the police were called to North Pear Street by a neighbour. Officers who arrived on the scene found Cobain sitting on the grass under a sycamore tree, holding a baseball bat; a teenage girl was crying nearby. There were rumours that he was regularly beating his women friends. The same neighbour was woken one evening that winter by a girl pounding on his door, wearing only a rain-soaked T-shirt and tights, shrieking, 'He's going to kill me!' as she cowered inside. Another night Cobain was found in the Weathered Wall, a barn-like Seattle club, coiled in the foetal position under a table, whimpering and sobbing that his mother had 'fucked' him. These were the times when he should have been writing, when it might have been possible to scale down if not vanquish his furies and acquire much-needed perspective on the trials of his youth; but not for the son of Wendy O'Connor.

Part of Cobain's problem was his dissatisfaction with unpublicized opinions. Of course it was possible for him to have had intensely unhappy memories as a result of his boyhood. But complaining about his mother while standing on the brink of material success was Cobain taking experience to the realm of obsession. 'Kurt lacked the ability to make light of misfortune,' says his cousin, or to 'channel grief into something good.' According to Julia Levy, 'It was perverse how he refused to let go of his childhood. It was a badge of honour for [Cobain] to be always suffering.' Robert Gess, a musician who 'helped cool Kurt off' at the club, believes 'some of the demons that killed him were there that night at the Wall.'

Like the 'stump-dumb rocker dudes' he despised, Cobain wound up conforming to a stereotype. From early 1991 he became almost a cliché of the violent punk devotee and drug-addled misfit, swaggering through Olympia and Seattle, bellicose, drunk, and constantly antagonistic to those who befriended him. Levy was violently jettisoned. Marander was again dropped. A member of Cobain's family who visited him in North Pear Street was met at the door by a 'naked Kurt, shaking his fist and howling abuse at me for hassling him'. A delegation from the new-wave K Records was also among the victims of this vendetta motivated by Cobain's punk sensibility. On that occasion a warning shot from the BB gun was enough to clear the front porch of visitors. For those who encroached more persistently, Cobain reserved harsher punishment. In August 1992 *Vanity Fair* described his pregnant wife as a 'train-wreck personality', whose penchant for cigarettes and heroin had led 'industry insiders' to fear for the health of her child. (The Los Angeles County Children's Services Department would force the couple briefly to surrender custody of their daughter.) Cobain chafed under the attack, promising 'ultra violence' on the guilty journalist, Lynn Hirschberg. 'I want to kill her,' he told Azerrad. 'I'm going to kill this woman with my bare hands. I'm going to stab her to death. First I'm going to take her dog and slit its guts out in front of her and then shit all over her and stab her to death.' When it was pointed out that such a move would have implications for Cobain's career, he considered sub-contracting the act to a hit-man, then, in more serious vein, began a long and unrelenting campaign to have Hirschberg fired. At the very end of his life Cobain was engaged in elaborate calculations, with the aid of a book of magic numbers, to determine a formula to 'hex the bitch' whose article so pained him.

Later that autumn two British journalists, Victoria Clarke and Britt Collins, earned Cobain's lasting hatred for the provocative ambition of writing a book about Nirvana. According to a police complaint signed by Clarke on 26 October, Cobain 'called and left a long, hostile and threatening message on her answering machine ... [Clarke] stated that she and [Collins] are writing a book about the suspect and his rock band and the suspect is upset about some of the book's material ... She is afraid the suspect will take action on his threats.' Unspecified, but audible on tape were the exact words Cobain chose to express his concern: 'If anything comes out in this book which hurts my wife, I'll fucking hurt you ... I'll cut out your fucking eyes, you sluts ... whores ... parasitic little cunts ... I don't give a flying fuck if I have this recorded that I'm threatening you.'

As a boy Cobain had had no shortage of enemies, but they were enemies other misfits respected him for making: parents, teachers, ministers, policemen. To be nonconformist as a teenager had not been a bad tactic. Cobain always seemed to be fleeing from a confrontation with the authority-figures he loathed; he was in that category of male most likely to be a victim of bullying. This gave him the advantage of the underdog.

By the 1990s Cobain was still re-living his childhood, fighting the battles that were as much a part of him as an arm or a leg. Five years after he left it, Cobain was still railing against Aberdeen, and remained as sensitive to criticism as he had been there. By the time *Vanity Fair* and the biographers took an interest in his career he was among the most respected and best-selling names in rock. Yet artistic and financial security did not satisfy Cobain for long. His double life as a punk agitator and retiring family man took on a new complexity when it was pointed out that Cobain all too rarely practised what he preached. Here was something new in the grunge world: a figure who epitomized the new-wave ethic, yet haggled for hours over the fine print of a recording contract, who leavened the art-noise experiments of his youth with Squeeze-like pop melodies and deserted his feminist and peace-loving effusions in favour of a violent, sexist harangue that would have turned heads in an Aberdeen bar. 'A pathological malcontent, inspired more by his hates than his loves,' his cousin calls him. Cobain himself would describe peace of mind as 'something that happens to other people'.

One of the ways Cobain isolated himself from the world was by keeping hours that would have crippled a hardened insomniac. It is not exaggerating to say that he saw sleep as a release from the paranoid rejection he felt by others, or that he dozed by day and worked at night in order to minimize his exposure to his enemies. By 1991 his most common guise was his pyjamas. 'I just like to sleep,' he explained. 'I find myself falling asleep at times when I'm fed up with people or bored ... For so many years, I've felt like most of my conversation has been exhausted, there's not much I can look forward to. Everyday simple pleasures that people might have in having conversations or talking about inane things I just find really boring, so I'd rather just be asleep.' When a photographer named Kirk Weddle shot a session with Nirvana in a swimming-pool that summer, Cobain surprised him by stretching out on the wet concrete surround and nodding off. A BBC engineer, Miti Adhikari, had the same experience when the group recorded in London that November: 'While everyone was arriving, unloading equipment, banging drums and tuning guitars, Kurt lay there in a corner snoring.'

A popular theory at the time was that Cobain was narcoleptic, and that sleep overcame him arbitrarily, without warning, sometimes in mid-sentence. Another version was that his body-clock ran to a timetable largely determined by his drug habit, and that he not so much slept as anaesthetized himself. Cobain may also have chosen silence for the simple reason that he had nothing to say. As an enthusiastic punk activist Cobain's pride had been stung by the knowledge that others were saying and doing equally outlandish things. Presumably he would have lost his hard-won credibility had he learned to look down on his supporters with a critical eye, but his capacity for identifying with them was costly, for it gave them not so much leadership as expression. Cobain spoke for them so perfectly that he never spoke to them. In his long years of subversive rhetoric he communicated only what thousands already thought.

Cobain chose to be mute because his ego could be gratified by appearing laid-back in relation to others. In this there was another parallel to Hendrix. Both men could strike an interviewer like Peel as so distant 'they seemed not to be there', and both achieved feature-length coverage of their 'self-effacing' and 'unpretentious' natures as a result. It was true, of course, that Hendrix and Cobain were poorly educated and in some ways unworldly men who let their music speak for them. 'It's all on the vinyl,' Hendrix once insisted. Yet a simple heart was not always matched by an unsophisticated mind. In claiming that he had nothing to say, Hendrix concealed the extent to which he chose his silence. According to his father, 'one of the reasons Jimi laid low was to stand out, be different'. To Hendrix a display of inscrutability and truculence, even to his friends, was neither surprising nor illogical. Rather, he saw it as the best way to be noticed in an industry already teeming with self-confident personalities. As with Hendrix, so with Cobain: 'There *was* a genuinely shy, chary side to Kurt,' says his cousin. 'There was also a part of him that pushed those qualities as a way of standing out and achieving his lifelong motto, "I'm not as you are".'

Cobain's health, precarious as a child, deteriorated in adulthood. He suffered renewed bronchial attacks and intense, chronic stomach pain. By the early months of 1991 it became obvious that Cobain was injecting himself with heroin partly because he wished to and partly because it helped relieve his gastric problem. Of this period in his life he told David Fricke, 'For five years, during the time I had my stomach (pain), I wanted to kill myself every day. I came very close many times . . . It was to the point where I was on tour, lying on the floor, vomiting air because I couldn't hold down water.' Cobain's suicide note would end with the words, 'Thank you from the pit of my burning, nauseous stomach.' He blamed 'a lot of [his] mental problems' on the fact that he awoke each day 'with a better than even chance of feeling dead'. On many of those days Cobain would have to give a concert, shoot a video or subject himself to an interview. In retrospect it was astonishing that his 130-pound frame would bear such stress and such a relentlessly full life.

There was inevitable scepticism about whether Cobain's addiction was the cause, not the result of his condition. This was a view that pulled heavily with Levy, who believes: 'Kurt over-medicated . . . the solution became the problem.' Novoselic and Grohl, on the other hand, agree that the stomach cramps were real enough, and Cobain himself hastened to join the consensus. 'There's been so many times when I'll be sitting there eating and having massive pain and no one even realizes it,' he told Azerrad. 'Halfway through the European tour, I remember saying I'll never go on tour again until I have this fixed because I wanted to kill myself. I wanted to fucking blow my head off.' Cobain's mother adds that she, too, suffered stomach pain in her early twenties. At least one of her brothers 'spent years in agony' with a similar complaint. According to Beverley Cobain, 'The problem was bad enough, but both for that and his depression Kurt paid the price of self-medicating. Heroin wasn't the answer. Lithium and a change of diet might have suited him better.'

Cobain's appearance was striking. Short, slight, waiflike – his clothes always seemed to swallow him – he was voluptuously abandoned to his own image, which, as Levy says, 'became another cage he couldn't break out of'. Over his shredded pyjamas or jeans Cobain wore an ever-present mohair sweater and, on the relatively few occasions he chose to be anonymous, a plaid hunting cap. A sign that he was entering one of his nostalgic, back-to-the-roots incarnations would be the removal of the sweater to reveal a flannel shirt. An observer watching Cobain perform in Seattle might have had difficulty deciding whether this was an actor burlesquing a punk or a punk burlesquing an actor. *People* once described him quite seriously as 'a typical in-your-face grunge exhibitionist'. With his trademark lank hair, unwashed but frequently dyed, his bloodless complexion and the surprisingly elongated feet forced into the black-and-white sneakers he bought from Payless Shoe Source, there was a touch of the prankster about Cobain, the clown. It was surprising that so many of his devotees failed to see it. Cobain himself realized the comical side of his personality and played on it intuitively. By 1991, says Moon, he was the 'lead card' around Seattle and Olympia. His clothes and looks became the butt of the mainstream media's laboured humour. He would turn up at meetings with Geffen in a pink bathrobe or a pair of women's underwear. When the 'austere look' was required by a photographer Cobain arrived in a fur stole and *Gone With the Wind*-era ballgown. He experimented with make-up and jewellery. If all this was supposed to induce a sense of levity, it seems to have failed badly. At the end of his life critics and fans were still scouring the horizon for evidence of Cobain's 'androgyny', or the 'meaning' of his blurring the sexual divide. 'He was pushing it,' says Levy. 'Seeing what he could get away with before someone rumbled him.' 'It was a joke,' said Cobain.

On 1 January 1991 Nirvana assembled in Seattle and recorded 'Aneurysm' and 'Even In His Youth', which appeared as a joint B-side that summer. The A-side was 'Smells Like Teen Spirit'. The songs were significant for the harnessing of punk energy to the user-friendly delivery Cobain made his own, and the wry comment offered by

'Aneurysm', in particular, on the whole history of pop. They also re-introduced Nirvana to Butch Vig, producer of the Smart session and a vital player in the group's breakthrough. Vig, if nothing else, had a clear idea of how successful rock albums should sound. The upshot would be a scientific and quite deliberate smoothing-down in the mix, resulting in an end-product in which echo, digital enhancement and special effects boxes dominated the true spirit of grunge. According to Peterson: 'Vig and Andy Wallace [his engineer] were indispensable. With them, Nirvana transcended punk.'

Nirvana's other advantage was the songs. By the first weeks of 1991 the near-nightly rehearsals in Tacoma had yielded 'Come As You Are' and 'Smells Like Teen Spirit', both in the accessible mould of 'Dive' and bulging with the promise of mass appeal. 'We knew that the stuff we were coming up with was catchy and cool and just good strong songs,' says Grohl. As well as Cobain's mounting confidence as a cannily melodic writer, there was a second, practical source for the new material. In the very week Cobain penned 'Teen Spirit' Allied aircraft launched the Gulf War and bombed Baghdad. When even a corporation like the Rolling Stones was moved to record a protest song it was inevitable that Nirvana would garner their remaining principles into a one-off display of genuine punk spirit. There was a rumbling note of fury in the lyrics. 'When we went to make the record,' Novoselic recalled, 'I had such a feeling of us versus them. All those people waving the flag and being brainwashed.' Whatever Cobain's motives, there is surely poignancy to be found in his writing the youth anthem of his day at the very moment society was more polarized than at any time since his birth. In the mid-eighties Cobain had declared that the Vietnam war, for all the misery that accompanied it, was not an unmitigated disaster of humanity, because it 'threw up some great pop'. The same creative process was at work on Nirvana's new single. It is uncertain whether Cobain intended a literal application for 'Teen Spirit' or, more plausibly, shunned altitude in favour of a middlebrow, mainstream rock song. What is clear is that the chorus, scrawled in a car speeding between Olympia and Tacoma, would achieve an almost sacramental quality in the nineties; and that Cobain himself had no idea of the demons he was unleashing. 'As far as I was concerned,' he said, 'it was just a tune. A time-marker. What I was into was making money and abusing people's trust.'

On 30 April 1991 he became a Geffen recording artist.

6

Nevermind

In the same month they collected their advance, Nirvana played a sold-out Canadian tour and a single date in Seattle where they debuted 'Smells Like Teen Spirit'. This was the year of his life Cobain always spoke of nostalgically. His worst problems with his family were behind him, he and Geffen had arrived at a deal, and his fame as a rock star grew, like his favourite sycamore, from a small seed – a handful of singles and one cult album. Yet that tiny output, coupled with curiosity about Cobain himself, was enough to excite interest in magazines and trade publications all over Europe and to raise a few murmurs of enthusiasm even in New York. According to a profile that summer in *Village Voice*, Cobain was a 'rising star', someone for whom 'alienation was paying off' and, in point of family background, 'an enigma wrapped in a riddle inside a mystery'.

In fact, by the time the article appeared, Cobain and his father had reconciled. Despite giving one interviewer the impression that they 'talked for over an hour, just catching up', Don later admitted that the phone call had been 'hard', with no effort made to subsequently meet. In one version, 'Kurt did everything to rub it in that he, Don, had been wrong about him'. Yet there was also a sense in which, merely by speaking to his father for an hour, Cobain acknowledged that as he grew nearer them in experience, he began to value his parents more highly. It was because he prized their approval so much that he was so resentful of their having withheld it. Cobain's relationship with Don went unresolved, but that it continued to haunt him was evident from the clues sprinkled throughout his lyrics. Both *Nevermind* and *In Utero* were concerned with fathers and sons, like a shadowy presence of subjects Cobain could not speak of directly. At the very end of his life he admitted that his relations with Don were one area 'we both screwed up, and royally'. According to Cobain's grandmother, 'They never admitted it, but they were too similar.'

Nirvana recorded their debut Geffen album at Sound City in suburban Los Angeles for $65,000, roughly a hundred times more than had been spent on *Bleach*.* During his six weeks in California Cobain stayed in a furnished apartment provided by Gold Mountain. After the technical matter of renting drums and guitars and a week's rehearsal overseen by Vig, Cobain got down to the business at hand. Tony Selmer, a neighbour of Nirvana's in Van Nuys, recalls this as 'drugs, drugs and drugs again' although Cobain's voyeuristic hobby was also seen to. An elderly woman in the same complex, hearing that 'really crazy musicians' were living above, invited Cobain to visit her one night after practice. He opened her door to find the woman sitting on a chair completely nude. According to Selmer, 'She was a sixty-year-old lady with glasses. Buck naked, she sat there smoking with a long cigarette holder and drinking out of a shot glass. Perfectly relaxed – there was nothing sexual about it at all. It was just another of Kurt's turn-ons, and this old girl made it come true.'

A second recurrent fantasy surfaced when, after days of haggling, Cobain persuaded two local twins to join him in bed. Even this relatively familiar arrangement was complicated by the additional presence in the room of a camera, which one of the women objected to. In the imbroglio that

---

* *'Nevermind* was better,' says John Peel. 'But not *that* much better.'

followed, a window was smashed and the entire complex's fire alarm set off. After that, says Selmer, 'the next thing anyone knew, this blonde girl came rocketing down the stairs screaming, "He hit me, he hit me," followed a minute later by her sister, silhouetted by the porch light, making off with Kurt's camera. That was the last we saw of the twins.'

Cobain also found time for music. Over six weeks Nirvana rehearsed and practised ten hours a day to record thirteen usable tracks and accompanying out-takes, of which there were many. As well as the new material, Cobain revisited much of the work from the Smart session a year before, while 'Polly' and 'Stay Away' had existed, in various forms, since *Bleach*. Much was later made of the apparent conflict between Cobain's impulsive, one-take approach to recording and the hard-fought perfectionism of Vig and Andy Wallace. Formidable melodies notwithstanding, too much of the material on *Nevermind* came across as self-conscious and canned. In those moments where it did take on muscle, it served only to betray Wallace's surprisingly inanimate mixes. Thus, 'On A Plain' emerged as a triumph of improvisational brilliance over lush production values, while on 'Territorial Pissings' Cobain reverted to garage-band status by plugging his guitar directly into the seventies-era mixing board, in the style of the early Sex Pistols. A song like 'Lounge Act', on the other hand, was perhaps too cleverly titled for its own good. While it was true that most of the studio friction was resolved ('For the most part,' says Vig, 'when I asked him to do stuff, he'd do it') and the commercial achievement was undeniable, critics would still ponder what might have happened had Cobain and his producers set out to make the same record.

One reason *Nevermind* became so immediately successful on release was that it touched on a world that had gone sour. Cobain's timing was impeccable. His grasp of the way many of his countrymen felt was perfect. After a few years of optimism in the mid-eighties, Americans saw one conflict overseas and another at home that threatened peace. Abroad, the West engaged in the largest military deployment since the Second World War. Domestically, an army of 42 million disaffected slackers formed a willing audience for the potpourri of pseudo-anarchist mumblings and droll sarcasms of *Nevermind*. Cobain's lyrics skewered the sense of defeat that foreign and civil war had brought to America only a few years after a presidential campaign had been won on the basis of 'peace and prosperity'. It became, then, a document: not only expertly put together, but touching on people's needs. Cobain was a master of the bleak metaphor for his times, and a virtuoso at tapping the eternal vein of one generation's desire to be different from another.

Cobain's other strength was his willingness to compromise. For all his talk of improvisation in the studio, it was clear that Vig and Wallace were free to work their brand of sorcery on at least half the tracks. Even 'Teen Spirit' itself, far from being a model of punk spontaneity, evolved over a period of weeks of rehearsals and torn-up arrangements. The second a version emerged into the world (reminding some of Boston's 1976 hit, 'More Than A Feeling') it was rushed to Wallace and Vig like a sickly child to the incubator. When critics first heard 'Teen Spirit' that summer, much was made of the distance between the song's upbeat delivery and its message. One was sunny, one was dark, but the music and lyrics had this in common: both were superior to anything that Cobain had done before, so full of gloomy utterances, so rich in manic energy that they might almost have been written by a different person. In a sense, they had been. The words were the very ones Cobain had scrawled one night on his way to the studio. That long and hard winter on North Pear Street had enabled him to throw off the yoke of what he thought was the acceptable way to write a song and so discard the claustrophobic themes of *Bleach*. In what seemed like a moment, Cobain had made a breakthrough, leaping from conventional topics like barbers and swap-meets into a stylistic and original world of his own. Much of Nirvana's music, however, remained in the most conservative rock and roll tradition, and Wallace's electronic embellishments rooted 'Teen Spirit' firmly in the mould of Deep Purple and Aerosmith. The contrast between the song's subject matter and its execution made the record seem oddly disjointed, and in later years Cobain would disown 'Teen Spirit's' production as a 'sell-out'.

Although Cobain gave a biographer the impression he rarely drank, his behaviour at Sound City proceeded along conventional rock star lines. As well as his favoured cough syrup, he downed a bottle of Jack Daniel's every night in the studio and refused all nourishment unless it was accompanied by an equivalent dose of alcohol. Once he was settled in his apartment he began taking antibiotics for his stomach, washing the tablets down with bourbon and wine. At first light Cobain would sit down to dinner with friends like Novoselic, Vig and Gary Gersh, where, according to Selmer, 'the booze flowed like Niagara', despite repeated warnings about the hazards of mixing alcohol and pills. This was a favourable situation for Cobain to drink in, because virtually everyone there was a potential nurse: he could be well guarded and cared for if he collapsed. He drank.

In later years Cobain enjoyed the reputation of an ascetic, someone whose worst vices were cigarettes and strong cups of cappuccino. An image took root which portrayed him as a latter-day saint of rock legend. That the heroic view of Cobain was something of a simplification the story of his youth perhaps demonstrates. In addition to the criticisms of his friends and contemporaries, his own paternal grandmother describes him as 'fractured'. But the rebellious child inside him had usually been kept in check by an adult of exceptionally strong ambition and, until 1991, a lack of funds to indulge himself fully. Poverty and a remarkably sensitive mind prevented him from drifting too far down the road of real excess.

In the years after *Nevermind*, that mind became less dependable and at last broke down altogether. With fame and money Cobain reverted to the habits of his youth, but now the dissipation was on a broader scale and the cost to his health was greater. Contributing to the cloudiness of his judgement was an increasing dependence on alcohol and drugs. Not only did Cobain drink cough syrup, whisky and wine in the studio, but by August 1991 Nirvana's contract specified the provision of one bottle apiece of vodka and Glenfiddich at each concert – modest by the standards of the Rolling Stones, but notable for a trio of which only two members drank. At the launch party for *Nevermind* that autumn Cobain celebrated as only he could: a banquet of junk food chased down by glasses of bourbon and beer. At Thanksgiving, he and his girlfriend were on a heroin binge in London and Amsterdam. By Christmas it had become obvious to Cobain, as well as to everyone else, that he could no longer exist without the bottles in either his medicine chest or his liquor cabinet.

One of the reasons for Cobain's behaviour was, of course, its genetic basis. As a boy he had learned to dose himself with Ritalin and sedatives, then travelled a well-beaten path through marijuana to substance abuse and finally addiction. As an adult he sought purpose in music, only to disown the results in much the same way, as a six-year-old, he had repudiated his prize-winning artwork. The pressure of his fame reopened Cobain's childhood wounds. Put simply, his cousin's verdict is that 'success only made Kurt a prisoner of his situation', someone who was pathologically incapable of enjoying the present, just as he was of abandoning the past. On this reading Cobain had ample reason for devising a form of oblivion. With alcohol and drugs, he found the middle ground or perfect balance between life and death. Suicide by direct means was out, but suicide through addiction was a way of dealing with life, especially now he had the money to indulge himself. Cobain drank and took drugs more for relief than for pleasure, and, according to Selmer, 'grew more friendless as he grew better known'.

That left the question of Cobain's love-life. When Nirvana had played the Satyricon Club in Portland in 1989 they met a woman with striking punk-rock hair, a tattoo and the sort of implausible name given to musicians' wives in Jackie Collins novels. Courtney Love, born on 9 July 1965, was the predictably troubled scion of a marriage between an experimental psychologist and a man who lived with the Grateful Dead. Asked in later life what associations her childhood called up for her, Love replied

> Guys in stripy pants in a circle around me, and my mother telling me to act like spring. Then to be summer and fall. Interpretive dancing. People in tents with wild eyes, painting my face.

Love herself first entered therapy at age three, then began a long downward spiral, by way of England and New Zealand, eventually leading to a shop-lifting conviction and a term in the Oregon reform school. She supported herself as a stripper, sang in a series of forgettable punk bands and, after coming to the attention of Alex Cox, won the lead role in his pop-spaghetti-western *Straight to Hell*. Before that, Love had taken a cameo in Cox's *Sid and Nancy*, a part she might have been born to play. In early 1990 she founded the hardcore group Hole.

Those who met Love in and around Los Angeles had no trouble recalling her. As well as the eyeliner and bleached hair, and the trim, exotic dancer's build, Love was unblushingly frank in her self-promotion. By late 1990 she had only one wish: despite the problems she was facing with Hole, she still hoped to make a name for herself as a musician. 'Courtney was vividly nonconventional,' says Celia Grech, a woman who met her that winter. 'She was hyped up on energy and self-confidence, and quite theatrical, a show-off. She had a sense of herself as a special person, [something] she made no effort to conceal. There were two possible reactions to Courtney – either you noticed her and loved her, or noticed her and loathed her. Unlike Kurt, she wasn't crushed by bad notices.'

What did crush her was to be ignored. When Love met Cobain again in Los Angeles in 1991 she chose to announce herself not with the traditional greeting, but by punching him in the stomach. Despite this unpromising introduction, the two stayed in touch while Nirvana recorded their album. Soon, Love began appearing at the Van Nuys apartment to exchange drugs. 'We bonded over pharmaceuticals,' she told Azerrad. 'I had Vicodin extra-strength, which was pills, and he had Hycomine cough syrup. I said "You're a pussy, you shouldn't drink that syrup because it's bad for your stomach."' In a short time the meetings and chemical exchanges evolved into dating, sex and a full-blown affair. The relationship with Love strongly influenced Cobain's outlook, directly affecting his career at several turns. It was not simply a hit-or-miss event in his life; she made a profound impression, and he arranged aspects of his work – even to their discussion of whether he should leave Nirvana – as the consequence of their mutual devotion. For all the lies, half-truths and skewering of Love as a drug-fuelled opportunist who bought into celebrity, it is certain that she stuck with Cobain when even his immediate family and colleagues deserted him. That her relationship with Cobain would help her career did not escape notice.

* * *

187

'I can see Kurt now, sitting on the floor,' says Charles Peterson. 'He would lay out what he called his art – foetus models, plastic bones, intestines – and call for a photograph.' Peterson is among those who think Cobain to have been 'less gifted visually' than some believed. It has been said to his credit that Cobain was prepared to oversee details of his albums which other musicians tended to ignore; it can also be said that his talent for design was at best subjective, an attempt to raise the bittersweet spirits of childhood memories, and at worst cloyingly self-indulgent. Cobain did, however, add one telling detail to the much-acclaimed cover of *Nevermind*. It was at his suggestion that the underwater photograph of five-month-old Spencer Elden was doctored to show him swimming towards a fishhook with a dollar bill on it. When the album was first released as much comment focused on the imagery and symbolism of the sleeve as on the contents. An entire PhD thesis was published on the 'allegories of Kurt Cobain's grand design', and wondered how much of the cover was metaphorical and how much objective truth. To Michael Azerrad the picture symbolized 'a departure from the acquisitive, yuppie eighties, a rejection of the materialism which backfired', while even the *New York Times* found in it a 'transforming shift' from the old decade to the new. What all of the critics missed were the cover's three simple themes – and the themes that dominate all of Cobain's writing: the sacredness of youth, whatever its form; the disappointment that invariably follows high expectation; and the corruption of innocence.

There was also the possibility that the cover was a joke. According to Levy, 'Kurt said that since everything was real as a form of perception, literal truth couldn't be distinguished from theory; in some images, speculation *was* literal truth.' Put bluntly, Cobain had certain symbolist-surrealist pretensions. He enjoyed the idea that sociologists and lifestyle writers could ponder the meaning of his work. A man present at the meeting to decide which picture to use for the cover – there were five contenders – recalls 'Kurt rolling about with mirth', and Nirvana themselves would do an underwater photo-shoot that, despite the sturdy work of the Rutles and the definitive heavy-metal spoof of Spinal Tap, took the send-up of rock and roll to new depths. According to Robert Fisher, an art director at Geffen: 'It was really stormy the weekend before and the pool got really clouded up . . . The pump broke two days before so the water was really cold and Kurt was really sick and they were hating being in the water. It was kind of a nightmare. Kurt had a hard time – it seemed like he had a real buoyancy problem – he'd kick and thrash and he'd still be on top of the water.' Later, Cobain finished a fifth of Jack Daniel's and plunged through a sheet of plate glass in search of further poolside refreshment.

One of the ironies of Cobain's sexual development was a taste for a particular type in women – the assertive, self-confident, physically striking type epitomized by his mother – so at odds with his own deeply reserved nature. By the time he was twenty-four Cobain had had half-a-dozen serious affairs, as well as the largely voyeuristic episodes with women like Donna Kessler. Now, as he returned to Olympia from California, he entered a brief relationship with a singer named Mary Lou Lord. 'It was intense,' says a friend, but the intensity was all on his side. Somewhere in the recesses of his mind, Cobain was 'transforming himself'. Lord, on the other hand, presented a more straightforward image: the outgoing young musician with a love of people. Her inner life, while rebellious, found its outlet in social activity.

He was disguised, veiled, going through social motions; she was enjoying herself, displaying what she was, opening herself up to immediate experience. One was playing for time, the other was full of life for the moment. Predictably

Lord joined the list of ex-lovers. From the summer of 1991 Cobain, finally departing from North Pear Street, would spend six months living in rented rooms, hotels and, on more than one occasion, bedding down among the hollow-eyed vagrants who traditionally haunted Pioneer Square.

'During that time that I attempted to be a bachelor and sow my oats and live the bachelor rock and roll lifestyle, I didn't end up fucking anybody or having a good time at all,' Cobain complained. It was inevitable that, sooner or later, his thoughts would return to Courtney Love. As a boy Cobain had craved attention; as a man he looked for empathy. Love gave them to him. More than once he said that he was truly alive only when he was playing music; but the fact remained, towering over him, as stubborn and irrefutable as Gibraltar, that he wanted to be truly alive in that way for only a few hours a week. The rest of the time Cobain preferred the more stimulating company of a woman who (as Love assuredly did) 'knew her mind'. From August, when she joined him on tour in England, the couple would be together near-continuously in the remainder of Cobain's life.

Love effected an immediate and lasting change to the way Cobain lived. Gone for ever were the sexual experiments and random voyeurism of his years in Olympia. Former girlfriends like Marander and Vail were discouraged from visiting. According to Wheeler, Love was 'always uptight around Kurt's past' and began a rigorous appraisal of old friends, long used to an open invitation, who now found their way barred at Cobain's door. More attention was paid to the way he looked and dressed, to what drugs he took and where he ate. Some also detected Love's influence at work professionally. From 1992 Cobain's lyrics would lose some of their scathing irony in favour of a petulant feminism, while punch-drunk noise and what Peel calls 'thrashing about' were allowed to dilute the winning mix of melody

Kurt Cobain in 1972, aged five. The same photograph was given to mourners at his funeral twenty-two years later.

Below 1000½ East 2nd Street, Aberdeen, filled with piled dishes, festering laundry and a tankful of turtles. (*J. Prins*)

'*Twin Peaks* without the excitement' – Aberdeen, Washington. (*J.Prins*)

Below The North Aberdeen Bridge, immortalized by Cobain in 'Something In The Way'. (*J. Meyersahm*)

114 North Pear Street, Olympia, Cobain's home
from 1987–91, where he wrote most of the songs on
Nevermind. (*W. Larkins*)

Cobain took the title of his biggest hit from a
teenage girls' deodorant. (*J. Meyersahm*)

Left Nirvana's 1989 line-up: Kurt Cobain, Chas Channing, Jason Everman, Chris Novoselic. *(Ian Tilton/Retna)*

Right 'Furiously catchy pop songs set to monster heavy rock riffs' – and an anarchic stage act; live with Nirvana, 1990. *(Ian Tilton/Retna)*

Below Seattle's Crocodile Café. *(C. Sandford)*

Left The launch of *Nevermind* – as close as Cobain ever came to being happy. *(Chuck Pulin/Starfile)*

Right A new guitar, purchased from the royalties of *Nevermind*, invokes grunge's 'negative, anti-state, Utopian rumblings'. *(Niels van Iperen/Retna)*

Right The 'next big thing' in rock and roll. *(Ed Sirrs/Retna)*

Left Courtney Love on stage with Hole. 'They are happening like war happens,' one critic wrote. *(Mick Hutson/Redferns)*

VANDALISM:
BEAUTIFUL AS A ROCK
IN A COP'S FACE

The Globe story on the Cobains.

and fury. Later, Cobain would fall out with Novoselic and Grohl over money. Those over thirty made the link to John Lennon, another artist thought to have been unusually influenced by his wife, and suggested that, now as then, a disintegration of the male ego was taking place. Though few openly said so, there was a feeling in Seattle that, figuratively as well as sexually, Cobain was the submissive partner.

In a sign of which way the rock *zeitgeist* was moving, meanwhile, Love and her group experienced the same fate as Nirvana, first attracting an enthusiastic club audience and then being discovered by the British weeklies. By 1991, in phrases that echoed those of 1989, *Melody Maker* was writing of Hole:

> They mangle a tune with *passion*. During 'Dicknail' Courtney touches her breasts, parts of her thighs, breathes hard and arches her back right over. A real suicide blonde if ever there was one.
>
> Hole are dangerous and inevitable. They are happening like war happens and nobody, not even they, can understand how powerful they are. They'll accept any label you want to give them – pop, rock, punk, whatever – and then throw them away like so many useless bits of paper.
>
> Yeah, I think they can change the world, so no, I don't think they are a pop group.

One of the reasons Cobain was technically homeless from July 1991 to January 1992 was the hectic touring schedule imposed on Nirvana by John Silva. In June, after leaving Sound City, they played in Mexico, California, Oregon and Colorado; on 20 August they joined Sonic Youth on a European festival tour; and from late September the phenomenon known as Nirvanamania took them from

America to Canada, Europe, Australia, New Zealand, Japan and, eventually, home via Singapore and Hawaii. As he grew richer and better known, Cobain chose to spend large parts of his time among people who shared none of the advantages of his profession. He was proud of this fact and sought to capitalize on it; yet his explanation for his 'downward urge' and liking for hostels and missions seems unconvincing, especially when he chose to live among real vagrants. Had Cobain thought about it deeply, he would have realized that his income and celebrity would always guarantee him a special place in the soup queue. In practice, therefore, his decision to live at 'ground zero', while touring or in Seattle, led him into situations where his superiority would be effortless and unrivalled. It is clear from the comments he made to friends in clubs and bars that he made no attempt to evade this special status; on the contrary, he relished it. In 1985 Michael Schepp had found Cobain 'living like an experiment' in the shack on East 2nd Street, while others spoke of his 'slumming it' around Aberdeen. The same whiff of play-acting was apparent six years later. This pattern of behaviour suggests that Cobain suffered from a deep sense of insecurity.

In Europe that summer he also announced a longing to live life among 'real people'. Kate Rous, one of the promoters who met Cobain at St Henry's Club in Cork, remembers him 'giving a really epic speech about how he was "just one of the guys" and then throwing a fit because the backstage Scotch wasn't Glenfiddich'. Indeed, Cobain went out of his way to act, some said over-act, the part of the 'grabola rock star' he soon styled himself, setting up a lifelong contradiction between what Rous calls the 'humble artisan' and the 'arrogant fuck whose ego doubled with each day on the road'.

The other thing Cobain developed during his eight months on tour was his ability to engage an audience. It was a tribute to his relentless insistence on rehearsal and practice that Nirvana's stage act went from enthusiastic to consistently brilliant in less than a year. By using his voice to build upon rather than drown the melodies, by his growing competence as a guitarist and above all by his famed ability to 'put himself across' (sometimes literally so, by diving into the crowd), Cobain's live performances would, within months, penetrate rock culture so deeply as to become lore. By the time *Nevermind* was released, Nirvana already enjoyed a fan-base out of all proportion to their modest record sales. On tour of Britain they were hailed as 'the next big thing', 'contenders', and the rightly dreaded 'future of rock and roll'. Even as critics applauded Sonic Youth, they reserved a special footnote for their support act. By late August, when Nirvana appeared at the Reading Festival, *Melody Maker* was writing of the still-unheard album as 'the finest straightforward rock record of the decade' and Cobain as possessing 'one of the finest "hurt" voices present in rock today.' In *The Times*'s simple view, 'Nirvana [had] arrived.'

This was the period of his life of which Cobain would always speak fondly. In an interview shortly before his death he told David Fricke: 'The best times were right when *Nevermind* was coming out and we went on that American tour where we were playing clubs. They were totally sold out, and the record was breaking big, and there was this *massive* feeling in the air, this vibe of energy. Something really special was happening.' As well as a word-of-mouth following in the US and Europe, Cobain had attracted media attention and photo coverage in titles like *Billboard* and *Rolling Stone* for the same reason that *Forum* had printed two pictures of him in a full-page profile on Seattle the month before: he looked unusual, which is to say, newsworthy. Giving the appearance of a jaded and world-weary child as he sat pouting among his clay dolls and bric-à-brac, Cobain was the only one in the feature who would make a reader stop before turning the page. Most of the other 'Grunge Activists', a selection that included Mark Arm, Chris Cornell and Jeff Ament, could just as easily have illustrated a story about young football players. Only Cobain knew instinctively how to seduce the camera, when to stand and when to sit, when to scowl and when to frown, and the editors at *Forum*, like other such editors in the future, could scarcely avoid giving him the spotlight he craved.

Fame also came to Cobain as the result of being in the right place at the right time. 'After the Gulf War everyone was waiting for the next MC5–Stooges generation to appear,' says Grant Alden in partial explanation. 'That's why so much attention was devoted to punks, and why a new album by any of them was considered an event.' Along with their growing support base and the buzz generated by the Geffen marketing department, Nirvana enjoyed the reputation of being plain-spoken about the way they saw life, both at home and overseas. *Nevermind* benefited hugely from this sense of being an alternative State of the Union address. It was seized on by critics, like *Forum*, seeking to explain 'young people's attitudes' to the war (never once mentioned in the lyrics), while others sought to promote the album as a manifesto for disaffected youth. Added to the cult following the group had attracted since *Bleach*, it was possible to see why Nirvana had every reason to suppose their move to Geffen would work to a commercial good, or why even Cobain's formidable reserve melted when he told Azerrad, 'Every time I look back at the best times in this band it was right before *Nevermind* ... It was awesome. That's when the band is at its best – they're really trying hard and there's so much excitement in the air you can just taste it.'

For Cobain to speak thus proved that he, too, was susceptible to 'Nirvanamania'. Friends confirm that the summer and early autumn of 1991 was 'the closest Kurt came to being happy' (between crippling bouts of stomach pain), and a Geffen executive remembers him 'bursting with pride' at the feature in *Forum*. The ragged, anti-social misfit framed the article and hung it in his hotel room. It was a fitting conclusion to the first phase of mainstream media interest in Cobain's life. His next major coverage would all be headlines, editorials and obituaries.

Nirvana's live performances were a new pioneering form, a new communications medium, a new affirmation of rock's raucous, liberating power. As with groups in the early 1960s, their tours had an enormous attraction for young people seeking role models, and their concerts did as much to polarize society in the early nineties as any satirist, agitator or political activist. Every town and city and hamlet, every nook and cranny eventually became accessible to the subversive movement that was flying under the banner and the appeal of grunge rock. In Los Angeles the Coalition Against Foreign Wars adopted *Nevermind*'s swimming-baby cover as the logo of its advertisements. The Peace Action Group, lobbying every congressman in the Union, quoted Cobain as 'one of [those] giving voice to how millions of Americans feel today'. And in Seattle the Workers World Party chose a picture of Nirvana onstage to illustrate its manifesto *Now What is to be Done?*

Cobain was widely praised for daring to show his more passionate side in public. Part of his appeal lay in his lack of ironic detachment, his commitment to what he called the 'top priority' of changing society. To his credit, he quietly supported charities and gave thousands of dollars to fringe groups. Yet even in his attempts to summon up the true spirit of anarchy, Cobain's talent for sleight of hand and ambiguity were at work. *Now What is to be Done?* praised Nirvana's stage act as a 'symbolic release of pent-up fury and rage at the capitalist machine'. In fact, the auto-destruction had begun as a simple effort by Cobain to maim his drummer. By 1992 Nirvana had taken instrument smashing to an art, piling up the equipment with special care and loosening bolts on guitars and drums to ensure they broke cleanly. In so far as there was ever a motive for Cobain's aggression, it lay in drunkenness rather than any wish to illustrate his commitment to change society. At the De Doelen Club in Rotterdam Cobain appeared dressed in matching pink lingerie, clutching a bottle, and invited the crowd to 'fuck themselves' while he writhed in front of them. Six weeks later he took the stage in Dallas, where, in the middle of 'School', he embedded his favourite Mustang guitar in the monitor board, apparently amusing himself but setting up a chant of 'BullSHIT' from the house. At the Hollywood Palace Cobain harangued the crowd from behind a brandy bottle, dropped his trousers, then began kicking and smashing the drum-kit, lying on his back in the debris and thrashing his legs like an upended insect. In August he tried the same trick at the Reading Festival and ended up dislocating his shoulder.

Play-acting and excess are always occupational hazards for anyone in the performing arts. Even so, Cobain's track record bears comparison to the great rock and roll carica-tures. During Nirvana's long months of touring he became monumentally drunk, one of his typical binges being when he stopped eating and drank himself into oblivion. These were virtually acts of self-destruction, since he needed to be saved by others, who, fortunately, always appeared in time. Two friends, Mike Coffey and Frank Medina, pulled Cobain off the diving board of his hotel swimming-pool, which had been closed and drained for the winter. Julia Levy entered his room in Seattle and found him unconscious, malnour-ished and too weak to walk. The pattern became a familiar one, especially after a particularly long and difficult time on the road.

While there was a suicidal component in some of these binges, Cobain did not consciously intend to die – the musical urge was too powerful for him to give up that critical part of his life. But he depended for his survival on good Samaritans like Coffey and Medina, and could be outstandingly churlish to those who helped him. He reduced a woman to tears backstage at the Reading Festival. Later in the week he left a club in London with two English girls, whom, he paused to inform Love, had 'tits like Washington cows'. In Bremen Cobain not only destroyed his guitar, amplifier, and most of the dressing-room but set fire to the tour bus. (This was the moment when even Nirvana's manager John Silva insisted, 'You guys have *got* to take it easy.') As the royalty flow from *Nevermind* increased and Gold Mountain's purse-strings loosened, Cobain celebrated by purchasing a new guitar with a sticker that read 'VANDALISM : BEAUTIFUL AS A ROCK IN A COP'S FACE'. Because he could finally afford it and because the audiences expected it, instrument smashing degenerated into a crowd-pleasing nightly ritual. When Coffey went to congratulate his friend on an outstanding show, Cobain swung at him with his fist, then sat sobbing with remorse and crying that 'self-parody' had ruined the performance. The dangers of mass-popularity and uncritical acceptance were recognized by Cobain when he told Azerrad, 'I found myself being overly obnoxious during the *Nevermind* tour, because I noticed that there were more average people coming into our shows and I didn't want them there. They started to get on my nerves.'

A sidelight on Cobain's reaction to fame is provided by Monty Lee Wilkes, Nirvana's tour manager from September to October 1991. As Wilkes told Azerrad, his first thoughts as he watched Cobain step off the plane were, 'There's something not right about this guy.' Things deteriorated from there. Even friends like Coffey found 'something sick' in the way Cobain delighted in tormenting his colleagues. 'Everything you fix,' said Wilkes, 'a guy like Kurt goes and deliberately unfixes it because he's a cutie pie, you know?' According to Frank Medina, 'Cobain could be a shit to anyone who knew him.'

As Cobain himself admitted, his rational motives for his behaviour were barely sufficient, and he was undoubtedly influenced by other factors which were to some degree subconscious. Among these were psychological problems that had existed since childhood. Although he sometimes made light of Aberdeen, he would often speak of it bitterly to close friends. Likewise, it was his tormenting knowledge that Nirvana were musically average that made public adulation so intolerable. The association between praise and guilt had been forged in Cobain from an early age, when he had rebelled against the misdirected approval of his parents. His tendency to use others for his own ends and to put too low a price on friendship also dated from his boyhood policy of self-containment. The result was an increasingly belligerent and drink-fuelled abuse of men like Wilkes (to whom Cobain 'never did say much unless he wanted something') and a high-handed rejection of others, like Silva, who sought to warn him about his behaviour.

The statement that Cobain 'didn't want average people at the shows' is symptomatic of the unhappiness with his audience that marked his later life. By 1991 he was regularly bemoaning the demands placed on him by his fans. 'Famous is the last thing I wanted to be,' he insisted; yet Cobain had wanted to be something similiar – rich, respected and talked about – for years. As he grew older he resented the intrusions on his private life more and more, while still seeking feature-length coverage of his every public act. Nothing was more characteristic of Cobain than this desire to disconnect his behaviour from its consequences. It was the same tendency that led him to blame 'unscrupulous dealers' for his drug addiction, or to threaten to sue his doctor for not explicitly warning him against mixing powerful antibiotics with heroin. According to Coffey, 'The good side of Kurt was a childlike innocence and a determination not to be corrupted by the world. The ugly side was a childish dependence on others, and an absolute refusal to take the blame for his fuck-ups.'

Cobain may not have wanted to be famous, but he went out of his way to attract a mass following. For all his battles with Vig and Wallace, he was willing and even eager to compromise on the production of *Nevermind*. The stories of 'creative differences' circulating later were wildly distorted, an effort to boost Nirvana's credentials as their art dwindled. Vig was an ideal colleague for Cobain: low-key, hardworking, accommodating and familiar with the quirks of difficult musicians. Cobain himself would comment that 'the stuff done [at Sound City] doesn't sound too bad. Worse shit's been released'. His representation of his work contained a good deal of truth; 'worse shit' had been released, but so had much better. The end-result was a characteristically sleek, seventies pop sound, the vocals layered lavishly on top, compared by Azerrad to 'a jagged stone encased in Lucite' and by Cobain as 'closer to Motley Crue than to punk'. The same recipe had worked, more or less, over the course of twenty-five years of rock history. It was not impossible, as this writer did, to buy *Nevermind* at the same time as the latest Rolling Stones record. While most critics were warm with praise when the album appeared that autumn, there were those who felt Cobain had all too willingly sacrificed principle for profit. 'It is ridiculous and debasing of us to call this grunge rock,' trumpeted the *Source*. According to Slim Moon, Cobain's friend and neighbour in Olympia, '*Nevermind* seemed dated almost as soon as Kurt made it.' Without the 'cathartic genius' of the single, it would have flopped.

When *Nevermind* reached the shops, the American publicity machine – magazines, newspapers, MTV and commercials – became a giant band that played only one tune: Kurt Cobain. With some minor exceptions, he relished the attention and played up to it. At the Reading Festival that summer, Cobain boasted to Courtney Love, '*I'm* going to be a star soon.' A stringer for the Seattle *Post-Intelligencer* remembers being invited to interview Cobain over dinner: 'It was hard for Kurt to sit through the meal. He was just like a little kid you bring to the table and prop up on the top of a phone book. He played with his food and talked non-stop about his favourite subject, namely himself.' Alice Wheeler believes 'there was a part of Cobain that wanted to be an old-fashioned rock star'. An Aberdeen woman, Randi Hubbard, was told by Wendy O'Connor that 'Kurt's all-time hero was John Lennon, not only for his politics, but because he made great pop music.' To another interviewer Cobain reacted angrily to a question about 'the falling-off in standards since *Bleach*' by asking, 'What's wrong with having a hit? What's wrong with liking the Beatles?' On Nirvana's tour bus that summer, Cobain took the point a step further by listening continually to *Abba's Greatest Hits*.

Cobain later described *Nevermind*'s production as a 'sellout' and worried that he should have 'aimed less high and hit my mark squarer'. Despite this intellectual self-justification, the album was a perfect example of the direction he was heading, and *Nevermind* would be understood as wholly Cobain's even without his name on the sleeve.* According to a friend, 'In some ways he was more like McCartney than Lennon, in his military attention to detail and the way he got what he wanted.' A BBC engineer,

* To illustrate the point, Cobain now dispensed with his alias.

Miti Adhikari, met and recorded Cobain in London that November: 'Kurt may have been laid-back and passive as a man, but as a musician he was focused, clear-headed and domineering. Whatever he wanted he got, and nothing happened without his say-so.' For all the talk of production problems that dogged Nirvana from *Bleach* to *In Utero*, it was clear that little if anything was done over Cobain's veto, and that his striving for commercial success was deliberately willed, whipped up and played for. As a misfit child, Cobain had inherited no sense of security or social position from his family. His future public status, no less than his self-respect, would depend on what he made of himself. Although he despised conventional work, he strove for personal distinction, and *Nevermind* seemed to offer such a chance. He later wrote that in May 1991 he 'had seen the opening and grabbed it'. Grant Alden is among those who believe 'Kurt tended to disown every album he did a year after he made it. They still all made perfect sense at the time.'

Cobain's 'military attention' to detail was at work when he supervised the video for *Nevermind*'s first single. Although he later fell out with the director Sam Bayer, Cobain declared himself 'knocked out' and even 'impressed' by the collage of fast cuts, swirling camerawork, superimposed effects and disturbing close-ups of 'Smells Like Teen Spirit'. The finished product, fondly described by Grohl as a 'pep rally from hell', was firmly in the tradition of *Blackboard Jungle*, a teen drama dealing with student anarchy, the theme reiterated in *Rebel Without a Cause*. Musically, 'Teen Spirit' tapped most of the roots of Cobain's own rock and roll education: as well as the familiar references to Boston and Aerosmith, the song bore more than a passing resemblance to the Pixies and reminded some of the primer for all Northwest rock, 'Louie, Louie'. A simple, vamp-like tune (Grohl and Novoselic playing a repetitive theme under the vocals), 'Teen Spirit' was saved by a brilliant Led Zeppelin-style guitar hook, setting up a swaying, singalong chorus more than enough to offset the maudlin lyrics. Even the fifty-year-old Patrick MacDonald remembers 'dancing around like a kid' when he heard the song's early chords.

'Smells Like Teen Spirit' allowed the audience to cross the punk-mainstream divide and, in crossing it, blur it. In MacDonald's words, 'it was a classic, old-fashioned rocker with new-wave appeal'. Part of the song's attraction lay in its pop-symphonic discipline and the carefully controlled ingenuity of the arrangement. Its other charm was the lyrics. Cobain himself described these as 'weird and different and spacy', something cobbled together on the dashboard of his car, full of improvisation and meaningless, and he proved not to be wrong. Despite its rallying title, 'Teen Spirit's' message was characteristically vague, a random sampling of surrealist-nonsense verse without any plot or location. The reference to 'A mulatto/An albino/A mosquito/My libido' might have been lifted from Edward Lear. Where Cobain *did* apply himself to direct comment, too much of the theme was given to demonology, preferring good and evil stereotypes to the complexities of human nature. In this, ironically, the song had much in common with the older American dreams it was thought to have rejected.

'Smells Like Teen Spirit' was a raucous, exhilarating, well-crafted rock anthem. It was also, like Cobain's career as a whole, a miracle of timing. In the weeks before Christmas 1991, MTV was a haven for Jason Donovan and Kylie Minogue, bland re-packagings of Phil Collins and Rod Stewart and recycled black and white clips from the sixties. 'Teen Spirit', the video and the song, struck an immediate chord with the audience. The station launched it in its 'Buzz Bin' in September; by October it was being aired eleven or twelve times a day. When, in the past, a song like 'My Generation' or 'Layla' had attracted such praise and hyperbole, certain critics had become tetchy, making it a point of honour to show their independence by finding fault. That was not the case with 'Teen Spirit', and most notices were all that Cobain could have hoped for. With the print reviewers and programmes like *Video Soul* dancing attendance, MTV (the station that had gone on the market the very day Cobain discovered punk) created a momentum for the single that lifted it into the realms of Michael Jackson and Madonna.

While MTV and the others pushed 'Teen Spirit', there was, as Gillian Gaar noted, 'endless speculation over what the song "really means". There were few clues to be gathered from the lyrics', and the ambiguity was the key to the appeal. 'It was possible to read anything you wanted into the lyrics, thus ensuring a wider audience.' (When MTV sent their cameras onto the streets to ask people what they thought Cobain was singing, not one quoted the words correctly.) The vagueness and slurring of the vocal hooks was a calculated ploy by Cobain, who felt the song was 'basically a scam', with the one redeeming feature of expressing the frustration of belonging to an underclass. Tim Arnold agrees that 'The lines about "I feel stupid/And contagious" were a deliberate playing for support, an avowal by Kurt that he knew how the kids felt. That sense of empathy, that he was just like them, was a huge factor in Cobain's popularity.' 'Smells Like Teen Spirit' may have been a defining moment in rock history, but it became one despite the haziness of the lyric, the shameless craving for sympathy and the familiarity of the central theme, which was 'Satisfaction' updated for the nineties.

'Teen Spirit' had begun life as writing on the wall, a slogan scrawled in North Pear Street comparing Cobain to the scent of a girls' deodorant. It was no less portentous for his career. The song, at a stroke, dragged Cobain out of his mewling years and pushed him to stardom. *Nevermind*, the album from which 'Teen Spirit' was taken, hit gold a month after release, and the Top Forty a month after that; by Christmas 70,000 people a day were buying the record. Cobain's face looked out from the covers of *Melody Maker*, *New Musical Express*, the *Rocket* and *Musician*. *Rolling Stone* ran a long review, unique for a group with one coolly received punk album on Sub Pop. In early 1991 Cobain had been locally known but destitute. A year later he was rich and internationally famous. 'Teen Spirit', he told his mother, would mean 'never having to eat corn dogs again'.

In fact it meant something far worse, as the song became first a cliché, and then a positive ordeal for Cobain to sing onstage. Everywhere he went, critics pressed him to 'explain' the song's chorus. A line he wrote in jest, his opening quip at parties, came back to haunt him as crowds stood at concerts, waving inanely beneath banners bearing the words 'HERE WE ARE NOW, ENTERTAIN US'. By 1993, Cobain could barely bring himself to play the song with any enthusiasm. On certain nights he refused to sing it at all, setting up a rumble of anger in the house and running the risk of alienating the very people 'Teen Spirit' had aimed to please. In Chicago there was a near-riot when Cobain mimicked the cry of 'Spi-rit' from the crowd, whom he characterized as 'fuckheads who [didn't] get the point'. Instead of the intended anti-social snarl of frustration, the song had become the totem of a generation, and the spectre of 'yuppies singing along to [it] in their BMWs' haunted Cobain until his death.

To the millions who bought 'Teen Spirit' and the accompanying album, Cobain was a defining symbol, a spokesman and, crucially, a purveyor of good tunes. First and second albums tend to be regarded primarily as pointers to the future, but *Nevermind* was the finished article. The true irony of the record is that it is as much a self-contradiction as anything Cobain ever did: a so-called 'cult classic' that reached the slopes of commercial triumph; praised for its spontaneity, yet nearly two years in the making. The tension between the grunge activist and the expert craftsman of pop standards was, of course, the chief dilemma of Cobain's life. The fates had showered upon this unlikely recipient creative gifts that were almost unparalleled. Yet he also worked at his music with unusual care, moulding and teasing the raw material of 'Sheep' into the end-product of *Nevermind*. Thus, 'Pay To Play', a song that had been around for years, evolved through a thematic make-over and a significant name change into 'Stay Away'. 'On A Plain' and 'Something In The Way', both dealing angrily with Cobain's time in Aberdeen, received the same melodic treatment. From the naggingly familiar riff and typically opaque lyric of 'Teen Spirit' to the caterwauling finale of 'Endless, Nameless', *Nevermind* was an attempt by Cobain to stick to the pop-rock songbook while re-emphasizing his punk credentials.

In effect, this meant collecting influences and making something entirely fresh and new out of them, a feat not achieved by most of Cobain's highly touted contemporaries. 'Lithium', 'In Bloom' (Love's favourite) and 'Breed' (previously 'Imodium') all coated enviably simple tunes in a blizzard of super-distorted guitar noise and ingenious arrangements, each recalling Nirvana's droll self-portrayal as 'the Bay City Rollers being molested by Black Flag'. 'Come As You Are' was like nothing at all. With its subdued two-chord guitar, murky sound and paradoxical urging to 'Take your time, hurry up', Cobain threw aside the stylistic straitjacket to create a new genre that fell somewhere between the two influences. If *Nevermind* acquiesced to Cobain's sweeter side and ultimately felt like the result of a record company compromise, at least one of its tracks drew blood with nine repeats of a line – 'I swear that I don't have a gun' – that cut to the emotional bone. This was the song that exemplified Cobain's skill at instilling meaning into dense, noisy rock, and one quoted incessantly in the days following his suicide.

It does nothing to diminish *Nevermind*'s appeal to say there was a formula at work; a formula in both the production and the music, which *Rolling Stone* described as 'sturdy melodic structures (being) attacked with frenzied screaming and guitar havoc'. This was Cobain's staple songwriting technique: a spoken or strummed intro, the blackboard-scratching screech of the chorus catching its breath back into a mumbled, and often incoherent finale. 'It was "tension and release" epitomized,' says Warren Mason. The multi-million-selling triumph of *Nevermind* had begun, almost incredibly, exactly ten years earlier, when he first gave the teenage student guitar lessons in Aberdeen. The sound Cobain had been chasing for a decade turned out to be a raw, grunge-tinged rock with conventional pop undertones and a lavish mix. *Nevermind* captured this crossover perfectly – every chorus was hummable, every solo was inventive and Cobain's voice was so versatile it effectively served as a fourth instrument. 'All we did was just put out a record,' Novoselic would insist in dazed response to the worldwide Nirvanamania. With its classic, three-minute singles, lusty swings of Cobain's guitar and, above all, in the impeccable timing of its release, *Nevermind* was, however, much more than 'just a record'. Like all genius moves, only in hindsight does the result seem inevitable. When the history comes to be written, *Nevermind* will be a contender for the album of the decade, an all-things-to-all-people confection with the weird, and much admired ability to shift seamlessly from sarcastic to caring.

On 24 September 1991, the day the record was released, 46,000 copies were shipped to stores around America and 35,000 to Britain. By mid-October the album debuted on the *Billboard* charts, and Nirvana moved up the west coast on the last leg of a gruelling tour. Guns N' Roses requested backstage passes for themselves and entourage, while Metallica faxed their congratulations and offered Nirvana a support spot. The Seattle trio soon eclipsed them both. Outstripping *Metallica* and *Use Your Illusion 1* & *2*, *Nevermind* sold 400,000 copies a week during the Christmas season, and within a year went on to gross $50 million. According to Grant Alden, 'The Geffen marketing department, notorious for not knowing a good thing when they see it, were caught cold by *Nevermind*. When the madness started they had to pull other new albums from the presses, to try and keep pace with the demand for Nirvana.' In the last weeks of 1991 and early days of 1992 it was impossible to avoid the plethora of cover stories and articles about the group, to ignore the critical plaudits, or to switch on MTV without seeing the 'Teen Spirit' video. Alden himself believes that in the way *Nevermind* became a unifying link between 'the millions of twentysomethings opposed to the war and depressed by conditions at home', it coalesced a 'general feeling of anger and boredom into the determination that something should be done'. According to this reading, *Nevermind* was as responsible as anything else for a huge upswing in anti-Republican sentiment, and ultimately for the election of Bill Clinton as president.

As critics pondered the 'strangely riveting' and 'mesmerizing' mix of upbeat songs with aggressively melancholy lyrics, and *Nevermind* dragged alternative rock into the mainstream virtually overnight, one man stood aloof from the outpouring of praise compared by *The Times* to Beatlemania. Cobain's creative pride was limited. When the members of Nirvana had been rehearsing *Nevermind* in North Pear Street, they occasionally filled in time between sessions by firing guns at the Washington State lottery building. By an ironic twist, Jonathan Poneman now described the group as having 'won the lottery'. Poneman's and Sub Pop's view was that all the pieces had fallen into place to allow a record like *Nevermind* to 'happen', and Cobain hurried to join the consensus. In an interview that October, he struck Patrick MacDonald as 'genuinely surprised that a song with the same name as a deodorant was a hit', excited but bemused by the prospect of success, and unresponsive and unwilling to explain the meaning of an album whose very title was, after all, a shrug of indifference.

Nirvana began a six-week European tour in Bristol on 4 November 1991. When Cobain had first played in Britain two years before, he complained of being homesick and depressed, and angry at the lack of opportunities to boost his album. Now he was meeting fifteen journalists a day and 'Teen Spirit' was aired on the radio continually. The 'shitola' surroundings of 1989 had become the luxury hotels of 1991, and as *Nevermind* rose in the chart the group's *per diem* grew proportionately. For the first time in his life, Cobain's reputation matched his self-image. He was, it appeared, a far better politician than he let on. As he told Tim Arnold, he was busy advertising himself. He had made 'people talk' about him. It was all paying off.

Cobain reacted to fame by a spree of drugs and drink, by renewing his affair with Courtney Love, and by distorting his stage act to the edge of madness. Later that month, Nirvana arrived in London. One evening, after a full day of drinking, Cobain began to experience delirium tremens in front of his colleagues and friends, crying out that rats were leaping at him. Arnold telephoned Nirvana's tour doctor and learned that Cobain's alcohol consumption had already damaged his liver. When he confronted him about the matter the next morning, Cobain flew into a rage. 'Kiss my ass,' he shouted. After a time, Novoselic angrily shoved a bottle of whisky in front of his old friend and told him to drink it without further ado.

In Amsterdam Cobain and Love graduated from alcohol to heroin abuse. By Thanksgiving he was taking the drug so often that close friends and a few journalists recognized the signs of addiction. He slurred his words and regularly fell asleep in the middle of conversations. A *Vrij Nederland* reporter called on Cobain at nine one morning, finding him lying dazed on his hotel room bed holding a needle and phial. Press Association reporter Graham Wright saw him eat six or seven pills, and snort from off a £5 note for breakfast. An ex-girlfriend watched Cobain down a bottle of cough syrup before stepping on stage in France.

Love's introduction to Nirvana greatly contributed to Cobain's self-projection as aloof, different and more impulsive than his colleagues. 'They're all so fucking boring,' he told Azerrad. 'There's no one willing to take risks, like "Let's just take off". It's always such a strict regimen – "Let's get to the show, let's play, let's eat dinner and go to sleep". I just got tired of it.' Now, in order to register protest, the couple were 'scoring drugs and fucking up against a wall outside and causing scenes'. In Holland there was a morning when Cobain arrived at his hotel, stark naked and dripping with blood, and in response to the manager's request to get dressed, re-appeared at the desk moments later clothed in Love's underwear. 'I think everyone was taken aback a bit at first,' says Nirvana's road manager Alex MacLeod. '[Love] would appear and it was like a tornado coming.' Even this pales by comparison to the memory of a second member of the entourage: 'You know those experiments where two elements react to each other? Kurt and Courtney related in the way petrol relates to a naked flame.' On 5 December, as they lay in bed in Rennes, the couple decided to get married.

While they were in London Nirvana recorded another session, this time for the disc jockey Mark Goodier. Miti Adhikari remembers Cobain appearing at the studio in Maida Vale fuming that he'd been 'treated like shit' the previous night on *The Word*, and spending the hour prior to recording curled up in a ball on the floor. When the time came to play, 'Kurt was a changed man, leading the band through an electric version of "Polly", cueing in the solos, scowling at Grohl, and generally coming across like a typical rock star.' As the music faded Cobain was back to his previous tack, commenting disparagingly on his hotel, refusing to join Adhikari, Novoselic and Grohl for a drink, and brightening only when an assistant arrived with news that *Nevermind* had reached the *Billboard* Top Ten that morning. 'He was quite separate from Dave and Chris,' says Adhikari; 'like someone in a different dimension. Kurt could come across as the angry punk, or equally as the mumbling sleepwalker. There was no middle ground to him.'

During his earlier years, even though he sought to epitomize violence, ambition and drive, Cobain was relatively stable, clear-headed and usually mild-mannered. He drank and took drugs, he was outspoken and could be cruel, but he tried to avoid rock star conceits. Quiet, diffident and sometimes affable, he carried within himself seeds of his later appearance, and these had blossomed by 1991 and turned him into an exaggeration, a self-caricature. Whereas Cobain's concerts had always been hit-or-miss affairs, it would have been unthinkable, a year or two earlier, for him to have cancelled a tour of Scandinavia on the grounds that he 'didn't give a shit'. Now, when he returned to his hotel after the BBC session, Cobain took one of his six custom-built Stratocasters and smashed it repeatedly into the wall, splintering the frame and throwing the debris out of the window into the street. Later that night he had to be treated in hospital for a drug overdose, described to reporters as exhaustion.

Cobain had achieved celebrity on a scale unprecedented in punk-rock. But he paid the price of being famous as much for his anarchic lifestyle as for his work. For the rest of his days Cobain would complain about the burden of success. The dark path of public exposure would lead to a dead end. Mobs followed him about and Cobain, who only a year earlier had been known to amble onstage from a place in the crowd, learned to hurry out of the stage doors of amphitheatres and skating-rinks and make his way to safety through side streets and blocked-off alleyways. 'He began to lose track of his audience,' says a friend. 'Self-doubt set in, and Kurt found himself the object of curiosity of people he hated.' A fan club was organized, and according to its president Nils Bernstein, 'most of the letters were along the lines of "Hey, dude, I saw your video and bought your tape! You guys kick ass!"' It was inevitable that, in successfully raising his profile, Cobain ran the risk of attracting an equally raised interest from the public and press. Stories began to appear about him in the tabloids, hinting at his heroin habit and, in one case, accusing him of having become an 'American celebrity'. Cobain responded by dyeing his hair red, by promoting the 'revolutionary debris' of his lyrics (like his music, rarely more than a clever combination of opposites) and by straining for punk credibility on a track like 'Beeswax', included on the *Kill Rock Stars* compilation that summer. All his life Cobain had sought acceptance and support. Now, when his own mother congratulated him on the success of *Nevermind*, he flew into a rage, smashing the window of his old bedroom in Aberdeen and complaining that the record was 'crap'. In a few moments Cobain would calm down sufficiently to tell Patrick MacDonald, 'I'm here because my Mom feeds me.' But the incident reflected in miniature the conflict that was being enacted inside East 1st Street. To Wendy O'Connor, it was obvious that fame was a reward worth having at any cost. To Cobain, nothing made up for the intrusion into his private life. Realistically, it would be impossible for him to ever recapture the feeling of freedom he had known before *Nevermind*, but it did not stop him fighting the battle to the death.

One reason Cobain railed against success was that it came to symbolize a barrier between himself and his original audience. As *Nevermind* went gold and platinum, there were mutterings in Nirvana's home town that the group had cashed in and Cobain himself become 'Johnny Superstar'. In late August a six-day alternative music festival had drawn thousands of fans to Olympia, where groups like the Melvins and L7 performed under a sign proclaiming 'No lackeys to the corporate ogre', while Nirvana played in the ballrooms and opera houses of Europe. By December, when *Nevermind* was jostling with new releases by Garth Brooks and Michael Jackson, the letter pages of the weeklies had begun to bristle with accusations of selling out. According to Johnny Rotten, a punk icon with first-hand knowledge of the mainstream, 'It must have stuck in Kurt's craw to become a pillar of the establishment overnight.'

Despite their impeccable grunge credentials – low-slung guitars, volume and the titanic aggression that fuelled *Nevermind* – Nirvana would never escape from the taint of commercial success. In Graham Wright's words, 'it tortured Kurt that he'd been taken up by people he loathed, and forced to tone down his music'. According to *Rolling Stone*: 'Alienation [had] paid off for Nirvana with *Nevermind*, a wail from the Washington State wilderness that [was] equal parts complacency and rage.' Another critic likened Cobain's voice to a 'Sinatra-meets-Satan growl'. In Europe that winter Nirvana made their own comment on artistic compromise by playing a version of The Who's 'Baba O'Riley', illustrated by Cobain spitting or shaking his fist at the crowd. As self-parody was followed in turn by confusion, Novoselic was heard to complain, 'I wish we could have a time machine and go back to two months ago', while Cobain muttered gloomily, 'It won't last very long' and 'We'll do something to fuck up, I know we will.'

It was an important part of Cobain's self-esteem that he never wanted to be seen as a conventional, grasping rock star. From his public shows of indifference, his apathetic dismissal of 'Teen Spirit' and his tendency to sleep through press conferences, the intended image was of a self-contained young stoic. A snapshot of Cobain as *Nevermind* was released appeared in *New Musical Express* on 21 September 1991:

> Anyone who's ever seen Kurdt Kobain [*sic*] on stage will concur that hot fires burn barely below the surface, but in person Kurdt is on some permanent audition for the part of the dormouse in *Alice In Wonderland*.
>
> 'Urm,' he mumbles. 'I'm narcoleptic, so I have a hard time being motivated at anytime.
>
> 'It's just that we don't have the patience to deal with all the managerial problems and the business part of the band,' says Kurdt. 'I don't care enough about it to deal with it. I forget things all the time. When people would call up and try to book a show, I just wouldn't give a fuck.'

Three weeks later, after a concert at the Cabaret Metro in Chicago, Cobain attended the opening of *My Own Private Idaho* (a film he admired) and secured a front-row seat on the basis of being 'the guy from Nirvana'. After the performance he heckled a singer in a local club with the words, 'Betty! I wanna suck your pussy!' When bouncers suggested that Cobain's presence would be more sparingly required, a punch was thrown which, according to one witness, 'Kurt countered by bawling "Don't hurt my hands! Don't hurt my hands!" The whole place was cheering when he was thrown out.' Next, Cobain woke his tour manager with a violent harangue about the quality of the previous night's sound-mix. After it was agreed that, in future, the guitar and vocals would be highlighted at the expense of the bass and drums, Cobain left to place a call to the Geffen sales department. He went nearly berserk, according to the man who took it, that *Nevermind* had only just that morning reached the chart. 'In Kurt's view of the universe, it should have been number one the day of release.' The evening supposedly ended with Cobain and Love having sex in the closed but not deserted hotel bar, then engaging in an equally public row as to which of the two was the bigger star.

His colleagues regarded Cobain with ambivalent feelings. They accepted him generally with affection and respect for his sincerity, talent and sensitivity. They smiled in condescension over his naïve earnestness and self-promotion. They believed that he tried too hard and had too much 'front', and they were uncomfortable with his obsessive concern with future glory, which he could not resist confessing from time to time.

He had no close friends.

The generally admiring tone of the press and public was not shared by all who knew Cobain professionally. After an anarchic performance on *The Jonathan Ross Show* (when Cobain refused to play the agreed 'Lithium', substituting an off-key version of 'Territorial Pissings'), a stage-manager commented that this was 'infantilism raised to an art' and that, so far from not caring, Cobain's behaviour backstage was like a spoiled brat. He performed the same trick on *Top of the Pops*, where Cobain chose to sing 'Teen Spirit' in a voice like Captain Beefheart's and expressed his disgust for his hosts by being violently sick in the dressing-room.

Late in 1991, a religious-rock group named Nirvana had issued cease-and-desist orders against TV and radio stations playing *Nevermind*; the suit was eventually settled for $50,000. Meanwhile, Cobain's British fame had brought him to the attention of Patrick Campbell-Lyons, coincidentally also the leader of a group called Nirvana, this one dating from 1967. The solicitor to the Musicians Union despatched a polite letter of protest on Campbell-Lyons' behalf, to no avail. The British Nirvana then hired a west coast lawyer with the striking name of Debbi Drooz to hurl writs at Cobain and his record company. After two years of what Campbell-Lyons calls 'legal nonsense', the case was settled. According to well-informed sources, Campbell-Lyons and his partner were paid $100,000 (minus Drooz's 30 per cent fee) and an agreement was reached for the two groups to co-exist. Campbell-Lyons has two observations: that the 'head-banging' nature of the negotiations proves that 'Cobain and Geffen certainly weren't disinterested when it came to money', and that *Nevermind* had a startlingly similar front cover to Campbell-Lyons' own LP *Simon Simopath*, which he thinks likely influenced the later work.

As part of the settlement Cobain also gave an undertaking not to trespass on the British group's territory by dabbling in psychedelic rock. Since the chorus of a typical Campbell-Lyons song runs, 'Many miles to go/How many bridges do we cross?/Winter rain and snow/Over mountains high and low' it can be taken that Cobain willingly agreed to the condition. Not much confusion could have existed, either, between Campbell-Lyons' *Top of the Pops* performances with classic 1967 regalia – paisley tunics, frills, and heels stacked like tower-blocks – and Cobain's own drug-ravaged appearance. Apart from spitting into the crowd and the lens of any photographer brave enough to film him, Cobain's stage-act included exposing himself, openly swallowing drugs and alcohol, and regularly taunting the stewards forming a thin line between himself and the audience. This last tactic back-fired at a show in Dallas, where Cobain jumped into the crowd and was forcibly pulled back by his hair by a bouncer. In the ensuing fracas Cobain swung his guitar at the man's face, gashing him on the forehead, and a full-scale brawl erupted onstage. The edited footage of the incident later won an award in the category of 'best rock documentary'. These images of Cobain stage-diving and manhandling his guitar, being passed from head to head as he played the madcap solo to 'Love Buzz', achieved an almost iconographic quality in the early nineties. Nirvana's world tour from September 1991 to February 1992 won Cobain more publicity than any activity he had undertaken since forming a group. The principle was not lost on him: he could labour for months over a song with barely a ripple of attention in the press, but by being photographed at the centre of a mob orgy he became an overnight celebrity. For three years titles like the *Rocket* and *Melody Maker* had talked about Nirvana. Now the *New York Times* devoted 2,000 words to the 'Cobain phenomenon' and smaller newspapers all over the country followed suit.

Cobain began to play up to the myth. When he walked on stage, wearing a weird mixture of deliberately cheap clothes and outré touches like a woman's necklace or tiara, his first priority was to pinpoint the number and location of the cameras filming him. Next, looking as humble as a man in costume jewellery and a glaring spotlight can, Cobain would mumble the mocking lyrics to 'Lithium', howling the mammoth chorus before accelerating into a wild race to the song's finish. With the exception of the unnervingly stark 'Polly' and the occasional acoustic ballad, the assault kept up through fifteen numbers and ninety minutes of tightly packaged theatrical rock, climaxing in Cobain stabbing his amplifier with his guitar neck and hurling the instrument into the drums. While there was praise for the 'pure punk ethos' Nirvana still embodied, there were others, like Cobain himself, who saw touches of self-parody in the performance, and at least one critic who believed 'Kurt was making something essentially easy look hard'.

Contempt for ordinary folk who had gone in for things like jobs and marriages was much to the fore in Cobain's tirades. In one outburst he spoke of 'suburban fuckwits', 'the masses – fobbed off with gadgets' and 'office geeks' before introducing 'Teen Spirit'. Along with reporters, another target of knee-jerk recoil, such types were stigmatized as 'dead to the world'. A sure sign of these devitalized specimens, Cobain continued, was that they clung like leeches to the routine and familiar. Since he himself – parroting routine punk-rock poses – was doing precisely this, it seemed an unwise attitude to adopt. A reaction against the sight of a half-educated twenty-four-year-old hectoring the crowd was inevitable, and even as the first wave of Nirvanamania broke, a backlash had set in. According to the *Source*, buffoonery now entered the performance. In Graham Wright's view, 'Kurt went mildly crazy in the six months after *Nevermind*, at which point he went insane.' In his calmer moments Cobain himself recognized the problem, opening his concerts with The Who's self-scoffing anthem, and admitting to *Rolling Stone* that he was in danger of 'blowing it'.

One of the cameramen regularly stalking Cobain that winter went on to release the documentary *1991: The Year Punk Broke*. (As well as Dave Markey's footage of Nirvana at the Reading Festival, there was the offstage moment when Love spat straight into the lens, 'Kurt Cobain makes my heart stop. But he's a shit.') The film was only part of the lurid mix of media circus and cultural theatre that descended on Seattle. For weeks at a time in the winter of 1991–2 the runway at Boeing Field was clogged with executive jets bearing television crews and record moguls from New York. The parking lot on the east side of the Crocodile Café was jammed with as many satellite dishes and microwave trucks as normally attended the Super Bowl, and the lobby of every hotel was lined end to end with journalists seeking an interview with Cobain. Just as it had three years before, Seattle became the latest city to sell, and in the wake of *Nevermind* hometown groups were being signed at the rate of more than one a week. Within a year six albums with local connections appeared simultaneously in the Top Forty, and Nirvana were being aired not only on MTV, but also on *20/20* and *Nightline*. According to a BBC profile, Cobain 'transformed the rainy backwater of Seattle into youth culture's newest capital city, and led the biggest and most successful assault in years on the corporate pop mainstream'. Meanwhile, in September 1992 Cameron Crowe's *Singles*, sometimes uncharitably subtitled *Shiftless In Seattle*, went on worldwide release. The central theme of the picture, dozens of emotionally unfulfilled characters linked by the burgeoning local music scene, struck an immediate chord with the critics. To *Variety*, *Singles* gave 'proof positive that the spiritual and physical home of grunge rock [had] arrived'. According to *Time*, the film achieved the 'same freewheeling power of the city it celebrates'. In Britain the reviewers were more guarded, focusing on the satirically inept dialogue (including such lines as 'Are my breasts too small for you?') and wondering why, when the characters had so much, were they so unhappy? Eighteen months later, the same question would be asked, unanswerably, about Cobain.

In the wake of Nirvana's success and the renewed media attention that followed, ridiculous claims were made for Seattle. 'What had been a local scene evolved into a global phenomenon,' says Charles Peterson; 'and became a joke in the process.' *Vanity Fair* ran a fashion spread entitled 'Society Grunge', but *Vogue*'s 'Grunge & Glory' feature in 1992 took the send-up of the Northwest to new heights, with celebrity models posing in 'grungy' dresses that sold for the price of *Bleach*'s entire recording budget, and an accompanying article written by Poneman. According to Alice Wheeler, 'every band in town now expected to be signed for $500,000' and any musician with long hair and a plaid shirt was snapped up as the 'next Kurt'.

Ironically, probably the only people who were not overjoyed about Nirvana's good fortune were the group themselves. *Nevermind* had the inevitable effect of loosening the knot that had tied the three together. In his worsening drug addiction, in the pressure on him to perform and the need to 'explain' his latest lyric, Cobain became a being apart from Novoselic and Grohl. 'We're just now coming into doing so many interviews that we're becoming exhausted by it, at least I am,' he told the *Rocket*. 'I mean, every waking day of my life is Nirvana now. Phone interviews and just constantly being tooled around.' One of the results was that Cobain, always wilful and now for the first time with the money to indulge himself, became a sort of parody of backstage excess. As well as liquor in London and heroin in Amsterdam, there was an incident in Belgium where, spurred by a bottle of brandy, Cobain posed a pair of visiting fans, two fireworks and a can of shaving cream in a striking combination, then demanded the women perform cunnilingus on one another while he watched with the inevitable polaroid. Even this was mild compared to the scenes witnessed by one Nirvana-watcher involving Courtney Love and her fiancé on tour in Europe.

The other effect of Cobain's fame was that he began to lose touch with his audience. Before a homecoming concert at the Paramount in Seattle, Nirvana were visited by a photographer named Darrell Westmoreland. 'I told Novoselic they were unprepared for what was about to happen,' he recalls. 'Chris was pretty receptive, but Kurt was just kind of in and out. He'd joke around, then go into himself . . . sort of in a shell-like daze.' According to Tim Arnold: 'The hall that night was like a giant psychiatrist's office, with

Kurt spitting out his anxieties to the fans. This was [Cobain] pleasing himself, not the crowd.' Slim Moon, Cobain's friend and neighbour in Olympia, believes he 'got more and more paranoid about what people wanted, and what direction they expected him to go in'. 'Kurt lost his bearings,' says a friend.

When Love returned from her own tour in December 1991, she and Cobain moved from hotel to hotel in California, taking what she calls 'bad Mexican LA heroin', which Cobain injected into them both. He also spent two weeks on the streets of Seattle. One winter evening he appeared in the Canterbury, a bar and grill decorated incongruously with a suit of armour, a fireplace, a high ceiling with exposed beams and a clientele of sightseers. The place was silent as Cobain made his entrance: the flannel shirt, the unwashed blond hair, the torn jeans and sneakers all gave the tourists instant visual gratification: this was what they had come to see.

Cobain was pale and obviously ill. He sat alone in a corner of the room, sipping a coffee which he fortified from a bottle in his pocket. In the course of an hour he smoked a dozen cigarettes, burning them right down to the knuckle, with another lit before the first was out. From time to time he would half-smile or roll his eyes, all to his own thought process. His only comment was a grunted acknowledgement of well-wishers and the mumbled word 'Daddy' repeated to himself over and again. On his way out of the room he signed an autograph for a middle-aged fan and walked quickly into the street, leaving the door open behind him. The signature he gave the man was passed around the bar. It read, 'Fuck you. Kurt.'

When Cobain was thirteen his cousin Toni remembers him having spent one evening talking to a boy half his age, showing the 'unwittingly tender' side his fans still claimed on his behalf. In 1989 Cobain had befriended a six-year-old named Simon Fair Timony, a would-be pop singer who before his tenth birthday fronted the Nirvana-inspired group the Stinky Puffs.* At the 1992 Reading Festival, seconds after destroying the set and putting the finishing touches on his guitar by hurling it to the ground, Cobain walked offstage hand-in-hand with a small boy suffering from terminal cancer. According to a critic backstage: 'Kurt slowly descended a set of stairs as one klieg light beamed down on him. A crowd of people surrounded him, but somehow the light never touched them. It was very quiet, especially after the thunderous noise of the show. The crowd followed him down an alleyway made by the backstage tents. Then Kurt turned a corner, still hand in hand with the boy, and was gone.'

That Cobain was fond of children, particularly those with an illness or handicap, is certain. That he saw in them traces of his own childhood is also certain, but is not a phenomenon limited to Cobain. Where he differed from other punk-rockers was in his longing for roots and domesticity. His comment about Tobi Vail – 'I was definitely looking for somebody I could spend quite a few years with. I wanted that security' – will be remembered. Whatever the cause (and Love herself would say it was because it was 'a bad time to do it, and that appealed to me') Cobain and his fiancée began to engage in unprotected sex, even though they were mainlining heroin. By Christmas the couple knew what the world learnt in the New Year: Love was pregnant.

As 1991 ended Nirvana were on tour with Pearl Jam, the Seattle group formed from the ashes of Mother Love Bone, and a particular target of Cobain's scorn. Before a New Year's Eve concert in San Francisco, Pearl Jam's Eddie Vedder accepted an invitation to a drink with an attractive

* They actually exist.

female fan backstage. Apparently for her own amusement, the girl also invited Cobain, choosing to greet him with the words, 'Kurt, Eddie says you suck dick.' Cobain then informed his rival he was going to drag him out onstage and 'beat him to shit' with his guitar. The details of what followed are unclear, but it seems fairly certain that Vedder remonstrated with Cobain, and that the two fell into a noisy quarrel. At one point, according to the girl, Cobain pinned back Vedder's arms, kneed him twice in the groin and took a swing at him. (The man who broke up the tussle says 'Kurt aimed a wild punch, missed and fell into a bowl of dip on the buffet.') Cobain staggered back to Novoselic immediately after the incident and bragged that he had just kicked Vedder 'in the nuts'. He made a similar boast to Frank Hulme, a reporter present backstage. According to Hulme, 'when Kurt talked about it, his voice went high-pitched and he giggled like a girl'. Many in the Nirvana camp shared Cobain's glee over his random act of violence. 'Vedder was just asking for it in those days,' says a source connected to the group. To a man like Hulme, it was yet another example of Cobain's 'mounting rock-star psychosis'.

According to *Rolling Stone* the forty-five-minute concert that followed 'completely wrecked what was left of the audience's composure ... Members of the mosh pit, which stretched from the stage to the back of the arena, were being thrown in the air like clods of dirt caught up in a live minefield ... [Cobain], his hair dyed purple for the occasion, vacillated onstage between nearly cataleptic detachment and unnerving inner intensity. The instant the set finished, he and his band mates destroyed their instruments in a cheery display of wanton violence. They didn't just throw them around, either – they lovingly unscrewed each piece, the better to batter them into tiny little shards, while the audience howled with glee.'

There was no encore.

After Cobain (*above* with Novoselic and Grohl) cut his hair and donned glasses, the family commented on how much he resembled his father. *(Steve Double/Retna)*

The 'elegant din' of the 1992 Reading Festival. Cobain played the entire show in his hospital smock. *(Mick Hutson/Redferns)*

Kurt and Frances Cobain, 1992. The slogan on his T-shirt was premature. *(Stephen Sweet/Retna)*

Below In the studio at a Dutch radio station, November 1992. *(Michael Linssen/Redferns)*

Cobain arrives with his family at the MTV Music
Awards, September 1993, a changed man from the
year before. Nirvana won Best Alternative Video
for 'In Bloom'. *(Steve Granitz/Retna)*

The *In Utero* set, decorated like a wood and flanked
with winged mannequins, like the one on the
album's cover. *(Ebet Roberts/Redferns)*

A ritual exchange of a painting and a Leadbelly biography, but not drugs, took place with William Burroughs. *(Steve Speller/Retna)*

STAN BAKER SPORTS
10000 Lake City Way N.E.
SEATTLE, WASHINGTON 98125
(206) 522-4575

The receipt for the gun with which Cobain killed himself was made out to his friend Dylan Carlson, shown below on his own band's publicity sheet. *(Sub Pop)*

DYLAN CARLSON   DAVE HARWELL

EARTH

SUB POP RECORDS
1932 First Avenue
Suite 1103
Seattle, WA 98101
TEL: (206) 441-8441

171 Lake Washington Boulevard East, Seattle. The detached room where Cobain killed himself is in the foreground. *(J. Farrar)*

8 April, 1994. *(Seattle Times)*

Love and her friend Kat Bjelland leave Cobain's public wake. *(Gamma)*

The crime laboratory report proving that Cobain wrote the note found at the suicide scene. *(L. Poort)*

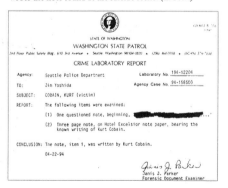

STATE OF WASHINGTON

WASHINGTON STATE PATROL

2nd Floor Public Safety Bldg. 610 3rd Avenue • Seattle, Washington 98104-1820 • (206) 464-7038 • (SCAN) 3's-7038

CRIME LABORATORY REPORT

Agency:	Seattle Police Department	Laboratory No.	194-12204
TO:	Jim Yoshida	Agency Case No.	94-156500
SUBJECT:	COBAIN, KURT (victim)		

REPORT: The following items were examined:

(1) One questioned note, beginning, ▄▄▄▄▄▄▄▄▄▄▄▄..."

(2) Three page note, on Hotel Excelsior note paper, bearing the known writing of Kurt Cobain.

CONCLUSION: The note, item 1, was written by Kurt Cobain.

04-22-94

Janis J. Parker
Janis J. Parker
Forensic Document Examiner

STATE OF WASHINGTON
DEPARTMENT OF HEALTH

Health

CERTIFICATE OF DEATH

LOCAL FILE NUMBER: 3471

146

STATE FILE NUMBER: 4 09454

1. NAME First	Middle	Last	2. SEX (M / F)	3. DEATH DATE (Mo, Day, Yr)
KURT DONALD		COBAIN	Male	4/5/1994

| 4. AGE LAST BIRTH 27 | 5. UNDER 1 YEAR MOS / DAYS | 6. UNDER 1 DAY HOURS / MINS | 7. BIRTHDATE (Mo, Day, Yr) Feb 20, 1967 | 8. BIRTHPLACE (City, State or Foreign Country) Aberdeen, WA | 9. WAS DECEDENT EVER IN U.S. ARMED FORCES? (Yes / No) No | 10. COUNTY OF DEATH King |

| 11. CITY, TOWN OR LOCATION OF DEATH Seattle | 12. PLACE OF DEATH—XX BOX FOR PLACE THEN GIVE ADDRESS OR INSTITUTION NAME 171 Lake Washington Blvd East | 13. SMOKING IN LAST 15 YEARS? (Yes / No) Yes |

| 14. MARITAL STATUS Married | 15. SURVIVING SPOUSE (if wife, give maiden name) Courtney Love | 16. SOCIAL SECURITY NO. 536 90 4399 | 17. DECEDENT'S EDUCATION Elementary/Secondary (0-12) 12 | College (1-4 or 5+) |

| 18. USUAL OCCUPATION Poet/Musician | 19. KIND OF BUSINESS OR INDUSTRY Punk Rock | 20. Was Decedent of Hispanic origin or descent? (Ancestry) (Yes / No) Specify: No | 21. RACE (Specify) White |

| 22. RESIDENCE—NUMBER AND STREET 171 Lake Washington Blvd E. | 23. CITY/TOWN, OR LOCATION Seattle | 24. INSIDE CITY LIMITS? (Yes / No) Yes | 25A. COUNTY King | 25B. LENGTH OF RES. 3 Yrs | 26. STATE WA | 27. ZIP CODE 98112 |

| 28. FATHER'S NAME—FIRST, MIDDLE, LAST Donald Cobain | 29. MOTHER'S NAME—FIRST, MIDDLE, MAIDEN SURNAME Wendy Elizabeth Fraidenberg |

| 30. INFORMANT—NAME Courtney Love Cobain | 31. MAILING ADDRESS Codikow-Carroll 9113 Sunset Blvd, Los Angeles, CA 90069 |

| 32. BURIAL, CREMATION, REMOVAL, OTHER Cremation | 33. DATE (Mo, Day, Yr) 04/14/1994 | 34. CEMETERY/CREMATORY—NAME Uniservice Crematory | 35. LOCATION—CITY/TOWN, STATE Seattle, Washington |

| 36. FUNERAL DIRECTOR SIGNATURE | 37. NAME OF FACILITY Bleitz Funeral Home 316 Florentia St, Seattle, Washington 98109 |

TO BE COMPLETED ONLY BY CERTIFYING PHYSICIAN | TO BE COMPLETED ONLY BY MEDICAL EXAMINER OR CORONER

| 38. TO THE BEST OF MY KNOWLEDGE, DEATH OCCURRED AT THE TIME, DATE AND PLACE AND WAS DUE TO THE CAUSE(S) STATED. SIGNATURE AND TITLE X | 43. ON THE BASIS OF EXAMINATION AND/OR INVESTIGATION, IN MY OPINION DEATH OCCURRED AT THE TIME, DATE AND PLACE AND WAS DUE TO THE CAUSE(S) STATED SIGNATURE AND TITLE Nikolas Hartshorne MD |

| 40. DATE SIGNED (Mo, Day, Yr) | 41. HOUR OF DEATH (24 Hrs) | 44. DATE SIGNED (Mo, Day, Yr) April 9, 1994 | 45. HOUR OF DEATH (24 Hrs) 2PM |
| 42. NAME AND TITLE OF ATTENDING PHYSICIAN IF OTHER THAN CERTIFIER (Type or Print) | | 46. PRONOUNCED DEAD (Mo, Day, Yr) April 8, 1994 | 47. HOUR PRONOUNCED DEAD (24 Hrs) 1030 h |

| 48. NAME AND TITLE OF MEDICAL EXAMINER OR CORONER (Type or Print) NIKOLAS J. HARTSHORNE, M.D. ASSISTANT MEDICAL EXAMINER 325 9th Avenue, Seattle, WA 98104 | 49. ME/CORONER FILE NUMBER KCME 94-399 |

50. ENTER THE DISEASES, INJURIES, OR COMPLICATIONS WHICH CAUSED THE DEATH:

		INTERVAL BETWEEN ONSET AND DEATH
IMMEDIATE CAUSE (Final disease or condition resulting in death)	A. Contact perforating shotgun wound to head	
DUE TO, OR AS A CONSEQUENCE OF	B. (mouth)	
DUE TO, OR AS A CONSEQUENCE OF	C.	
DUE TO, OR AS A CONSEQUENCE OF	D.	

| 51. OTHER SIGNIFICANT CONDITIONS—CONDITIONS CONTRIBUTING TO DEATH BUT NOT RESULTING IN THE UNDERLYING CAUSE GIVEN ABOVE. | 52. AUTOPSY? (Yes / No) Yes | 53. WAS CASE REFERRED TO MEDICAL EXAMINER OR CORONER? (Yes / No) Yes |

| 54. ACC, SUICIDE, HOM, UNDET, OR PENDING INVEST. (Specify) Suicide | 55. INJURY DATE (Mo, Day, Yr) 4/5/1994 | 56. HOUR OF INJURY (24 Hrs) ?PM | 57. DESCRIBE HOW INJURY OCCURRED: Self-inflicted shotgun wound |

| 58. INJURY AT WORK? (Yes / No) No | 59. PLACE OF INJURY—AT HOME, FARM, STREET, FACTORY, OFFICE BLDG, ETC (Specify) Residence | 60. LOCATION—STREET OR RFD NO, CITY/TOWN, STATE Seattle King County Washington |

| 61. RECORD AMENDMENT (Register use only) ITEM | DOCUMENTARY EVIDENCE | REVIEWED BY | DATE | 62. REGISTRAR SIGNATURE X | 63. DATE RECEIVED (Mo, Day, Yr) APR 14 1994 |

FOR INSTRUCTIONS SEE BACK AND HANDBOOK

DOH 110-006 (Rev. 7/91) (formerly DSHS 9-150)
DOH 01-033 (5/9)
A

The death certificate. *(L. Poort)*

Come as you are. *(Michael Linssen/Redferns)*

Eleven days later Nirvana recorded a live set for MTV and played *Saturday Night Live* in New York. By then Cobain's rock-star conceits went further than even Frank Hulme knew. Grohl remembers 'walking into [Cobain's and Love's] hotel room and for the first time, really realizing that these two were fucked *up*. They were just nodding out in bed, just wasted.' When a *Saturday Night Live* staffer went to deliver a package to Nirvana's dressing-room he found 'Kurt giving [a woman] oral sex on the edge of the sink', a procedure he interrupted long enough to spit in the stagehand's face. At a session with the photographer Michael Lavine, Cobain, in his favourite Flipper T-shirt, squabbled furiously with Novoselic and Grohl, lifted up the shirt to expose the various bruises, welts and track-marks on his chest and arms, then fell asleep in front of the camera. According to the same *SNL* employee, 'Kurt may have been about punk rock once, but by the time I saw him he was swaggering about, stoned, like one of Led Zeppelin.' Even when Cobain sought to protest his becoming a 'corporate whore' and to 'fuck Aberdeen' by french-kissing Novoselic during the show's closing credits, he only succeeded in raising the spectre of superstar rock: Mick Jagger had done the same thing, on the identical programme, thirteen years before.

The next morning, 12 January 1992, *Nevermind* went to number one on the chart.

7

Wasted

Cobain, Love and their heroin supplier spent a week in New York following *Saturday Night Live*. It was suitably debauched. When the dealer proved unreliable Cobain himself bought drugs on the street while his pregnant fiancée waited in their hotel. In the months that followed there were dramatic reports of binge drinking, violence and sexual involvement with third parties as the couple moved first from Manhattan to Seattle, then to an apartment in the Fairfax area of Los Angeles. Despite giving an interviewer the impression that his day-to-day existence was 'fairly routine', Cobain struck at least one visitor as 'wild . . . a virtual lunatic'. According to Frank Hulme, 'Kurt was doing $100-a-day of heroin, chasing it down with cough syrup, then falling asleep with a lit cigarette in his mouth.' Diagnosis was simple: 'A young man in despair.'

There are a thousand ways for a twenty-four-year-old to find unhappiness, and few of them involve making millions of dollars. The money merely adds poignancy. But relentless pressure – to fulfil his ambitions and to make the record company rich – had done the job in Cobain's case. No one who starts taking drugs ever thinks they will get addicted. It just happens. In the last days of 1991 and the first weeks of 1992 Geffen and Gold Mountain continued to insist Cobain was happy, healthy, writing new material and 'enjoying the chance to live quietly with his girlfriend'. The reality was that he was almost constantly stupefied by drugs. In the intervals when he was not buying heroin and methadone, Cobain devoted extended passages of his day to self-flagellation and fascinated self-analysis. 'I'm too much of a creepy, negative person . . . A sicko . . . Desperate . . . The pathological type.' He also described himself as 'ugly, awkward, uptight and socially retarded'.

By the time Nirvana met to shoot the video for 'Come As You Are' Cobain was unrecognizable from the man of a year before. He arrived on location in the Hollywood Hills wearing a heavy overcoat – to face 70° weather. He seemed listless and detached, and his sole comment to the director was that he wanted himself 'blurred'. (This was achieved by filming Cobain's face through running water.) According to Grohl, Cobain 'looked bad. Grey. I didn't understand addiction and so I just thought, "What the fuck are you thinking? Why are you doing this?"' Even that paled by comparison to Novoselic's reaction. At one point he looked wearily at his old friend and said, 'Why not put us all out of our misery?' Later that night he made it clear to Cobain he was 'fucked up and needed help'.

On 24 January Nirvana began a six-week tour of Australia, New Zealand and Japan. It was a disaster. Within a week even Grohl was forced to admit 'everyone knew it was a mistake'; Novoselic's views can only be guessed. Apart from the anxiety and risk of drug-trafficking in a foreign country, Cobain's stomach pain now returned with doubled intensity. He made an appointment with an unsympathetic Australian doctor who assumed – wrongly, Cobain insisted – that his real problem was his addiction. A second GP, with a picture of himself and Keith Richards on his wall, prescribed methadone. By the time the tour ended in Hawaii Cobain was back to his daily dosage of opiates.

All the capacities of psychotic rage and hysteria he had enlarged through heroin were stretched to the limit on tour. For years Cobain had ended his concerts by splintering his guitar and amplifier, taking wild offence at the drums and screaming at Novoselic like a madman. Now, the stage persona became the reality. In New Zealand Cobain pushed a table laden with bottles and plates out of his fifteenth-floor hotel window. This piece of what Hulme calls 'rock-star psychosis' was followed by another. At the next stop in Singapore, Cobain informed Novoselic and Grohl he was 'fucked off' at being 'the fall-guy for Nirvana', and insisted he receive a higher share of the group's publishing royalties. 'Not only that,' says a witness to the scene. 'He had a roadie bring Chris to his hotel suite to tell him.' Throughout the Far East tour Cobain prompted instant dislike as well as intense devotion. When Nirvana reached Japan he ignored the record company representatives sent to meet him at the airport, stepped outside the terminal, belched theatrically, and announced he was there to 'repay the cunts for Pearl Harbor'.

Part of Cobain's behaviour was undoubtedly beyond his control. A sick man like himself, who once informed his mother nonchalantly that he woke up every day of his life in pain, who spent five years with chronically bad digestion, was likely to show personality defects for another reason. As he dosed himself with heroin, valium, cocaine and marijuana, Cobain aggravated not only his stomach, but what the doctors now call a bipolar disorder.

According to the US department of health, the condition shows itself in 'alternating bouts of dejection and mania'. When depressed, the sufferer is likely to have 'persistent sad, anxious or "empty" feelings', 'a general sense of hopelessness and pessimism', decreased energy, and sleep disturbances characterized by 'insomnia, early-morning waking, or oversleeping'. In the manic phase, individuals typically feel an 'unrealistic belief in their own abilities', 'swings of mood elevation and irritability', increased energy, and an 'aggressive response to frustration'.

This was Cobain's lot. To say that he might have benefited from some strong, humanly sympathetic figure only states the obvious. To Beverley Cobain, 'it was Kurt's greatest tragedy that no one was there to save him from himself'. Neither Nirvana's manager, nor David Geffen – and certainly not the friends who laughed and applauded as he vomited in front of them – ever plausibly suggested he curb his drug use. This conspiracy of silence applied equally to Cobain's entourage. 'I couldn't understand,' says Grohl. 'If something like that is destroying somebody ... I guess I don't understand addiction.' Michael Lavine admitted 'I didn't have enough guts to [confront him.]' Cobain himself, he told Azerrad, would remember only, 'Dead silence. Dirty looks and dead silence. [Novoselic and Grohl] weren't the type to confront anyone about anything. They were so passive-aggressive that they'd rather give off bad vibes than talk about anything.' For years Cobain had admitted to a crippling inability to address a problem until it was too late. This ironic light had now to be cast on his own treatment by others. For the rest of his life – over two years – almost all Cobain's friends would staunchly deny that he ever had a serious drug problem.

When, in 1994, every newspaper headlined the news of Cobain's violent suicide, a campaign began to preserve the myth; to die at the height of his power, escaping the horrors of middle age and decreasing fame, to end not with a whimper but with a bang that reverberated around the world – that truly was the fate Cobain's friends would have chosen for him. The role played by drugs was discounted. 'Just blaming [Cobain's death] on smack is stupid,' said Novoselic. 'People have been taking smack for a hundred years. It was just a small part of his life.' According to this version, Cobain took heroin for its analgesic qualities, not to enjoy himself, and along with the feelings of anger and betrayal, went a broad streak of denial that his addiction had hastened the end. In a long harangue in *Spin*, Love would complain,

'All they want to talk about is how much drugs Kurt and I did. That is not all we did. We had a life. We ate breakfast. We ate lunch. We ate dinner. We rented movies, and ate ice cream. We would read out loud to each other almost every night, and we prayed every night. We had some fucking dignity.'

All of those things were true. Until he was nine, Cobain was raised in a normal working-class home; although he could never reject Aberdeen enough, some of its habits and customs stuck with him. Among these was a refreshing humanity and simplicity of outlook that survived the ravages of his later fame. When in the mood, he could be exceptionally kind, sensitive and considerate of others. He was, in some senses, the antithesis of rock star vanity.

Only after he was twenty-five would Cobain the man clash seriously with Cobain the rock icon. With the release of *Nevermind* and 'Teen Spirit', with Love and drugs, he seemed to abandon himself to his own self-image: his determination to be, without adequate moral or intellectual equipment, absolutely different from everybody else. It comes as no shock that Cobain's private life was rooted in his need for family and domesticity, or that he reserved his most jaw-dropping behaviour for the times someone was watching. It was the particular tragedy of Cobain's life that he lost the ability to separate the public, performing image and the man himself.

A mark of his efforts to do so came in his periodic cries for help. In the fortnight between *Saturday Night Live* and Australia, Cobain and Love had decided to detox together. He submitted to a week of alternating sleep and nausea before catching the plane to Sydney, where he did, for a day or two, swear off drugs. That spring he checked into the Exodus Recovery Center in California, a facility popular with celebrity addicts. This, too, proved an inadequate response: in an ominous foreshadowing of his escape from the same hospital two years later, Cobain told the clinic staff he was stepping out for a walk and promptly scaled the wall. Then he flew to Seattle and bought more heroin. Meanwhile, despite relentless pressure from his management and colleagues, Cobain refused to countenance touring with Nirvana, a decision that brought an angry phone call from Novoselic and more than one clash with Geffen.

Another feature of Cobain's life was his insistence that he could 'handle' his habit. In fact his chronic heroin dependence was the genesis of almost daily conflict. Cobain was both the instigator and victim of violent arguments with dealers. He told interviewers, 'It wasn't a heavy addiction at all' and persuaded a biographer to write that 'detoxing was easy', but in truth Cobain was among the most notorious users in the industry, something he made almost no effort to conceal, even in public. He regularly bought heroin on the streets, and once startled the night-clerk of the Olympus Hotel in Tacoma by crashing through the front door, carrying a small paper bag and wildly demanding the bathroom. A locked cupboard in the Fairfax apartment contained what a guest calls 'a whole pharmacy' of supplies – there were needles, spoons and phials, as well as the heroin and a bottle of rubbing alcohol. In January Cobain had been spending $100 a day on his habit. By July the figure had risen to four times that – relatively modest by Hollywood standards, but enough for the nickname 'Kurt Cocaine' to be revived behind his back.

In the days after Cobain's suicide his widow characterized Seattle as a drugs mecca, where heroin was more plentiful than in New York or Los Angeles. Others in the local community agreed with the police that the magnifying-glass of media attention had distorted the reality of drugs in Seattle. 'It wasn't more of a problem here than anyplace else,' says a former manager at Sub Pop. Nor, however, was it any less of a problem: heroin-related deaths in Seattle jumped by 90 per cent in the 1980s, while a single local hospital recorded 830 life-threatening overdoses in 1993, the most recent statistics available. Seattle police handle 6,000 drug cases a year. On University Avenue, from 3,500 to 5,000 dirty needles are exchanged weekly at a stand run by a volunteer named Bob Quinn. Most needles are for shooting heroin, Quinn says, although amphetamine use is 'big among teenagers'.

If all this falls short of Love's claim that heroin in Seattle is 'like apples in the orchard', it tends to support Cobain's view that 'with dope, supply leads to demand'. When, like most things Cobain wanted, success turned to ashes in his mouth, he soon resumed the drug habit of his youth. The difference lay all in the scale. Suddenly the weak, naïve Aberdonian was keeping company with crack dealers and pimps. As Cobain's interest in music dwindled, so his love of drugs grew proportionately greater. No one attempted to stop him: some actively encouraged his habit. By late 1992 he was a shambling parody of the author of *Nevermind*, stumbling from one heroin fix to another and submitting to visits from a social worker in order to keep custody of his daughter. Although the outcome would have been the same in Pittsburgh or Kansas or Cleveland, it was unfortunate that Cobain spent the last two years of his life in a town notorious, in his widow's words, for 'grunge, cappuccino and heroin'; and ironic that he came to epitomize the thing that ruined him.

Nirvana had barely made their breakthrough before Cobain threatened to destroy the group.

The incident took place against a backdrop of increasing irritation between Geffen and Gold Mountain on one side and the band on the other. Preparations were under way for a US arena tour that spring when Cobain, wanting to be with Love during her pregnancy and in no condition to leave home, refused to travel. It was not impossible to feel sympathy for the decision. Since 1989 Nirvana had toured America, Canada, Europe, Australia, New Zealand, Singapore and Japan, released two albums, given countless interviews and appeared on the cover of every music title in the world. According to Frank Hulme, 'Dave rued the lost sales of *Nevermind*, but agreed they needed a break.' There was grudging acceptance of the decision from Novoselic: 'The tour just seemed like a lot more pressure. Before, we were just vagabonds in a van, doing our thing. Now you've got a tour manager and a crew and it's a production.'

Less easily accepted was Cobain's enslavement to drugs. As well as the now 'shitty atmosphere' at group meetings, there was Novoselic's outburst to his wife, 'Kurt's a fucking junkie asshole and I hate him!', and a falling-out between Nirvana's two founders. Here, some discrepancy exists between Cobain's account ('All Chris did was give me bad vibes and dirty looks') and Novoselic's ('I tried to help'). Later that spring Cobain screamed at Novoselic's wife for the tactless remark, 'Kurt, I just hate to see you doing this to yourself.' By the time they returned from the Far East Nirvana had divided into two warring camps, Cobain and Love versus the Novoselics, with Grohl unhappily bringing up the middle.

The result was a bitter clash about publishing royalties. What incensed Novoselic and Grohl was not so much that Cobain would demand more than twice their share on the grounds that 'I'm under pressure' – they were used to that – but that he asked for the new arrangement to be retrospective. Neither of his colleagues would see another penny from *Nevermind* until Cobain had finished collecting his due. In extreme circumstances, had the album stopped selling as dramatically as it had started, it could have left them in substantial debt to Cobain.

To see their career turned into *cinéma noir* was an appropriate enough fate for Nirvana. Practically alone of rock groups, who rarely have much interest beyond the surface, they did almost exactly resemble a film. In fact they closely echoed the plot of one particular picture, a favourite in the rock business, and one that Frank Zappa could never see without recalling the happy likeness – *Spinal Tap*. Nirvana avoided the more laughable extremes of that group's saga, but they had the disputes about vision, the warring girlfriends and even, insofar as Grohl was the sixth such musician, the multiple drummers. It is uncertain whether Cobain prompted the crisis because of Love, because he needed the money, or, more plausibly, because he feared his talent had gone sour and he was terrified of the future. 'I can't handle work,' he admitted in 1989. A year later Cobain told *Sounds*: 'I don't want to have any other kind of job. I can't work among people.' By 1992 he struck Hulme as 'morbidly scared' of losing his money and restarting a 'slow and ugly life' in Aberdeen. If Cobain had disliked the town as a boy he positively repudiated it as an adult. 'I'd literally rather kill myself than go back there,' he told his cousin. When a dispute between the Weyerhaeuser company and its workers was reported in the press Cobain was quoted as saying, 'I'd blow my brains out, living like that.' On taking off in a plane, he liked to look down at the rows of identical houses and make a gesture like the pulling of a bomb lever. Cobain's motives for reneging on his agreement may never be known, but by the time the dust had settled and he collected his money, he was married to a woman whose rejection of the 'slow and ugly life' matched his own.

On 24 February 1992, in a ceremony attended by Grohl, three Nirvana employees and a passing drug dealer (though not Novoselic and his wife), Cobain married Love. The service, on a cliff overlooking Waikiki Beach, was performed by a non-denominational female minister found by the bride through the Hawaiian wedding bureau. The groom, high on heroin, wore green and white check pyjamas and a lei;

at the phrase 'man and wife' he broke down and cried. By the time they retired to a local bar to celebrate so many of the party were weeping that, as Cobain put it, had Love shown any public emotion 'it would have been a wake'.

Love did not show public emotion. Methodical, capable, icily efficient, she made other rock wives look almost shamefully self-effacing. Even Yoko Ono appeared low-key and shy by comparison. While it seemed to Grohl that 'Courtney was the ideal mate for Kurt', the idyll soon proved more apparent than real. Once the first delights of marriage had worn off it became obvious to both that, although they complemented each other in many, perhaps most, respects, in others they were woefully incompatible. Love rebelled fiercely against the shackles of domesticity, while Cobain's vision of a perfect match was of a relationship so close that every confidence was shared, no private agenda pursued. He wanted to possess and to be possessed. This vision filled his wife with horror. Not only was there the matter of her career, there was also the threat of Cobain's drug habit.

Looking back on the ceremony three years later, Love told David Fricke:

> If you don't think I knew what I was getting into when I married Kurt ... I mean, the lack of credit I get. Kim Gordon and Julie Cafritz told me when me and Kurt got serious, 'You know what's going to happen?' They spelled out everything. Not taking into account Kurt dying, obviously. Actually, in Cafritz's version Kurt would OD: 'You'll become junkies. You'll get married. You'll OD. You'll be 35, you'll try and make a comeback' ... I knew [what was] happening.

Looking at Cobain's life in full, it is tempting to see a kind of insecurity of which his need for a strong wife was typical. He honestly thought he was marrying above himself. Love compensated for his crippling lack of self-esteem. 'She's my one and only chance,' Cobain described her to Grohl. What he wanted from marriage was constant encouragement, loyal support, affection. Within reason, Love gave them to him. That she also valued her independence and her career was understood, and in July 1992 Hole signed to Geffen for a sum that led one cynic to tell *Newsweek*, 'sleeping with Kurt Cobain is worth a million dollars'. 'They jogged along,' says a man who knew the couple in London. Although one was 'passive-aggressive' and the other 'a thug', they enjoyed a 'punk contempt' for the world. According to Hulme, 'They were compatible. They may have loved one another. I doubt they'd have won the Nobel Prize for chemistry.'

The headline in *Rolling Stone* that April read: 'Inside the Heart and Mind of Nirvana.' The tone was scrupulously upbeat. Cobain assured the magazine he was happier than he'd ever been. (According to *Rolling Stone*, 'whenever Love walks into the room, even if it's to scold him about something, he gets the profoundly dopey grin of the truly love struck.') He dismissed rumours of a rift inside Nirvana; his attitude to fame was 'pretty relaxed'; he admitted to mellowing with age and not blaming 'the average seventeen-year-old punk-rock kid for calling me a sellout'. The hoped-for impression was of an affable family man, studiously calm, a husband who worshipped his wife and praised his friends and fellow musicians (with the notable exception of Pearl Jam). Unmentioned was Cobain's collection of drugs and guns, his sudden mood swings and his violent outbursts against his group. He may not have been able to control his anger – it was a form of addiction – but Cobain went too far in claiming, 'I don't even drink anymore because it destroys my stomach. My body wouldn't allow me to take drugs if I wanted to, because I'm so weak. All drugs [do is] destroy your memory and your self-respect and everything that goes along with your self-esteem. They're no good at all.' Anybody reading the article would have come away thinking Cobain to be a civilized and rational adult with a conservative outlook on life, and a new-found self-restraint; it was a marvellous performance. No one would have guessed there was a supply of heroin, needles, spoons and rubbing alcohol in the cupboard behind him.

Inside Cobain's heart and mind was not a comfortable place to be, nor easily reached. When other rock stars talked about themselves it was usually in the context of self-exposure – they were pleased to be famous, and they wanted to share their good fortune. Now, Cobain came forward, and pleasure was the last thing on his mind. On the wide canvas of his unhappiness, his reaction to fame loomed among the largest.

There were those, of course, who saw Cobain as a symptom of a disease that had eaten at the body of society, mainly through rock music, for years. When the obituaries came in they used words like 'tragic' and 'dysfunctional' to describe behaviour that, to others, was cynical and self-indulgent. In the latter view, Cobain had embraced his fame all too willingly. 'He claimed to be put upon,' says Hulme, 'but he was hopeless without attention.' Cobain's advisers had evolved into his servants. Hard-headed businessmen running record companies had become doting sentimentalists and fed his belief that he was beyond rebuke, that even mild criticism was part of a plot. It was enough to make Cobain paranoid, and it did. He also became a show-off and a bore. After a three-hour dinner that summer at Quaglino's in London, Cobain and a girlfriend went to great lengths to avoid being photographed on their departure. Yet the restaurant, as he well knew, was high in the top ten of paparazzi haunts;

hence the reason for its star-studded clientele. In the imbroglio that followed, punches were thrown and insults exchanged with photographers. ('I have absolutely no respect for the English,' Cobain said later. 'I thought I'd never say anything racist in my life, but they're the most snooty, cocksure, anal people. They make me sick.') There were other signs that he was not entirely free of rock-star vanity. When Cobain returned to Aberdeen in 1992 he did so in a stretch limousine. By flying into New York wearing a false beard and a hat he achieved more public scrutiny than would have resulted from his normal appearance. He treasured every scrap of praise, never forgot a word of criticism, and would do anything to attract publicity without ever admitting it.

Cobain never sought to be a youth spokesman. Insofar as he was taken up by ambitious critics, disc jockeys and impressionable fans, he *was* unlucky: he suffered the fate of a symbol. In one of innumerable articles on grunge, *Atlantic* commented that 'Twentysomethings ... have become a Boomer metaphor for America's loss of purpose, disappointment with institutions, despair over the culture and fear for the future.' According to this view, the times had come into alignment with Cobain's gloomy vision, rather than the reverse. As a friend says, 'He was the perfect role model for the nineties. That pressure, in the form of constant demands that he act in type, finally broke him. But for a year or two, no one summed up the times better than Kurt.' He became the first superstar of both punk and the new decade.

By degrees, predictably, Cobain became convinced by his own press. He began to deny more and more being a figurehead, with the inevitable result that he became one. It was a particular hallmark of Cobain's life that he showe: virtually no capacity for power. As a musician he had breathtaking leadership skills. But in most other respects he was cruelly handicapped. Easily led, self-obsessed, over-indulged, Cobain lacked anything resembling an ethical centre. He was incomplete – someone with personality but no character. That flaw led Cobain to deny the consequences of his own actions, and to accept the privileges of fame even as he shunned the responsibilities. Other than a hazy allegiance to left-wing politics and feminism, he had few personal beliefs outside of music; and it always surprised him that, as he said, 'people looked for a deeper meaning' of his role. 'The idea that getting high wasn't enough shocked Kurt,' says Hulme. 'No one had warned him that he might have to give a moral lead.' It was ironic that after the years of work Cobain had done to become famous, when it happened it caught him unawares.

When Geffen had first released *Nevermind*, they thought it might sell 50,000 copies. That level would have been the right one for Cobain; high enough, but not so elevated that he became a Messiah figure. There was always a deep-seated and nagging part of him that wondered if the game was worth the candle. In the end Cobain could see the truth of what he had long dimly known and perhaps hopefully suppressed – that for a compassionate and sensitive man to be treated as a god can be a disagreeable experience. Instead of happiness, he once said, he found only a kind of 'giddy high'; instead of glory, only 'ashes and muck'.

Cobain always spoke of his success as a joke, proof that fate regarded him with satirical malice. It was bad enough that 'Teen Spirit' went platinum on April Fool's Day; to have the single parodied by 'Weird' Al Yankovic and covered as a piano sonata by Tori Amos merely added to the irony. In concert the song quickly achieved anthem status, and the sound of 10,000 voices gently crooning the chorus proved a surreal and, to Cobain, deeply traumatic experience. 'He began to think of himself as no more than a ringmaster in a circus,' says a friend. According to Hulme, 'He never thought the audience actually felt like he did. To Kurt, they were just singing along.'

By the time Cobain toured Europe in June, even hearing the song was too painful, a reminder of the old days when everything lay ahead. According to Grohl, there was 'crazy shit going on' that summer in Sweden, Spain and France; in Belfast, after a concert described by the *Telegraph* as containing 'the traditional trashing the equipment spot' and 'no real surprises', Cobain was rushed to hospital suffering from, in his version, methadone withdrawal; in his management's, a bleeding ulcer; and, in reality, a heroin overdose. When Cobain and Love reached Paris they were kept under lock and key by two bodyguards hired by Gold Mountain. The faintly poignant sight of a man synonymous with personal licence being 'grounded' by his own staff was admitted by Cobain in an aside to Azerrad: 'I was being monitored by two goons . . . I had absolutely no desire to do drugs but I was being treated like a fucking baby. They were turning this band into everything it wasn't supposed to be.'

There was further irony awaiting Cobain and Love when they returned to Los Angeles. Before flying to Europe the couple had stored their favourite clothes, guitars and, more significantly, notebooks full of half-written songs in the bathtub – the idea was that no one would think of looking there. Instead, a burst pipe during their absence had flooded the room with slime and mud, completely ruining the journals. There was dark humour to be found, some thought, in the prince of grunge and his self-styled 'greaseball queen' being driven from their home by sludge. The pair moved to a new apartment in the Hollywood Hills, where Cobain promptly befriended the local heroin dealer.

'We went on a binge,' Love admitted when she was asked about the couple's habits in the early months of 1992. 'We did a lot of drugs. We got pills and then we went down to

Alphabet City and we copped some dope. Then we got high and did *Saturday Night Live*. After that, I did heroin for a couple of months.'

That was enough to persuade the journalist Lynn Hirschberg to speculate that Love may have been taking heroin even after she knew she was pregnant, the exact date of which remains unknown. The September issue of *Vanity Fair*, published in early August, duly posed the question, 'Are Courtney Love, lead diva of the postpunk band Hole, and her husband, Nirvana heartthrob Kurt Cobain, the grunge John and Yoko?' before giving itself over to unnamed 'industry insiders' who regarded Love's intrusion into the Nirvana camp as the seed of the group's downfall. Among the more damaging quotes was one describing Love as 'not particularly interested in the consequences of her actions' and the Cobains' home life as a 'sick scene', raising 'fear[s] for the health of their child'. The article failed to mention, however, Cobain's resilient ties with his family and his love of children generally. For good measure the magazine chose to illustrate the piece with a photograph of Love stripped of her clothes and also, it emerged, of a cigarette airbrushed out on the editor's orders.

It would be hard to overestimate the grief caused to Cobain by *Vanity Fair*. The profile describing his wife as a 'charismatic opportunist' and implying that he was a drug addict and unfit father galled and hurt him. He seemed unable to believe that a responsible journalist could write about him thus. As soon as Cobain and Love saw the piece they issued a statement denying the central allegation, while in private Cobain raged at Hirschberg and (unsuccessfully) attempted to have her fired. The article dramatically increased his paranoia about the press. Previously trusted friends, long used to open access to Nirvana, now found their way barred at the stage door. Keith Cameron, one of the first reporters to write about the group in Britain, was left in tears by a comment Cobain made to him that August. Beyond the range of the media, Cobain also fumed at 'gossip by people in the rock world who want desperately to pretend they have some information' and sent an early Christmas card to Soundgarden's manager Susan Silver addressed to 'our favourite inside source'.

Theoretically, Cobain might have shrugged off the attack and gone about his business. He stood accused on the basis of unsourced quotes and charges that were often flagrantly inaccurate. He also stood condemned by industry figures who had not always been strangers to drugs themselves. These were not matters weighty enough to halt the march of the 'king of the scene', as Cobain had long been portrayed. As things stood, he could have resumed his career and scoffed at those who had wasted his time and trivialized his life for the benefit of their readers.

Instead, the article destroyed Cobain's spirit, hastened his physical decline and almost crushed him financially. In part this was due to the irrational fear that the world was out to ruin him. There was also the 'suicidal grief' of losing old friends. Cobain was hurt deeply when his own colleagues began to turn their backs on him, leave the studio when he arrived, and make excuses to be elsewhere when he invited them to dinner. Then, too, the financial and mental strain of fighting the Department of Children's Services played a role. When the couple's baby was born (just eight days after *Vanity Fair*'s publication), a hearing in Family Court ordered Cobain to detox once again, and to surrender care of the child to Love's half-sister. For five weeks after that, neither of the Cobains were allowed to be alone with their daughter. After a series of interviews with social workers and a urine test for both parents, the family was reunited in September, by which time Cobain had spent $300,000 on legal fees and was almost incoherent with self-pity. ('It was an attempt to use us as an example because we stand for everything that goes against the grain of conformist American entertainment,' he told one interviewer. 'It was a witch hunt.') Paranoia and despair, never far removed from Cobain, deepened with each passing month. He often rose late in the afternoon, watched television sit-coms during the evening, and stared for hours at the makeshift Buddhist shrine in his living-room. He frequently refused phone calls, even from colleagues. 'A kind of neurosis began to set in,' says Hulme. For the rest of their marriage Cobain and Love, whose own reputation became proverbial, were rarely out of the limelight. No doubt remembering their vital role in the group's success, rock journalists began to speak of Nirvana as having been 'lost' to their audience. At about the same time, the mainstream media started writing about the heady mixture of sex, drugs and rock and roll swirling around the group. Old lovers were coming forward with gossip about the Cobains, *Time* and *Newsweek* had both mentioned the couple, and tabloid reporters were already at work investigating new rumours about heroin addiction. Cobain himself was heartbroken and increasingly suicidal.

By the time Cobain flew home from Madrid in July 1992 he knew he needed help. The concerts in Europe had been widely criticized as stale and formulaic. Cobain was as aware as anyone that 'last year's shows were way better'; he began talking about remodelling the group, or breaking it up altogether. The 'shitheads and scribblers' who so vexed him were agony to one of his sensitive temperament. Moreover, Cobain was now beginning to break down physically and mentally, and this, in turn, contributed to his often choleric behaviour. By midsummer he was taking so many drugs that even distant friends and a few fans recognized the signs of dementia.

The result was Cobain's latest effort to stabilize his health, a three-week stay in Cedars-Sinai hospital in Los Angeles.

Both his gradual withdrawal and a renewed interest in food suggest that, even before the Court-imposed programme, another sea-change, illustrated by Cobain cropping his hair to 1981 length, was under way. When the photographer Darrell Westmoreland met him later that autumn, Cobain said 'he'd woken up one morning, looked in the mirror and said to himself, "Man, I need help. I need to turn my life around." He told me, "Look, man, I put weight on!"'

Cobain enjoyed such admissions and always shared his outbreaks of sanity with others. Unusually for a rock star, he was sensitive and self-aware. His years in the limelight were characterized by frequent confessions of weakness and of his need to change. The problem was that Cobain never sustained the momentum. Every advance was matched by a relapse. His insights were marred by paralysing bouts of blindness and self-deception. Cobain might have slowed down, taken more holidays and enjoyed a more detached view of his life. Instead, he worried more about himself every day. The paeans about his wife and daughter turned to tirades about journalists and double-dealing friends. The flashes of optimism were snuffed out by his dim view of humanity. According to his cousin, 'Kurt always longed to accentuate the positive. But he was fighting an almost allergic reaction to the rest of the world.' Even in the first flush of fatherhood, Cobain admitted he was 'back in that state of mind every few months'.

Frances Bean Cobain was born three weeks early but perfectly healthy on 18 August 1992. She was named after the musician Frances McKee and her resemblance, much remarked on by Cobain, to a kidney bean. According to a published report, Love had continued her drug use until two weeks before giving birth. The American *Globe* claimed she arrived at the hospital 'so spaced out she had no idea what she was doing ... (Love) was totally incoherent ...

She would demand food, eat some and then throw the rest against the wall.' Even that sorry nadir paled in comparison to Cobain, detoxing in the same hospital, who attended the birth semi-conscious and vomiting throughout because of withdrawal symptoms.

Both parents denied this report, and the fact that their child was born in good health casts doubt on the *Globe* story. To judge by the article in *Vanity Fair*, Love herself had helped to foster the rumours. She was, as she admitted, 'one of the most sarcastic people in the world'. Some of that satire was taken by the media at face value. For instance, there was the couple's exchange of faxes while in Europe in 1991, likening their feelings for each other to 'being on acid', but appearing in the *Sun* as 'proof that both [took] LSD'. Love's quip that 'If there's ever a time that a person *should* be on drugs, it's when they're pregnant, because it sucks' was also widely quoted. By the time her baby was born there were reporters hiding in corridors and squatting in laundry hampers in the hospital basement; one photographer tricked his way in dressed as a doctor. Transcripts of Love's phone calls and faxes would appear in the press. The spate of hostile coverage continued with a full-page splash in the *Globe* under the headline 'Rock star's baby is born a junkie'. According to the paper, 'Love was still smoking (in hospital), but compared to the other ways she was abusing her body, the smoking was minor ... When her rock and roll friends came around, they would sit cross-legged and chant. A few times, there was a frantic alert after she wandered off barefoot in her nightgown.'

In the explosion that followed, Cobain and Love were forced to hire a lawyer to regain custody of their daughter. Love also sued her doctor and the hospital on the grounds of invasion of privacy and negligence, a case that was settled out of court. Meanwhile, Gold Mountain issued a statement insisting that 'the vicious rumours that Frances was suffering any withdrawals at the time of birth are completely false, and in fact, she has not suffered any discomfort since delivery', an assurance that only fed the tabloids' insatiable appetite for gossip, including the rumour, later confirmed, that Love had had her breasts lifted after giving birth.

The press entirely missed the real crisis. On 19 August, the day after Frances's birth, Cobain appeared in his wife's hospital room holding a handgun. His intention was to kill first Love, and then himself. Cobain looked ill and seemed to stagger slightly. He announced he was 'sick and tired of being shat on' by the media. 'They're murdering me,' he sobbed. It took all Love's efforts and the help of her friend Eric Erlandson to persuade Cobain to give up the gun. Then he shuffled out of the room and summoned his heroin dealer, a woman by whose own admission he looked 'dead'. Immense effort went into portraying Cobain as a man revived by the birth of his daughter. 'He looks at Frances all the time and he says, "That's the way I used to be! That's the way I used to be!"' Love told a reporter. Cobain himself would insist, 'having a child and being in love is something that everyone wants. It's the only thing I feel I've been blessed with.' Yet Frances's birth also had a negative effect on Cobain, calling up his old feelings of inadequacy and self-doubt. According to his cousin, 'a voice would tell him that he wasn't a good enough daddy. He never wanted her to see the dark side.' Along with his own insecurity went the fear that Frances had inherited the same bleak characteristics as her father. 'He was tormented that he and Courtney would divorce, Frances would begin the downward spiral, and history would repeat itself,' says Graham Wright. Less than two years later, Love read out parts of her husband's suicide note at his memorial service. 'I have a daughter who reminds me too much of what I used to be,' Cobain had written.

* * *

Ten days after Frances's birth Cobain was on a plane to London. On 30 August Nirvana headlined at the twentieth annual Reading Festival. In the week before the event both the *Source* and the *Enquirer* had confidently announced the group had broken up. This fact presumably needed confirmation, since both those enterprising titles sent reporters to Reading. The British press had also published tales of Nirvana's woes, one paper suggesting that a stand-in, not Cobain himself, would actually appear on stage. There were still rumours circulating around the crowd as the lights went down and Cobain, in his own droll comment on his ordeal, rolled out in a wheelchair and wearing a hospital gown.

The concert that followed was vintage Nirvana. The *Nevermind* material was so strong that it could sustain even quirks such as mindless riffing, rewritten lyrics and pain-threshold volume. The result was organized chaos – what one critic called 'an elegant din' – as Cobain's guitar and rabble-rousing vocals were seized on by the crowd's head-bangers. Those dozing in the park's furthest reaches were rudely awoken by an 80,000-strong cry of 'Nir-VANA' as 'In Bloom' was followed in turn by 'Lithium', which gave way to 'Rape Me'; by 'On A Plain' the fists shaken aloft stretched back to the far reaches of the site. Miti Adhikari, who recorded the concert for radio, calls it 'punk heaven', marred only by the fact that 'Kurt was cooler towards his friends. The old camaraderie was missing.' John Peel (whose small daughter's foot was accidentally bruised when Cobain leapt offstage) agrees: 'You could tell the ways of the industry, and all the negative coverage, were getting to him. He seemed to have aged a hell of a lot in a year.' Later at the Reading Ramada, and minutes after befriending a young cancer patient backstage, Cobain was shown an article by Nirvana's British amanuensis Keith Cameron. 'Right away,' says Graham Wright, also present in the hotel, 'Kurt started screaming blue murder, threatening to throw Keith out and have him worked over by the heavies.' Cobain and Eric Erlandson then threw their drinks in Cameron's face. Wright was not alone in finding something disturbing in the way 'Kurt went from Dr Jekyll to Mr Hyde in the space of a minute'.

On 9 September Nirvana played the MTV Video Music Awards in Los Angeles. The performance was dramatic enough: minutes before the live broadcast, MTV vetoed the group's preferred choice of 'Rape Me'. 'Either the song goes,' the producer boomed, 'or you go.' It was close; in the end Cobain compromised, seguing into 'Lithium' after playfully strumming the first few bars of the offending title.* Nirvana then gave a performance that raised admiring eyebrows in the Seattle *Times*:

> The beleaguered band, beset with rumors of drug abuse and breakups, answered all the doubters and rumor-mongers the best way it could – by delivering a moody, blistering, explosive version of its current single . . . One thing that will no doubt help its future was the revealing of singer Kurt Cobain's boyish handsomeness. He used to try and look as punky as possible, with garish hair colors, sunglass-covered eyes, overgrown stubble and rag-pile clothes. Last night his cropped hair was a natural shade of blond, his big blue eyes were unshaded and the Kirk Douglas cleft in his chin was plainly visible. His mostly white clothes looked not only clean but bleached.

* More or less the same scene had, of course, been played out virtually nightly on countless mid-sixties variety programmes. It was probably a coincidence that Nirvana's next video was a satire of the *Ed Sullivan Show*.

Cobain refused to go onstage to accept the prize for Best Alternative Music Video, sending a Michael Jackson impersonator in his place. He did, however, collect the Best New Artist award, thanking his family, Geffen, Gold Mountain and the group's 'true friends' before staring deep into the camera and muttering, 'You know, it's really hard to believe everything you read.'

Cobain might have left it there. It had been an emotional performance, a reminder of Nirvana's power, and proof that Cobain had a wry and even lucid slant on his fame. Instead he gave in to his obsession with confronting his enemies. Earlier in the year Cobain had run down Pearl Jam to *Musician*, and told *Rolling Stone*, 'I would love to be erased from my association with that band . . . They're jumping on the alternative bandwagon.' According to the sound engineer Alan Wineberg, 'sparks flew when Kurt ran into Vedder backstage. He told him, flat out, that Pearl Jam stank.' That was as nothing compared to the Cobains' reception of Axl Rose. A month earlier, Rose, still fuming at Nirvana for refusing to supply him with backstage passes, had asked an audience in Florida, 'Don't you think Kurt and Courtney should be in jail for doing drugs while she was pregnant?' Now, when Love greeted Rose with the question 'Will you be our baby's godfather?', his reply, screamed an inch from Cobain's face, spun heads the length of the room: 'Shut your bitch up or I'm taking you down to the pavement.' The two most popular rock singers in the world then engaged in a shoving match. Cobain later told a journalist that Rose had been 'bug-eyed' and 'literally foaming at the mouth'. By his own admission, he described the incident to anyone who listened during the next few weeks. One reporter heard Cobain say that he had enjoyed the fracas thoroughly. A manager at Gold Mountain gloated in a private memo, 'If, as quoted, Axl gave Kurt "a piece of his mind", we should have the specimen put in a jar.'

Someone in Seattle sent Cobain a bracelet inscribed, 'For services to Punk above and beyond the call of duty. September 9 1992.'

Friends noticed Cobain's habit of deprecating himself, of running himself down, and some admonished him for being too slow to anger. According to Love, 'his largest problem in life was *not* being able to say, "Fuck you". "Fuck you, Courtney. Fuck you, Gold Mountain. Fuck you, Geffen – and I'm gonna do what I want".' But Cobain's diffidence went skin deep. A part of him loved to provoke, and that part had spoken when, as early as 1986, Cobain picked a fight with a neighbour in Aberdeen. 'It was a really scary reminder of how violent I can be when I want to hurt somebody. It actually felt good, I was actually laughing about it,' he told Azerrad. (Cobain's victim suffered a concussion and lapsed into a brief coma.) Years later there was his threat to his would-be biographers and his reaction to Lynn Hirschberg, of whom Cobain said in print, 'I'll fucking get revenge on her. Before I leave this earth, she's going out with me.'

Part of Cobain's temper stemmed from his paranoia, his sense of the world closing in. 'No matter what we do or how clean we live our lives, we're not going to survive this because there are too many enemies and we threaten too many people,' he said. 'Everyone wants to see us die.' A key factor in turning mere distrust into dementia was Cobain's growing anger at the media. Love no doubt captured this mood when she spoke of a 'vindictive desire for revenge' against the couple. One of the results was that Cobain cordially returned the journalists' suspicion. With a few notable exceptions, his press relations sank to zero in the wake of *Vanity Fair*. Another consequence was a growing rift between the public figure and the private man.

For years Cobain had preached the gospel of non-violence. He almost defined the role of the refusenik, someone with a Gandhi-like tolerance of his enemies. His confidence that in so doing he was recapturing 'the whole point of religion' won widespread support. Now, on the questionable grounds of 'needing to defend myself', Cobain justified ownership of a virtual arsenal of guns. 'I believe in them for protection,' he said in 1992. 'I'm not as much of a hippie as some people would want me to be. I could blow somebody away easily, no problem.' That August he had to be talked out of turning his revolver on both his wife and himself. Within a year Cobain would tell David Fricke, 'I like guns. I just enjoy shooting them.' On 18 March 1994 police removed four firearms and no fewer than twenty-five boxes of ammunition from the Cobains' home after a panic-stricken call from Love, revealing many things his fans did not want to know about her husband. According to an officer who attended the scene, 'I've never seen so many loaded weapons in a private house. There were literally Berettas lying around on the table.' A therapist who worked with Cobain that spring also noted him as 'an acutely paranoid young man'.

Paranoid about what? As well as his treatment by the press, there was Cobain's fear of becoming a cartoon, a caricature of himself. 'Teen Spirit' had already been covered by Al Yankovic and Tori Amos. Now Hard Rock Comics published an unauthorized story of Nirvana, 'Smells Like Territorial Pissings', and Cobain jokes began to air on late-night TV shows. The governor of Washington referred admiringly to Nirvana in his annual State of the State address. *Time* ran a headline suggesting 'The Puget Sound is the hottest in rock'. All this led Cobain to complain bitterly that 'self-parody [had] set in' to the Seattle scene. Nineteen ninety-one may have been 'the year punk broke' but only twelve months later its sole local expression was the daily arrival of sightseers at the Crocodile Café and a booming tourist industry centred around Nirvana. For years Cobain's clothes had sported hand-written slogans protesting something, or chastizing a new-found enemy. This hostile light was now forced to be cast on himself, and Cobain took to wearing a T-shirt proclaiming GRUNGE IS DEAD. Likewise, though he derived moments of enjoyment from his fame – as when he cashed a six-figure cheque or sent a limousine to pick up his mother – he was also horrified to discover 'yuppies in their BMWs' among his fans. The liner notes to a Nirvana anthology that Christmas included the claim, 'I don't feel the least bit guilty for commercially exploiting a completely exhausted Rock Youth Culture, because at this point in rock history, Punk is, to me, dead and gone', and ended with a plea for fans lacking racial or sexual tolerance to 'leave us the fuck alone – don't come to our shows and don't buy our records'. The message was signed, 'Kurdt (the blond one).'

Cobain's songwriting worked in close conjunction with his experience. And now the whole saga had been, as it were, chewed and spat out. His childhood and early life had been vented in *Bleach*. Then America and all its problems, together with all Cobain's problems, had been anatomized, summarized and brilliantly distorted in *Nevermind*. That as sensitive and self-aware a person as Cobain did not know that he was, to all intents and purposes, finished as an artist, defies belief. He certainly knew. The knowledge, along with his growing aversion to his audience, caused Cobain to retreat. In June 1992 a Nirvana press release spoke of their plans to 'strip away the pretensions' on their next album. In July the group released 'Lithium' as a single, along with a consciously, some thought self-consciously, dated video. In October Cobain recorded with Jack Endino for the first time in two years. According to Graham Wright, 'Despite record company hassle, Kurt was doing *Bleach*-like songs, playing what he liked, with the confidence of a man letting his dog run,' a dog that had always come back before. One of Cobain's most appealing qualities as a superstar was to never forget and actively promote the musicians he admired. Now he began to talk up the rootsy groups that had most inspired him – the Breeders, Shonen Knife, Jad Fair, the Vaselines, Sonic Youth – and to agitate for a 'return to basics'. Despite grappling with problems of his own he gave up weeks of his time to co-produce the Melvins' LP *Houdini*; he appeared on stage with Mudhoney. Meeting the Raincoats, Cobain announced, was 'one of the few really important things that I've been blessed with since becoming an untouchable boy genius'.

In early September Nirvana played two concerts in support of the aggressively non-profit Washington Music Industry Coalition. ('The terrible trio is alive and well,' noted Patrick MacDonald. 'Kurt Cobain and Dave Grohl stayed on the stage a good ten minutes after the last song, tossing, smashing, totally annihilating their instruments. Grohl's whole expensive kit was demolished, and Cobain banged his beautiful white guitar on the stage until it splintered.') They played two further Northwest dates in October, unscheduled appearances at Western Washington State University and the Crocodile. Here, as at Reading, the crowd was noisily expectant as Cobain climbed on stage; the torn angora sweater and Cobain's own promise to 'rock the Croc' both hinted at an evening of enjoyable nostalgia. (Cobain's good mood did not, however, extend to Victoria Clarke; the luckless biographer was denied entry at the Crocodile door.) The performance that followed reminded some of why they liked Nirvana in the first place. Cobain had once described the group's formula as 'musical anarchy' – it had become a straitjacket. Now, freed from the irksome job of travelling around the world, having hit albums and generally being a global icon, Cobain was happy to sit in with old friends like Mudhoney and puckishly ask the crowd,

'Any requests?' If his modesty occasionally smacked of play-acting (he took to setting up his own equipment and performing menial tasks that might have been done better by roadies), there was also something appealing about Cobain, something honest and natural, which made one wonder how he could ever have been a rock star in the first place.

Nirvana's homecoming led to a revival of interest in their roots. The Seattle *Times* dispatched a reporter to Aberdeen, where one resident spoke of Cobain as 'intelligent and talented', and another compared knowing him to 'living with the devil'. (The paper's verdict: 'Even then he had a certain spark ... a strong sense of outrageousness.') The *Daily World* interviewed Cobain's mother, rejecting the 'cartoon neurosis' of his public persona in favour of an 'artistic and musical prodigy' whose inspiration came from his unhappiness as a child. Something of this pain communicated itself to *Rolling Stone*'s Michael Azerrad, who was traumatized by Aberdeen's 'perpetually rainy, gray climate' and run-down wooden shacks, where people lived on bully-beef and corn dogs 'with only the prospects of unemployment or risking life and limb hacking down beautiful, centuries-old trees'. Even in this joyless scenario there was a touch of myth and invention. Grant Alden, who accompanied Azerrad to the Pourhouse, remembers him as 'staggered to find people sitting down with a jug of beer apiece. That struck Michael as the worst kind of evidence of alcoholism. It never occurred to him that it's the most economical way to buy a drink.' The whole visit convinced Alden that 'not only *Rolling Stone*, but the rock press generally' were taken in by the image of the 'stump-dumb rocker dude', a stereotype most natives were all too eager to perpetuate. 'I was there when that kid made his famous crack about Kurt, "We *deal* with faggots here. We run 'em out of town." It was mean. as a joke at the expense of what he saw as an effete New York writer, and of course Mike swallowed the bait.' The quote duly appeared in *Rolling Stone*'s cover story and was later widely used to illustrate the tale of Cobain's childhood.

Nineteen ninety-two also saw a gradual acceleration of the process by which Cobain became a community celebrity. His hostility to Aberdeen softened, and twice that summer he was seen arriving in a chauffeured car to visit his mother. It seemed to some in his circle that Cobain valued Wendy's raw attitude and blunt speech both as a link with his past and as evidence of how far he had come. Don Cobain also tried to repair relations with his son. In January 1992 he sent letters to Geffen and Gold Mountain ('neither of whom gave a damn about him', a cousin notes) before talking his way backstage at Nirvana's Seattle concert that September. After an hour of 'hassle and bullshit', Don briefly saw his son for the first time in seven years and was introduced to his daughter-in-law and grandchild. The scene was exactly what was expected: a crowded, unattractive VIP suite, with people tugging at Cobain's arm even during his few minutes with his father. 'I felt sorry for him,' said Don. 'It didn't look that glamorous to me.' After the meeting had ended in tears Cobain told his heroin dealer, 'I'm a pathetic person.' 'Kurt, you're not a pathetic person,' the woman replied. 'You're a pathetic junkie.' This time, Cobain laughed.

Historically, apologizing for himself was not a tactic that Cobain had had much opportunity to use, as others had tended to pre-empt him. In a long article in the Los Angeles *Times* that September, Robert Hilburn applied the latest spin control, describing Cobain as 'a shy, sensitive man [who] admits that he's used drugs, including heroin, but never as much as has been rumored or reported in the rock press. He also says in a quiet, but forceful way, that he is now drug-free.' In November Love did her first major interview since *Vanity Fair*, in which she told the *Rocket*: 'The heroin thing is just so stupid.' And Jonathan Poneman emerged to write a cover story for *Spin*'s December issue, proclaiming Nirvana 'artist of the year', and fronted by a heavily doctored photograph of the Cobains cradling a healthy-looking baby.

None of the interviews produced any fresh information concerning Cobain's disastrous flirtation with chemicals. He confirmed that heroin was 'dumb'. He mentioned the calming influence of his daughter. More revealing than anything Cobain actually said was the aggrieved, slightly raised tone of his voice, and the way in which, despite the overwhelming evidence of his habits, he persisted in regarding his claim to have been 'raped' as self-evident. 'I feel totally violated,' he told Hilburn. It did not take a genius to deduce that it was the blows to Cobain's ego and pride that had been more damaging than those dealt to his private life, let alone his professional standing. What little Cobain did say was that familiar cocktail of the defensive, the self-pitying and the plain unbelievable. How often, Hilburn wondered, had he dabbled with heroin? 'Maybe once or twice a year,' said Cobain, the man with a $400-a-day habit. His inventions about his health were among the most fertile of a mind not always given to factual exactitude. In 1991 Cobain had told interviewers 'I'm a narcoleptic', only to admit a year later that it was a fabrication. 'I don't have narcolepsy,' he told *Melody Maker*. '[Sleep's] the only defense mechanism I have.' When Cobain nearly died from an overdose the official line had been a collapse 'possibly related to fatigue'.

Heroin, marriage, fame, money – things were closing in quickly. In Cobain's cheerier moments, he would speak touchingly of the changes his new family had wrought in him: 'I was an extremely negative person, but my attitudes and opinions have only got better. I've become more optimistic.' Along with Cobain's lifelong tendency to 'say a giant fuck-you to the world' came infusions of love for his wife, mother, daughter, and for Seattle, where he could still occasionally be seen walking the streets unmolested. 'The old Kurt was still there – ambitious, focused and plotting his next move,' says a friend. He pushed himself still, as he always had, and he realized, no doubt better than anyone else – with the single exception of Geffen – the challenges he would face in the coming year: the challenges of his private life, of recording a follow-up to *Nevermind*, and his career. He was twenty-five, the age at which Hendrix had recorded *Electric Ladyland*, or that Lennon had been in 1965 (the year of *Rubber Soul*.) It was not too late for him to have built on his success.

He had wasted time, it must have seemed to Cobain, since becoming famous. His self-advertising at drug-taking and debauchery had backfired. The last year of his career had been aimless – a regression. He was intense, fanatical, and sometimes enthusiastic, even boyish. He was also chastened, less outspoken, more sceptical, less spontaneous, more calculating. Cobain had suffered the bitterness of a backlash, and it had scarred and tempered him. He was psychotically angry at Hirschberg and his detractors in the press. He continued to rage at biographers and to renounce what he called the 'soap-opera side' of his life, while striking the author William Burroughs as 'acting out a kind of morality tale about rock'. Essentially, the plot was a simple one: the mother-dominated yet wayward boy from the wrong side of the tracks, discovering a talent to amuse, knows enough to turn it into money and stardom, but would always rather be elsewhere, doing something else. As fame struck, Cobain returned to his painting and sculpture, learned to enjoy classical music, read authors like Joyce and Beckett and wrote to Burroughs asking him to collaborate on a project. These were all diversionary tactics – distractions from his own talent and career, and from the bitter feeling that everyone seemed to enjoy themselves more than he did.

'Every night,' he told Azerrad, 'I think, "God, my life is so fucking boring compared to so many people that I know".'

It was an important, perhaps vital part of Cobain's self-opinion that he saw himself as a 'chosen reject'. He sometimes had to strain for evidence to support the image. He told one journalist, '[As a child] I'd rather hang out with the kids who didn't get chosen for the baseball team'; yet others remember him as an enthusiastic member of the local league. According to the Seattle *Times*, 'An [Aberdeen] librarian says she once saw Kurt when he was very down. She asked him what the matter was and he said his father had smashed his guitar because he was playing too loud'; nothing of the kind happened. Many of Cobain's lyrics show that he was rarely enamoured of himself, either. 'I'm so ugly,' he moaned on 'Lithium', or 'Everything is my fault/I'll take all the blame' ('All Apologies'). The working title of his new album was *I Hate Myself And I Want To Die*. Yet even here Cobain's talent for sarcasm and sleight-of-mouth was at work. The 'ugliness', it turned out, applied equally to Cobain's listeners. 'One more special message to go/And then I'm done, I can go home' he sang on *Nevermind*'s penultimate track. *I Hate Myself* became a celebration not of death but of birth, *In Utero*. Anyone looking at Cobain's songs as a dark prophecy of his suicide should remember the delight he took, in interviews as well as his lyrics, in laying false trails about himself. 'It's your crossword puzzle,' he told his biographer.

Calling Cobain a chameleon implies there was something false about each appearance he took on, as if such identities were motivated by an impulse toward subterfuge. There *was* play-acting and vanity in his internal make-up. But it was also the case that all the facets of the prism produced an equally true picture of Cobain, and that the real man was the sum total of everything he did. 'Kurt could just be very outgoing and funny and charming, and a half-hour after he would just go sit in the corner and be totally moody and uncommunicative,' says Butch Vig. According to Kate Rous, 'he was a composite, a mix of stupefying blandness and egotism'. 'Kurt went up and down,' notes his grandmother. The most shocking feature of Cobain's outbursts was not his savaging of Nirvana but his scornful dismissal of the world. Cobain recognized that, though 'one or two people' were worth saving, 'the same fuckwits [were] always around', that 'ninety-nine per cent of humanity could be shot if it was up to me', and that rock music had done 'literally nothing' to transform society. Graham Wright then asked if it were true that 'every abused kid in the country had probably bought a copy of *Nevermind*'. This was the signal for one of those sudden reversals in behaviour that constitute the basic pattern of Cobain's life. 'He went completely out of control,' says Wright. 'He shouted at me, his eyes bulging out of his head, and said: "Fuck you! I changed America! Kiss my ass!" He told me to turn off the tape recorder and get out.'

All rock stars carry a strong potential for disaster. On top of their youth and volatility, already a poisonous combination, they develop guilt pangs about their money. Add the constant proximity of drugs, sex and other inducements, and it is possible to see how a stronger man than Cobain could have developed identity problems.

In the sixties rock was makeshift, catering to an audience in their teens and younger, with none of the marketing and PR techniques so prevalent later. Even at the end of his life, a man like Hendrix never resorted to mind-numbing reshuffling of stale formulae, nor stooped to competing with his own past. He merely made music. He had, to use an overworked term, artistic control. Hendrix, a close relative insists, 'knew none of the record company bullshit' familiar today. It was enough that 'he put out a record and did the gigs'. Not only that: Hendrix never generated an obsessive local following. When he visited Seattle he was as anonymous as a man in hip-hugging crushed velvets, unbuttoned satin shirt and a bare chest can be. A family member speaks movingly of collecting his famous relative at the airport before a homecoming concert in February 1968. 'Jimi carried his own bags, spent the night in his old bed, and walked to the store the next morning to buy eggs for breakfast.' For all his own vaunted forays to the Crocodile or his dealer's home on Capitol Hill, it was impossible to think of Cobain enjoying the 'free and easy time'. His relative claims for Hendrix even in his adopted home of London: 'In the sixties, Jimi was only "on" for an hour or two a day. Otherwise the [rock] business and the people let him be. He'd no more take his work home with him than I would.'

Twenty-five years on, the industry had become mature and sophisticated in its machinations. Cobain's record company talked about his music in terms of 'demographics' and 'market penetration' and Gold Mountain were already agitating for 'another *Nevermind*'. A sense of mounting urgency had been instilled by his management in the latter half of 1992. Cobain was convinced that by fixing Christmas 1993 as the date for Nirvana's next album, Geffen had set the group an impossibly hurried task; now Gold Mountain had satisfied themselves that they could not afford to wait so long. As well as writing and recording new material, Cobain was obliged to make good his promise to tour the US and Europe, to subject himself to interviews and to cooperate in a lengthy published history of the group, *Come As You Are*. There was also the question of his daughter's custody, and of his own self-fulfilling reputation. In New York and London drug dealers followed him around. During the long periods he spent in Los Angeles Cobain could barely set foot from his door. His car was mobbed, he was recognized by everyone, and his daughter was not neglected – 'a man once put his head through the window and, grinning madly, shouted "Frances!",' Frank Hulme remembers. Cobain, unlike Hendrix, was 'on' twenty-four hours a day. When Hulme was invited to lunch at the Hollywood apartment he found 'Kurt and the nanny sitting on the floor chanting, with two phones ringing unanswered, and a fax (later destroyed by Cobain) buzzing in the corner.' Fans and curiosity-seekers stood waiting at the door and a photographer talked himself inside in the guise of a delivery-man. When Cobain saw the camera he had to be restrained from getting his gun. 'That was typical,' says Hulme. 'It went on like that every day, until Kurt started staying in his room like Howard Hughes, just on the phone all the time. It was crazy.'

A mark of Cobain's growing international fame came when Nirvana played in Buenos Aires that October. Fifty thousand fans became delirious at the sight of the three musicians arriving backstage, then kept up an impatient chant of 'CO-*bain*' during the opening act by Calamity Jane, an all-female group from the Northwest. 'It was the largest display of sexism I've ever seen at once,' Cobain said, promptly adding Argentina to his long list of pet hates. Nirvana then devoted almost their entire set to baiting the crowd, all of whom stood up in the fast numbers and sat down again when introspection called, ending with a free-form, improvised version – surely the definitive treatment – of 'Endless, Nameless'. There was no 'Teen Spirit'.

This was Nirvana suiting themselves, not the crowd. As 'School' followed 'Aneurysm' and gave way to a perfunctory 'Dive', Cobain wore the distracted, embarrassed look of someone flicking through an old family photograph album. Even the more recent additions to the repertoire received scant attention. It was only in the extended finale that Cobain came alive, flailing his guitar, taunting the audience with his single word of Spanish (*Cabrónes*) and spitting lustily into the upturned faces in the front row. Where once fans had clambered onstage and slam-danced, now a retinue of floor-managers and bouncers, responding to Cobain's snarled command to the crowd to 'leave us the fuck alone', beat back intruders with broom-handles. 'For the first time,' Grohl complained, 'I didn't even know the names of the crew members.' 'It was a sick scene, those goons strutting around and Kurt standing there laughing,' says Wright. 'The whole gig was like Nuremberg.'

There were two other results of the débâcle in Buenos Aires. Love was reconciled to the Novoselics (whose falling-out in Hawaii was deemed 'a big misunderstanding'); Cobain then spoilt the effect by setting off a cherry bomb in Nirvana's dressing-room, causing his colleagues a moment of panic and bringing the attention of the muscular 'security consultants' so recently vented on the crowd. In the scene that followed Novoselic was forced to explain the discharge as 'a prank' and Cobain, rapidly losing his good humour, was ejected by the police, screaming, 'Fascists! Nazi bastards!' and threatening a lawsuit.

Cobain then put his MTV Awards experience to good use by parodying the *Ed Sullivan Show* in the video for 'In Bloom'. Kevin Kerslake was dispatched to find authentic, Kennedy-era Kinescopes and Nirvana performed in slicked-back hair and matching suits, Cobain himself sporting glasses. Some detected irony in the compère's introduction of 'These three fine youngsters from Seattle' and his urging the audience to 'Let's hear it for these nice, decent, clean-cut young men.' After the shoot two of the trio mingled with the crowd, signing autographs, posing for amateur photos, while Cobain insisted that a female extra, whom he accused of 'bugging me', be thrown off the set. He then stalked into a local bar, still wearing his suit and glasses, and complained to the owner, 'People expect me to pay for my good luck –

they'd like me to fuck up so they can say, "Kurt's finally paying for his success". Well, I am.' The bartender had never heard of Cobain. As far as he was concerned, 'I thought I was dealing with a store-clerk or an accountant. I only realized [Cobain] was a celebrity of some sort when his agent called on me and said I shouldn't say anything about him because he was paranoid about the press.'

On 3 November America went to the polls and elected a new president. Only twelve months earlier the incumbent had had an approval rating of 90 per cent. Efforts to explain why the impossible had happened began at once, as did, understandably, a great deal of soul-searching among reporters, editors and broadcasters who had underestimated the Generation X-vote so woefully. Grant Alden is not alone in believing the cumulative protest triggered by *Nevermind* to be a significant reason for the result. Youth support for Bill Clinton had been 'overwhelming', said the *New York Times*. According to *Newsweek*: 'The precarious state of the world appeared to have benefited the challenger's campaign, and particularly as it became clear that eighteen- and nineteen-year-olds, led by activists in the rock industry, had voted *en masse* for the Democratic candidate.'

This was heady stuff, particularly as Cobain was not really political. Rather, he was romantically attached to certain personal principles which were not necessarily owned by the left or right. In his belief in the timelessness of these views, he was, if anything, a conservative in the classic sense. He believed in freedom of speech and in equal rights: in September Nirvana had played concerts to protest Oregon's Initiative 9 (designed to limit homosexual rights under the law) and to support the anti-censorship Washington Music Coalition. Inspired by women like Kathleen Hanna and, latterly, his wife, Cobain had taken up feminism, although it seemed to Frank Hulme that 'he approved of the cause in principle, and in practice not at all'. Cobain himself did not vote. He was not the intuitive moral crusader that some claimed. He was not ideological. In so far as there was a driving force behind his protest, it was a widespread and increasingly desultory rejection of the rest of humanity. Throughout his life he contained the contradiction of a popular spokesman sometimes made inarticulate by the intensity of his desire for personal revenge. Cobain's most telling protest came in neither speech nor song, but in the mute raising of a finger in the time-honoured gesture of contempt for the world.

On 15 December Geffen released *Incesticide*, a compilation of out-takes, doodles and unreleased tracks from the BBC sessions. The chaos of the collection proved Cobain's repudiation (as though not already familiar enough) of *Nevermind*. It also showed him at the end of his famously short tether with his fans.

If ever there was any doubt that, at bottom, Cobain despised his core audience, the liner notes of *Incesticide* dispelled that notion for ever. The original version had carried a lengthy harangue of Lynn Hirschberg and 'aspiring groupie writers who surround us now like celebrity-worshipping jackals moving in for the kill'. When the lawyers objected, Cobain substituted a paragraph in praise of his wife and daughter, and 'a big "fuck you" to those of you who have the audacity to claim that I'm so naïve and stupid that I would allow myself to be taken advantage of and manipulated.' Finally, for sheer pent-up anger there was Cobain's advice to the homophobic, mysogynist fans who had bought *Nevermind*: 'Leave us the fuck alone.'

In the late 1980s Cobain's songs, singing, and especially guitar – raging slabs of it, played at ear-ringing volume – had ensured Nirvana cult status, if not sales. Some of that frenetic primal energy was captured on *Incesticide*. There were 'Aero Zeppelin', 'Hairspray Queen' and other elementary, ragged tunes recorded in an era of archaic remoteness at Reciprocal; a whimsical cover of Devo's 'Turnaround'; revivals of 'Sliver' and 'Dive'; and an electric version of 'Polly' its producer recalls having been 'played strictly for laughs – until Kurt caught on to the joke'. *Incesticide*'s qualities were Cobain's own stocks-in-trade: anger, irony, arrogant self-pity, narcissism, fun. Less convincing were Nirvana's art-noise experiments, clunky, monotonous reworkings of a formula best left to Sonic Youth. According to *Rolling Stone*, 'Nirvana was a great band before *Nevermind* topped the charts. *Incesticide* is a reminder of that and – maybe more important – proof of Nirvana's ability, on occasion, to fail.' The album languished in the lower half of the chart until February, and went gold only when Geffen released a video promoting 'Sliver'.

Incesticide also famously included a cover painting by Cobain (a mutant baby clutching a skeleton), thought by Azerrad to be 'incredibly revealing', by Dylan Carlson a portrayal of 'innocence and authentic vision beset by a cruel and uncaring universe', and in Charles Peterson's view 'utter crap'. Finally, in the latest of a flood of open letters lauding his favourite groups, Cobain ended the album with a note from 'bloody exhaust grease London' celebrating the Raincoats. Finding their out-of-print LP had made him 'happier than playing in front of thousands of people each night'. It was typical of Cobain that he responded so strongly to the lure of nostalgia. At the time of which he wrote he was in Britain to promote *Nevermind*. He enjoyed a far-flung reputation as a rebel, and Cobain was besieged by people in fringe political groups to lend his name to their causes. Almost without exception, he turned them down. He regarded himself as 'an artist', not 'a missionary'. He would quietly give money to a charity, but rarely spoke out on an issue. When one teenage boy asked Cobain his views on the Gulf War he exploded that it was 'none of [his] fucking business'. A woman named Celia Ross remembers 'Kurt just shaking with mirth when, backstage before a show, he was introduced to some gay rights people.' Cobain himself would later call the 'spongers and fuckwits' he met in London 'the biggest assholes in the world'.

Nineteen ninety-two ended with an accounting of the first full year's royalties from *Nevermind*. At the time he signed with Geffen, Cobain had supposed 'a million dollars was more money than anyone could ever have. I thought a million would support us and the record label for the rest of our lives.' Now, to his horror, he found that it did nothing of the sort. Merely buying a new home, paying taxes, and hiring a lawyer to fight for custody of his daughter was enough to put Cobain heavily in debt to his record company.

Whenever he spoke of 'musical anarchy' and 'the punk ethic', Cobain was forced to conceal the extent to which he was swayed by commercial factors. Not only was a million dollars insufficient for a lifetime – it barely covered expenses for a year. Cobain had postponed a follow-up to *Nevermind* planned for the previous summer. Now he informed Geffen that recording would begin immediately, and that they, the record label, had 'the duty to talk up the album and the group'. The truth, it became clear, was that, for all his emphasis on the punk ethos, Cobain yearned to be recognized in shopping malls and to earn serious money before the intervention of middle-age. It was the cruellest lesson of a year not untouched by shadow that 'If [the new] record doesn't sell, I'm not going to be set for life. I'm going to have to get a job.'

8

Something in the Way

To many who had attended other festivals over the years, Nirvana's two concerts in São Paulo and Rio de Janeiro in January 1993 were as bungled, as badly managed as any in memory – *The Times* called them a 'catalogue of ineptitude' – and the idea that the headliners had to fetch and carry their own equipment, as Nirvana did, seemed the final straw. By the time the group arrived in Rio there was a near-mutinous atmosphere backstage, where neither food nor drink had been provided, but a longtime, nameless friend had been arrested in Nirvana's dressing-room. He had a large quantity of heroin in his possession. Geffen's lawyers put in a full night of arguing and pleading to prevent Cobain himself being charged. The friend was escorted to the airport and effectively deported for ever from Brazil. There was no publicity about the matter. But it set a suitably ominous tone to what became known as the Hollywood Rock Festival.

Cobain ended the Rio concert crawling offstage, wearing a woman's black slip, to the curses, boos and catcalls of the mob. While most jeered, others felt Cobain deserved credit for what *Forum* called 'bringing his femininity to the fore', for 'daring to be different'. Yet a longing to shock, and to dress up in his wife's lingerie, was only one side of Cobain's personality. When he was with street people he was the epitome of the street, just as when he was in the Pourhouse he was the epitome of Aberdeen, or in Los Angeles, the epitome of the jaded rock star. Clearly, Cobain took his

265

identity from the company he kept. It was significant that he was joined on the tour of Brazil by Love. According to a senior executive at Geffen, 'It was obvious Courtney was never just "Mrs Kurt Cobain", and that if anything she saw herself as the big star and him as the groupie. He hero-worshipped her.' Cobain clung to his wife's hand ('like a man under arrest', says the same source) for all but the two hours a day he was actually onstage, and she in turn took responsibility for literally everything that it was not vital for him to do himself. While in Brazil the couple rehearsed material for what Cobain assumed would be a solo album, but which Love considered releasing as a joint project two years later. (It would be 'aesthetically right' to do so, she told *Rolling Stone*.) Cobain also completed a song which hinted at his deepening emotional dependence on his wife. 'I've been locked inside your heart-shaped box' and 'Throw down your umbilical noose so I can climb right back' were only the most graphic lines of what one critic called 'a harrowing public admission of impotence'. The greatest of Cobain's strengths as an artist, and not the least of his weaknesses, was his ability to see his own predicament. At the same time as he wrote 'Heart-Shaped Box' he recorded a second number, dedicated to Love onstage at Reading in 1992, in which Cobain sang simply, 'I'm married. Buried.'

Both songs were among the material recorded by Nirvana at Pachyderm Studios, Minnesota, in February 1993. As producer Cobain chose Steve Albini, a man of impeccable punk credentials, who 'hated *Nevermind*' and even 'felt sorry' for Nirvana: 'There was a bunch of bigwig music industry scum whose fortunes depended on [the group] making hit records. It seemed obvious to me that fundamentally [Nirvana] were the same sort of people as all the small-fry bands I deal with. It was sort of a fluke that they got famous.'

Cobain should have been delighted. He considered the

importance of the producer's role second only to his own, and had filled the job three times now with men of proven ability and strong personality. Endino and Vig had served their purpose, but each had been slighted by Cobain only months after parting company. In Albini he had found his most devoted ally in retrieving the primal, back-to-basics sound lost on *Nevermind*. For two weeks Cobain arrived early at the snowbound wooden house, shunning electronic gadgetry and technique in favour of the deliberately crude, one-take tradition of *Exile On Main Street*.

Cobain still voiced the reflex pessimism that so wearied his friends. 'I'm equally as pissed off about the things that made me pissed off a few years ago. It's people doing evil things to other people for no reason. And I just want to beat the shit out of them,' he told one interviewer. Albini himself remembers Cobain's mood as 'sombre when we were recording, but I think that was pretty much the case all the time . . . He was a very pleasant, likeable, witty man. It was just that he never seemed to be *thrilled*.' After only six days twelve basic tracks had been recorded, and Novoselic and Grohl were virtually redundant. But there was very little in the way of completed lyrics, and what Cobain saw of his own notebook, he didn't like. 'Good God, what crap!' he scrawled across the top. A visitor to Pachyderm recalls 'Kurt off to one side, *sobbing* with anger that the words wouldn't come. Even when everything else was going great, he still found something to gripe about.' According to Hulme, 'Kurt had changed his mind before, but in making an ordeal of [the studio] he turned his back on his greatest love.' Cobain's suicide note would complain that 'I haven't felt the excitement of listening to, as well as creating music, along with really writing, for too many years now.'

A practical joker, Albini was in stark contrast to Cobain and had the knack of pricking his balloon of inflated cynicism. 'A nasty rumor's floating around that you were actually seen happy,' he told him. Another night the producer urged Cobain, to no avail, to 'for fuck's sake, loosen up'. To mark the end of recording, Albini handed out exploding cigars – 'everyone laughed except Kurt'. The same visitor to Pachyderm felt there was something 'whipped up and fake' about Cobain's low spirits in the face of so much celebration. Yet if a man chose pessimism, there was evidence for it to feed on in the studio. Time after time Cobain had run down *Nevermind* as a 'sell-out' and 'a complete betrayal of the punk ethos'. Now, within days of leaving Pachyderm, he began to worry that the new material was 'mushy' and 'not musical enough'. He fell into violent dispute with his producer, and complained bitterly that 'no one can hear my fucking voice'. When Albini refused to make the necessary adjustment, Cobain lobbied for Andy Wallace – the very man he blamed for 'ruining *Nevermind*' – to be hired to remix the album. After Novoselic protested he settled on R.E.M.'s producer Scott Litt, thus achieving a sound described by one critic as a 'reckless compromise' and by another as 'proof that Cobain, having started out a lover of all things punk, [had] finally joined the rock mainstream he despised'.

Cobain lifted his media ban long enough to speak to the *Advocate*, a gay rights magazine, that February. It emerged in the course of the interview that he had thought of himself as homosexual in high school, and that 'I'm definitely gay in spirit'. Cobain's admission that 'I probably could be bisexual' was widely vented by the press. As well as his youthful dabblings in Aberdeen, there were the occasions when, as an adult, he formed physical relationships with men in bars or in gay clubs around Europe, where one friend remembers Cobain's love of drink, drugs and indiscriminate oral sex as 'squalid rather than wicked'. There was also a side of Cobain that loved to shock by his accounts of deviant sex and 'being different'. In October 1991 he appeared on

MTV dressed fetchingly in a yellow silk ballgown and flirted throughout with Novoselic; two months later they french-kissed on *Saturday Night Live*. With Love came the opportunity for Cobain to extend his experiments in cross-dressing into ribbons, bows and frilly underwear. He began to appear on stage wearing his wife's lingerie. Love's own group would release a single called 'Beautiful Son' in April 1993. 'You look good in my dress/My beautiful son', she sang to the epicene teenager on the record sleeve, an exact double of her husband. A year later she told *Out* that Cobain had 'made out with half the guys in town' and that she, Love, had 'slept with about fifteen women'. A man in Seattle named Mike Collier speaks of the time he saw Cobain enter the men's room of a club, 'hand-in-hand with a truck-driving or logging type' and emerge with a 'matter-of-fact air of completion'. A woman watched 'Kurt dance with one guy after another' in the Vogue, and 'a girl in a drop-dead dress' fail to even interest him – he drifted off alone. In early 1993 Cobain told a close friend in Los Angeles that 'he'd had sex with three or four men', that it was 'no big deal', and he 'wanted the subject closed'. He thereafter made frequent allusions to his heterosexuality and complained of the 'bad impression' given by his comments in the *Advocate*. Cobain struck Frank Hulme as 'deeply embarrassed by the rumour that he was gay'. According to Collier, 'As his marriage progressed, so Kurt grew less and less enamoured with being branded a fag.' His Los Angeles friend also believes Cobain 'never got over the shame, beat into him in Aberdeen, of being queer. For all he said to the contrary, Kurt was hyper-sensitive to people ragging him.' By a quirk of timing, Nirvana's next single after the *Advocate* interview would be 'Oh, The Guilt'.

There were no lack of humanizing contradictions about Cobain. He was the egalitarian who fought with his friends over money, the hairshirt ascetic with a taste for drugs, the pacifist who stockpiled guns. In so far as he had a professional reputation, it was as a wry observer with an all too evident modesty about his work. Yet as early as 1989 there were signs that Cobain also possessed a healthy ego. Reflecting on his firing from Nirvana, Jason Everman told Azerrad, 'I probably wanted to do things that were not simple enough for them, ideas that were *mine* as opposed to Kurt's ... Maybe it was just a control thing.' Even on heroin Cobain exercised day-to-day supervision of video shoots, interviews and his own appearances. (When MTV first asked Nirvana to play the Video Music Awards in September 1992, Novoselic and Grohl went to Cobain's hospital room to get his approval.) Albini would tell *Q* that 'what surprised me was how efficient Kurt was, how together his music and his band were. He was an easy person to work with: perceptive, capable of speaking his mind, describing what he wanted.' Danny Goldberg was not alone in comparing his client's single-mindedness to John Lennon's. Yet even that fails to do justice to Cobain's self-awareness and flair for publicity. Almost as soon as Azerrad's biography was published, Cobain was making plans to commission a book 'telling the whole truth' and outlining to Kevin Kerslake his idea for a video history of Nirvana. Much as it went against his image, Cobain's management of his career exceeded even typical rock star standards. In 'always knowing what he wanted and getting it' he was 'near unique,' says Hulme. Only one other performer came close to his exceptional grasp of detail – Mick Jagger.

Almost all Nirvana's songs were built of a collaboration. Andy Wallace and Butch Vig had embellished the basic tunes on *Nevermind*. Novoselic offered advice in the studio and wrote part of 'Heart-Shaped Box'. Grohl contributed the melody to 'Pennyroyal Tea'. Yet all those tracks were credited solely to Cobain. Old friends in Seattle had taken photographs and helped design album covers because, as Alice Wheeler says, 'everyone believed in the group'. According to Peterson, 'the whole idea of Nirvana, and punk generally, was that anybody could share in the band's success.' By 1993 it appeared that Cobain had deserted collectivism in favour of a more individual approach. 'It's mindboggling,' he complained. 'I come up with every idea for everything we do . . . it just pisses me off to see on the back of the *Bleach* album, "art direction by Lisa Orth", and everyone thinks that Lisa Orth came up with that picture . . . I came up with the whole idea and they get credit for it.'*

Cobain and Love worked hard for their enmity. They were involved in several lawsuits in the early part of 1993. The comment of one writer that 'they communicated with the world through litigation and press releases' may be unfair. Even so, by choosing to fight their battles publicly, in court, they risked not only financial loss but their own reputation.

Over Christmas Love had filed suit against her doctor for medical fraud and negligence, unlawful disclosure, and intentional infliction of emotional distress. (The gist of the complaint was that during her confinement Love's medical file had been leaked to Los Angeles *Weekly*.) The action was settled out of court. Similar invasion of privacy claims, never tried, were made against Lynn Hirschberg and the *Globe*. Meanwhile, Victoria Clarke, the Cobains' would-be biographer, alleged that Love had attacked her at a Los Angeles club. Love countered that Clarke had started the brawl. The case had a preliminary hearing in early 1993, although it, too, was later dropped. Cobain himself settled

* According to Orth, 'the *real* unsung heroes' of *Bleach* were Tracy Marander, who took the cover photograph and Bruce Pavitt, who designed it.

with Patrick Campbell-Lyons in the same month. He made an *ex gratia* payment to a former colleague who had threatened to sue. According to Albini, Cobain was 'very conscious of his predicament' and 'horrified' by the mounting litigation: 'People were trying to find some excuse to get a chunk of Kurt's money, most of it almost certainly shysterism.' As one final indignity, a fan now filed suit against Nirvana after being struck in the face by flying shards from Cobain's smashed guitar.

By threatening to sue *Vanity Fair*, Cobain and Love had forced one of the country's oldest and most resourceful publishing companies to pore through the couple's lives in search of dirt. It was no wonder that they came to feel paranoid about the media. Nothing was more typical of Cobain than this tendency to divorce his behaviour from its consequences. When he railed at Hirschberg or Clarke he said he had the right to be two people, the public performer and himself. It was Cobain the family man who promised to 'fucking get revenge' on his detractors. But even to his friends at Geffen, this inclination to see himself as both Cobain the celebrity and Cobain the human being was not entirely a virtue or necessarily an admirable characteristic. As one executive put it, Kurt 'would forget that the rest of the world might not make the distinction'. Moreover Cobain, as a public figure, could not win a libel suit unless he could prove either that the press knew what they wrote was false, or that they wrote it with reckless disregard for the truth. This theory – that certain people have chosen to lead highly visible lives and therefore voluntarily sacrifice much of their protection from criticism – comes from the 1964 decision in *New York Times v. Sullivan*. Public figures, the judge in the Sullivan case reasoned, have ample opportunity to rebut any false allegations. But Cobain denied that he was a public figure.

On 23 March 1993 the Cobains finally won a legal battle

when the accusations brought against them by the Department of Children's Services were dropped. The couple could now raise their daughter without supervision by social workers.

A sign of Cobain's determination to lead 'some sort of normal family life' was his purchase for $400,000 of an eleven-acre estate in Carnation, a small community twenty miles east of Seattle. The weathered two-storey house, connected by a bridge to a guest cottage, was reached by a dirt road rising from the Tolt river between forests and the lush pastures of Carnation Farm. Buying the property may have been the most sensible thing Cobain had done since becoming famous. 'He just dreamed of going out there and never coming back,' says his mother. 'He loved to stay there with Courtney and Frances, and maybe a few close friends and family, grow vegetables and flowers, make a little music for himself, and never go back.' Cobain bought Love a new car, a Lexus, and started driving himself again. He sometimes appeared in the tavern next to the Carnation Bible Church and struck one woman as 'no different from any young man who came in for a beer and a hamburger'. According to a local man, 'the very idea that he was somehow different, or special, was ridiculous to him. He was the most down-to-earth guy in the world, even when people hassled him'. This was perhaps where the image of Cobain as a shy, unassuming man of the people was most real. Often tourists from Seattle stood outside his property, gazing through the trees. 'Is this where Nirvana lives?' a woman shouted at him one morning with a camera in her hand.

Cobain also rented a four-bedroom house overlooking the water in Seattle. From the outside, at least, the property at 11301 Lakeside Avenue NE conformed to the 'normal family life' he wanted. There was a rock garden, rhododendron bushes, a view of the lake, a boat garage and even a basketball hoop for the Cobains' entertainment. Among their neighbours were a university professor and an executive vice-president of Boeing.

With two homes in the area Cobain became a more familiar figure on the streets of Seattle. Despite all his wealth he still shopped at the local Safeway, bought his own petrol and took time to speak to fans and well-wishers. Later that June Gillian Gaar saw him waiting patiently to use his ATM card outside a bank on Broadway, and was struck by his 'darting blue eyes' and the way 'he shuffled forward with round shoulders'. A writer named David Haig met him at a convenience store and remembers 'Kurt answering questions about himself and the band for ten minutes', and then incongruously refusing to sign an autograph. A teenage boy approached him at the airport and was rewarded by 'a long conversation about how much Kurt dug Seattle and wanted to raise his family here'. He then carried his own luggage out to the street. As Cobain's taxi pulled away from the curb, a young woman squeezed her bare breasts against the car window and mouthed 'I love you' through the glass, gestures Cobain returned by merely 'smiling calmly'.

Lest this be taken as evidence of deeper stability, Cobain continued to lead an exotically chaotic private life. His Seattle home combined the found-art experiments of Olympia with the rampant drug use of Los Angeles. One corner of the house, designated the 'mess room', contained books, papers, decaying food, empty bottles, cigarette butts, guitar parts and Love's Buddhist shrine. Gold and platinum discs, their glass frames shattered, covered the floor. A bedroom had been converted into an artist's studio and repository for tin cans, lengths of pipe and broken crockery. Cobain himself held court at the kitchen table, building a plastic anatomical model while washing down his morning valium with champagne. 'His wig-outs were legendary around here,' says a neighbour in the otherwise quiet, semi-private street. 'One night Kurt stood on the porch screaming at [Love] and threw all her clothes into the road.' On another occasion Cobain attacked his car with a tyre iron, smashing the windscreen, before charging off towards the lake 'like a bull'. Police called at the house twice in the space of five weeks in response to complaints. Within a year the Cobains would leave the property and buy their own home.

On 9 April Nirvana gave their first American performance in six months, a charity event at the Cow Palace in San Francisco. The bulk of the proceeds went to Balkan rape victims. At the pre-concert press conference Novoselic (restoring the Bosnian spelling of his first name) spoke movingly of the plight of the Tresnjevka Women's Group and, with Love in attendance, insisted that 'the whole point of punk' was to 'empower women to lead their own lives'. Cobain neither endorsed nor disputed the view, but there were those, like Wright, who thought 'the political aspect of the show meant less to him than the chance to play'. On some issues, such as abortion, Cobain was undoubtedly a feminist. In other areas, however, he was a far from whole-hearted supporter of women's rights, refusing on occasion to read a magazine because it was 'full of shit about dykes'. In December Love would tell the journalist Kim Neely, 'Kurt's one of the most liberal people I know, but he looked at me one day and [said], "I hate it when you read those fucking feminist books".' It was noticed that Cobain never opened a book of photographs of Bosnian women given to him in San Francisco, and that after the show he left the album in the dressing-room.

The concert itself opened with 'Rape Me' and included seven other new songs recorded at Pachyderm. There was much to admire in Nirvana's performance. Cobain remained an unlikely success on stage, overcoming his natural shyness and playing off Novoselic and Grohl to create an engagingly wry review of his now-panoramic background. The bludg-eoning guitar and deadpan lyric of 'Blew' gave way to the

275

anthemic 'Lithium' and a chilling, half-spoken 'Polly'. But Cobain was not one to dwell on his past glories to the exclusion of a fresh creative stance. The old material was well complemented by songs like 'Heart-Shaped Box' and 'Scentless Apprentice'. If the resulting mix occasionally jarred – 'melodies emerged and sank again', noted *Rolling Stone*; 'the band's new songs resembled alternative cuts in *Incesticide* rather than the hits on *Nevermind*' – the energy of the performance held its own pleasures. Cobain's stage act infused the set with a true sense of abandon. At the climax of the seven-song encore he stood howling on his amplifier, screaming and stamping his foot before diving headlong into the drums, collapsing in a great crash of mangled steel and wood.

Cobain had one year to live.

Charles Peterson, summoned to Lakeside Avenue to take photographs for *In Utero*, understood what success had done to Cobain spiritually as well as physically. 'Before, Kurt had looked on adversity as a test that strengthened him. Becoming a professional musician gave him a sense of power and control over his life.' But the test of fame had left him worse off, not better, feeling weaker instead of empowered. As well as succumbing to the 'parasites and hangers-on', Cobain had chronically abused his already frail body. As 1993 ended he all but gave up alcohol, a notable reversal for one previously fond of champagne and whisky. But he still chain-smoked both marijuana and his Winston Lights. According to Hulme, Cobain kept a packet of cigarettes at hand 'as a security blanket'. He also, of course, took heroin, indiscriminately and with rapidly diminishing returns for his health. Most evenings when he was in Seattle Cobain drove to a derelict yellow-sided house on Harvard Avenue where he bought his supplies. David Haig saw him 'stagger out, almost bent double, and lean on his car, choking' before driving off. Another man met Cobain on Broadway, 'slurring his words and barging into people on the street'. According to Wright, 'it got to the stage where Kurt was staying up all night, smoking, and killing himself.' He rarely ate.

Though few publicly said it, it was clear Cobain was becoming mentally unstable. 'He was afraid, he thought he was being threatened by people following him, he thought he was being bugged,' says Frank Hulme. He was 'acutely paranoid'. When telephone engineers called at Lakeside Avenue Cobain locked himself in the basement, accusing the men of being 'agents' sent to harass him. In turn he developed a 'fatal attraction' form of mental illness, erotomania, and sent a young art student 'seven or eight love notes', a hand-drawn Valentine's card and an invitation for the woman to join him in a Seattle hotel. When she refused Cobain phoned a dozen times in a day, followed her home and sent a brick wrapped in a piece of paper with the message: 'I'm not obsessed with you. I just wanted to talk to you about conceptual art.'

Underlying Cobain's erratic behaviour was his nagging dread of growing older, and the fear that, at twenty-six, his best days were already behind him. Although millions still enjoyed Nirvana's music, others judged the group's once-unique mix of apathy and anger to be old-hat. By 1993 a backlash had begun against the generation of Americans who took Cobain as their role model, culminating in an *Atlantic* article chiding the 'whiny pusillanimous purveyors of pseudo-pop' whose sole achievement to date had been 'something called grunge'. Moreover, many of Cobain's own fans had grown weary of a relentless diet of unmitigated gloom. 'Cyberia' was the new buzzword of the young who surfed the Internet, head-banged to industrial rock and, in the words of Lucas Barr, editor of the cult magazine *KCB*, 'kind of enjoy[ed] rushing towards oblivion'. Cobain, in short, was in danger of losing his audience – too mainstream for the thirteen- to nineteen-year-olds coming up fast behind Generation X, not ancient enough to tap the nostalgic vein worked by the likes of Pink Floyd and the Rolling Stones. 'He saw himself being marginalized,' says a friend. 'A large part of his problem was, simply put, an artistic crisis about the future. Musically speaking, Kurt was on the way down, rather than the way up.' He had already lived a modern saga. Cobain had been present at the birth of grunge – indeed, more than anyone else, was its creator. He had had the advantage of writing on the slate when it was virtually clean. Now a slew of new groups had sprung up to challenge him, Cobain faced a demoralizing and even debilitating crisis. It was widely noted that Nirvana had not released an album of new material in nearly two years. There was renewed talk about the group breaking up. Novoselic spoke openly about the prospect of a solo career, while Cobain himself, he insisted, wanted to start his own label 'to record street bums and people with deformities and mental deficiencies'. Whatever the cause, it was hard to deny that by 1993 the first wave of the group's fame had broken, or that the question posed in *Select*, 'Nirvana: What's Gone Wrong?', was widely asked.

The transformation of Cobain from wicked rebel to icon was a peculiar American phenomenon, and his worth, in both musical and social terms, was still the most hotly debated issue in rock. 'Kurt shaped the thinking of millions who never heard of any other group,' says his friend. To others, as Cobain himself well knew, he was at best a figure of fun – rich, cosseted and (the ultimate insult) bourgeois. Those of his contemporaries who most fiercely affected the punk or anarchist styles of music, dress and rhetoric were the most scornful of him. 'A cop-out' was the fell phrase used by the *Facts*. It must have been galling to Cobain, as he sat in his waterfront mansion, to realize he had become what he most despised, a famous American personality. Overall, he took a poor view of celebrity and often had a hard time convincing himself that his own fame was worth it. 'It's become a job, whether I like it or not,' he told an interviewer. To the question 'What's it like to be famous?' he answered, 'The only thing I can think of is paranoia . . . it makes you feel like someone's watching you.' Nor did Cobain take much comfort in the support of his colleagues. According to Albini, 'Literally every person involved in the enterprise that [was] Nirvana, besides the band itself, were pure pieces of shit.'

That Cobain was cynical about his management is certain, but he was also a realist. 'I'm a whore for my music. I'll do anything to get it out,' he told Hulme. That his career showed many of the characteristics of a dog being wagged by its own tail – specifically, Geffen – is also certain but was not a problem confined to Cobain. Despite his friendship with Mark Kates and Gary Gersh, Geffen 'didn't understand' *In Utero*, he thought, a feeling shared by the record's producer. In May the Chicago *Tribune* quoted Albini as saying, 'I have no faith this album will ever be released.' *Newsweek* then ran a piece under the banner 'You Call This Nirvana?', describing Geffen as 'horrified' by the grunge-rock quality of the mix. Others suggested there were insufficient potential singles for the label's taste. Items in *Rolling Stone* and *Entertainment Weekly* also reported Cobain as 'at loggerheads' with his employers, who, he told Azerrad, 'want another *Nevermind*. I'd rather die than do that . . . [*In Utero*] is exactly the kind of record I would buy as a fan,' he insisted. 'I couldn't be truer to myself than to put this out the way it is. It's my favourite production and my favourite songs.'

Within a month Cobain changed tack and, showing what Hulme calls 'his obsessive need to communicate with the people he despised', sent a long rebuttal to *Newsweek*. 'Jeff Giles has written an article on our band which was not based on the band's views nor on information provided by our representatives,' the letter opened, in tones that could only have been supplied by Gold Mountain. 'Most damaging of all is that Giles ridiculed our relationship with our label based on totally erroneous information. Geffen Records has supported our efforts all along in making this record.' In a press release, Cobain went further in openly attacking Albini: 'Steve has made a career out of being anti-rock establishment, but being commercial or anti-commercial is not what makes a good rock record, it's the songs. And until we have the songs recorded the way we want them, Nirvana will not release the record.' With a deft change of position, Cobain now pronounced the new album 'not as good' as *Nevermind*. He seriously considered hiring Andy Wallace to give *In Utero* the same user-friendly mix as the earlier work, in the end settling for Scott Litt. Cobain and Albini never spoke again. When *In Utero* was released in September (debuting at Number One), the expected controversy centred less on the music than the refusal of two national retailers to carry the album. The stores' chief objection was the back cover, a collage of plastic foetus models, lilies and orchids, arranged by Cobain and photographed by Charles Peterson, which the one thought depicted 'sex and woman and *In Utero* and vaginas and birth and death' and the other considered 'junk'. Geffen also changed the song title 'Rape Me' to 'Waif Me', a name that Cobain picked, according to the record company's Ray Farrell. 'At first, Kurt wanted to call it "Sexually Assault Me",' Farrell says, 'but it took up too much room. In the end he decided on "Waif Me" because *waif*, like *rape*, is not gender specific. *Waif* represents somebody who is at the mercy of other people.'

After his confessional interview to the Los Angeles *Times*, Cobain never admitted to using heroin again. 'He'd been badly shaken,' his cousin says. 'And he still seemed deeply shocked. You got the feeling he only had to say one word out of place and Children's Services would have been back for Frances.' According to David Haig, 'Kurt didn't want the expense, hassle and trauma of another custody battle. Officially, he was off dope. The feeling [in Seattle] was that it was only now that his addiction really took hold.'

On 2 May 1993 Cobain came home to Lakeside Avenue pale, shivering and dazed. 'The victim suffered symptoms associated with an overdose,' the police report says. 'Victim was conscious and able to answer questions, but was obviously impaired to some degree.' Love told police that Cobain had been at a friend's house, where he injected $30–40 worth of heroin. Later in the evening, in the course of a family dinner, his condition deteriorated 'to the point that he was shaking, delirious, and talking incoherently'. As Cobain's mother and sister watched, Love injected her husband with buprenorphine (an illegal drug sometimes used to revive overdose victims), before giving him a valium, three Benadryls and four codeine tablets, causing him to vomit. Cobain was treated at Harborview Medical Center and released. Love told the police that 'this type of incident' had happened before. No charges were filed.

On Friday, 4 June police returned to Lakeside Avenue to answer a domestic disturbance call. According to the official report, 'Suspect Kurt Cobain and victim Courtney Love had gotten into an argument over guns in the household. Victim Courtney stated that she threw a glass of juice into suspect Kurt's face and that suspect Kurt pushed her in turn. Victim pushed suspect back, at which time suspect pushed victim to the floor and began choking her, leaving a scratch.' In the unofficial version, Love had started the fight over her husband's 'suicidal' drug use.

Cobain was arrested and locked in King County jail, where he spent three hours before being freed on $950 bail. The incident was investigated by Seattle police's criminal division, which later decided against pressing charges.

According to a memo filed by the division's director on 9 September:

> The victim will testify that nothing happened, contrary to the police report. Additionally the [emergency] tape is probably not admissible because it neither describes an assault, nor do her hearsay statements fall under an exception to the hearsay rule. Most notably, her statements do not fall under the excited utterance exception because her speech gives no indication that she was under the stress of a startling event such as an assault . . . Since we are unable to prove that an attack causing bodily injury occurred and that there was an absence of self-defense, the City declines to file.

Unmentioned by the report but widely aired in Seattle was the condition of the Cobains' home found by the police. According to one source, the first officers to arrive at the scene were staggered by the sheer filth and air of decay: 'There was a powerful, unpleasant smell, as if there was a dead cat somewhere.' The chaos of the house was of a piece with Hulme's description of the couple's life in California. In both cases the phone rang unanswered, a fax machine chattered in the corner. There were no pictures on the walls, and heavy sheets at the windows instead of curtains. 'I could just imagine Kurt walking around there being really depressed,' says one Seattle friend. 'You couldn't get in to see him. He had all these people around him – plastic people from LA, keeping his old friends away.' Other reports had Cobain wandering around his home dressed in pyjamas (when the police arrested him he was wearing a bathrobe) or locked in a dark room playing the guitar. Rumours that he regularly hid from his wife in a closet are probably groundless. There was, however, an occasion when a friend arrived at Lakeside Avenue to find 'Courtney throwing everything that was loose against the wall, and screaming at Kurt for being useless. His fault, as she saw it, was not being able to come up with a song.'

Some of Cobain's domestic chaos was captured in the video promoting the re-released 'Sliver'. Much of the footage was shot in the garage at Lakeside Avenue. As well as the debris of Cobain's experiments in clay dolls and models, the eight-month-old Frances also appeared, apparently dancing although actually propped up in her father's arms. (Love was away with her group in Britain.) For someone who had spent nearly ten years in the rock business, Cobain had few close friends and no real confidants among the men he knew or worked with, any more now than in boyhood. It was the three women in his life, his mother, wife and daughter, who mattered, whose company and approval he most valued. Over the next year Cobain regularly appeared with Frances in public, earning reproof from some for exploiting his child and praise from others for his willingness to be photographed holding formula bottles and nappies. None of the networks objected to Frances's cameo in 'Sliver', although a collage of magazines had to be cut from the video because of rules about product placement.

On the morning of 23 July Love heard a crash in the bathroom of the New York hotel where the couple were staying. She opened the door and found Cobain unconscious. Only hours after being treated for yet another drug overdose he was onstage with Nirvana at Roseland, reminding the *New York Times* of the 'perfectly realized formula' that made the group famous in the first place:

> Mr Cobain sings in a voice that moves from haggard complaint to threat, the voice of someone growing angrier as he realizes he has nothing to lose. It's a voice millions can identify with, particularly when carried by

Nirvana's music. Mr Cobain's guitar parts, with chords and riffs and noises, are a razor-wire topping to the brick wall solidity of Dave Grohl's drums and Krist Novoselic's bass.

Less impressed was the critic who thought 'Kurt spent most of the night looking like a man whose dog had just been run over,' or the fans who booed and whistled when Cobain sat down with an acoustic guitar and was joined by a cellist. If it was true, as they insisted, that Nirvana wanted to be 'taken seriously as musicians', it was also true that Cobain was a guitarist whose authority depended on the sort of sonic assault shunned at Roseland. His modest unplugged work was a mere shadow of his electric virtuosity. Worse still, Cobain and the cello were strangers to each other's time scales. This accounted for the rambling songs, fussily. arranged, elaborately introduced, conveying a sense that everything Cobain now did, everything he thought, said and played was of importance because he was important. A number of reviewers pointed to this, and none of them too kindly. 'Well, aren't we clever?' was the refrain of *Guitar*, while the *Forum* critic thought Cobain made too much of his 'contented-daddy-mature-musician act' and pleaded for a return to 'sanity'.

Cobain spent the next three days doing interviews in New York. According to a piece filed by Amy Raphael in the *Face*:

He pushes Frances Bean about in her pushchair, big grins on their faces. He jokes around with Courtney, kissing her very publicly and proudly. Does he feel he can live forever? 'Sure. I believe if you die you're completely happy and your soul somewhere lives on and there's this positive energy. I'm not in any way afraid of death.'

To another writer, Cobain added:

> I've been suicidal all my life. I just don't want to die
> *now*. Having a child and being in love is the only thing
> I feel I've been blessed with.

Two weeks later, on 6 August, Nirvana gave their final performance as a trio. At the last minute they joined a Seattle benefit for Mia Zapata, a local musician found murdered the previous month. According to Gillian Gaar, 'You could tell Kurt was enjoying himself by the way he threw in a Zeppelin number and a hilarious cover of "Seasons in the Sun".' To the photographer Michael Andeel, the same song was 'actually poignant' in its sense of 'time moving on, life closing down'. After years in which they played drug-addled grunge to packed houses, and adulatory coverage, Nirvana faced the ironic possibility that they might be falling from favour just as they strove for respect as musicians. 'Kurt was hurt that people were laughing at him,' says Andeel. Backstage, the photographer found a 'roaring drunk' Cobain refereeing a fight between Love and Tad Doyle's girlfriend, ending in a lamp being knocked over and a fire starting in the dressing-room. Cobain then drove off to meet his heroin dealer and finished the evening in the bar of a downtown hotel, acting out of character, signing autographs for tourists and businessmen and insisting that Seattle, despite its 'shitty weather' was 'the greatest place in the world'.

Cobain's enthusiasm for his adopted home came as the original novelty of the town gave way to self-caricature and parody. Events elsewhere, in cities like Atlanta and Minneapolis, had helped transform the once-arcane world of grunge into a national fad. Another five years of deterioration of the American social fabric since 'Love Buzz' had helped to disseminate Nirvana's values. The dress code varied from coast to coast, but the guiding beliefs – the air of screwed-up nihilism, of limited prospects, of contempt for the phoniness of 'establishment' rock and the hypocrisy of family life – were now the dominant standards of the age. Meanwhile, Nirvana itself had become a successful mainstream group, dominated by lawyers and accountants, a tabloid gossip item and, to some, a travesty of the late-eighties original. Many of the band's own disciples had grown disillusioned with its success. Less than a week after the Zapata benefit, Smashing Pumpkins' Billy Corgan (the man Love left for Cobain) told a cheering capacity crowd in Chicago, 'As far as I'm concerned, "fuck Seattle".' The feeling that Cobain might be an ephemeral figure, reduced to imitating his imitators, was lent ironic weight by *Rolling Stone*'s placing an indifferent review of the Roseland concert next to a glowing profile of Corgan: 'Determined to prove that they are creating some of the toughest, most dynamic rock around – without the hoopla of a scene to buoy them – Smashing Pumpkins blasted through an exhausting ninety minutes of music that left the entire all-ages audience physically fatigued and sonically exhilarated. Nevermind Nirvana; the Pumpkins are the real deal.'

Two writers chose this moment to publish biographies of the group, Michael Azerrad's *Come As You Are: The Story of Nirvana* and *Nirvana and the Sound of Seattle* by Brad Morrell. Although 'officially unauthorized', Azerrad's book enjoyed its subjects' cooperation, and tackled (in one review) 'Cobain's troubled upbringing; the group's troubled early years; the troubles incurred by a meteoric rise; and drug trouble'. Less harrowing – to some laughable – was the author's treatment of Aberdeen, which Grant Alden believes 'reflected Mike's own values' and Lamont Shillinger calls 'patronizing and wrong'. Both Azerrad's and Morrell's books were welcome relief from the sense of embattlement Cobain felt over media coverage of his marriage. Since *Vanity Fair* both he and Love had been demonized in the tabloids. For twelve months the campaign had been relentless, and the effect on Cobain shattering. According to Moon, 'Kurt had known all along what might happen', but however dark his premonition, he could not possibly have measured the outcome. No one could have. A few trade papers and fanzines had supported Cobain, even through the low-point of 1992. To *Rolling Stone* he was 'one of the major figures to emerge from rock's first thirty years', someone whose 'misanthropic view seems to inspire his remarkable gift'. But such voices were lost in a tempest of journalistic outrage. 'LOCK UP THE JUNKIE ... SEND THE CHILD ABUSER TO HELL ... SUGGEST YOU COPY ARTICLE ON JUNKIE LOVE TO AUTHORITIES' read telegrams typical of those pouring into *Vanity Fair* and the other titles. While by far the greatest clamour came from those who wrote in criticizing his heroin use, there was no lack of editorial comment on the 'pissy, complaining, freaked-out schizophrenic image', as Cobain quite accurately put it. It is not exaggerating to say that he seized on almost every critical reference as evidence of a conspiracy. Even mild rebuke was torture to one of his hypersensitive nature. By late 1993 Cobain's chief concern was with finding a way to 'speak direct to people' without the distorting influence of either the music industry or the press. It was to this concern that his plans for his own label were a response. Cobain also spoke about commissioning book and film treatments of his life, showing the compulsive need to 'convert his enemies' for which friends still remember him.

Cobain had only played a few concerts in a year, but even this effort had exhausted him. He looked cadaverous (his weight fell to 115 pounds), his voice a barely audible growl. All his life, Cobain had bridled at the attention given to his looks, but now he was self-conscious about his appearance. He began to go out more often wearing a hat or sunglasses.

A make-up artist called at Lakeside Avenue before Cobain's public engagements. According to one visitor, 'it was a shock that this beautifully made man had wasted away to a shell' through drug use. To compound the problem, Cobain's stomach cramps now returned. Literally everything he did, said and played from 1993 on would be affected by physical pain. Cobain saw half-a-dozen specialists in the first half of the year alone. He also experimented with a virtual reality machine, a small box taped to his stomach supposedly to help him relax. 'He seemed to go from bad to worse,' says Frank Hulme. 'I doubt whether Kurt had more than a few normal days for the rest of his life.'

It was now that he began a downward spiral of chronic heroin use. As well as the near-fatal overdoses in May and July, there was an incident in San Francisco when he was rushed to a clinic blue in the face and barely breathing, where a doctor not only revived him but extracted two broken needles buried inside his arm. 'Everything you did, Kurt had to do six of,' says David Haig. Even Love would later describe her husband as a wholesale 'gobbler' of drugs. He was seen buying heroin outside a drive-in hamburger stand on Broadway; in a park near his home; on the steps of the Seattle public library. A friend of the couple's told the journalist Mick Brown, '[Cobain and Love] kept on announcing that they were clean and everything, and that made it worse in Kurt's mind because he knew they weren't, or that he was only clean for a short time and he'd be back on it.' In September Cobain – yet again – underwent detoxification before a winter tour of the US and Europe.

As his health deteroriated, so his irascibility and obsession with his rivals worsened. An important part of Cobain's character was his need, almost a compulsion, to publicize his views about his enemies. To David Fricke's question, 'Where do you stand on Pearl Jam now?' he answered, 'I don't want to get into that', then a moment later added 'I'm pretty sure that they didn't go out of their way to challenge their audience as much as we did with [*In Utero*]. They're a safe rock band.' Cobain claimed to be 'purposely naïve', yet his ego was famous even in an industry proverbial for its self-promotion: 'a tyrant', according to one colleague. By the time of his death two distinct pictures had emerged of Cobain. Those who preferred not to be named spoke of him as manipulative, self-obsessed, 'passive-aggressive', with an erratic temperament frequently bordering on the neurotic. To Azerrad, the biographer who became Cobain's friend, he was 'a very sensitive person, sweet and bright'.

Love herself recognized the paradox when she described Cobain as 'addicted' to his own press, someone who 'wanted to be popular', 'very much a people pleaser', a man who physically fought with his wife over the magazine articles she hid from him. Almost without exception, journalists who interviewed Cobain commented on his seemingly conflicting love of publicity and fear of exposure. *Rolling Stone* encountered this contradiction as early as November 1991: 'Having already shunned the *New York Times* and the *Los Angeles Times*, he at first refused to be interviewed for this article, changed his mind, then failed to surface two other times, in one instance hiding in a locked hotel room.' Even Michael Azerrad was left waiting by Cobain to go 'Inside the Heart and Mind of Nirvana'. When a Seattle journalist named Jo-Ann Greene arranged to meet the group in 1993 she found the three waiting for her in a downtown hotel:

Kurt, standing between Krist Novoselic and Dave Grohl, spotted me immediately. I smiled, and he immediately dropped his gaze.

As the distance between us shortened, Kurt's unease became apparent. His eyes darted back and forth, he hunched deeper into his own shoulders. By the time I was half way there, Kurt was beginning to sidle backwards. I kept walking – our gaze met again. This time, his eyes showed naked terror. He looked like a cornered animal.

For years Cobain had struggled to convince himself that things, though black, would eventually lighten. 'All I need is a break, and my stress will be over with,' he told *Rolling Stone*. 'I'm sure it will just be a matter of time,' he added to his biographer. 'If people just keep their fucking mouths shut and stop the accusations ... I'll probably be okay.' Now, after more than a year of tabloid scrutiny, Cobain was no longer so sanguine. According to Haig, 'It was the thought that the unbearable, instead of getting better, was likely to deteroriate that so bothered him.' As he prepared to tour again in October 1993 Cobain seemed to have lost even the hope of professional fulfilment. 'We're almost exhausted,' he told an interviewer. 'We've got to the point where things are becoming repetitious. There's not something you can move up toward, there's not something you can look forward to.' To this writer Cobain expressed the melancholy thought that 'I'll be totally forgotten in five years'.

His group's ballistic rise to the top unsettled Cobain deeply. 'Teenage angst has paid off well/Now I'm bored and old' he sang in the opening lines of *In Utero*. 'I'm only in it for the money,' he told his cousin. That one theme – the perversion of innocence – would recur in almost everything Cobain wrote. His own suicide note read as a morality tale ('wearisome in its familiarity', according to Mick Brown) of mercurial rise and instant burn-out; of the conflict between the creative process and the corruption of its rewards; of hope and disillusionment. For years Cobain had said that he 'didn't want to be famous'. What he really objected to was becoming a sort of cartoon rock star. *Nevermind* had lifted him to true celebrity, in the peculiarly American sense of the word. He crossed over the line separating those who are well known for doing something from those who are famous for simply being. Cobain worried constantly about being characterized as no better than a spectacular abuser of drugs, a schizophrenic and an unfit father. Yet it would be wrong to suppose that he wished to avoid the limelight altogether. Famous, life was difficult; unknown, it was impossible. By 1993 Cobain had leavened his rage against the media with a new sense of civility and after chiding a reporter, he was likely to add the rider: 'Don't take it personally.' One or two journalists broke through his reserve, and he struck *The Times* correspondent as 'playing the press like a fiddle'. On 1 July Cobain invited the visiting *New Musical Express* stringer to Lakeside Avenue for a preview of *In Utero*, handing the magazine a major scoop and causing palpitations for the Geffen publicity department.

Cobain also developed a much-needed streak of irony about his own plight. 'Wait/I've got a new complaint,' he sang on 'Heart-Shaped Box'. The bridge of 'Serve The Servants' contained the line 'The legendary divorce is such a bore'. ('I'm a product of a spoiled America,' Cobain told a reporter. 'Think of how much worse my family life could be if I grew up in a depression or something.') The final chorus of 'Frances Farmer will have her Revenge on Seattle' was 'I miss the comfort in being sad', a subject he evolved into a whole song in 'Dumb'. For all his worsening health there was evidence that happiness and fulfilment were threatening to break out in Cobain's life. He craved success – the fans and the music press gave it to him. The look, the familiar soiled jeans and dirty hair, the lyrics and the epigrams Cobain polished against his next interview made him a surpassing symbol, and the major icon of the age. He was respected, as well as vilified – 'one of the most polarizing figures in America,' according to *Spin* – and his ability to chart trends had given him a unique place in the cultural drama of his time. One thing Cobain had never done, how-ever, was to laugh at himself. With acceptance came self-confidence. He referred wryly to his lifelong habit of 'brooding and bellyaching'. He made self-mocking quips to the media. He was 'no better than the average redneck', Cobain told the *Sun*. He insisted a local photographer shoot him 'looking as dumb as possible'. He even kept the glasses he wore on 'In Bloom' for months afterwards, cultivating what Cobain called his 'nerdy look', and reminding some of his father at the same age.

Don himself visited Lakeside Avenue in late 1993. He spent an hour talking to Love and Frances while Cobain hid in a bedroom upstairs – a tactic a relative later called 'humiliating'. (Cobain told another man that the real fault had been Don's for visiting in the first place.) Relations with Wendy, though warmer, followed the same unpredictable course. Despite having a son whose records sold in the mil-lions, the woman Cobain called 'a saint' still lived in the four-room house in the Aberdeen flats. A plan to build a new home with O'Connor in Olympia had to be abandoned when the marriage failed. Cobain lent his mother money, called her from around the world and still appeared at East 1st Street to visit his family. But there was rarely intimacy on either side. Wendy took inordinate pride that 'Kurt had made it' and 'gotten out of the *Peyton Place* of Aberdeen'. She never missed his press cuttings and appearances on TV. But she followed them as though he had a permanent star-ring role in a school play. Beverley Cobain sensed that Wendy, given her constricted world, never fully grasped the size of the stage her son played on. To Claude Iosso, 'she was proud of Kurt, but couldn't come to terms with his success'. A neighbour on East 1st Street remembers Wendy berating Cobain as 'Johnny Superstar' after an argument triggered by his arriving for dinner wearing his stage clothes and make-up.

Apart from drugs, Cobain's only other long-term relationships were with his wife and daughter. According to Hulme, 'Kurt was dominated by one and worshipped the other'. He was uncharacteristically dutiful and responsible about all kinds of family matters, the sort of parent who warmed his daughter's milk and made sure the nanny prepared only wholesome meals. Cobain acted like any doting father, handing out Frances's photograph to friends. 'Pictures, always pictures,' Hulme remembers. On 8 September Cobain arrived at the annual MTV Awards wearing a modish striped jersey and red bug-eye sunglasses, carrying Frances and assuring the crowd he was 'just dandy'. The event was in stark contrast to the 1992 ceremony. Although Nirvana again won the award for Best Alternative Video ('In Bloom'), there was no backstage fracas. Where previously Cobain had taunted Eddie Vedder and squared off with Axl Rose, now he cheerfully signed autographs and introduced well-wishers to his wife. Alan Wineberg remembers 'Kurt fishing about in a bag for Frances's diapers' and an atmosphere 'more akin to a picnic than a rock show'. The only moment of tension came when a security guard, apparently surprised by the smiling figure carrying his small daughter on his shoulders, asked Cobain for proof of identity before allowing him onstage.

Two weeks later Nirvana made their second appearance on *Saturday Night Live*. The drug-addled chaos of their first performance gave way to a mood of efficiency and professionalism. The group arrived, enhanced by a rhythm guitarist (Pat Smear), played two tracks from *In Utero*, bowed and left. No instrument smashing, no French kisses. Cobain's friend Jane Kinnear, who witnessed both programmes, describes how 'Kurt had seemed listless, out of it' on the previous broadcast. By 1993 he appeared 'sharp', joking with reporters backstage, 'promoting the group, but not taking himself too seriously'. In dealing with the press

Cobain now made self-deprecation the dominant theme. 'It's not like I really matter,' he told the *Source*. That autumn Cobain even allowed a Muzak-style version of 'Teen Spirit' to appear on Sara DeBell's anthology *Grunge Lite*.

All this activity preceded the release of Nirvana's first new album in two years. Originally titled *I Hate Myself And I Want To Die* (Cobain's pat response to enquiries about his health), and then *Verse Chorus Verse* (a dig at production-line songwriting), the final choice ended up being *In Utero*. The record debuted in the *Billboard* charts at Number One. Even that rare achievement dismayed Cobain. Never in the history of rock and roll had an artist repudiated his success as violently as he did now. From the world-weariness of 'Serve The Servants' to the self-lacerating theme of 'All Apologies', *In Utero* was rife with gibes at Nirvana's enemies, themselves included, and snide references to the anonymous 'inside sources' who passed judgement on the Cobains in the media. The operative words to describe the album were petulant, enraged and self-obsessed. Fans who wanted reassurance that all was right with their hero would have found disappointment in *In Utero*. Cobain saw deep strains of cruelty everywhere. But his cynicism stopped just short of bile. Along with the unrepentant punk went snatches of blues, folk and Sonic Youth-type rock, while Cobain's pop sensibilities surfaced even in the throes of his Lear-like rants. Although for much of the album Nirvana's needle seemed stuck in the usual groove of fame-bashing and introversion, *In Utero* teemed with guitar-driven energy, sounding at times like White Album-era Beatles, and striking one reviewer as Cobain 'exorcising his discontent with bristling, bull's-eye candour'.

The album opened with 'Serve The Servants', a lyric so angst-ridden that in mainstream terms it might as well have been Nico singing in the original German, but with a naggingly catchy tune. It gave way to 'Scentless Apprentice', a song inspired by Patrick Süsskind's novel *Perfume*, and also informed by Cobain's own feelings of 'quite a few years ago' when 'I was so disgusted by human beings that I felt, How do I get away from *everybody*?' With its snarling raw-throated chorus – 'Go away, get a-way' – 'Apprentice' aptly yielded to the album's most bare-knuckled track. 'Heart-Shaped Box', whose morbid theme and claustrophobic feel owed something to the fact that it was written in Cobain's closet in Los Angeles, was the very essence of the Nirvana playbook. There was the familiar strummed guitar and muttered verse, erupting into a power-chord frenzy that came on ambient and emerged as pure pop. No matter how hard he tried, Cobain's commercial instincts still dogged him. 'Heart-Shaped Box' was eloquent, fiery and fully human. The unsettling lyric was matched by a melody that came close to capturing some of R.E.M.'s grandeur – the fat bass, jangling guitar and dense percussion would all have suited *Out Of Time*. 'Box' was released as a single in Britain, where it quickly hit the Top 5. A video for the song was shot by Anton Corbijn, a typically bleak treatment with the same crucifixion theme as the album's next cut, 'Rape Me'. This was the song Cobain meant as a commentary on life in the post-*Nevermind* madhouse. (There was even an echo of 'Teen Spirit' in the opening guitar.) With his stock for the album still high, Cobain next indulged in a four-minute rant on the life of Frances Farmer, a local film star committed to an asylum in the 1940s (and Seattle's patron martyr), before seguing into 'Dumb', a slab of cello-and-guitar chamber music reminiscent of 'Eleanor Rigby' and *Nevermind*'s own 'Polly'.

From then on things went downhill. Four of the remaining tracks on *In Utero* lacked punch and clarity. Albini's back-to-basics production, which could achieve effect through simplicity with an artist like PJ Harvey, emerged here merely as simple. Without an Endino or Butch

Vig, Cobain's emotional display degenerated into self-indulgence. The scatological lyrics of 'Milk It' ('Her milk is my shit/My shit is her milk') came across as the attention-seeking ravings of a ten-year-old. There was *fin de siècle* dissolution of reason, images twisted with lurid expressionism to represent moral decay – and then there was the abject dross of 'Radio Friendly Unit Shifter', of which Cobain's reference to 'Bi-polar opposites' was the sole point of interest. For sheer feral rage (and another guitar part lifted from *Kimono My House*) there was 'tourette's', a hoarse tirade against the media. Lyric: 'Fuck, piss, shit'. This wasn't a musician writing for an audience, it was Cobain venting his spleen on the world. 'Very Ape', although in the same dismal mode, at least showed a grasp of the basic tenet of modern pop stardom: exploit your pain. Cobain's self-portrayal as the 'king of illiterature' was a pre-emptive strike against the barbs of his critics. The second half of *In Utero* was rescued by the trump cards of 'Pennyroyal Tea', a folk-punk fusion that, with a friendlier mix, would have had a chance as a single, and 'All Apologies', another R.E.M.-manqué ballad, closing the album with the cryptic revelation, 'All in all is all we all are'.

From the title to the cover art of a transparent woman, the theme of *In Utero* was the familiar cry of horror at the barren world outside the womb. There was also a shout of rage violent even for one of Cobain's capacity for self-pity. Farmer's story, with her downfall precipitated by disillusion with Hollywood and the pressures of fame, was an obvious comparison. Cobain had read William Arnold's biography of the actress as early as 1978, told relatives in Aberdeen he was 'obsessed' with the story, and in the last month of his life contacted the author to arrange a meeting. (Arnold was set to return the call on the day he heard Cobain had committed suicide.) Some of the same self-indulgence spilled over into the music. At its worst, *In Utero* was hollow, retrograde, monotonous, an empty roar warped by what Peel calls 'thrashing about' and lacking the economy or exuberance of, respectively, *Bleach* and *Nevermind*.

On the credit side, much of the album was rooted in proven pop values. Although twentysomethings hailed the group's originality, older listeners could still recognize Nirvana's reference points – the screaming guitars, the maniacal vocals, the incessant drums. For all its moments of experimentation, there was a curiously old-fashioned feel to *In Utero*, at least half of which was anchored in the hoary rock and roll tradition of 'Twist and Shout'. The artwork would have fitted almost any post-*Sergeant Pepper* sleeve design. There was even a diagram showing 'suggested bass and treble positions'. This struggle to accommodate the nineties to the sixties was, writ large, Cobain's whole musical dilemma. At its best *In Utero* crossed the nihilism of punk with raw pop energy and an unbeatable ear for a hook. With 'Dumb' and 'All Apologies', Cobain seized the chance to pen the Beatles pastiches that had always threatened to emerge from his songs anyway. 'Heart-Shaped Box' was an altogether darker experience, which later took on new relevance. 'Serve The Servants' was a model of songwriting economy. For these and the ferocious intensity of the playing throughout, *In Utero* was a deserved critical and popular hit.

In his desire to experiment, his attitude to fame and his rampant paranoia, Cobain again recalled Jimi Hendrix at the same age. By summer of 1969 Hendrix had parted with the group that first brought him to success and announced his intention to wed jazz freedom to the dignity of acoustic blues, thus bypassing the electric virtuosity of his best work. He was also becoming increasingly distrustful of those around him. According to Hendrix's biographer Harry Shapiro, 'He told another musician that for a time he thought the conga player was a spy for the office; he told Billy Cox that he dropped $100 bills on the ground to see who would pick them up; he told his girlfriend [that] Mike Jeffrey [Hendrix's producer] would kill him rather than release material that Mike didn't think was commercial enough.'

This was familiar territory. As with one singer, songwriter and guitarist from Seattle, so with another. According to John Peel, 'Jimi seemed to be wondering out loud about how he'd found himself in a world where he was always performing.' Cobain, too, took a rueful view of his life since becoming famous. The honours heaped on him by others failed to silence the small, nagging voice that whispered within that he had never done enough. His chronic discontent drove him to succeed, yet robbed him of the capacity to enjoy success. When Hendrix visited Seattle for the last time in July 1970 he quoted Mark Twain to Mike Collier: 'Any life is a failure in the secret judgement of the man who lives it.' Twenty-three years later Cobain told the same critic that he was 'no fucking good' and in need of change. That his future depended on the hated 'verse chorus verse' formula of *Nevermind* was unthinkable, but a career outside of music was impossible. For Cobain, as it had with Hendrix, life was closing down.

One of the most curious episodes of Cobain's search for new horizons was his involvement with William Burroughs. This singular collaboration came about through the offices of a mutual friend, Thor Lindsay of the independent Tim Kerr Records. Although self-admittedly 'not into grunge', the author of *Naked Lunch* 'admired the spunk' of Cobain's work. Burroughs in time sent a recital tape to Tim Kerr, where it was mixed with a sampling of Cobain's guitar and released, to a largely indifferent world, as 'The "Priest" They Called Him'.

Next Cobain sent a fax to Burroughs's home in Lawrence, Kansas, asking if he would appear as the crucifixion victim in the video for 'Heart-Shaped Box'. Burroughs turned him down. After another exchange of faxes (in which Cobain expressed the hope that 'you won't think I'm trying to exploit a drug connection'), a meeting was arranged in Lawrence. Thus it was that, one evening in October, Burroughs watched a limousine pull into the small driveway of his home.

> I waited, and Kurt got out with another man [the road manager Alex MacLeod]. Cobain was very shy, very polite, and obviously enjoyed the fact that I wasn't awestruck at meeting him. There was something boyish about him, fragile and engagingly lost. He smoked cigarettes but didn't drink. There were no drugs. I never showed him my gun collection.

The evening ended with a ritual exchange of gifts: a painting for Cobain, who in turn produced a Leadbelly biography, which he signed. Burroughs watched the limousine pull away before remarking to his secretary, 'There's something wrong with that boy. He frowns for no good reason.'

The crowds at Finsbury Park, London, where Nirvana played that autumn, bore testament to the fact that their concerts were no longer ad-hoc, underground get-togethers. Commerce, most pertinently drug trading, had arrived, and the T-shirt and souvenir hawkers lining Seven Sisters Road would have done credit to the Rolling Stones. As if in further comparison, the concert itself was a disappointment.

On 18 October Nirvana began a full-scale American tour, their first in two years. Cobain had wanted to return to the road with a show that would appeal to punks by confining itself to small clubs where everyone could dance and nobody need bring binoculars. Unfortunately, it was too late for Nirvana to beat the economics they themselves had largely created. The end-result was a forty-five-date itinerary, performing in a mix of arenas and theatres, to audiences among whom it was now commonplace to snort cocaine and wave banners calling for 'Teen Spirit'. There was a matching expansion in production and stagecraft. Previously Nirvana had played to a backdrop of soap bubbles or psychedelic pink circles in whose glow a teenage girl had sometimes shrugged, apparently indifferent, like a dancer on *Ready Steady Go!* Now the group ran on, spotlit and over-amplified, to a shouted introduction and the manic roar of the crowd. There were other embellishments. The set was ludicrously decorated like a wood, with dead-looking trees and paper birds. Cobain had lifted an idea from the film director Wim Wenders and flanked the stage with winged anatomical mannequins, like the one on the cover of *In Utero*. In a final upscale progression, the group changed its own line-up, adding a second guitarist, Pat Smear, and the cellist Lori Goldston from Seattle's Black Cat Orchestra.

For a man who spoke of killing himself in 1992, Cobain was remarkably cheerful only a year later. 'I've never been happier in my life,' he told David Fricke. To another reporter he spoke of having 'recuperated' from both drug addiction and his chronic stomach pain. Some of these high spirits came across on tour. Though now protected by a phalanx of bodyguards, publicists, cooks, chauffeurs and personal assistants, Cobain could still put on a crowd-pleasing display of punk informality, as when he wandered on stage in Kansas while the house lights were still on and asked, 'Is Kevin here?' He even urged audiences to join in the chorus of their favourite songs. The sound of 6,000 voices duly crooning the lyrics of 'Rape Me' provided the tour's most surreal moment.

Kim Neely met Cobain after a concert in Davenport,

Iowa, where she was struck by the 'childlike' and 'lost' qualities also noted by Burroughs. So much had been written about Nirvana in 1992, about their success and the surly antagonism that followed, that the group's other qualities had sometimes been overlooked. First and foremost, they were and remained outstanding musicians. On the whole *In Utero* brought off the rare feat of combining moments of experimentation with a general restatement of first principles. Cobain was still a thrilling live performer. He was also an inveterate crowd-pleaser. When not going out of his way to offend them, he actively sought the approval of the masses. David Haig heard Cobain worry out loud if he was 'still in touch with ordinary kids'. Kim Neely watched him enter a taco restaurant, sign an autograph for the one fan who mustered the courage to approach him, then sit happily at the public counter. The churlish attributes, the self-indulgence and backstabbing, were matched by the qualities of freshness and naïvety that made him popular in the first place. From a low point in July 1993 Cobain seemed actually to improve during the rest of the year. He could be egocentric, but there was a selfless side to his nature. He gave countless interviews stressing his commitment to Nirvana and his affection for his family. He talked up his wife as 'cooler than I'll ever be', a view Love gave him no reason to retract, and actively encouraged her own *Rolling Stone* interview, 'Courtney Speaks Her Mind'. Haig would later call this 'the very moment the feminist icon was born'. Others credited Love with greater insight than her husband into the quality and trustworthiness of the people around him.

An interviewer backstage in Chicago found Cobain discoursing wryly on life in the rock fast lane. 'It was so explosive,' he said of his early fame. 'I didn't know how to deal with it. If there was a rock star [class] I would have liked to take it. It might have helped me.' After listing the reasons for his new-found content ('Pulling this record off. My family. My child. Meeting William Burroughs and doing a record with him') and admitting that 'every month I come to more optimistic conclusions', Cobain ended with the line later held to presage his suicide: 'I just hope I don't become so blissful I become boring. I think I'll always be neurotic enough to do something weird.'

It says much for Cobain's sorry view of life that even as he was praising his colleagues, he confessed to 'getting tired with the Nirvana formula'. His had been the voice raised loudest when deciding to add an acoustic set for the appearance at Roseland. Some of the simple appeal of that concert was retained when, on 18 November, Nirvana joined the long list of those succumbing to the MTV *Unplugged* series. The performance at New York's Sony Studios was notable for the feeling of cosy well-being engendered by the group and the self-deprecating humour ('I guarantee you I'll screw this song up') shown by Cobain. There were competent versions of 'About A Girl', 'Polly' and 'Come As You Are'. In 'Pennyroyal Tea', played solo, Cobain's riveting voice won over even the hardened grunge rockers in the crowd. The concert's uncongenial format worked best when Cobain sat alone, hunched with his acoustic guitar, dragging back his earliest songs from the archive. There was also an unprecedented number of covers: six in all, including 'The Man Who Sold The World', in which Cobain chose to ad-lib a line about the 'gazeless stare' of material success.

MTV Unplugged In New York was released a year later. There was also a widely shown TV broadcast. To some like Patrick MacDonald, 'Cobain seemed out of place, sitting on a stool, quietly crooning some of the slower songs ... The numbers don't stand up well by themselves. They're part of a whole package that includes the full force of live, electric rock.' Lovers of 'Teen Spirit'-era Nirvana were also among those insisting that the group's volume was no optional extra but a musical must. Others found poignancy in the sound of the familiar doom-laden voice echoing, as it were, from the grave. In Aberdeen, Cobain's grandmother 'could hardly bear' to listen.

Cobain ended 1993 headlining MTV's 'Live and Loud' New Year's Eve special held on the Seattle waterfront*. Backstage, Alice Wheeler was staggered by the 'Hollywood atmosphere' surrounding her old friends, with rock groupies vying with celebrities and 'no one giving a shit about the band'. Wheeler took photographs of Cobain in his trailer. He was, she says, in 'excellent humour', catching up on gossip, and his 'usual opinionated, intelligent self'. Cobain discussed the Kinescope lenses used on the 'In Bloom' video with all the enthusiasm of a renowned camera buff. In Wheeler's view, there were 'three basic Kurts: the big rock star, the family man, and the Aberdeen misfit. All of them were in conflict.'

Later that evening Cobain walked down a darkened street to the yellow-sided house on Harvard Avenue. According to the woman who sold it to him, he left with a tinfoil package of heroin 'with no more fuss than if he'd bought a pizza'. At Cobain's next stop he drank a cocktail of tequila and gin, chased down by cough syrup. Midnight had already struck before he was persuaded to rejoin his family. Walking unsteadily down a flight of steps, Cobain fell and rolled – 'like a thrown rug', according to one witness – into the gutter where, smiling gently, he saw in the last new year of his life.

* The widely anticipated meeting between Nirvana and their support act, Pearl Jam, never happened. At the last moment Eddie Vedder refused to appear, forcing that part of the show to be cancelled.

9

'Thank You. I'm a Rock Star.'

It was fitting that Nirvana's final American shows should be in Seattle. Supported by the coyly abbreviated BH [Butthole] Surfers, the group ended the tour with hometown concerts on 7 and 8 January 1994. Cobain retained his upbeat mood. To Patrick MacDonald in the Seattle *Times* the *Unplugged* session had shown Nirvana to be a 'fun, non-threatening group' and Cobain himself 'not only healthy but good-looking enough to be a heartthrob'. To the *People* stringer, Nirvana were all about 'old-time rock and roll' and a 'Led Zeppelin groove'. Michael Andeel saw Cobain and Love standing backstage before the first of the two concerts. 'I told him I'd enjoyed the Mia Zapata gig the previous summer. Kurt couldn't remember the show until Courtney reminded him. Then he kind of brightened up. "Oh," he said. "*Mia*."' According to the disc jockey Marco Collins: 'He was in a different world, but he was happy. Whatever demons caught up with Kurt, they weren't there in early January.' Cobain came onstage to a standing ovation, went directly to the microphone, lit a cigarette and began talking, addressing not just the packed hall but an enormous radio audience. The speech, telling the fans how much he loved them, lasted just two minutes. Speaking slowly and carefully, Cobain was interrupted by applause again and again, six times before he finished. After the show Alice Wheeler once again found herself backstage. Cobain was 'unassuming, genial' and eager to see the photographs of his New Year's Eve concert. An 'uptight' Love told Wheeler that the family were planning to move, and that a change-of-address card would be forthcoming. It never arrived.

The Cobains' new home was at 171 Lake Washington Boulevard East, in Seattle's affluent Madrona district. As with other houses on the street, security arrangements were elaborate. The grey, shake-sided mansion was hidden behind a brick wall topped by a thick screen of bushes. A sign read 'Beware of the Dog'. The detached garage above which Cobain shot himself was, however, fully visible from the road. Standing on a neatly manicured lot landscaped with rhododendrons and azaleas, the three-storey house enjoyed a view over the water to the mountains and forests of west-central Washington. Had the Cobains chosen to, they could have watched the sun rise over the snow-capped Cascades from their front window.

Cobain liked to refer to the place as a 'log cabin'. It was indeed made of logs, solid cedar. The house had been built by Swedish carpenters brought to Seattle expressly to develop the area for the city's first world fair in 1909. There was no shortage of luxury fittings. The oak floors were covered by expensive rugs. As in the Lakeside home, a room had been set aside for Cobain to paint in. The basement included the familiar clutter of books, records, broken guitar parts and wine bottles. The extensively modernized kitchen was the size of a studio apartment. A large open fire (dangerously exposed, some thought, for the baby) crackled in the living-room. Despite the congenial setting of the home, visitors found it a strangely depressing place. There were no pictures on the walls. As before, sheets hung at the windows instead of curtains. Black plastic tarpaulins were draped from the trees to thwart photographers.

Cobain bought the property, through his lawyer Allen Draher, on 19 January 1994. The selling price was $1,485,000. According to a close friend, 'Kurt liked having doctors and investment bankers as neighbours. "Solid, successful folks," as he called them. By then, someone who made money struck him as more worthwhile than a punk rocker.' The feeling of respect was mutual. 'They were exemplary neighbours,' says William Baillargeon, whose home was adjacent to the Cobains'. 'We were very happy to have creative and interesting people here.' Only a month earlier Cobain had told a reporter that '[As a child] I'd rather hang out with the kids who didn't get chosen for the baseball team.' For years he had made a virtue out of his hatred of sport. Now, in a dramatic feat of upward assimilation, Cobain wrote to the Seattle Tennis Club, a few streets away from his home, asking about membership for his family and himself.

Cobain had worn his celebrity as a burden. His songs frequently spoke of the corrupting influence of fame. Despite having spent tens of thousands of dollars on drugs, for a rock star he remained blushingly normal in his habits. His personal tastes were not extravagant. 'I still eat Kraft macaroni and cheese – I like it, I'm used to it,' he told David Fricke. Cobain's wardrobe was famously meagre. A few weeks before his death he traded in his Lexus for a grey Volvo (whose licence number, 175 EYA, he used to worry added up to thirteen). All the same, with the Lake Washington home Cobain took a step nearer becoming an affluent American celebrity. By 1994 he was a rich man; he needed to be, and never felt himself well-off, but his life in Seattle was unrecognizable from the Bohemian existence of only two years before. Certain friends, like Tracy Marander, alienated by Cobain's wealth, began to speak of his 'blowing it' with his old circle. 'He was impossible to get through to,' says Wheeler. 'Kurt by himself was one thing. With his cronies, he was something else.'

This was Cobain three months before he killed himself: successful, prosperous, emotionally fulfilled, competitive. Early in the new year he announced that Nirvana would headline the 1994 Lollapalooza tour, a sort of travelling Reading Festival, with the wry dig, 'But we have to sell more records than Pearl Jam'. No one who saw his final concerts in Seattle suspected a crisis. 'Just the opposite,' says a friend. 'For the first time, Kurt actually worked up some enthusiasm for life. He was getting his act together.'

As the moment of relapse loomed, Cobain spoke warmly of his happiness as a husband and father. He stressed his loyalty to Nirvana. With the addition of a second guitarist, a doom seemed to have lifted from Cobain onstage. Some of the humour of his earliest performances returned. He regularly doodled the 'Twilight Zone' theme between numbers. He took requests. He even added an off-key 'If You're Going To San Francisco' to Nirvana's set. Before leaving the stage on 8 January he dedicated the restored 'Teen Spirit' to 'Seattle – the most liveable city in America.' Then he stood outside in the rain for forty minutes signing autographs.

At a party that night Cobain spoke about death. Not his own, but those of four just-departed role models: Frank Zappa, the actors River Phoenix and Fred Gwynne (Herman Munster of *The Munsters*), and the radical, seventies governor of Washington, Dixie Lee Ray. 'There was nothing morbid about it,' says Mike Collier. 'Kurt was rueful they'd gone, not aiming to join them.' Another guest at the party remembers Cobain humming a tune – 'so catchy it was like Abba' – he planned to include on Nirvana's next album. According to Collier, the impression was of a 'blissed-out family man, at the peak of his powers', who spoke only half-jokingly about being 'the next Paul McCartney'.

What went wrong? It was assumed that, because of his family and the success of *In Utero*, Cobain had finally thrown off the 'pissy, complaining, freaked-out schizophrenic' image of old. A close study of his actions that month shows that this was not true. After he returned from the post-concert party, Cobain sagged visibly, as though he had emptied himself by being sociable. Friends found him chronically depressed and unhappy at the prospect of touring, 'back on the beat' as he put it. In late January, Haig remembers, 'Kurt seemed down the whole time. The energy level was not all that great. The flame was spluttering. He saw himself serving time.' Rumours began to circulate that all was not well with the Cobains' marriage. The cycle that had emerged early in their relationship persisted, now under greater stresses. Cobain would do or say something thoughtless that hurt Love; her hurt would put her in a peevish mood; and her moodiness would then annoy him. He promised one day that he would give away all the guns in the house. She told a friend he was donating them to Mothers Against Violence. He never did it. When Cobain returned home, Love was crying and 'looking like shit', which irritated him. Love was opposed to having loaded weapons under her roof. Cobain said he needed them for protection, and because of his enemies. 'Fame was heady wine for Kurt,' another friend observes. 'Fame led to paranoia. And with that came the guns.' All that Love could hope for was that the wine would run out.

Cobain also kept up his prodigious drug intake. According to Alice Wheeler, 'There were rumours that he was no longer using just to help his stomach. The cure had become the disease.' Marander called Wheeler to discuss Cobain's health, and was 'shocked at the tales of Kurt's and Courtney's mutual interest in heroin'. According to the journalist David Gardner, a delivery boy arrived one afternoon at Lake Washington Boulevard. 'The scene could have been from almost any middle-class home in the US. After a few moments, the door was opened by a blousy young woman clutching a baby. She gave the delivery boy a cheque for $250 and a further $150 in cash. Then, grabbing the package he gave her in exchange with her free hand, she turned and called upstairs to her husband: "Honey, your stuff is here."'

'Kurt had a serious habit,' says a thirty-three-year-old former computer analyst who sold him heroin. 'I did drugs with them and a male friend who was often at the house. From the outside it looked impressive, but inside it was like a pigsty. Clothes were strewn everywhere. Kurt would need someone he trusted, but he was still pretty naïve. He would sometimes pay me by cheque. But we knew his money was good. He had so much coming in he didn't know what to do with it.'

Sam Mayne, a regular at the Tacky Tavern on Seattle's Capitol Hill, says he saw Cobain make 'three or four cash deals' in a room off the bar. According to Mayne, 'Kurt would come in, wearing a ridiculous hat with earmuffs, hand over the money and fix himself up right there in the corner.' A second source says that 'Kurt was taking sleeping-pills and tranquillizers, but in such huge quantities that he was effectively a junkie. We always called them "sedatives" to Kurt, and he would too, to fool himself, but it wasn't true.'

The fact is that, for the last two years of his life, Cobain was a mental cripple. His doctors needed four to six weeks to prepare him for a tour, and even then things would go wrong: film of Nirvana's last concerts in Europe shows a decrepit amnesiac who could hardly remember even the famous catchphrases of his own songs.

Cobain emerged from Lake Washington Boulevard on 28 January and spent three days with Nirvana in the studio. On the 31st he made his final effort to rationalize his feelings about his father, placing an hour-long call to Don, of which Jenny Cobain says: 'He actually got to tell Kurt that he loved him, and he felt good afterwards, and cried.' But the reconciliation was only skin deep. On 'Serve The Servants' Cobain had sung, 'I tried hard to have a father/But instead I had a dad/I just want you to know that I don't hate you anymore/There is nothing I could say that I haven't thought before.' Whatever he said to the contrary, Cobain's feelings about his parents were at best ambivalent, at worst implacably hostile. Don himself admits that 'things were never resolved'. As Cobain boarded the plane to Europe on 2 February he told a friend that 'rage sometimes exploded in him and he never wanted to see his family again, only to find himself lonely and miserable the moment they were gone'. Cobain's cousin compares him to 'a man sitting in a furnace, shrieking for an iceberg, who after an hour in the cold was panting to get back to the furnace again. He never made up his mind about people.'

By early 1994 Gold Mountain had forgotten their earlier high sentiments. They had forgotten their promise never to schedule so many consecutive dates for Nirvana overseas. Nor did they heed the words of a Seattle friend who urged against Cobain being cut loose from his support-base. 'It was too much, too soon,' says Mike Collier. 'It was folly to send Kurt back on the road, and I said so.' Nirvana's record company and management seem to have ignored the risk that Cobain's health might not stand the test of thirty-eight concerts spanning a dozen European countries. In fact, even at his appearance on a TV show in France, he was complaining of being exhausted and in no mood to sing. By the time the tour itself opened in Lisbon on 6 February Cobain was tense, withdrawn, travelling in a separate bus to Novoselic and Grohl, and striking even Alex MacLeod as 'tired'. For all his well-documented capacity to self-medicate, he still seemed unlikely to get through the tour without outside help. When, ten days later, heading back through France, Cobain began to lose his voice, a second member of the group was heard to comment on this typical example of 'Kurt need[ing] to be nursed' in order to perform.

Love would later say of Cobain's mood in Europe: 'He hated everything, everybody. Hated, hated, hated. He called me from Spain, crying. I was gone forty days. I was doing my thing with my band for the first time since forever.' As well as what a group member calls 'sheer boredom, home-sickness and downright fatigue', Cobain's manic behaviour on previous tours had set up expectations he had no wish to satisfy – 'sowing a wind to reap a hurricane', as Haig puts it. New light was now cast on Cobain's perceived glamoriz-ing of drugs to his fans. 'He called me from Spain,' Love told *Rolling Stone*. 'He was in Madrid, and he'd walked through the audience. The kids were smoking heroin off tinfoil, and the kids were going, "Kurt! Smack!" and giving him the thumbs up. He called me, crying . . . He did not want to become a junkie icon.'

While Nirvana were in Paris a photographer named Youri Lenquette asked Cobain to strike up different poses with a newly purchased sports pistol. (He was 'all high', according to Love.) In an eerie foreshadowing of his own suicide Cobain inserted the barrel in his mouth, pretending to pull the trigger and miming the impact of the gunshot to his head. That was the most widely publicized instance of behaviour that swung between manic and depressive, with bewildering speed. Some of the same volatility was obvious in the music. By the time Nirvana appeared in Rome on 22 February the set had given way to the cartoon props and stagecraft that the group's public persona had become, as all five musicians played extended free-form solos and took deep ironic bows after each rendition. Cobain's voice had deteriorated to a throaty, stylized snarl. His comments between numbers, once seized on almost as eagerly as the songs themselves, veered from the mundane ('You're very quiet tonight') and clichéd ('This is one off the new album') to a bizarre brand of self-mocking ego ('Thank you. I'm a rock star'). But nothing made Cobain appear so strange as his own naïvety when combined with his stubborn determi-nation. While in Paris he met a homeopathic doctor who demonstrated his miraculous machine, the 'transfuser', that he claimed cleansed electrically all traces of drugs from the bloodstream. Cobain was ready to part with a $10,000 fee to undergo treatment when saner heads intervened. That so devout a cynic as Cobain should fall for so obvious a fraud was hardly startling. Throughout his life he contained the paradox of a sceptic sometimes made credulous by his urge to experiment. And Cobain would automatically be favourably disposed towards anyone who was, like this man, struck off by *L'Ordre des médecins*.

Miti Adhikari, the BBC engineer who befriended Cobain, was at Nirvana's performance in Ljubljana, Slovenia, on 27 February. By then, he says, 'it was pretty obvious Kurt was floundering. If anyone was in charge, it was Novoselic. He was the one calling the shots, introducing his family, discussing the war in Bosnia like someone from the State Department. The whole time, Cobain sat backstage and said nothing. He looked like a ghost. Pale. Shrunken. Eventually he did mumble something about getting together in London, but I would've taken odds against it ever happening. He had that deathly pallor about him, and it obviously hurt him to speak, let alone to sing.'

Adhikari, who had produced Nirvana in 1991 and recorded their triumphant return to the Reading Festival, was saddened by the 'crude, aimless blurting' of the Ljubljana show. It was a 'stunning plummet' from the standards of only eighteen months before. According to Adhikari, 'It wasn't as though it was a wild, strange gig that didn't work. It was worse than that: a mediocrity.' There were some familiar touches – the hard-rock drums and choppy guitar (not Cobain's, but Smear's) – and the cello highlighted the group's virtues: tunefulness, audacious content, innovative arranging. But all too often the best material from *Nevermind* and *In Utero* degenerated into lazy ad-libs that would never have been considered worthy of release on the original albums. Previously Nirvana had been better live than on record, now they were worse. Three-minute classics like 'Drain You' and 'Rape Me' became protracted, elemental jams, and the musicians themselves appeared to have no higher ambition than to fill out the required hour on stage. They seemed, says Adhikari, 'not to much care'. As Cobain would write only weeks later: 'When we're backstage and the lights go out and the manic roar of the crowd begins, it doesn't affect me in the way in which it did for Freddie Mercury.'

On Tuesday, 1 March Nirvana performed at Terminal Einz in Munich. Cobain lost his voice after the third number, howled a few improvised lyrics, and went to see a throat specialist the next day. 'He was told to take two to four weeks' rest,' says Alex MacLeod. 'He was given spray and [medicine] for his lungs because he was diagnosed as having severe laryngitis and bronchitis.' The group then rescheduled the remainder of the European tour. While much was made of the fact that Nirvana had postponed, not cancelled, the outstanding twenty-three concerts, Cobain's own doctor believed he needed to 'take at least two months off and learn to sing properly'. His response was to self-medicate with heroin. Though Cobain had been familiar with the drug for nearly ten years, it was only now that he crossed the threshold to permanent, final slavery. While Novoselic flew back to Seattle and Grohl took part in a video shoot for the film *Backbeat*, their colleague spent the day trawling the crack houses and subway alleys of Munich. On 2 March he flew to Rome. There was no chance of the tour now resuming, he told a reporter. Cobain had heard the 'manic roar' for the last time.

The story had a familiar ring: the Seattle rock star with a history of drug abuse succumbing to an overdose in his European hotel room. On the evening of 2 March Cobain checked into suite 541 of the Rome Excelsior, across the street from the American Embassy. The next day Love, Frances and the baby's nanny arrived from London. That same evening, Cobain sent a bellboy out to fill a prescription for Rohypnol, a valium-like tranquillizer sometimes used to treat heroin-withdrawal symptoms. He then ordered two bottles of champagne from room service.

What happened overnight in the Cobains' suite was variously described as 'a mistake', an 'inadvertent overdose', and a collapse 'related to severe fatigue'. Early in the morning of 4 March Love found her husband unconscious. 'I reached for him, and he had blood coming out of his nose,' she told *Select*, adding, 'I have seen him get really fucked up before, but I've never seen him almost eat it.' (Love would tell Robert Hilburn of the horror of finding Cobain slumped on the bedroom floor: 'I thought I went through a lot of hard times over the years, but that was the hardest.') At first the incident was passed off as an accident. It was later revealed that Cobain had unwrapped and swallowed no fewer than fifty pills and had left a suicide note. Although the crisis had its origin in a marital row and his fear of being divorced, the exact cause, Love told David Fricke, was more mundane:

He'd gotten me roses. He'd gotten a piece of the Colosseum, because he knows I love Roman history. I had some champagne, took a valium . . . I fell asleep.

I turned over about three or four in the morning to make love, and he was gone. He was at the end of the bed with a thousand dollars in his pocket and a note saying, 'You don't love me anymore. I'd rather die than go through a divorce . . .'

I can see how it happened. He took fifty fucking pills. He probably forgot how many he took. But there was a definite suicidal urge, to be gobbling and gobbling and gobbling. Goddamn, man. Even if I wasn't in the mood, I should have just laid there for him. All he needed was to get laid.

Cobain was rushed to Rome's Umberto I Polyclinic and then transferred to the American Hospital. After twenty-two hours he awoke from a coma and scrawled his first request to his wife: 'Get these fucking tubes out of my nose.' 'The vital signs came back, and he's opened his eyes,' Gold Mountain's Janet Billig reported on 5 March. 'I don't know if he's talking lucidly, but he's moving his hands. His wife and daughter are with him.'

Rome was never the ideal place for a celebrity to enjoy the 'total peace and quiet' Billig requested on Cobain's behalf. This particular celebrity had already brought a flock of photographers as he lay unconscious in the ambulance speeding him to hospital. Now, as Cobain's doctor Osvaldo Galletta assured the press his patient had suffered 'no permanent damage' ('I had hope for him,' the surgeon added. 'Some of the people that visited him were a little strange'), the paparazzi arrived in force. Raiuno TV showed dramatic footage of Cobain being carried from the hotel and Love shouting abuse at reporters. CNN interrupted a newscast to announce, erroneously, that the singer had died. The story made the front page of the Seattle papers. And in Aberdeen, Cobain's mother tempered her joy at his recovery by the conviction that 'he's in a profession he doesn't have the stamina to be in'. 'It was a real bad night,' Wendy told Claude Iosso. 'I took one look at Kurt's picture (in Rome) and saw his eyes, and I lost it. I don't want my son gone.'

The spin control applied by Cobain's management was quick to portray Rome as an accident. 'It was definitely not a suicide attempt,' Gold Mountain would say. 'He wanted to celebrate seeing Courtney after so long.' Like many of his close friends, Charles Peterson regrets that neither Cobain nor his family told him that he had already tried to kill himself – 'I would have at least tried to see him.' Slim Moon also believes that 'communication just broke down' after Rome. To Collier, 'the Kurt I knew went south, and there was no way to reach him.' For the remaining month of his life Cobain's idealism soured into fatalism (Nirvana had become a 'Nazi state', he told one friend) and his old self-destructiveness returned with a vengeance. He made arrangements to buy a gun to replace those confiscated by the police. David Haig had to stop him from stepping into a busy street in the path of oncoming traffic. A Gold Mountain employee walked into Cobain's kitchen and saw him turning a bread-knife over in his hand, then give her a 'drop-dead look' before leaving the room. Late in 1993 Cobain and Love had spent time at Canyon Ranch, a health resort where Cobain's doctor had told him, 'You can choose to live, or to die.' Now, it seemed, the decision was made. William Burroughs is not the only one bitter with regret that 'no one took responsibility' for keeping Cobain in hospital after Rome. Instead, just five days later he was put on a plane to Seattle and left to his own desires.

Among those who knew the truth about Cobain was, of course, his wife. Nine months after the event she would tell *Rolling Stone*, 'Yeah, he definitely left a note in the [hotel] room. I was told to shut up about it.' (The letter, written on Excelsior notepaper, ran to three pages.) The charge of negligence levelled against Love is undoubtedly misplaced. She had her own problems with drugs, and there was her career to distract her. It would be wrong to suggest that she could have foreseen the outcome. That Love at least feared the worst, however, is shown by her request, after returning from Rome, that Cobain freeze his sperm for her future use.

A friend who met the Cobains that March recalls Love 'giving Kurt projects, like a kid being bought a colouring book, so that she, Courtney, could get on with business'.

Often this diversion was not necessary because Cobain would nod off and sleep through the afternoon. It bore in on him, says Collier, 'that Courtney found being in Hole preferable to being his nurse'. On 18 March a Seattle policeman named Von Levandowski, responding to an emergency call, 'found Kurt locked in a bathroom, hiding from Courtney' – there were scratches on Cobain's back – at Lake Washington Boulevard. According to Levandowski: 'I asked Kurt what was going on, and he stated that there was a lot of stress in their relationship currently. [Cobain] said that they would seek marriage guidance and I advised him to do that.' A month later Love herself would tell police, 'The relationship was going through hard times because of Kurt's frequent use of drugs and the fact that [I] tried to get him to stop.' Tom Grant, a private investigator hired by Love in April, adds that 'Courtney and Kurt had not been getting along. They'd been talking about divorce. Within weeks before Kurt died, Courtney called one of their attorneys, Rosemary Carroll, and told Rosemary to get the meanest, most vicious divorce lawyer she could find. Courtney also asked Rosemary if the prenuptial agreement could be voided.'

According to Beverley Cobain, 'Kurt was sinking into a manic depression and, like most sufferers, didn't seek help.' Because his condition was a 'whole-body' illness it affected not only his mood but the way he ate and slept. An employee who visited Lake Washington Boulevard recalls Cobain 'dazed with fatigue' and 'floating about like a zombie'. Mike Collier doubts that 'Kurt ate anything but wolfed-down junk food' during his last month. With his physical resistance lowered and his self-mockery become masochism, it was hardly surprising Cobain was susceptible to the pull of mainstream American hobbies – among them, of course, drugs and guns.

After Cobain died his widow spoke of his 'sweet, Jimmy

Stewart' side and his love of sixties TV programmes that 'represent[ed] his lost boyhood'. But the childlike man was a step away from the dysfunctional adult. For years Cobain's songs had been dotted with tart references to both friends and enemies. He had always been uneasy about the godlike esteem in which some fans held him. Now, as they returned to Seattle, the Cobains were deluged with faxes and phone calls, most of them concerned, others actively deranged, from worried disciples. The majority were intercepted by Love but Cobain saw some and was aghast: a ten-year-old boy had written asking, 'If you die, how do I go on?' The very 'accessibility' Cobain insisted on resulted in hundreds of messages from people he felt unable to help, but about whom he worried endlessly. Love would remember Kurt 'finding a hidden stash [of articles about himself] that I put away, about three months' worth. We got into a physical fight. I was trying to tear them away. He was ripping pages out on the floor . . . I tried to say to him: "It's a cloud; it'll pass." [Cobain said] "Damn right, it'll pass. I'm not gonna make any fucking music ever again. I'm not gonna fucking be here to see it pass."'

Cobain wanted, if not to quit the rock business altogether, then to become a working musician, someone with respect rather than adulation, free to collaborate with old friends like Mudhoney and the Melvins. Grant Alden calls him 'the most reluctant superstar since Frances Farmer'. If the Cobain legend gathers strength from its similarity to the actress's story of shame and degradation, there was another strain in Farmer's experience that it represents equally well. Although his habitat was Seattle and not Hollywood, Cobain had the typical starlet's ambivalence towards the audience. He fretted about them and their image of him; but it tormented him that they were, at bottom, redneck, fist-pumping morons with no sense of his message. Cobain's liner notes on *Incesticide* were a way of testing his fans by confronting them. They also showed self-destructive skills of a high order.

Hopelessly adrift from his career, Cobain had turned inwards to his family. On 28 February he called his cousin, Art Cobain, to say 'he was getting really fed up with his way of life'. Among his numerous concerns was having 'sold out the punk ethic' (something Alice Wheeler also recalls Cobain saying) and becoming no better than the 'kiss-ass careerist' he deemed Eddie Vedder. To another relative Cobain uttered the fell phrase, 'I'm just recycled Lennon.' Truly it must have seemed that, from Pete Townshend's stage act through to a Keith Richards-like drug habit, to say nothing of Cobain's personal affection for the Beatles and Sex Pistols, all that had been done was cleverly imitative. The 'Led Zeppelin groove' had come back to haunt him.

It was hard to think of Cobain growing old gracefully. Watering down his greatest hits and adapting 'Teen Spirit' for cabaret would have removed the last vestige of meaning from his life. 'It's impossible for me to look into the future and say I'm going to be able to play Nirvana songs in ten years,' Cobain told a reporter. 'There's no way. I don't want to have to resort to doing the Eric Clapton thing.' Love would say of her husband's suicide, 'It could have happened when he was forty.' Cobain himself used to insist that life ended at thirty-two, and by totalling his Social Security number (536 90 4399) in the same way he studied his licence plate, swore he would be 'dead for sure' at forty-eight. With 'fuck-all to show for it', he used to complain. It depressed Cobain beyond words that Nirvana's three years at the top, while ushering in groups, like Hole, previously on the hard-core fringes, had done nothing to derail the likes of the Rolling Stones, Pink Floyd, the Eagles, Fleetwood Mac, Elton John and Barry Manilow, all of whom played to packed houses in 1994. 'I feel like I've gone backwards,' he told his cousin.

Those who knew Cobain and Love feared for the sanity of both. There were daily domestic rows at Lake Washington Boulevard, and at least one occasion when Love fled the home in order to escape her husband's erratic behaviour. When Haig met him in a downtown hotel he found Cobain tense and emotional, and weeping openly when discussing his marriage. He also complained of partial memory loss, insomnia, fatigue and 'a buzzing in the top of my head'. 'One could wonder about impairment of judgement [after Rome],' says Dr David Bailey, chairman of the department of psychiatry at the University of California. A man who met Cobain in mid-March remembers his 'cussing and vile language'. He believed his music was being suppressed by the CIA, and that he was excessively tired because 'all America [was] on my back'.

On 18 March police responded to yet another emergency call from Love. The officer who arrived at Lake Washington Boulevard found Cobain locked in a bathroom, hiding from his wife and insisting he was neither suicidal nor planning to hurt himself. Due to the 'volatile situation', the police did, however, confiscate four guns, twenty-five boxes of assorted ammunition and a bottle of unidentified pills. Cobain was interviewed, released, and spent the remainder of the week-end alone in Carnation. Love would later tell *Rolling Stone*, 'The reason I flipped out [on the 18th] was because it had been six days since we came back from Rome, and I couldn't take it anymore. When he came back from Rome high, I flipped out . . . I wish to God I hadn't. I wish I'd just been the way I always was, just tolerant of it. It made him feel so worthless when I got mad at him.'

Four days later the Cobains appeared at the American Dream car lot on Westlake Avenue, where they struck the owner Joe Kenney as 'upset' and Love as 'unstable', dropping a bottle of pills as she walked towards the bathroom. Another man heard the couple 'snarl at each other like wild dogs' while out walking their daughter near their home.

By the fourth week in March Cobain's family, colleagues and management all admitted what ordinary fans had known for years. According to Steven Chatoff, an intervention counsellor in Port Hueneme, California, 'They called me to see what could be done. [Cobain] was using, up in Seattle. He was in full denial. It was very chaotic. And they were in fear for his life. It was a crisis.' As Tammi Blevins, a Nirvana spokeswoman, put it: 'People close to him definitely did not want him on drugs.' A friend of the Cobains is blunter. 'The message came down to Kurt, from the highest authority – "Clean up or kiss goodbye to your career".'

On 25 March Love, Novoselic, Smear, John Silva, Danny Goldberg, Janet Billig and Cobain's old friend Dylan Carlson staged their own ad-hoc intervention. One by one each threatened in turn to leave him or to fire him. Cobain, who his wife says was 'out of his tree' by this time, sat impassively through the five-hour session. (According to one party present, 'We all made our pitches. The trouble was, nobody pointed out that kicking [heroin] was in *Kurt*'s best interests too.') Chatoff's services having been declined, Love persuaded her husband to re-enter the Exodus Center in Marina del Ray. Once at the airport, however, Cobain changed his mind and refused to board the flight. Love flew to Los Angeles alone with her manager. She would never see her husband alive again. In 1985 Wendy O'Connor had tried to shock Cobain into action by moving his belongings out of the house on East 1st Street. Nine years later, history was repeated with the same dire results. 'That eighties tough-love bullshit – it doesn't work,' Love would say at Cobain's vigil two weeks later. 'I got angry, and it was the first time I ever had,' she told *Rolling Stone*. 'I did not even kiss or get to say goodbye to my husband.'

Cobain's family had, at the twelfth hour, resorted to drastic measures. They were too late to save the man who six months earlier had sung 'Look on the bright side is suicide' on *In Utero*, and who struck his own uncle as 'unbearably discontent' and 'oppressed by some sense of not having done right in life'. Love, Novoselic and the others had at least tried to mediate. In the days following Cobain's death, when judgement, understandably, could be impaired by emotion, the hardest words were for those who had known the truth and denied it. Both Gold Mountain and Geffen refuted charges of having done too little, too late. Industry insiders were also blamed. In the August issue of *Request*, Jerry McCulley chided Poneman for his flattering *Spin* interview with Cobain and Love eighteen months before. 'Objectivity and journalistic ethics had been jettisoned,' according to McCulley. He also took to task Michael Azerrad and the *Los Angeles Times'* Robert Hilburn. In a bitter moment months later, Love herself would remark that her husband might have been better served: 'He didn't have any real friends.'

Cobain spent the last week of March alone in Seattle. He struck Alan Moeur, a drinker in Linda's Tavern (part-owned by Poneman and Pavitt), as sick and tired-looking. His 'organic connection' to life had been snapped, and all that were left, he complained, were box-office receipts. Cobain, says a spokesperson for Gold Mountain, had gone 'cuckoo'. Seattle police believe he wandered around town with no clear agenda for several days. On the evening of 26 March Cobain appeared at his drug dealer's house on Capitol Hill and asked the woman, 'Where are my friends when I need them? Why are my friends against me?' The next day he was seen in Ohm's comic-book shop on Pine Street. He spoke of flying to Atlanta to visit Michael Stipe.

Later that month, the *Los Angeles Times* reported that Nirvana had withdrawn from the Lollapalooza tour. The *Rocket* went one further by announcing that the group had broken up. For years Cobain had lost himself through his art, allowing him to cope with pain and suicidal fantasies. Now he seemed disillusioned not only with Nirvana, but the 'blatant typecasting' of his music. In an echo of his *Incesticide* sleeve notes, Cobain left a message on the Internet warning fans, 'If you're expecting the same verse-chorus-verse, you have but two choices. Don't buy the [next] album ... or get used to the fact that the band is changing.' A Geffen executive reports 'celestial panic' that the winning formula of *Nevermind* had become 'more avant-garde kitsch', with a consequent falling-off in sales. At the time of Cobain's death, not one of Nirvana's albums was in even the Seattle Top Ten. A critical backlash had begun in Britain, where the group had cancelled the tour scheduled for mid-April. It must have irked Cobain, the man who feared rejection, to read reports of Nirvana being dropped by their label and replaced on Lollapalooza by the very group led by Love's ex-boyfriend Billy Corgan, a man she praised in print as 'great in bed'.

On the afternoon of 30 March Cobain and Dylan Carlson pulled into the driveway of Stan Baker Sports, a pre-fabricated shack overshadowed by a tall billboard on Lake City Way NE, a zone of industrial stucco, fast food and failed beauty salons. Baker's assistant Del Olson found nothing suspicious about the two men with long hair who entered the shop and asked to look at shotguns. 'They seemed like perfectly ordinary young people,' Olson says. Baker himself remembers 'asking what the hell are these kids going to do with that gun? It's not hunting season.' Nor was it his concern, however. At Cobain's request, Carlson made the actual purchase, paying $308.37 cash for a Remington M11 20-gauge shotgun. He wanted it for protection, says Carlson, who insists 'neither Kurt nor anyone close to Kurt' told him that Rome had been a suicide attempt. According to Seattle police, 'Cobain did not want to buy the weapon in his name as officers had recently confiscated four of his weapons ...

Cobain was asked by Carlson to wait [before buying the gun], but Kurt wanted the weapon now.'

Cobain was again suffering from stomach pain and spoke of being 'shanghaied' by Gold Mountain to enter drug treatment. 'He felt that he had no habit,' Carlson says. 'That was more like what management wanted him to do.' In the remaining few hours of 30 March, Lake Washington Boulevard was a place of perpetual ferment. In quick succession Cobain was visited by a Geffen employee, his agent, a doctor and his heroin dealer. He took calls from Novoselic and Love, finally agreeing to his wife's ultimatum that he re-enter Exodus or face the prospect of divorce. Later that evening a limousine driver named Harvey Ottinger, after waiting for an hour outside the house, drove Cobain from Lake Washington Boulevard to the airport. On the way his passenger told him that he had just purchased a gun, that he had a box of cartridges with him and was worried about boarding the plane with live ammunition. Ottinger says he took the bullets for safe keeping.

Once in Los Angeles Cobain was met by Smear and a Gold Mountain manager who drove him to Exodus. He spent two days in room 206 of the twenty-bed clinic. Two years earlier Cobain had described the facility as 'disgusting' and staffed by 'forty-year-old hippie long-term-junkie-type counsellors' for whom he had 'no respect at all'. Time had done nothing to modify this bleak assessment. Dressed in olive-green pyjamas and dressing-gown, but without a sash to prevent any attempt at suicide, Cobain paced his nine-by-six-foot cubicle. Allowed only two meals a day and a packet of cigarettes, he was tortured by the constant glare of a reflected light set up to shine directly into his room at night while he tried to sleep on the rock-hard mattress. On 1 April, Good Friday, Frances's nanny Jackie Farry brought the baby to visit her father. According to an Exodus employee, 'it pissed Kurt off that Courtney [a few miles away in the Beverly Hills Peninsula] never came.' Later that afternoon Cobain called Love at the hotel. 'He said, "Courtney, no matter what happens, I want you to know that you made a really good record",* she later told the Seattle *Post-Intelligencer*. 'I said, "Well, what do you mean?" And he said, "Just remember, no matter what, I love you."' That was the last time Love spoke to her husband. Later that evening, after a visit by Gibby Haynes (of the Butthole Surfers) and a woman Exodus describes as an 'enabler' (someone who encourages a patient to take drugs), Cobain dressed, climbed the six-foot-high wall surrounding the centre's patio and headed for the airport.

Bypassing Nirvana's usual travel agency, Cobain bought a first-class seat on Delta flight 788 to Seattle, paying with his credit card. Before boarding the plane he called the limousine company to meet him on arrival. He then tried to draw $150 cash, only to find that Love, told of Cobain's escape, had stopped his card and hired a private investigator, Tom Grant, to track him down. At one o'clock the next morning Linda Walker of Seattle Limousine saw Cobain speaking normally to other passengers after leaving the plane, and approach her with a thin smile. Walker dropped her fare at the gate of Lake Washington Boulevard and watched him walk up the driveway. Frances's former nanny Michael De Witt, who was staying in the house, woke up to find Cobain sitting on his bed. 'I talked to Michael, who said he had seen Kurt on Saturday [2 April],' says Carlson, adding that De Witt described Cobain as 'looking ill and acting weird'.

At 7.30 that morning Cobain took a taxi into town to look for bullets. A receipt from Seattle Guns for twenty-five shotgun cartridges would be found in his pocket. After a desultory breakfast and a visit to his heroin dealer, Cobain

---

* Hole's *Live Through This*, released on 11 April.

spent six minutes vainly trying to contact Love at the Beverly Hills Peninsula. (The hotel switchboard, told to hold all calls except from Love's husband, failed to make the connection.) Later in the afternoon he met a friend on Capitol Hill, gave her the keys to his Volvo and made a sign to her with his hand signifying a gun held to his head. As Cobain walked away from the bar he paused at a sycamore tree, bent down, picked up one of its seeds and put it in his pocket. He spent the night walking the streets of Capitol Hill. Nirvana's manager, John Silva, saw Cobain briefly on 3 April, Easter Day. A neighbour found him in Viretta Park, an open space on Lake Washington Boulevard, looking ill and wearing an overcoat despite the unseasonable weather. Charles Peterson also saw Cobain in downtown Seattle and thought him 'gone'.

In mid-afternoon a male voice called Seafirst Bank's twenty-four-hour number and attempted to make several charges to Cobain's credit card. A $1,100 debit was rejected at 3 pm, as were several later efforts to draw cash. Cobain, now dressed in a heavy military jacket under his black over-coat and a hunter's cap, next met a woman named Sara Hoehn on Broadway. He was in a 'foul temper' about a report that 40,000 fans had lined up on the street that morning to buy tickets for an Eagles concert in Los Angeles. 'We might as well not have happened,' is Hoehn's memory of his words. Cobain then disappeared from Seattle for forty-eight hours. The police believe he was driven by a woman to Carnation. According to Love, a blue sleeping bag she had never seen before was found in the house, along with left-over food and CDs. Next to them was a picture of the sun drawn in ink above the words 'Cheer up' and an ashtray of cigarette ends. One brand was Cobain's, the other, smudged with lipstick, wasn't.

At 9 am on 4 April Wendy O'Connor filed a missing person report with the police. According to the official complaint, 'Cobain ran away from [a] California facility and flew back to Seattle. He also bought a shotgun and may be suicidal.' The report went on to say that Cobain might be at a Capitol Hill apartment, describing it as a 'location for narcotics'. Police patrol units began making periodic checks on Lake Washington Boulevard and found only building labourers there. The workmen were asked to call the authorities if Cobain showed up. To Brent Wingstrand, commander of Seattle's East Precinct, 'It was not unusual that he would disappear like that . . . I thought he may not have been truly a missing person, but a person who didn't want to be found.' Ernest Barth, a private eye working for Tom Grant, also set up surveillance at Lake Washington Boulevard and outside what he terms a 'dope house' on Capitol Hill. No one fitting Cobain's description appeared. The bureaucratic intricacy of America's intervention system, enough to bring four policemen to Lakeside Avenue when, in June 1993, Love had complained of a scratched arm, broke down completely.

In stark contrast to the police's description of their quarry as 'not dangerous' was Cobain's own admission to a friend in Carnation, 'Other people make me reach for my gun.' After Rome he found he could tolerate human company only if he was loaded with drugs. 'How to face life with the fun gone?' he asked rhetorically on the evening of 4 April. Cobain found the answer in a syringe of heroin. 'It cheers me up for the brainlessness of people,' he told his friend, who has a last memory of Cobain leaving the diner to shuffle up Entwistle Street: 'His face was grim, heavy and set, and his feet were dragging.'

On Tuesday 5 April Gillian Gaar tried to interview Love by phone in Los Angeles. She was told by Hole's guitarist Eric Erlandson that 'Courtney was ill and not taking calls'. Frances Cobain was in the hotel with her mother. In

Aberdeen Wendy O'Connor, between fielding enquiries and offers of help and support, visited her therapist and 'asked her advice about what I should do if Kurt called me. She said I must tell him how much I and others loved him, ask him where he was, make some polite chit-chat, try to find out for sure whether he planned to kill himself – then hang up and call the cops straight away.' Cobain's mother spent the following three days by the phone.

By noon on the 5th, two electricians sent to install an alarm system had surveyed the Lake Washington property and left. Ernest Barth had gone off duty at 7.30 that morning. Michael De Witt was elsewhere in Seattle. No one saw Cobain return to the house. It was a cloudy day, mild with patchy rain – typical springtime weather for the area.* Cobain sat in his study watching television. Towards evening, with the rain strengthening and the lake murky grey through the cloud and fog, he walked outside into the room above the garage. Cobain was wearing a long-sleeved white shirt over a Japanese print T-shirt, blue jeans and a pair of loosely-laced athletic shoes. He was carrying a shotgun.

Cobain barricaded himself in by locking one French door and propping a stool against the other. He completed a one-page note addressed to 'Boddah', his invisible childhood friend, smoked a half-dozen cigarettes and drank from a can of root beer. Reaching into a cigar box containing syringes, burnt spoons and cotton he injected 1.52 milligrams of heroin, three times the normal fatal dose, into the crook of his right arm. Then Cobain drew a chair up to the window, threw his disguising hunter's cap and sunglasses on the floor, laid down two towels and a brown corduroy jacket, and opened his wallet to show his driver's licence. If he saw the

---

* Alice Wheeler is among those who think the steady rain in Seattle over the previous week had been the 'final straw for Kurt'.

lights coming on across the water in Bellevue or heard the schoolchildren running down Lake Washington Boulevard to their dance class, neither stopped him raising the barrel of the shotgun to his mouth and, by using his free thumb, pulling the trigger.

On 6 April Barth, the private investigator, took up position in a car outside the house. Two employees of Veca Electric worked in the grounds. A newspaper and letters were delivered to the door. Michael De Witt came and went. A patrol car from the East Precinct reported 'nothing unusual' about the scene. Elsewhere in Seattle, a woman tried to charge a $1,517 cash advance on Cobain's credit card, a last effort to settle his unpaid drugs bill.

Early the next morning Tom Grant*, letting himself in through an open window, twice checked Cobain's house, the second occasion with Dylan Carlson. They failed to search the room above the garage. Grant did, however, find a note on the stairs from De Witt, advising Cobain to 'take care of business' and accusing him of mistreating his family. At 1.30 pm Barth was relieved and the watch transferred to Carnation. The police again visited and found nothing amiss. Later that afternoon De Witt, indignant that 'Courtney [had] accused me of hiding Kurt', flew to Los Angeles to protest his innocence. By the time he arrived Love herself had been taken to Century City Hospital, apparently suffering from an overdose, and while there arrested for possession of drugs. (All charges against her were later dropped.) After posting $10,000 bail, Love immediately checked into Exodus, the same facility from which her husband had escaped six days earlier. She stayed only one night.

At 8.40 on the morning of 8 April Gary Smith of Veca

---

* According to Grant, Love's last words to him before he flew to Seattle were 'Save the American icon, Tom.'

Electric arrived at Lake Washington Boulevard. After checking the main house he walked upstairs to the balcony outside the garage, looked in, and saw the body through a glass opening in the door. 'At first I thought it was a mannequin,' Smith says. 'Then I noticed it had blood in the right ear. Then I saw a shotgun lying across his chest pointing up at his chin.' Smith raised the alarm after paging his boss, who in turn contacted Seattle radio station KXRX-FM. By the time the police arrived at 8.56 the news had already broken that there was a body at the Cobain house and speculation as to its identity.

Two officers broke into the room and visually confirmed that Cobain was dead. In forcing the French door they spread glass fragments, several of which struck and cut the body. According to the pathologist Nikolas Hartshorne, 'Kurt was cold, in the early stages of putrefaction, and there was already skin slippage.' Dr Hartshorne also noted that the webbing of Cobain's left hand bore the impression of a shotgun barrel. The suicide note was stuck into a planting tray by a red pen. Detectives spent only a few minutes at the scene, during which an enterprising Seattle *Times* photographer took a shot from above the glass doors of the garage, revealing Cobain's body from the waist down, his right fist clenched, the cigar box open at his side. The corpse, which was removed from the house by the King County medical examiner, was later identified through fingerprints.

News of Cobain's death was first reported by KXRX, told by Veca they had the 'scoop of the century' and that 'you're going to owe [us] some pretty good Pink Floyd tickets for this one'. After the network called the Associated Press, TV and radio stations across the country began flashing the news. The Seattle *Times* made the first printed announcement. Later in the afternoon the medical examiner issued a press release indicating 'the body of Curt [*sic*] Cobain has been positively identified by fingerprints'. Love, contacted by Cobain's lawyer, chartered a plane from Van Nuys airport to Seattle. After viewing the body, she cut a lock of her husband's hair and, remarking how much he hated shampoo, carefully washed it. Love kept the bloodstains on her hands for three days. Cobain's mother, father, and sister all heard the news on the radio.

The next two weeks revealed much about the workings of the media under pressure. On 10 April the Seattle *Times* carried a mock advertisement on its front page under the headline 'Business Opportunities':

> Distributorships wanted. I can cure insomnia with my special formula developed over many years of experimentation. You'll sleep like a baby for days: Contact Kurt Cobain, c/o whatever hospital room I'm currently at

– a lapse for which the paper later apologized. *People* ran a sour review of Michael Azerrad's *Come As You Are* on 18 April, similarly prompting a boxed explanation about deadlines in the next issue. While Nirvana's British fans held heartfelt vigils to express their grief over Cobain's loss, sections of the press left readers cringing with a series of mistimed commentaries. The day after the singer's death, the *Guardian* was unable to pull its interview with Love, which summarized Cobain's Rome overdose with the words: 'Awww, shucks – he coulda been a legend.' More than a week after Cobain's suicide, the *Sunday Mirror* ran a full-page preview of Nirvana's (cancelled) concert at the Brixton Academy, which warned: 'Beware of low-flying guitars and don't forget your gum shield.' The June issue of *Q* included an interview with Cheap Trick's Rick Nielsen in which he reported two absent colleagues to be 'in an Italian hospital with Kurt Cobain'. A song by the California group the

Sleestacks called 'Cobain's Dead', also a commentary on Rome, was released on schedule and sold 300,000 copies in a week. In Britain *New Woman* ran a piece prescribing Cobain 'a hair and body shampoo to get rid of that grime'.

The funeral took place in Seattle's Unity Church of Truth on 10 April. According to the minister Stephen Towles, Soundgarden's manager Susan Silver, not Cobain's favourite person, suggested the venue. 'She set up a meeting between Wendy, Courtney and myself on Saturday. We held the service the next evening, not so much as a wake but to share each other's feelings.' There was no casket; Cobain's body was still in the custody of Dr Hartshorne. The 200 invited guests heard Towles describe suicide as 'no different than having your finger in a vice. The pain becomes so great that you can't bear it.' Novoselic, clad in a dark suit, delivered a brief eulogy. 'We remember Kurt for what he was: caring, generous and sweet,' he said. Dylan Carlson read verses from a Buddhist monk. Bruce Pavitt made a short speech to his departed friend: 'I love you. I respect you. Of course I'm a few days late in expressing it.' According to Alice Wheeler, 'It was noticeable that the old cronies like Dylan, Bruce and Slim Moon were all there, but none of Kurt's so-called friends since he became famous.' Towles continued the service with the 23rd Psalm and by inviting Love to read passages from the Book of Job and tell anecdotes about her husband. Danny Goldberg closed by saying, 'You got us hooked, Kurt. It's unfair to split like this,' and playing a tape of the Beatles' 'In My Life'. As Love left the church she stopped at the door to speak to Cobain's father. According to Don's wife Jenny, 'Courtney made a point of saying she wanted him to see more of his granddaughter. Frances smiled at him and called him Papa.'

While Towles met with Love and Wendy O'Connor, the disc jockey Marco Collins had been organizing a public vigil to 'help kids vent their sense of betrayal'. On the same evening as the funeral, 6,000 mourners gathered outside the Flag Pavilion in the shadow of the Space Needle. As the loudspeaker system played 'Serve The Servants' and other tracks from *In Utero*, weeping fans plunged into a nearby fountain, showed off the *k-u-r-d-t* tattoos scored on their arms with razors and, in perhaps the ultimate ritual sacrifice, publicly burnt their flannel shirts. According to *Spin*, 'It was a truly awesome moment of spontaneous, pagan catharsis.' 'Kurt would have loved it,' says Collins. 'It was just the sort of anti-establishment gesture he lived for.'

Later, a professionally recorded tape was played to the crowd. Love's voice was tearful and near inaudible as she began, 'I don't really know what to say. I feel the same way you guys do. If you guys don't think that I'd sit in his room when he played guitar and sing and feel so honoured to be near him, you're crazy.' After berating her husband as 'an asshole', Love then read part of Cobain's suicide note, interjecting her own thoughts into his, as if they were arguing.

'The worst crime I can think of,' Cobain had written, 'would be to rip people off by faking it and pretending as if I'm having 100 percent fun.' (*No, Kurt, the worst crime I can think of is for you to just continue being a rock star when you fucking hate it*) ... 'I can't get over the frustration, the guilt and the empathy I have for everyone. There's good in all of us, and I simply think I love people too much – (*So why didn't you just fucking stay?*) – so much that it makes me feel too fucking sad ... I have it good, very good, and I'm grateful. But since the age of 7, I've become hateful toward all humans in general only because it seems so easy for people to get along and have empathy – Empathy! – only because I love and feel sorry for people too much, I guess. Thank you all from the pit of my burning, nauseous stomach for your letters and concern during the past years. I'm too much of an erratic, moody baby, and I don't have the passion anymore, so remember – (*And don't, because this is a fucking lie*) – It's better to burn out than to fade away. (*God, you asshole.*) Peace, love, empathy. Kurt Cobain.'

There was a part of the note not read in public, described by Love as 'very fucked-up writing' and ending, 'You know I love you, I love Frances. I'm so sorry. Please don't follow me.' Just as Cobain had foreshadowed Neil Young's 'It's better to burn out' rock-star cliché in his line on *Nevermind*, 'It's more fun to lose than to pretend', so the private part of his note echoed that album's theme of corrupted innocence. 'It was all about Frances and Kurt not wanting to see her become like him,' says a woman who read it. 'I have a daughter who reminds me too much of what I used to be,' Cobain had written.

Nikolas Hartshorne, who performed the autopsy on Cobain, calls it 'the act of someone who wanted to obliterate himself, to literally become nothing'. Hartshorne is certain there were no suspicious circumstances about the death. The fact that the impact of a shotgun cartridge to the mouth left no exit wound – seized on by conspiracy theorists as evidence that Cobain was killed by different means – Hartshorne describes as 'a quirk'. On 9 April, the day after the body was found, the medical examiner announced a verdict of suicide, specifically a 'self-inflicted contact perforating shotgun wound to [the] head'. As part of their investigation, Seattle police compared the three-page letter addressed to Love in Rome with the note found next to the body, with the rapid conclusion that both had been written by Cobain. With the exception of the toxicology report – withheld by Dr Hartshorne, but widely thought to show evidence of heroin and the Valium-like drug diazapan – that closed the formal examination of Cobain's death.

Love, meanwhile, arranged for Stephen Towles, the pastor of Unity Church, to perform a 'cleansing' ceremony in the room where Cobain shot himself. 'Courtney, Kurt's mother and I sat on the floor and lit candles and chanted,' he recalls. Wendy herself remembers 'hav[ing] this vision of [Cobain] from the time of his death. He was in a kind of bright blue graduation gown and he had that familiar look on his face, a little smirky but kind of Jesus-like, and euphoric. During the chanting I let out this guttural sound, and the vision went flying like a rocket, further and further from my mind. Now I can't see him any more.' A few days after the exorcism Towles wrote to Cobain's widow offering to visit, but Love's brief experience at Unity apparently cured her of western religion. From then on, she always turned to her Buddhist beliefs for comfort.

After being released by the coroner, Cobain's body lay at the Bleitz funeral home before being cremated on 14 April. Part of the ashes were sent by Love to a burial site in India, part were meant to be scattered in a public cemetery in Seattle, if cost and crowd-control problems could be solved. The remainder she placed in a Buddha figure by her bedside. In an elaborate procedure, the gun with which Cobain shot himself was released to his lawyer, who in turn presented it to KIRO Television, who donated it to the pressure group Mothers Against Violence, who then returned it to the authorities (who destroyed it), all without the weapon physically leaving police custody.

There were different views and different constructions of Cobain's death. For most of his eleven- and twelve-year-old admirers, and there were many, it came as their first brush with mortality. At its most extreme, the reaction of his fans mirrored Cobain's own negative qualities, his emotional estrangement and the fierce undercurrent of his isolation, loneliness and despair, his fear of being used and then abandoned – just as his family had 'abandoned' him in Aberdeen. 'He left us,' was the verdict of one tearful girl standing on Lake Washington Boulevard. The Seattle Crisis Clinic received over 300 calls on the day Cobain's body was found, roughly twice the usual number. Hours after returning from the Flag Pavilion, a man named Daniel Kaspar committed suicide with a shotgun. Two teenagers, one in Australia, the other in southern Turkey, killed themselves in apparent tributes to Cobain. To those over thirty, 8 April 1994 recalled the days when Hendrix, Janis Joplin or other, earlier rock music icons had died. Karen Dyson, sales manager of Seattle's Tower Records, said it reminded her of 'when Elvis bought it'. Nirvana records, said Dyson, were 'flying out of the door'.

Of those who kept up a vigil that weekend outside Cobain's home, Laura Mitchell, who described herself as a 'diehard' fan, said Nirvana 'touched something deep inside me'. Her friend Renae Eli, also dressed in black, was shaking so badly she could scarcely speak. 'Kurt had something to say, especially to young people,' she sobbed. 'He helped open people's eyes to our struggles.' To Jim Sellars, a twenty-year-old nursing assistant, 'the bond [was] hard to describe, but he was a writer who could feel the way we do. I'm still in shock, I feel so numb that someone who helped us understand is dead.' A woman named Katie Hess expressed a popular view in her letter to the *Post-Intelligencer*:

I won't judge the circumstances or the pain of Kurt's leaving, though that pain must have been incomprehensible. Beautiful and gifted as he was, maybe there was no one who could have made him recognize it in himself, or bring him back from his despair. I will not judge, nor tolerate those who will. Rather, I stand with those who adored the poet, the sage, the wondrous minstrel that Kurt Cobain was. I stand in celebration of a bright and fleeting star who graced the planet with the song of angels.

A more cynical interpretation of Cobain's death was also forthcoming.

His suicide handed a substantial weapon to seventy-five-year-old Andy Rooney, who asked, pertinently enough, 'When the spokesman for his generation blows his head off, what is the generation supposed to think?' In Rooney's view, there was relatively little of interest in the life, and none at all in the death. Cobain himself had always said that no one over thirty-two could understand him, and a number of that generation now cordially returned his mistrust. Complaining on *60 Minutes* that Cobain had lived through neither a war nor a depression, Rooney then opined that 'if Kurt Cobain applied the same thought process to his music that he applied to his drug-congested life, it's reasonable for a reasonable person to think that his music may not have made much sense either.' The backlash continued with figures like Rush Limbaugh, the *McLaughlin Group* and countless newspaper columnists (many of whom admitted they had never heard of Cobain, Nirvana or even grunge) all angrily dismissing the dead rock star. To Rooney and the rest there was no way to torture the word 'model' to make Cobain into a 'role model' for his generation. In Britain, using the forum of *The Times*, Bernard Levin wrote: 'We all need idols, and some of us find them in the most extraordinary situations. Why should not ten million youths find theirs in a foul-mouthed, brutish, violent singer-guitarist, drugged to the eyebrows and hating himself and his way of life?'

Few would have expected Levin or Rooney to flatter Cobain. A more telling criticism was by those in their twenties and younger, for whom his suicide had its genesis in a lack of scruple and a preference for striking the lower notes of the human scale rather than the higher ones. In the words of the eighteen-year-old Sarah Murray, 'My first thought was that it was pretty selfish of Kurt, because of his family and his daughter and his wife. And it was selfish musically, too, because Nirvana was just beginning. He left everyone hanging.' 'He died a coward,' growled one Seattle disc jockey, 'and left a little girl without a father.' There were those even among Cobain's peers who saw nothing noble, still less original, in his going. 'The whole thing reeks of cliché,' said Chris Dorr, a twenty-three-year-old Seattle college student. 'It makes you wonder if our icons are genetically programmed to self-destruct in their late twenties.' Even Love, after a period of seclusion following her husband's death, saw the event in a more dispassionate light: 'There's definitely a narcissism in what he did. It was very snotty of him.'

In Lawrence, meanwhile, William Burroughs sat poring over the lyric sheet of *In Utero*. There was surely poignancy in the sight of the eighty-year-old author, himself no stranger to tragedy, scouring Cobain's songs for clues to his suicide. In the event he found only the 'general despair' he had already noted during their one meeting. 'The thing I remember about him is the deathly grey complexion of his cheeks. It wasn't an act of will for Kurt to kill himself. As far as I was concerned, he was dead already.' Burroughs is one of those who feel Cobain 'let down his family' and 'demoralized the fans' by committing suicide.

The emphasis of the press coverage was hyperbolic, sometimes fawning, often hysterical, invariably opinionated. MTV, the station that grew up with Cobain, went into mourning for twenty-four hours, prompting *Time* to compare their coverage with that which followed the Kennedy assassination thirty years before, 'with Kurt Loder in the role of Walter Cronkite'. The media frenzy got under way over the weekend of 8–10 April, with reporters from *Inside Edition*, *20/20*, *Hard Copy*, two *Rolling Stone* writers, a producer for NBC's 'First Person' and *People*'s Johnny Dodd all combing Seattle for stories. The three national networks, CNN and Fox began broadcasting live from Lake Washington Boulevard. For the first time in two years, the satellite-uplink trucks returned to the parking lot east of the Crocodile, while within, a reporter from the *Globe* – the paper that demonized Cobain in 1992 – brandished a cheque-book. Gary Smith, the electrician who found the body, was paid $1,500 by 'A Current Affair' and told the Seattle *Times*, 'I'm kind of waiting to see what other magazines, or the rest of the entertainment industry, wants' in terms of deals. A photographer had to be evicted from the medical examiner's office while trying to locate the corpse.

Cobain's life had been largely ignored by the serious media even after the release of *Nevermind*, but his violent death made headlines the world over. According to ABC News, he was 'another casualty of success'. The *New York Times* ran the story on its front page, above items on Rwanda and the resignation of the Japanese government. Across the Atlantic Cobain's death was reported on both the BBC and *News at Ten*, immediately after the story of Paul Gascoigne's broken leg. *The Times* and the *Telegraph* each ran long, if factually flawed obituaries. Elsewhere, there was reticence by those, like the London *Standard*, for whom Cobain's death lacked the 'epic drama' of Hendrix's or Lennon's, and an over-reaction by others, stigmatized in one paper under the heading 'Smells Like Dead Rock Star'.

In Britain, Cobain's face appeared on the covers of *Melody Maker*, *New Musical Express*, the *Face*, *Vox*, *Raw*, *Spin* and *Q*. As with Lennon in 1980, an entire issue of *Rolling Stone* was devoted to Cobain's life (proving, if nothing else, that Gold Mountain still denied that Rome had been a suicide bid), along with features in *Time* and *People*. The pack was led by *Newsweek*, which had the morbid good fortune to have had a suicide cover story on the presses when the news broke. *Entertainment Weekly* brought off the difficult feat of criticizing the 'crass profiteering' that followed Cobain's death while printing an advertisement, two pages later, for 'Nirvana collectibles'. Both here and in the other mass-circulation titles, virtues were discovered that had somehow previously failed to surface. The gap between how Cobain was judged in his lifetime and how he was depicted in death was not merely unusually wide, it was alarmingly so. It was obvious now that serious commentators in both Britain and America, of both sexes and all ages, took to this violent, self-loathing heroin addict in a way which few had ever suspected. He was valued, liked and admired. With notable exceptions, the mainstream media treated Cobain with a respect that was as exaggerated as, a month earlier, it would have been astonishing.

A number of Cobain's fellow musicians also spoke about him, and the tributes tended to be fulsome. 'I thought he was one of the more beautiful, quiet people,' said Curt Kirkwood, the singer-guitarist who joined Nirvana for their *Unplugged* set the previous autumn. To Cobain's friend Mark Lanegan 'he was an amazing guy, a complete gentleman'. Kevin Martin of Candlebox enthuses about 'everything Kurt ever wrote about. He took an easy chord progression and made it an intricate trip through life.' When Pearl Jam took to the stage in Fairfax, Virginia, on the evening of 8 April, Cobain's suicide had been public knowledge for six hours. 'I don't think any of us would be in this room tonight if it weren't for Kurt,' said Eddie Vedder, thus dramatizing a relationship that had, in the past, been fickle. Six months later Pearl Jam's album *Vitalogy* would contain lines apparently inspired by Cobain's death, including a reference to a cigar box on the floor, such as the one found next to his body in which Cobain kept his heroin kit. Among the elder generation, David Bowie calls 'Kurt's death one of [the] really crushing blows in my life'. 'He was quoted as saying things that I totally identify with,' said Eric Clapton. 'Like being backstage and hearing the crowd out there, and thinking, "I'm not worth it. I'm a piece of garbage. And they're fools, if they knew what the truth was about me, they wouldn't like me." I've identified with that a million times.'

There were musical tributes, including Neil Young's 'Sleeps with Angels', a reply to Cobain's ghastly perversion of Young's own lyric. Syd Straw unveiled a moving song titled 'Almost As Blue As Your Eyes'. Cobain's old guitar teacher Warren Mason wrote the self-explanatory 'Goodbye', while the British Nirvana chose to record their namesake's 'Lithium'. Sinéad O'Connor, who remarked that Cobain's death meant not having to commit suicide herself, covered 'All Apologies' on her *Universal Mother* album. Later in the year R.E.M.'s *Monster* would include a track called 'Let Me In' and a second song, 'Crush With Eyeliner', widely interpreted as a reference to Love.

A few dissented. Cobain's Aberdeen friends the Melvins gave Claude Iosso the impression they were 'less than enthralled' by his suicide. To Gilby Clarke of Guns N' Roses 'it was an act of selfishness'. Mick Jagger told a New York press conference Cobain's death was 'inevitable', while even Keith Richards, the sixties prototype of a wasted rock star, contemptuously believed he 'had a death wish'.

The scepticism that followed Cobain's suicide was also reflected close to home. Seattle's efforts to honour its dead son succeeded in only a handful of isolated projects. In October 1994 an artist named Amy Jo Merrick showed an exhibition of sculptures titled 'Never Fucking Mind'; there was an open-air reading of Cobain's lyrics; Seattle's booming spiritualist and channelling industry advertised a seance to 'reach Kurt'. The major reaction, not surprisingly, came from those who had known Cobain professionally. 'It's a much different thing here, with the rock scene,' says Sub Pop's Nils Bernstein. 'Kurt's death is an ongoing event.' Sub Pop itself was besieged for days by reporters, none of whom got past the receptionist's icy 'no comment'. By a quirk of timing, the Saturday after Cobain's death had long been scheduled as the label's sixth anniversary party. According to Gillian Gaar, there was 'a rather subdued feeling – "It had to happen and it's happened"' – that night at the Crocodile. A label representative named Pat Riley summed it up when, at some point in the proceedings, he mouthed 'How's it going?' across the counter to Poneman. 'Really shitty,' was the reply. Riley smiled quietly, and lifted his glass. 'Here's to tomorrow,' he said.

In fact, by the next morning Cobain's death was being jostled from the front page by the nearby unveiling of the first Boeing 777 and the opening of the baseball season.

Affection is an emotion as ephemeral in Seattle as elsewhere, but even Cobain, with his violent repudiation of his fame, might have been surprised by the apathy that followed. 'Fuck Kurt, I can't get a job' was the verdict of one local youth. After the initial shock had worn off, something like indifference, even among Cobain's diehard fans, set in. Exactly a year after his death, a small band gathered in Viretta Park, the open space bordering the home on Lake Washington Boulevard. 'We're here to gather our thoughts, to praise Kurt,' said one girl. At other times during the year, the park benches and the hedge and trees skirting the house had been defaced and vandalized by those holding a different interpretation of Cobain's history. 'You can't blame the kids for being unimpressed,' says Marco Collins. 'All I know is that people at every level of the community were willing to get involved in the public vigil.' Their willingness did not, however, extend to subscribing funds for a monument to

Cobain – perhaps unsurprisingly for a city still debating plans for a Hendrix museum.

The media descended on Aberdeen within a few hours of Cobain's death, looking not only for quotes but for signs of *Twin Peaks*-like abnormality. They found the stories they wanted. In *Rolling Stone* Mikal Gilmore located more of the low-life ambience also noted by Azerrad. 'Special correspondents' for the *Guardian* and the *Observer* flew in from London. Claude Iosso wrote a front-page obituary for the *Daily World*. He found a 'mute' response from even Cobain's friends, for whom he became 'an emblem of failure, not success', and a predictable hostility in City Hall. The *World*'s headlines would soon be given over to the proposal that Hoquiam co-host the 1994 Lollapalooza tour, in part to honour Cobain, and the immediate vetoing of the plan by the authorities. The only visible local tribute, one that would have pleased its subject, was the graffiti KURT COBAIN R.I.P. spray-painted on the wall of a downtown bank.

Meanwhile an Aberdeen woman, Randi Hubbard, working from her husband's muffler shop, sculpted a 'cement resurrection' of Cobain and offered it to the city council. This, too, was declined. At some stage in the debate Hubbard found herself on a live radio show with Novoselic, who threatened to smash up the sculpture if it was ever publicly exhibited (and then left the studio with the words 'I love you, Randi'). Elsewhere in Aberdeen, Cobain's old teachers Robert Hunter and Lamont Shillinger were surprised to hear plans for a 'Kurt Cobain Visual Arts Scholarship' aired on MTV. 'His management just laughed when I asked them about it,' says Shillinger. 'Personally, I haven't a hope it will ever happen.'

Perhaps the most poignant hometown comment of all was that by Cobain's mother, alluding to the pantheon of rock stars who died in their prime: 'Now he's gone and joined that stupid club.'

Love always insisted that something good would come from Cobain's death. It did: a new boom in Nirvana record sales and a new national forum on suicide. *Newsweek* led the way with their cover story, 'Why Do People Kill Themselves?' Linking the subject to the euthanasia debate, suicide, the magazine concluded, was 'just another human choice' in the 1990s. Cobain's death was compared to those of Abbie Hoffman, Marilyn Monroe and Ernest Hemingway. *Newsweek*'s efforts to 'explain' grunge and put Cobain 'in context' showed signs of being hurried, and none too approving: '99.9% of Americans don't kill themselves. For better or worse, they stick to the rules – the unspoken "covenant" we all have with each other to affirm life even, perhaps, when there's little left to affirm.'

Susan Eastgard, director of the Seattle Crisis Clinic, noting that their number of calls had doubled on the day Cobain's body was found, spoke of the 'deadly urge' among white males aged between twenty and thirty-nine to take their own lives. Elsewhere, Cobain's suicide ignited a flurry of speculation about what was happening to America's thirteenth generation. One conclusion: 'They [were] the first to experience the "Home Alone" phenomenon – latchkey kids . . . They grew up feeling limited and it's made many of them angry.' Then there were the guns and drugs. While the availability of both had long been debated, it would have been unthinkable, only a year or two earlier, for a petition of two million signatures to demand a ban on exactly the type of weapon with which Cobain killed himself, or for the Washington state legislature to stir itself to consider 'de-glamorizing' drugs by legalizing them. According to one Representative, 'It was precisely because of Kurt that these issues came to the floor.' With their campaign thus made viable, both sides of the House began to trade Cobain anecdotes and to interpret his death as their mandate for action.

* * *

Twenty-five years on, the rumours about Jimi Hendrix's death show no sign of seriously abating. To this day there are conflicting theories about the events of 18 September 1970, when Hendrix's girlfriend Monika Dannemann called an ambulance to London's Samarkand Hotel – in one version six hours after he stopped breathing. As recently as 1994, detectives from the International and Organized Crime Branch were trying to establish whether there was a delay in raising the alarm and whether any items were removed from Hendrix's room before police arrived. The new investigation was ordered after the Attorney General studied a dossier on the case compiled by another of Hendrix's ex-girlfriends, Kathy Etchingham. She has always claimed that the guitarist 'was in the wrong place at the wrong time'. According to yet another of Hendrix's lovers, Gale Frank, 'We may never know if he killed himself, or if someone else did it for him. Did he really die? It's a pretty safe bet that the tabloids will run at least one "Jimi sighted in Arizona" story before each year's out.'

Cobain's suicide attracted much the same speculation. In one frequently heard version, Cobain died not by suicide or neglect, but was murdered, shot by an unknown assassin, for a reason buried somewhere back in the madness of his twenty-seven years alive.

First of the conspiracy theorists into print was a Seattle man, Richard Lee, who aired his own public-access television show *Was Kurt Cobain Murdered?* and speculated, without foundation, as to whether Love was 'psychologically capable' of killing. Lee was also struck by the shooting death of a Seattle police officer, Antonio Terry, in June 1994. Terry had been among those looking for Cobain in the days between his leaving Exodus and the discovery of the body, and may have been, according to Lee, the last person to see him alive. Later in 1994 Tom Grant, the private eye who searched Cobain's house but failed to check the room above the garage, claimed on radio that 'Kurt was . . . drugged and shot . . . by someone who wanted to increase the value of his records.' He declined to give a name. Grant was sceptical that the suicide note found by the body, compared by the police to the one written in Rome, had, in fact, been left by Cobain. One aspect under investigation, by Grant if no one else, was that the letter had been forged by someone familiar with Cobain's thought-process, and the singer killed to preserve the legend and maximize his estate.

A more exotic theory was aired by an organization called Friends Understanding Kurt. According to this thesis, Cobain had been dabbling in the last days of his life with a so-called 'Dream-machine'. This device, described as a 'psychoactive hallucinogenic neocortex-pulsator' (basically a strobe light), designed by the late Brion Gysin and patented by William Burroughs, was allegedly shipped to Cobain in California. In the Friends' words, 'Kurt immediately commenced a habitual, perhaps maniacal use of the Dream-machine, then took it with him to his and Courtney's shared Seattle mansion, where he stationed himself with the device in a room above the garage. We construct his corpse being discovered sprawled across the floor, a symbol of darkness offset by a final, albeit misunderstood message to the living.' The group's construction did not, however, reach to the Seattle police's Incident Report, which fails to list a humming black cylindrical box among the items found at the death scene. Burroughs himself, noting the acronym formed by the Friends' initials, suspects an 'anarchic prank'.

Lee's and the other theories, tendered in the usual form of questions rather than answers, all raised the point why Cobain should have chosen a shotgun as well as a massive overdose. One explanation is offered by Wendy O'Connor: 'What happened was that shortly before he died, I begged him not to let drugs kill him like it had killed all the rest of them [Hendrix, Joplin, et al]. So, Kurt being Kurt, I guess he decided he didn't want to follow them. He wanted to do it his own way, and he shot himself to be *different* . . . If I hadn't told him not to join that club, he might have overdosed, as he had before, and we might have found him and saved him. A gun was so final.'

For the last three years of his life, an indication of a crisis in Cobain's mental health would be the complaint that 'jackals' were exploiting his name. The process accelerated after his death. At one extreme there were benign tributes like the repeated airing of the *Unplugged* concert, Beverley Cobain's design of a 'Kurt shirt' for his fans, and the setting up of a Kurt Cobain Memorial Project at the children's hospital in Minneapolis. At the other, there was the auctioning, for $17,000, of a smashed guitar with Cobain's blood on it.

For at least a year after the event, Seattle was inundated by journalists, screenwriters and authors seeking a morbid dramatization of Cobain's death. Some revived the 'stump-dumb rocker dude' myth Cobain had rejected; others found that the punk ethos of openness and candour did not extend to cooperating with unauthorized biographers. Eventually *Rolling Stone* was able to publish a coffee-table book commemorating Cobain's life. By late 1994 rumours had surfaced of a Hollywood 'biopic', with Brad Pitt or Stephen Dorff (Stuart Sutcliffe in *Backbeat*) in the title role. Meanwhile, hardcore fans could wear T-shirts printed with Cobain's final message, 'It's better to burn out than to fade away', or buy colour posters showing the corpse from the waist down.

Nirvana themselves, Novoselic and Grohl, announced plans for a thirty-song live album, then changed their minds, citing the difficulty of working on the project so soon after Cobain's suicide. 'I entered into [it] with an air of optimism and an overall good vibe,' says Novoselic; however, the 'emotional drag' proved too great. Charles Peterson, who sat next to Novoselic and Grohl on a flight to Los Angeles at the time, believes that 'hearing Kurt's voice again threw them for a loop. They were both badly shaken.' In the end the album (provisionally titled, yet again, *Verse Chorus Verse*) was released, in November 1994, as *MTV Unplugged In New York*. It wasn't that it was bad; merely that the group had neither the skill nor training to appear raw and unadorned before an audience. Nirvana were like professional footballers who had wandered inadvertently on to a junior-school playing field. The unlikely success and astonishing reviews of *Unplugged*, combined with the groundswell of sympathy for Cobain's colleagues, were enough to earn it a Record of the Year Award from MTV, and a 1995 Grammy.

'It doesn't really sink in that you're never going to see this person again – or there's never going to be another Nirvana record,' says Cobain's friend Mac MacCaughan. He may be surprised. As well as the double live album still promised for the future, there are at least fifteen unreleased songs, some given to friends like Michael Stipe, others retained by Geffen, in Nirvana's capacious vault. There must be a probability that, like Hendrix's, Cobain's work will be routinely recycled for years, if not decades to come. The Albini session yielded at least two out-takes, 'Two Bass Kid' and the tastefully named 'Moist Vagina', likely to herald a flood of 'newly discovered' recordings. There are ten hours alone of *Nevermind*-era rejects. In late 1994 Love began playing one of her husband's unreleased songs, 'Drown Soda'. In a friend's view 'the modern scourge of the record industry, repackaging and the scraping of the studio barrel' has already begun.*

At the same time as *Unplugged*, Geffen released the video

* By mid-1995 a 'limited tin' containing *Nevermind*, a T-shirt, badge, and post-cards was on sale for $100, while *Unplugged In New York* in a red heart-shaped box retailed for $152.99.

Live! Tonight! Sold Out!!, a haphazard mix of concert footage, TV appearances, and on-the-road flummery shot by Nirvana themselves. Neither of these products diminished Cobain's reputation – they may even have added to his place in pop history. With the video, however, an opinion began to form that Nirvana, post-Cobain, were no more 'alternative' than they needed to be. The joke in Seattle about 'into the chart with a bullet' was unfair, but the price of the film (higher than that of new releases by U2 and Madonna) and the use of the phrase 'Sold Out' in the title were thought, at the least, ironic. Both *Unplugged* and *Live! Tonight!* were substantial hits, while sales of *Bleach*, *Nevermind*, *Incesticide* and *In Utero* all tripled in the weeks following Cobain's death.

The prime beneficiary of all this activity was Cobain's widow. On 11 April Hole's second album, called by the cruellest of ironies *Live Through This*, was released to wild critical acclaim. It takes nothing from Love's songs and the record's *Nevermind*-like hooks to say there was a sympathy vote at work in some of the reviews: sympathy for the loss of her husband and for the ordeal she suffered elsewhere in the media. Even as a widow, Love was one of the most polarizing figures in rock. To millions she became an avenging angel, a feminist icon and at worst an object of curiosity and respect; to others (some of whom, in the days following Cobain's suicide, sported T-shirts with the slogan 'Courtney Did It') a different interpretation was apparently possible. What no one did was to ignore her.

After Cobain's suicide, his mother started to worry that Love might try to join him. 'I was so concerned about her that I stayed in her room,' Wendy told *Entertainment Weekly*. After a week at Lake Washington Boulevard, Love drove cross-country and spent the spring at a Buddhist monastery in upstate New York. Even behind the veil, she managed to attract the lurid attention of the press. One paper had Love 'spending thousands' on exotic lingerie in Manhattan, while another weighed her drug consumption as not far behind that of her ex-husband. ('I have used heroin,' she would admit. 'After Kurt died.') By the middle of May Love had begun venturing back into the public eye. She attended the MTV Movie Awards with Michael Stipe. A photograph was taken of her lying on a hotel bed with one of Cobain's friends, Evan Dando. Then, on 16 June 1994, Hole's bass player, Kristen Pfaff, was found dead of a drug overdose in her bath. She was twenty-four. The police and firemen who broke down her door came on a distressingly familiar scene. Pfaff was lying on her back, her arms slumped over the edge, with a box containing drug paraphernalia beside her. For the second time in ten weeks the press descended on Seattle, some seeking to 'explain' heroin addiction, others, no more successfully, to interview Love. Pfaff's death once again made Hole's future precarious, and there were reports over the summer that the group would disband.

Such rumours underestimated Love's ambition, resilience and need – almost a pathological demand – for attention. In July Hole hired a replacement bass player, and in August performed chaotically at the Reading Festival. On 11 September the group played in Seattle for the first time since Cobain's and Pfaff's deaths. Love told the hushed crowd that her late husband was listening as she sang a version of 'Where Did You Sleep Last Night'. Fans pressed close to the stage claimed they saw tears in her eyes. On some nights concert goers were confronted by a woman described as 'embarrassingly out of control', on others by America's 'most powerful, eloquent female rocker'. Both personalities surfaced at Hole shows over the autumn. In Cleveland, Love put down her guitar, pulled up her shirt and tore off her bra. 'She reverted almost completely to her stripper days, sticking out her belly and writhing,' said *Spin*. But the *New York Times* raved about Hole's show in that city. 'The songs balanced fury, defiance and craft like the best punk rock,' wrote John Pareles. He called Love brave and vulnerable, 'a punk anti-heroine in spike heels'. At a second Seattle concert in November, Love walked on, tossed her overcoat on a pile of dolls, stuffed bears and toys that filled the stage, lit a cigarette and told a television cameraman in the pit to 'fuck off'. That done, she strapped on her guitar and ground out the power chords of 'Plump'.

Some punk rockers, while forceful enough live or on record, are curiously shy of advancing their views on society. Love was not one of these musicians. In the year following Cobain's death she vented her opinions on drugs, sex, guns, fame, feminism and motherhood. She frequently brought the two-year-old Frances onstage, raising questions about the wisdom of letting her daughter be seen as a sympathy prop. Love was rarely without a dramatic gesture or a telling quip. Backstage at a concert in New York, she was asked by a security guard to show her pass. 'How about the tracks of my tears,' Love said, and walked by. It surprised no one that she won a role in the film *Feeling Minnesota* and *Basquiat*, or that *Time* described her as a 'safe bet' for future stardom on the big screen.

In the winter of 1994–5 alone, Love appeared on the covers of *Entertainment Weekly*, *Rolling Stone*, *Q*, *Spin*, *Village Voice* and, incredibly, *Vanity Fair*, dressed either in lingerie or the baby-doll dresses she described as her 'kinder-whore' look. In the rare moments she was neither onstage nor being interviewed, she began filing messages on the computer bulletin-board America Online. Rambling and strewn with expletives, they expressed all the anger, the pain, the bile and frustration Love felt in the first months of widowhood. Among her numerous targets were reporters and biographers ('All of you that ever denigrate or blaspheme Kurt

. . . be afraid, be very fucking afraid'), her father ('Biodad') and Seattle's drug dealers. Elsewhere she commented disparagingly on Novoselic, Grohl and Eddie Vedder. In a low point of petulance, Love got loudly drunk at the Oscars ceremony. She then chased Cobain's ex-girlfriend Mary Lou Lord, describing her as 'one of five people I'd like to fucking kill', down a street. Such was the pull of Love's name that a serious debate began as to whether her Online postings were drug-fuelled, exercising a deep Joycean stream-of-consciousness, or (as Love herself insisted) the product of a 'sticky, fucked-up keyboard'.

Love also spoke frequently, and affectingly, about her husband. She saw him as a victim of success. 'Ultimately his largest problem in life was *not* being able to say "Fuck you",' she told David Fricke. 'Kurt had a lot of personal inner fucking demons, a lot of frailties and physical ailments,' Love wrote on Online. 'He doesn't want to be known as a loser,' she told distraught fans camping in Viretta Park. Love continued to wear her engagement ring from Cobain until it was stolen from her New York hotel room. She also appeared in her husband's brown corduroy jacket police found at the suicide scene. ('I washed the blood off it,' she informed Fricke.) Love even slept in the now-bare room above the garage. If her decision to stay in the home at Lake Washington Boulevard was both brave and quixotic, there was a feeling among some that Love was neither unaware of her status as Cobain's widow ('People will refer to rock couplehood not just in terms of Sid and Nancy and John and Yoko, but Kurt and Courtney. We're in the pantheon') nor indifferent to its rewards (Cobain left assets of $1.2 million to his wife and daughter). There was also a price to be paid for remaining in Seattle. Another Online bulletin described Love's domestic predicament: 'surrounded by much-needed 24 hour security . . . a new cyclone electronic fence with sensors, a rottweiler, a german shephard.' And the letters from fans: 'No longer charming, guileless *kids*. Now it's the legitimately, intensely insane people ... the ones writing *those* letters, the ones in blood, the satan ones.'

The Cobains' legend drew strength from its compliance to the feminist ideal of a weak man and a strong woman. For Emma Forrest in the *Sunday Times* Cobain's suicide was 'The ultimate act of betrayal ... His wife, an important musician in her own right, would have died for him. The truth is she is stronger than he was. She had the same heroin habit to fight, the same personal demons, the same miserable upbringing.' He chose to kill himself 'at a crucial point in Courtney's career'. To Ann Powers in *Village Voice*, 'The dissolution of the Love–Cobain partnership [was] an artistic tragedy. These two were exploring the male–female dynamic together, as musicians and as public figures ... Just as it's mercilessly unfair to blame Love for Cobain's death, it may be in bad taste to point out that he committed suicide the week her album was to be released.' It became an axiom among the press to be either 'pro-Kurt' or 'pro-Courtney'; pop psychiatrists wrote columns about how he had done irreparable psychological harm to his wife and daughter. In a hasty revision of the Cobain myth, *Rolling Stone* now believed 'his tragedy was his inability to feel his own power; Love's achievement is to be able, across the black expanse of her sorrow, to maintain a sense of her own.' Only the public, it seemed, could hold in its head simultaneously the ideas that Cobain was a well-meaning man who did his best; that Love was an intelligent opportunist who had had a rough time and craved attention; and that they should probably never have married.

Among Love's antics were follies that made Madonna look positively dignified. In January 1995 ABC's *Inside Edition* aired examples of her 'bizarre and unpredictable behaviour', including her passing out on the floor of a nightclub, and eliciting on-camera advice from Love's father: 'If you're not getting help, Courtney, get some.' There was a report that Love had come close to immolating herself after falling asleep holding a cigarette. In late 1994 she was arrested on a flight to Australia for swearing at a stewardess who asked her to move her legs. The magistrate ordered Love to be of good behaviour for one month or forfeit a $380 bond. The following summer she was taken off a flight to Seattle suffering from an 'accidental overdose' and promptly arrested on an assault charge. She made the 1995 Ten Worst Dressed Women list. Finally, there were Love's close friend-ships with Dando and Michael Stipe, and an affair with Trent Reznor of Nine Inch Nails, supposed to have been cemented during a romantic weekend in New Orleans.

If Love was in revolt against the teenage fans to whom she screamed 'I've grown, you haven't', it was not from the standpoint of someone maturing gracefully. She despised naïvety, but she feared middle-aged atrophy. 'Any sign of growing old frightens her,' says a friend. 'A part of her is stuck at sixteen,' adds Mike Collier. According to David Haig, the 'teenage harlot look' may already be approaching expiry. On 9 July 1995 Love turned thirty, two years short of the age at which Cobain once insisted, and she never denied, it was 'all over'.

Among the others whose lives Cobain touched were, of course, the members of Nirvana. Novoselic and Grohl attended the funeral, white-faced, in suits – appearing not so much in mourning as deeply shocked – and paid moving tribute to their friend. 'Caring, generous and sweet,' were Novoselic's words. His only public comments on Cobain have been to threaten to destroy Randi Hubbard's statue and to discourage Love from erecting a similar monument. Novoselic's mother, Maria, describes him as 'still haunted'.

Grohl himself told a television audience in September 1994, 'I think about Kurt every day.' Other than a brief reunion to back Cobain's protégé Simon Fair Timony, the editing of *Unplugged* and *Live! Tonight!*, Novoselic's appearance in the trio Sweet 75, and a groundless rumour that Grohl would join Cobain's old enemies Pearl Jam – eclipsed by his success with the Foo Fighters – nothing has been heard in the year since. When a reporter asked music journalist Dan Lothian about Nirvana's future, Lothian enlightened the public with the knowledge that 'experts are saying there were only three people in this band, and without the lead singer [who also played the guitar and wrote the songs] it's doubtful that Nirvana will continue as it was known in the past'.

Opinions vary as to whether Cobain 'made' Sub Pop or vice-versa, but friends like Charles Peterson and Alice Wheeler agree that the label's hype was a vital factor in selling the Nirvana myth. Pavitt's comment to the *Sounds* reporter in 1989 was to the point. 'There's one thing I want you to know,' he said. 'I'll stake my life that Kurt will make it.' It was a personal commitment, and the response was personal. Until the day his ambition finally offset his talent, Cobain spoke of Sub Pop with almost touching gratitude. They gave him 'a life', he once told Collier. Cobain was provided with ample opportunity to exercise the gifts that had led people to call him a 'rising star' by the men who so desperately wanted to be starmakers. Slim Moon recalls that when, in the house on North Pear Street, Cobain began grumbling about his career, he always spoke of Pavitt and Poneman as 'the only two men who understood him'.

Five years later, Sub Pop may 'no longer have [had] any connection with the group' as they put it to reporters, but the penthouse office suite and the thriving souvenir shop were both testament to the healthy cash flow from Nirvana's first three albums. The idea that Sub Pop harboured commercial ambitions of their own, so apparently shocking in 1989, was confirmed in 1994. That Christmas the label sold a 49 per cent interest to Warner Music US, a division of the giant Warner Music Group. Under the agreement, Sub Pop were affiliated with Warner's Elektra label, 'while continuing to function as a wholly autonomous [business]' according to Poneman. Sub Pop's faux-Fortune 500 identity had long been an in-house joke, with the two principals wearing suits in their publicity shots and boasting about the 'limited edition of 500,000' sampler *The Grunge Years*. But with the Warner deal fantasy became reality. While once Poneman and Pavitt had sold records out of cardboard boxes on the street, they now employed a staff of forty in the Seattle office, another three in Boston and six in Europe. The label posted sales of $7 million in 1994. According to Pavitt, 'The [Warner] partnership helps us achieve our goal of building Sub Pop into a label that combines the vision of an indie with the clout of a major.' It also virtually guaranteed that Seattle would remain a centre of rock-business activity into the next century.

As the Cobain legend grew, his home town was careful to measure the distance between his violent, negative self-image and its own more measured one. There was praise for Nirvana's music in the year-end reviews in the Seattle *Times* and *Post-Intelligencer*, but the critics spoke of a 'wave of disgust' over the brutality of Cobain's death and the message it sent to his fans. The local readers' music polls were led by groups like Pearl Jam, Soundgarden and Hole, further proof that the underground had become the mainstream, where TV variety shows exposed glum, flannel-shirted rockers to millions. From the classic Seattle image that Love portrayed as 'grunge, cappuccino and heroin' to the popular film location and tourist spot, it is tempting to see the city's progress as that from lawless outpost to fashionable resort. By mid-1995 Pioneer Square had traded its itinerants and punks for a relentless lineup of artsy, trend-conscious shops. For years Cobain's own greatest ambition had been to headline at the Central Tavern. That was before Andrew Wood overdosed and the remnants of Mother Love Bone became Pearl Jam, Alice In Chains went double platinum with *Dirt*, grunge fashion was featured in couture collections, and even the Central was re-opened as a blues club. In late 1993 Cobain had told *Rolling Stone*, 'For a few years in Seattle, it was the Summer of Love, and it was so great. To be able to just jump out on top of the crowd with my guitar and be held up and pushed to the back of the room and then brought back with no harm done to me – it was a celebration of something that no one could put their finger on.' Just as it would be wrong to blame Seattle's commercialization for Cobain's depression, it may be unfair to point out that, for at least a year before his death, he complained bitterly that what had once been 'new and fresh and original' had become 'old and stale', and that, on top of his other frailties and ailments, he now plausibly added another: boredom.

Cobain's mother, Wendy O'Connor, broke her silence about his death when she told *Entertainment Weekly*, 'Kurt's problems were ongoing, and we struggled with them for years. I talked him through so many nights. He was probably a mis- or undiagnosed depressive, which runs in my family . . . The way I explain it is, have you ever been hit in the stomach and lost your breath? It's a horrible panicky situation. Can you imagine being in that state of mind, in that state of anxiety and fear for years? He was a wonderful person, but he just couldn't stand the pain anymore. That's why I'm not angry at Kurt.'

O'Connor herself has been through a divorce, breast cancer and the suicide of her only son. She still lives in the small, green-painted house on East 1st Street and is thought to be writing a book. After the initial shock and distress, she began to see Cobain's death as something horrific, but not wholly illogical: 'We all prayed Frances would save him,' she says. 'But in the end I think she was part of the reason he did what he did. Watching someone die slowly of heroin addiction is a sickening experience. He didn't want to put her through that ... Because of his own upbringing, Kurt was also frightened of being a father. He was actually very good at it – though I'd describe him as more of a mother to Frances, the way he always cuddled her and showed her affection – but he never felt he could give her enough.' Cobain himself touched on those fears in the private part of his suicide note, saying his baby's life would be 'so much happier' without him.

Don Cobain moved to Bellingham, north of Seattle, where in a career change that would have confirmed his son's worst fears, he joined the Washington State Patrol. He communicates sporadically with Love and his grand-daughter. Apart from one calculated lapse, Don refuses all offers to speak about his family, believing the press has stigmatized him as the 'big bad guy' in Cobain's life.

In the house on Lake Washington Boulevard, meanwhile, a three-year-old girl is learning to live without her father. According to O'Connor, 'Frances knew in the first week something was really bad. Then after a while she started hitting and pinching. It was like, "OK, the sadness has gone on long enough, bring back Daddy now".' Love herself told *Rolling Stone*, 'On some nights she cries out for [Cobain] ... And I thought she didn't know anything. So every couple of days I mention him.' O'Connor and Love believe that some day, when she is considered old enough to understand, Frances will be allowed to 'get to know' her father through video archives and tapes. In the meantime, despite periodic kidnap threats and the placing of a restraining order on one fan, she can still be seen around Seattle with her nanny, playing on the small lakefront beach, calling out to her unseen parents, raw-voiced, crying and with familiar piercing blue eyes.

In the fruitless search for clues to Cobain's death the conspiracy-mongers made much of the thesis summarized in the slogan 'Courtney Did It'. Their second theory was, if anything, even more arresting. Cobain, the suggestion went, was a repressed homosexual, someone whose youthful flirtations concealed a raging and confused libido, causing him unspoken grief and leading directly to his suicide.

This view struck a deep chord in broad-minded Seattle, where homophobia ranks as a vice behind only misogyny and racism. Ample evidence suggests that Cobain, in adolescence, experimented with different sexual experiences. There was an Indian boy in Aberdeen called Hard Rock with whom he was thought unduly friendly. Whatever the subsequent breach, he gravitated to the openly homosexual Myer Loftin. Then there were Cobain's dalliances in the back alleys of Seattle, London and Berlin: his tendency to wear dresses and lingerie, and to declaim on his 'lesbian side' in public. Love would muse that her husband had 'made out with half the guys in Seattle'. 'What else should I say/ Everyone is gay', Cobain himself sang on 'All Apologies'. 'I probably could be bisexual,' he told the *Advocate*. 'I'm definitely gay in spirit.'

Those were thought to be jokes, Cobain's familiar teasing of the press or, at best, youthful dalliances already forgotten by the time he met Love. On the other hand, there were certain patterns within his family which may have made Cobain more predisposed to a homosexual lifestyle. One of Don's family now considers himself 'actively gay', and Cobain's sister Kimberly has announced her lesbianism. A homosexual Los Angeles man told *Penthouse* that Cobain was the lover of a well-known male artist in the year before his death. The artist 'idolized Kurt', says the source. 'Kurt would refer to Courtney as "the dumb bitch", and I had the impression he was regretting the marriage.' A second man in Seattle, also speaking anonymously, insists that 'Kurt was frustrated trying to go straight. He wanted out of that marriage so bad . . . it killed him.'

Magazines like *Penthouse* can offer a number of motives for Cobain to have shot himself, but no specific reason. There may not be one. As a white male in the dreaded twenty- to thirty-nine-year-old age group with a history of both depression and drug abuse, he matched the profile of a suicide victim almost exactly. There was also his lifelong exposure to guns (mentioned in three songs on *Nevermind*) and a family flaw Cobain's cousin calls 'the Irish love of self-ruin'. Wendy O'Connor's grandfather had tried to commit suicide and eventually died from his injuries. In July 1979, one of Don's uncles, Burle Cobain, killed himself by a gunshot to the stomach. Five years later, Burle's brother Kenneth committed suicide in the same way. Beverley Cobain believes there were 'other bipolar victims' on both sides of the family. The very use of the word 'victim' encapsulates one of the greatest problems Cobain faced: that almost every form of unacceptable behaviour could be excused on the grounds that he was suffering from a medical condition. This condition could absolve him from responsibility and transform the threat of retribution into a demand for help. Well-meaning friends and Seattle's amenable drug dealers duly supplied him, in time setting up a vicious circle of manic depression, pain and heroin addiction. Add fame, fortune and success – the very things Cobain railed against – and the only surprising aspect of his suicide is that it should have occurred so late in his downward spiral.

Cobain saw himself as ill-placed in life's queue. Not only did he have the misfortune to come from a family of depressives, he chose a profession notorious for the brevity of its successes. 'It was hard to imagine Kurt growing old and contented,' says Nirvana's assistant Craig Montgomery. Cobain himself could never envisage 'doing the Clapton thing'. The prospect of playing 'Teen Spirit' to a crowd of paunchy, middle-aged fans in the year 2020 was unthinkable to the man who insisted life ended at thirty-two. Cobain's expectations may have been low, but his suicidal imagination had a dramatic twist. As his final words prove, Cobain believed it was better to go out young, before atrophy and self-parody set in, not with a whimper but a bang. If he chose not to kill himself earlier, it was because he felt he had important things to say, and still needed a stage from which to say them. At twenty-seven, Cobain no longer had such plans.

That he felt himself creatively exhausted hardly needs repeating. Like Hendrix at the same age, Cobain had grown tired of the need to burlesque himself onstage, exaggerating an ever-more flamboyant façade while privately lobbying for a return to the basics. 'We've gone to the point where things are becoming repetitious. There's not something you can move up to,' he told *Rolling Stone*. Cobain was not the first musician to feel trapped by a formula, but it surely contributed to the final crisis. One of the persistent rumours in Seattle was that he killed himself because of writer's block. In his suicide note, Cobain despaired that his muse had flown south – 'The worst crime I can think of would be to rip people off by faking it and pretending.'

Cobain's vision of himself as an inveterate misfit imposed an unduly high standard on him and contributed a good deal to his ultimate collapse. In any realistic sense he was rebellious enough, but Cobain could not live very long with a self that was also well-paid and successful. In the last two years of his life he constantly sought assurance that neither he nor those he admired had sold out – and was constantly disappointed. It is known that in March 1994, just days before he died, Cobain saw a photograph of his friend Mike

Mills, of R.E.M., happily playing in the MTV 'Rock n' Jock' Softball Challenge on a California beach. He was not merely surprised, he was shocked; it seemed to Cobain that trifling with elderly actors and celebrities was the worst kind of betrayal of the punk ethic. He felt that his own success was too easily come by, and all too susceptible to the same kind of perfidy. Even Cobain's Lexus seemed to him an unacceptable symbol of affluence. He took the car back. Cobain used to agonize about the relative opulence of the house on Lake Washington Boulevard and spoke about living among the street people on Capitol Hill. He took every opportunity to reproach his own fame on *In Utero*, singing 'I do not want what I have got' and 'What is wrong with me?' Put simply, Cobain found conditions in the real world to be different to those in his head. He never reconciled his life with his myth.

There were other theories, and other causes of Cobain's death, from the mythical (he was sacrificing himself to avenge Frances Farmer); the astral (Cobain's horoscope for April 1994 spoke of his being 'involved in a constant struggle between expressing personal desires and suppressing them . . . Friends have withdrawn themselves from you for a while. There is a crisis because you are so self-absorbed'); and the obvious (heroin addiction.) One fact, too little noted, was that Cobain may have come, literally and figuratively, to the end of the line. From Aberdeen to Olympia to Seattle, his journey had been a steady upward progress from the backwoods to the relatively bright lights and tolerant culture of America's most liveable city. Cobain tried to heal, in his idyllic lakeside home, his own deep-seated disgust with humanity. He managed, as his suicide note admitted, only to make it worse.

Finally, there was the fact that Cobain subscribed to the view that 'if you die you're completely happy and your soul somewhere lives on . . . I'm not afraid of [dying].' He called his group Nirvana in the first place because, to him, it meant 'total peace after death'. Cobain may have had his moral reasons for killing himself, including the belief that it would protect his daughter, but there was surely pathos in his line on *In Utero* 'Look on the bright side is suicide', and the claim, just before he died, that 'becoming someone else is the best hope I've got'.

Cobain struggled to square his love of purity with his ear for a tune. From the moment Nirvana put out a mainstream cover song as their first single, through to the compromise of *In Utero*, his whole career was an exercise in, as Grant Alden puts it, 'hammering melody to fury'. It is tempting to wonder where this conflict might have taken Cobain had he lived. As has been seen, he was already profoundly disillusioned with the Nirvana formula. 'I'd love to be able to play with other people and create something new,' he told Azerrad. 'I don't want to keep rewriting this style of music, I want to start doing something really different.' Charles Peterson agrees that Cobain's mind was 'already wandering' and 'what he really wanted was to get back to his roots'. Slim Moon believes the volatile chemistry of Cobain's songwriting – energetic optimism in uneasy cahoots with sedentary cynicism – suggests that his reputation would have grown.

Would it? Raw talent such as his often needs a favourable time and congenial surroundings in which to flourish, and creatively gifted as he was, Cobain was also what he most denied, lucky. In the first place, he grew up with rock and roll. His motive to be different in life met with opportunity. He also lived in Seattle, a city that, by the end of the 1980s, enjoyed the same reputation as a rock mecca once held by Liverpool. Cobain was even luckier in stumbling across two famously alert men who steered him through the shark-infested waters of the punk music scene. Without Pavitt and

Poneman he would almost certainly have never come to the attention of Geffen. Without Geffen his name might never have emerged from the pack of worthy-but-obscure cult groups of the early nineties. Cobain had a flair for singing and a genius for songwriting, but his greatest talent may have lain in his consistent, if unintentional, good timing.

By the time Jimi Hendrix reached twenty-seven, the age Cobain died, self-indulgence in drugs and groupies and sheer boredom at apeing himself onstage had led him to a demoralizing crisis: for the last year of his life he was welding the guitar style that had set London on its ear to acoustic blues and the free jazz tradition of Miles Davis. Cobain, it can be assumed, because of a series of unhappy pronouncements about his group, would have made a similar break from Nirvana.

Two results suggest themselves. The first is that Cobain might somehow have matched the obvious intensity of his music with a much-needed sense of detachment. It would be unfair to suppose he could have leavened the typically American passion of his work with an irony more frequently seen in Europe, but it is a British musician, Paul Weller, who comes to mind as a role model. The second possibility is that Cobain might have made an aesthetic connection to the Beat Generation of the 1950s. The notion that Kerouac's touch of insurrection and perpetual mobility had been handed down from poet-hipsters to punk-rockers like himself was immensely pleasing to Cobain. There was even the totemic plaid shirt in common to both generations. Cobain might have baulked at completing the ensemble of black polo-neck and wraparound shades, but it would have been entirely logical for him to have followed in the native tradition of Pete Seeger and Woody Guthrie.

When Cobain had complained in his suicide note, 'the manic roar of the crowd doesn't affect me the way in which it did for Freddie Mercury', his widow interjected, 'Well,

Kurt, so fucking what? Then don't be a rock star.' The truth is that he was chronically unsuited to be anything else. His career in music had been difficult, but a job outside it would have been impossible. Time and again, Cobain stressed his unfitness for conventional work, his loathing of drudgery and sweat. No one can say the direction in which his career might have gone; but it is certain that, if Cobain was ever tempted to quit his job, the alternatives would have raised his own deep feelings of despair.

Cobain often insisted that he found reviews of his work painful and never read them. Love's account of wrenching away magazine articles hardly supports this claim, though he certainly found even mild criticism unpleasant. The truth is that, at the time of his death, Cobain's reputation had dwindled from the heady days of *Nevermind*. The first three places in the *Rocket* chart in April 1994 were occupied by Soundgarden, Alice In Chains and Pearl Jam, reflecting a local feeling that Nirvana had been lost to an art-noise world more typical of New York. Much of the criticism suggested that Cobain had become unknowable and, in some eyes, irrelevant: no longer the punk icon and archetype of the unashamedly free spirit, but a monster of narcissism, deceit and vanity, whose desperate and bizarre behaviour verged on the pathological, who was greedy, manipulative and ruthless. National journalists who came to Seattle in the winter of 1993–4 were equally caustic. 'With *In Utero*, Nirvana have slid back into well-deserved obscurity,' said the Chicago *Tribune*. In Graham Wright's view, 'Kurt's star was waning near the end. He only became a "spokesman for a genera-tion" after he died.' According to this reading, it took the tragedy of Cobain's suicide to revive a name associated by some with the earlier, near-forgotten era of George Bush, the Gulf War and *Nevermind*.

The headlines over the weekend of 9–10 April 1994 were

in sharp contrast to the few obituaries of Lee Brilleaux, singer with Dr Feelgood, who died the day after Cobain. Brilleaux, the least pretentious man in music, spent twenty years barking no-frills R&B to overspill audiences in Canvey Island and Slough, occasionally threatening a national breakthrough, and paving the way for the likes of the Buzzcocks, Eddie and the Hot Rods, and punk – a chronological, logical development. When he died at forty-one of throat cancer, Brilleaux was forgotten by the critics but popularly admired for having ended rock's dalliance with Mud, Sweet and the rest in the early seventies. Here was a significant man, down to earth, easy in his own skin, who, neither representing 'a scene' nor taking his own life, was overlooked in the media stampede to Seattle.

Yet Cobain, by capturing the popular drama of his time, succeeded where Brilleaux failed. Nirvana, as William Burroughs puts it, may 'not matter a hill of beans next to Louis Armstrong'; it is a fair bet, though, that Cobain will prove as timeless as Hendrix and that a spate of books, articles and ever-recycled albums will assure him the same exalted status. It was not merely sentiment that led *Rolling Stone* to name Nirvana 'artist of the year' in 1994 nor *Spin* to list the group top among 'ten that mattered most' in the decade 1985–95. These were solid achievements, based largely on the distance Cobain's music went both forwards and back, linking pop with new wave, the sixties with the nineties. Even his critics conceded that Cobain had felt the past as few of his age had. If only as an intermediary between generations, he was among the most influential artists of his time. Add his harrowing lifestyle and violent death, and it is possible to see how he caught the public eye and why, when America came to mourn its famous dead in 1994, there was Cobain's name alongside those of Nixon and Onassis.

When Love said that 'something good' would come from Cobain's life, she may have been referring to the network of college radio, labels and clubs that sprang up partly due to Nirvana; to the sudden accessibility of family TV shows to alternative groups like Hole; or to the fact that *Nevermind* revived a faith in rock largely lost in the reigns of Michael Jackson and Madonna. Less beneficial was the doom, defeatism and despair that was the chief legacy of the grunge revolution. Cobain's life and death between them form what John Peel calls the 'ultimate rock and roll morality story'. 'Kurt won't be remembered as a loser,' says Slim Moon; nor as 'the spokesman for a generation' adds Peterson. The odds are short that Cobain's reputation will evolve into one of these extremes. History forgets most of us, then makes too much of those who remain. Fame buries the human contradictions: the gifted man unqualifiedly devoted to music; the victim and recluse; the addict; the self-lacerating cynic; the young activist Cobain used to talk about nostalgically, remembering the days when everything still lay in the future.

Coda

Seattle in the late eighties: fat, catatonically dumb and happy; non-stop 'hair farmer' pap on MTV and Michael Jackson hogging the radio: grunge music was well served by its enemies. Kurt Cobain, who handled opposition far better than he did fame, put enough rage and guilt into *Bleach* to blight an entire generation. The record crackled with self-loathing, as though the internecine struggle between Cobain the joker and Cobain the suicide had seeped into the vinyl. As Nirvana's debut played out, the punters enjoyed the spectacle of a man giving a tardy but well-aimed finger to polite society. It was the band's, and Kurt's, crowning moment. Eighteen months later the group and entourage stood spellbound, watching Cobain construct ever more fussy variations on the same basic theme in *Nevermind*. Surely this one would be so glib and over-the-top that even furtive pop dudes (like Kurt himself) wouldn't swallow it. Ah! But with a big enough beat almost any cobblers can become a singalong classic. Fifty million dollars duly rang up for the album within a year. Kurt drew a bead between fury and melody in the follow-up *In Utero*, where the bulk of the lyrics were consumed by tirades against fame: for a record about birth, it seemed dangerously obsessed with closing down. One spring evening six months later, Cobain barricaded himself in a room above his garage, took a shotgun and blew his brains out.

Three LPs, about two hours of music plus some recycled odds and sods – it's not much to show for the famed Mouthpiece of a Generation. Yet more than seven years after his death, and ten since *Nevermind*, Cobain is stubbornly proving as timeless as Hendrix or Lennon. Rock icons appear and flourish, and afterwards their imitators struggle to duplicate the weird alignment of forces with which a *Pepper* or *London Calling* captures the great average. In his time, nobody filled this role better than Kurt, whose paradoxical capacity for fun and innovation and life-is-shit credo kept him ahead of the curve until self-parody kicked in. Add drug addiction, clinical paranoia, an unhappy marriage and the awareness that rock longevity requires sacrifices he wasn't prepared to make – and it's possible, if not easy, to see why Cobain reached the end of his famously short tether in April 1994.

In the kingdom of grunge, the great and the small, the transient and the seminal, the putrid and the corny live side by side. The names on old Sub Pop posters loom like hieroglyphics on the wall of a tomb: Blood Circus, Cat Butt, the Fucks. Amid this roll call of dire comic-opera chancers, only Kurt and co. have any serious claim to durability, let alone permanence. Are they better, as he once crowed, than the Beatles? Is *Nevermind* a bigger deal than *Pepper*? I seriously doubt it, but it's close.

As with Lennon, everything people look for in and know about pop – the basic noise of life – is distilled in Kurt Cobain. If some cosmic Butch Vig figure were to lean over a mixing board and – *phhhht!* – delete everything known about music, leaving only Kurt remaining, you could still reconstruct from him every staple, every character and pose contributing to rock. He was, simply, that good.

Of the various sidekicks and myrmidons, Sub Pop itself imploded in the familiar corporate mergers and personal wranglings; Dave Grohl and Chris Novoselic disappeared, respectively, into Foo Fighters and down a deep hole; Courtney Love reinvented herself as an actress admired by virtue of her superior skill, professional class, lack of ambition, purity of heart and exquisite taste – particularly the last, in gracing a *People Vs Larry Flynt*. She sold the family home on Lake Washington Boulevard and moved to Beverly Hills. Seattle itself went through a municipal nervous breakdown in 2001, triggered by a dot-com surge as though fuelled by Viagra, and, inevitably, followed by rapid detumescence.

The clubs and firetraps where Kurt first plied his trade may still be there, but then so are the domes where a 'Layla' or 'Satisfaction' can be heard, windswept, echoing among the Bud cans and soggy programmes while officially tolerated old farts like Clapton or the Stones preen in the mid-distance. When Nirvana plugged in at the Crocodile in 1989, it seemed like most of the sixties élite were already dead. A dozen years on, the Croc is where Seattle bankers go for lunch, and all manner of dinosaurs are back roaming the earth. It never occurred to me when I first signed up for Sub Pop that one day I'd be able to write an epilogue on Kurt Cobain while simultaneously enjoying live prime-time video of Bon Jovi flouncing around on MTV. For a year or two, the 'Seattle scene' truly seemed to be changing the whole specific gravity of rock, but then it settled for recycling the careers of recently dead mavericks who lived wasted, misfit lives. The scene may be bigger than ever, but most of the acts aren't just theatre of the absurd – they're treachery to the cause. What's left of grunge itself is satirically dopey, banal and mainstream, not unlike its host town.

I happened to spend some time in Kurt's old Seattle haunts in 2001, listening to rosy-cheeked, faultlessly hep thirtysomethings, bursting out of their down-filled Eddie Bauer jackets and tan Dockers, conferring about fascism in America. Everybody always seemed to be discussing police repression and the anxiety and fear of life under the younger Bush. I couldn't make any sense out of it. Not only was money pumping into Seattle on a scale that would have glazed Ken Livingstone's eye, the thirtysomethings were still running wilder and freer than any generation, in any city, in history. For that matter, Seattle itself had just hosted a small protest against the new administration, burning the president's two teenage daughters in effigy under a banner wittily proclaiming FUCK YOU BUSHIES. The president, we're told, was briefed about it. Yet the ruthless SS dragnet somehow missed the prank's organizers, who cleverly laid low at a keg party on Capitol Hill. The word went round that the storm troopers were definitely out there, but the plucky situationists kept drinking Red Hook and trawling the buffet, until towards dawn most were able to slip away to their lakeside eyries with the stripped-pine work stations, hardwood floors and stacks of unread *New Yorker*s wedged in behind the Scandinavian latté machines.

Somehow, for them, the knock on the door never did come.

Back at the Sub Pop Mega Mart, skulking among the racks of neatly pressed LOSER T-shirts and 'special deluxe edition' CDs of *Nevermind*, I eavesdropped on a conversation between two young punters.

'Have you, like, dumped Chip yet?' said one girl.

'Kinda,' said the other. 'Like I'm gonna blow a whole week at the lodge? Not.'

'Skiing? He's taking you skiing?' The first girl nearly disapproved.

'He says if I don't come we're gonna miss the best snow, like that pass is really bitchin'.'

'It *is* bitching,' the first girl said primly. 'Y'know, everything's going to shit, and that lame-ass Bush an' all, but let's face it, round here these days the biggest deal, as far as I can see, is beating the fuckers out of town on a Friday afternoon.'

What a sorry pass. But it's not as if we weren't warned. 'Yuppies in their BMWs' crooning along to 'Teen Spirit' was a scene that haunted Cobain until his death. Even, or especially, at ground zero, in Seattle, Kurt's influence nowadays cuts wide but not very deep. There's no liberation to be gleaned from *Nevermind* and the rest – no liberation from greed or inanity, or from the larger quandaries of human suffering and injustice that Bush, father and son, allegedly represent. The original backwoods revolt in favour of (one of Kurt's pet words) authenticity might have, sure enough, saved rock from the clutches of Michael Jackson. It's done nothing at all for the wider landscape.

Finally, a confession. Seven years ago, when I first wrote his biography, I wanted to rescue Cobain from detractors and camp-followers alike. I admired Kurt's talent. His imagination's voyages, on the other hand, looked less like a dazzling breakthrough than the escapism of a man unequal to everyday life. I was, so it seemed to me, sympathetic.

When the book was published I was followed around, investigated by a private eye, my phone tapped and recorded. You get used to that. What stuck in the craw were the over-caffeinated Seattle hacks whose bombardment of my then editor, Liz Knights, continued unabashed in the knowledge that she was battling terminal cancer. (Liz, who often and eloquently defended her authors' right to an opinion, died in November 1996.) So far as these sages ever formed a consensus, it was the familiar one about the book's 'giving off vibes' (the exact wording of one complaint), its author a racist, sexist, gay-bashing thug who, the theory went, lied, cheated and – as if there could be anything worse – listened to the Rolling Stones at top volume. All in all, it seemed, a book about a man dedicated to the principle of self-expression was no place for free speech.

Of the many and varied depressing sub-plots of Cobain's life, the worst by far is the sort of left-wing apartheid embraced by some of his old court. (And I mean, like myself, *old*: had he lived, Kurt would be pushing thirty-five, and many of the lickspittles who made a mint off him are cruising serenely through middle age.) These gutsy radicals and free-thinkers evidently believe that anyone criticizing the lifestyle isn't just a fascist, nazi and other such mild epithets, but a non-person. I needed to be 'offed', wrote one of Nirvana's pony-tailed apologists when *Kurt Cobain* was first published. Another bard referred to me in print as a 'leech' for having 'spued [sic] a book of criminal slander.' Actual evidence of this criminality was apparently hard to find, but my critic did finally manage one example: 'Sandford compares Cobain-the-rock-star to . . . *Mick Jagger.*'

Guilty as charged. According to this reading, the author of *Kurt Cobain* wasn't only morally faulty, he had the gall to raise the troubling contradictions of being, simultaneously, the prince of grunge and a twenty-five-year-old pampered millionaire. That Cobain himself was well and cruelly aware of this contradiction needs no repeating. It's also painfully obvious that, with certain rare exceptions, Kurt was infinitely better than his disciples, for whom impugning the character and motives of their opponents takes the place of real argument. By and large these people have few actual duties in honouring such a vast legacy with such a captive audience, chief of which is to appear, like Cobain himself, both intelligent and semi-tolerant. For the most part they've proved incapable of either, but otherwise they carry the torch well.

In a culture where anyone voting Republican or, God knows, Tory is routinely vilified as somewhere to the right of Darth Vader, I can only say that in the year I wrote *Kurt Cobain* the funniest, kindest and most truly anarchic friend I had was seventy-three-year-old Al Meyersahm, a legendary conservative who embodied more of the freedom principle than any of grunge's loon-panted moguls with their ideologically right-on pieties. As with Liz Knights, it's a pleasure to pay tribute to Al, an American classic who died in December 1999.

Kurt Cobain has had exactly one good moment since he

committed suicide, and that came only a few weeks after the event. The occasion was the release of *Unplugged in New York*, which at its brooding core was one of the best albums, by Nirvana or anyone else, of its kind. Most of the rest of the projects, including the woeful *Live!* video, have long since metastisized into just another rock 'n' roll cottage industry. The continuing backbiting, log rolling and conspiracy theories about Kurt have proved to be media manna, and jam to the diehards. They've done nothing at all for Cobain. As for the big-ticket tributes: they're not much, but as models of the pathology of stargazing, they stand alone. The director Nick Broomfield cobbled together a film, the *Rocket*'s Charles Cross a new 'definitive' biography. I haven't seen it, haven't read it.

Kurt's redemption, such as it was, began simply with the first track of *Bleach* and ended with the last notes of *Unplugged*. In the early days he was a rare if uneven musical savant. Perversely, the amped-up production of *Nevermind* hurt him as much as it helped, and Cobain ended up chasing after some of the faux Led Zep numbers. But even then the best songs, including the stunning 'Polly', are reminders of his singular genius. Reviewers of *In Utero*, meanwhile, used the occasion to expound on Kurt-the-icon, and none did so more movingly than William Burroughs, who told me 'Cobain raised the bar for the way people relate to pop . . . He was all about letting kids recognize each other through their differences, not about buying limos and all the other junk.'

As a quick glance at the charts confirms, the market has, even in Seattle, warmly embraced the many sub-Nirvanas and Cobain types who followed. Still, Burroughs was only half right. Until *Bleach*, rock and roll was all about relentless hype and inwardly terrified (of being found out) saps striking poses. This *danse macabre*, which began with Elvis, is often understood to have been undone by Johnny Rotten and the original punks. But fifteen years later, there was Cobain and the marketing machinery grinding away feverishly on his behalf. His towering reputation, which (reversing everything Kurt stood for) depends on ruthless intolerance of any dissent, reveals the ugly side of an industry that, in subtler form, persists to this day.

C.S.
2001

Appendix 1

Chronology

20 February 1967	Kurt Donald Cobain born in Grays Harbor Community Hospital, Aberdeen, Washington.
August 1967	The family move to 1210 East 1st Street, Aberdeen, as near to a settled home as Cobain will have.
24 April 1970	Cobain's sister, Kimberly, born.
1 March 1976	Cobain's father, Don, leaves home.
9 July 1976	Don and Wendy Cobain divorce. Custody of the children is granted to their mother.
1977	Cobain's first, tentative exposure to punk rock, through the Ramones and the Sex Pistols.
14 June 1979	Don Cobain petitions Grays Harbor Superior Court for custody of his son, who now migrates between his parents, grandparents and other relatives.
20 February 1981	Cobain is given his first guitar, a second-hand, six-string Lindell. According to his music teacher, his main goal is to learn 'Stairway To Heaven'.
1982	Cobain's horizons expand when the Melvins' singer Buzz Osborne exposes him to new wave groups like Flipper, MDC and the Butthole Surfers.
1983	Cobain meets Chris Novoselic, a fellow Melvins habitué and aspiring punk rocker,

with whom he conducts graffiti raids around Aberdeen.

August 1984	Cobain finally hears a punk rock group play live, coincidentally on the very day MTV, with a sale document promising 'coverage of new wave and new talent everywhere', goes on the market.
May 1985	Cobain drops out of Aberdeen High School, only weeks short of graduation. He moves from home to home, spends several nights under the North Aberdeen Bridge and tries heroin for the first time.
1986	Cobain begins rehearsing with Novoselic and, in a rare excursion into the real world, takes a maintenance job at the nearby Polynesian Ocean Front Hotel.
September 1987	Cobain moves into his girlfriend Tracy Marander's apartment at 114 North Pear Street, Olympia. He, Novoselic and drummer Aaron Burckhard form a number of short-lived groups, finally settling on the name Nirvana.
23 January 1988	The trio (with Dale Crover replacing Burckhard) record a ten-song session at Reciprocal Studios in Seattle, with the 'godfather of grunge', Jack Endino.
Spring 1988	In a turnover worthy of *Spinal Tap*, Burckhard returns to Nirvana on drums, leaves again, rejoins, only to be in turn replaced by Chad Channing.
November 1988	Sub Pop releases Nirvana's first single, 'Love Buzz'/'Big Cheese', in a limited edition of 1,000 copies.
	Meanwhile the *Sub Pop 200* compilation, including Nirvana's 'Spank Thru', is written up by John Peel in the *Observer*.

25 February 1989	Nirvana play the University of Washington and other venues on the west coast.
18 March 1989	Everett True of *Melody Maker*, having flown to Seattle at Sub Pop's expense, describes Nirvana as 'the real thing' and Kurdt Kobain [*sic*] as 'a great tunesmith [who] wields a riff with *passion*'.
15 June 1989	Nirvana's debut album, *Bleach*, is released on Sub Pop.
	The group embark on their first extensive US tour.
30 October 1989	Nirvana begin their first European tour in Newcastle, are on hand for the fall of the Berlin Wall, and play a triumphant concert at the Astoria, London, on 3 December.
1 April 1990	The group launch a second major US tour, this time with the services of a road manager and two assistants. Channing is fired and Dale Crover returns on drums.
22 September 1990	Nirvana perform at the Motor Sports International, described by some as the high-water mark of the 'Seattle Scene'. Three days later, yet another drummer, Danny Peters, is replaced by Dave Grohl.
October 1990	The amended line-up – Cobain, Novoselic and Grohl – tour briefly in Britain.
1 December 1990	Sub Pop issue Nirvana's second single, 'Sliver'/'Dive', while Cobain resumes his search for a major record label.
Winter 1990–91	Nirvana conclude negotiations with David Geffen Company, eventually settling for a $290,000 advance. As part of the contract, Sub Pop receives an initial $75,000 buy-out fee, a percentage of the group's future sales and a chance to release a final Nirvana single, 'Molly's Lips'.

30 April 1991	Nirvana formally sign with Geffen.
May–June 1991	Sessions at Sound City Studios, California, for the record that will become *Nevermind*. Cobain is visited in California by Courtney Love.
20 August 1991	Nirvana play a nine-date European tour, including a landmark performance at the Reading Festival.
20 September 1991	A six-week US tour begins.
24 September 1991	Geffen issues 46,000 copies of *Nevermind*. By Christmas the album is selling 400,000 copies a week and grosses $50 million within a year.
31 October 1991	Nirvana return to play the Paramount, Seattle.
4 November 1991	The group play in Bristol, followed by other dates in Britain and Europe.
	Both *Nevermind* and the single 'Smells Like Teen Spirit' climb the charts. Cobain's choice of music on the tour bus is *Abba's Greatest Hits*.
12 January 1992	*Nevermind* reaches Number One.
24 February 1992	Cobain marries Courtney Love in Hawaii.
August 1992	With rumours rife of the couple's drug use, *Vanity Fair* publishes an article describing Love as a 'train-wreck personality' and 'not particularly interested in the consequences of her actions . . . raising fears for the health of their (unborn) child'.
18 August 1992	Frances Bean Cobain born in Los Angeles, while her father undergoes detoxification in the same hospital. The Children's Services agency immediately revokes custody of the child, an action that drags on until March 1993.

30 August 1992	Cobain, days out of hospital and after threatening to kill himself, headlines with Nirvana at the Reading Festival.
9 September 1992	Cobain tells an international TV audience: 'It's really hard to believe everything you read.' Backstage at the same awards ceremony, he engages in a shoving match with Axl Rose.
30 October 1992	Nirvana play to 50,000 fans in Buenos Aires, a show Cobain describes as 'the largest display of sexism I've ever seen at once'.
15 December 1992	Geffen releases *Incesticide*, a compilation of B-sides, out-takes and tracks from Nirvana's BBC sessions.
February 1993	Nirvana record their third album, *In Utero*, at Pachyderm Studios, Minnesota. The basic tracks are recorded in six days – the argument about production lasts six months.
9 February 1993	Cobain tells the *Advocate* 'I probably could be bisexual' and 'I'm definitely gay in spirit'.
March 1993	The Cobains buy an eleven-acre estate in Carnation, east of Seattle, and rent a lakeside home in the city itself.
9 April 1993	Nirvana regroup to play a charity show at the Cow Palace, San Francisco.
2 May 1993	Cobain is admitted to hospital in Seattle suffering from a heroin overdose.
4 June 1993	Seattle police arrest Cobain for assaulting his wife. The charge is later dropped.
23 July 1993	Cobain again overdoses, this time hours before going onstage with Nirvana in New York.

21 September 1993	Geffen releases *In Utero*. The album debuts in the *Billboard* chart at Number One.
18 October 1993	Nirvana begin a 45-date US tour to promote *In Utero*.
October 1993	Cobain visits William Burroughs at the latter's home in Lawrence, Kansas, striking the author as 'shy' and 'engagingly lost'.
18 November 1993	Nirvana play an *Unplugged* set in New York. The album is released commercially a year later.
7–8 January 1994	Nirvana perform at the Seattle Center Arena, their final US shows.
January 1994	The Cobains move into a home at 171 Lake Washington Boulevard E. in Seattle.
2 February 1994	Nirvana, along with two additional musicians, fly to Europe.
1 March 1994	The group play at Terminal Einz, Munich, their last-ever performance.
3–4 March 1994	Cobain overdoses on a combination of champagne and valium-like Rohypnol, described by his management as an accident, but actually a first suicide attempt.
18 March 1994	The police respond to yet another domestic disturbance call from the Cobains, home again in Seattle.
30 March 1994	Cobain and his friend Dylan Carlson buy a Remington M11 20-gauge shotgun at Stan Baker Sports in Seattle. Cobain flies to Los Angeles and spends two days at the Exodus Recovery Center in Marina del Ray.
1 April 1994	Cobain escapes from Exodus by scaling a wall. He flies to Seattle.
4 April 1994	Cobain's mother files a missing person report with Seattle police, describing her

son as armed with a shotgun and possibly suicidal.

5 *April* 1994   Cobain, evading the police, a private investigator and electricians working in the grounds, barricades himself in the room above the garage at Lake Washington Boulevard, writes a suicide note, injects himself with heroin, raises the barrel of the shotgun to his mouth and pulls the trigger.

Appendix 2

Discography

Nirvana Singles and EPs

UK	US
	'Love Buzz'/'Big Cheese' **(Sub Pop, 1988)**
'Blew'/'Love Buzz'/'Been A Son'/'Stain' **(Tupelo, 1989)**	
'Sliver'/'Dive' **(Tupelo, 1991)**	'Sliver'/'Dive' **(Sub Pop, 1990)**
'Sliver'/'Dive'/'About A Girl' (Live) **(Tupelo, 1991)**	'Molly's Lips' **(Sub Pop, 1991)**
	'Here She Comes Now' **(Communion, 1991)**
'Smells Like Teen Spirit'/ 'Drain You' **(DGC, 1991)**	'Smells Like Teen Spirit'/ 'Even In His Youth'/ 'Aneurysm' **(DGC, 1991)**
'Smells Like Teen Spirit'/ 'Even In His Youth'/ 'Aneurysm' **(DGC, 1991)**	
'Smells Like Teen Spirit'/ 'Even In His Youth'/ 'Aneurysm'/'Drain You' **(DGC, 1991)**	
'Come As You Are'/'Endless, Nameless' **(DGC, 1992)**	'Come As You Are'/'School' (Live)/'Drain You' (Live) **(DGC, 1992)**
'Come As You Are'/'Endless, Nameless'/'School' (Live) **(DGC, 1992)**	'Lithium'/'Been A Son' (Live)/'Curmudgeon' **(DGC, 1992)**

'Lithium'/'Curmudgeon'
                    (DGC, 1992)
'Lithium'/'Been A Son' (Live)/
'Curmudgeon'   **(DGC, 1992)**
'In Bloom'/'Polly' (Live)
                    (DGC, 1992)
'In Bloom'/'Sliver' (Live)/
'Polly' (Live)   **(DGC, 1992)**
'Oh, The Guilt'
          (Touch And Go, 1993)
'Heart-Shaped Box'/'Marigold'   'Oh, The Guilt'
                    (DGC, 1993)   **(Touch And Go, 1993)**
'Heart-Shaped Box'/'Milk It'/
'Marigold'   **(DGC, 1993)**

Nirvana Albums and CDs

UK		US	
Bleach	**(Tupelo, 1989)**	*Bleach*	**(Sub Pop, 1989)**
Nevermind	**(DGC, 1991)**	*Nevermind*	**(DGC, 1991)**
Incesticide	**(DGC, 1992)**	*Incesticide*	**(DGC, 1992)**
In Utero	**(DGC, 1993)**	*In Utero*	**(DGC, 1993)**
MTV Unplugged In New York		*MTV Unplugged In New York*	
	(DGC, 1994)		**(DGC, 1994)**

Related Recordings and Compilations

'Spank Thru' by Nirvana on *Sub Pop 200*
                    (Sub Pop, 1988)
'Mexican Seafood' by Nirvana on *Teriyaki Asthma Vol 1*
                    (C/Z, 1989)
'Bikini Twilight' by Go Team, featuring Cobain
                    (K, 1989)

'Do You Love Me' by Nirvana on *Hard To Believe*

(C/Z, 1990)

The Winding Sheet by Mark Lanegan, featuring Cobain on 'Where Did You Sleep Last Night'

(Sub Pop, 1990)

Bureaucratic Desire For Revenge by Earth, featuring Cobain

(Sub Pop, 1991)

'Beeswax' by Nirvana on *Kill Rock Stars*

(Kill Rock Stars, 1991)

'Return Of The Rat' by Nirvana on *Eight Songs For Greg Sage*

(Tim Kerr, 1992)

'The "Priest" They Called Him' by William S. Burroughs, featuring Cobain

(Tim Kerr, 1993)

'I Hate Myself And I Want To Die' by Nirvana on *The Beavis and Butt-head Experience*

(DGC, 1993)

Houdini by the Melvins, co-produced by Cobain

(Altantic, 1993)

'Verse Chorus Verse' by Nirvana on *No Alternative*

(Arista, 1993)

'Pay To Play' by Nirvana on *DGC Rarities Vol 1*

(DGC, 1994)

Sources and Chapter Notes

It is no secret that a book like this relies on the insights, ideas and recollections of a large number of people. The following notes show the principal sources used in writing each chapter. I also interviewed a number of individuals who prefer not to be named. Where sources asked for anonymity – usually citing friendship with Cobain's widow – every effort was made to persuade them to go on the record. Where this was not possible, I have used the phrase 'a witness' or 'a colleague' as appropriate. I am sorry that no acknowledgement thus appears of the enormous help, encouragement and kindness I received from a number of people. Where Cobain himself is quoted, the sources are his published interviews, my own notes or the memory of those who spoke to him.

Chapter 1

Compelling accounts of Cobain's suicide and the events that followed appeared in newspapers and magazines around the world. I should particularly mention the versions carried in the *Guardian*, *The Times*, *Today* and *Q*. Personal comment was supplied by Beverley Cobain, Gillian Gaar and Patrick MacDonald. For the rest of the chapter my own memory is entirely responsible.

Chapter 2

Various accounts of Cobain's childhood have been previously published, most notably in Michael Azerrad's *Come As You Are* (Virgin Books, 1993); it is a pleasure to acknowledge the debt to this, the most comprehensive story of Nirvana yet written. Dave

Thompson's *Never Fade Away: The Kurt Cobain Story* (Pan Books, 1994) also fills in a number of gaps.

For personal comment on the period 1967–86, I am grateful to: Les Blue, Beverley Cobain, Don Cobain, Ernest Cobain, Iris Cobain, Leland Cobain, Toni Cobain, Francis Coughlin, Amy Griggs, Tony Groves, Randi Hubbard, Robert Hunter, Claude Iosso, Betty Kalles, Megan Kern, Donna Kessler, Warren Mason, Maria Novoselic, Jeff Sanford, Michael Schepp and Lamont Shillinger. Myer Loftin was illuminating on Cobain's sexual identity as a teenager.

Other material was gleaned from: Aberdeen *Daily World*, Aberdeen High School, Grays Harbor County Court, Montesano High School, Seattle *Times* and Seattle *Post-Intelligencer*.

I am grateful to John Prins and Jim Meyersahm for steering me through Cobain's home town.

Chapter 3

Major sources for this chapter included Patrick Campbell-Lyons, Beverley Cobain, Jack Daugherty, Robert Hunter, Myer Loftin and Dale Poore. The job of describing the 'Seattle scene' of the late 1980s would have been infinitely harder without the help of Grant Alden, Tim Arnold, Gillian Gaar, Patrick MacDonald and Noel Tyler. Cobain's friends Slim Moon and Alice Wheeler provided insights into his life in Olympia.

An idea of Nirvana's early impact in the UK was supplied by Jeff Griffin, John Peel and by studying the back issues of *Melody Maker* and *Sounds*. Charles Peterson, whom I interviewed in Seattle, was intriguing and candid about Cobain's professional breakthrough. On that subject, I also relied on notes I made myself while living in Seattle in 1988.

Published source material included Suzi Black's *Nirvana* (Omnibus Press, 1992), Brad Morrell's *Nirvana And The Sound of Seattle* (Omnibus, 1993), magazines including *Rolling Stone*, *Q*, the *Face*, *Vox*, *Raw*, *People* and *Spin*, and, again, *Come As You Are* and *Never Fade Away*.

Chapter 4

Charles Peterson, the man Cobain credited with popularizing grunge, was again a major source for this chapter. Grant Alden, Cheryl Han, Julia Levy, Patrick MacDonald, Slim Moon, Lisa Orth, John Peel, Jeff Sanford and Alice Wheeler all made my research more profitable than it otherwise would have been.

Published sources again included the relevant issues of *Melody Maker* and *Sounds*, and Gillian Gaar's essay, 'The Dark Side of Innocence: Nirvana and the Rise of the Seattle Sound', published in *Goldmine*, December 1993.

'About A Girl' (Cobain) © 1989, Virgin Songs, Inc/The End Of Music.

Chapter 5

Among the sources consulted were Chuck Leavell, Slim Moon, Karen Pelley, John Peel and Kate Rous. Sub Pop being famously tight-lipped about their dealings with Cobain, I relied on anonymous, but corroborated, sources – and on the memories of Lisa Orth and Alice Wheeler – for the necessary material. Three women, Randi Edlin, Geraldine Hope and Julia Levy, spoke to me about their relationships with Cobain.

Published material was culled from *New York Times*, *Vanity Fair*, *BAM*, *Billboard*, *Melody Maker*, *Rolling Stone* and the *Rocket*. A number of the quotes by and about Cobain in this chapter first appeared in *Come As You Are.*

Gillian Gaar supplied me with a tape of Cobain's various comments to Victoria Clarke and Britt Collins.

Chapter 6

Invaluable help was given by Grant Alden, Mike Coffey, Randi Hubbard, Frank Hulme, Patrick MacDonald, Frank Medina, Slim Moon, Charles Peterson, Kate Rous, Tony Selmer, Alice Wheeler and Graham Wright. Don Cobain, while not going as far as a formal interview, allowed himself a number of comments about his son, as did Wendy O'Connor in conversation with Claude Iosso.

Quotes and background material on Courtney Love came from

Come As You Are and from the large number of her published interviews, notably *Rolling Stone* of 15 December 1994.

Miti Adhikari, who recorded Nirvana in London, and Patrick Campbell-Lyons, who fell into dispute with the group, both gave their help.

A useful but by no means comprehensive profile of Nirvana in these years can be found on the Geffen video, *Live! Tonight! Sold Out!!* I should also mention the Music Collection's *Tribute To Kurt Cobain*.

Additional research took place at the King and Paramount Theatres, both of Seattle, and in the Washington State lottery building.

'Smells Like Teen Spirit' (Cobain) © 1991, Virgin Songs, Inc/ The End Of Music.

'Come As You Are' (Cobain) © 1991, Virgin Songs, Inc/The End Of Music.

Chapter 7

Cobain's reaction to sudden fame and money was vividly recalled by Miti Adhikari, Grant Alden, Frank Hulme, Patrick MacDonald, Charles Peterson, Celia Ross and Graham Wright. I am grateful to a source at Harborview Medical Center, Seattle, as well as to the late Frank Zappa.

Published accounts of Cobain's life in 1992 were supplied by the Aberdeen *Daily World*, the *Globe*, *Rocket*, *Spin* and *Vanity Fair*. A source at the Washington Music Industry Coalition put that organization's view of Cobain at my disposal.

My own research for this chapter took me to the Olympus Hotel, Tacoma, the Pourhouse Tavern, Aberdeen, and Quaglino's in London.

Full acknowledgement is again made to Michael Azerrad's *Come As You Are* and to *Cobain* by the editors of *Rolling Stone* (Little Brown, 1994).

'On A Plain' (Cobain) © 1991, Virgin Songs, Inc/The End Of Music.

'All Apologies' (Cobain) © 1993, Virgin Songs, Inc/The End Of Music.

Chapter 8

It was among the greatest pleasures of the book to interview William Burroughs. I am grateful both to him and his secretary, James Grauerholz, with whom I must have exchanged two dozen phone calls in the winter of 1994–5.

Michael Andeel and Gillian Gaar both provided personal reminiscences of Nirvana's last performance as a trio in August 1993.

Other sources included Grant Alden, Beverley Cobain, Mike Collier, David Haig, Frank Hulme, Lisa Orth, Charles Peterson, Lamont Shillinger and Alice Wheeler. Monty Dennison and Jane Farrar provided help in locating Cobain's homes in, respectively, Carnation and Lakeside Avenue NE, Seattle.

Published material consulted included articles in the *Advocate*, Chicago *Tribune*, the *Face*, *Los Angeles Times*, Los Angeles *Weekly*, *Newsweek*, *New York Times*, *Rolling Stone*, Seattle *Times* and *Select*. The quote by Jo-Ann Greene originally appeared in Dave Thompson's *Never Fade Away*. It would be difficult to exaggerate the debt owed to Michael Azerrad.

Documentary material on Cobain's collapse in May 1993 and his arrest the following month was provided by the Seattle Police Department.

'Heart-Shaped Box' (Cobain) © 1993, Virgin Songs, Inc/The End Of Music.

'All Apologies' (Cobain) © 1993, Virgin Songs, Inc/The End Of Music.

'Serve The Servants' (Cobain) © 1993, Virgin Songs, Inc/The End Of Music.

'Frances Farmer Will Have Her Revenge on Seattle' (Cobain) © 1993, Virgin Songs, Inc/The End Of Music.

'Milk It' (Cobain) © 1993, Virgin Songs, Inc/The End Of Music.

Chapter 9

An analysis of Cobain's last weeks alive was supplied by sources including Miti Adhikari, Michael Andeel, Mike Collier, Gillian Gaar, Sam Mayne, Charles Peterson and Alice Wheeler. Again, the job of constructing the actual events of April 1994 would have been harder without the help of the Seattle Police Department and their legal adviser, Leo Poort.

For an account of the weeks following Cobain's death, I am grateful to Marco Collins, Gillian Gaar, Nikolas Hartshorne, Claude Iosso and Stephen Towles.

Other sources included *Cobain*, CNN, the *Face*, *Melody Maker*, *New Musical Express*, *Newsweek*, *New York Times*, *People*, *Q*, *Raw*, *Rolling Stone*, Seattle Department of Construction and Land Use, the Seattle *Times*, *Vox*, and the Washington State Department of Health.

A number of the quotes from Wendy O'Connor first appeared in *Today*.

Summaries of Cobain's life were provided by Grant Alden, William Burroughs, Beverley Cobain, David Haig, Randi Hubbard, Slim Moon and John Peel.

'Serve The Servants' (Cobain) © 1993, Virgin Songs, Inc/The End Of Music.

'All Apologies' (Cobain) © 1993, Virgin Songs, Inc/The End Of Music.

'Radio Friendly Unit Shifter' (Cobain) © 1993, Virgin Songs, Inc/The End Of Music.

'Milk It' (Cobain) © 1993, Virgin Songs, Inc/The End Of Music.

Index

405